CHINA IN WORLD HISTORY

By the same author

THE MODERNIZATION OF THE CHINESE SALT
ADMINISTRATION
PROVINCE AND POLITICS IN LATE IMPERIAL CHINA

China in World History

S.A.M. Adshead
Reader in History
University of Canterbury, Christchurch, New Zealand

MACMILLAN
PRESS

First published 1988

Published by
THE MACMILLAN PRESS LTD
Houndmills, Basingstoke, Hampshire RG21 2XS
and London
Companies and representatives
throughout the world

Printed in Hong Kong

British Library Cataloguing in Publication Date
Adshead, S.a.M.
China in world history.
1. China – Relations
1. Title
951 DS740.4

ISBN0-333-43405-6

To the memory of Joseph Fletcher Jr.

Contents

Introduction

This book presents a history of China which, it is hoped, will be more meaningful to Western readers than conventional histories. It is a history of China not as an isolated entity but as part of the world. Its subject is China's relations with the other major centres of civilization in Western Eurasia, Africa and America, and with what will be claimed to be an emerging world system or super-civilization. This is not the whole of Chinese history, but it is the most important part for a Western reader to know. The emerging world system is of primarily Western design and make, but China has contributed more to it than is usually realized and something is missing from any picture of modern history which does not take account of this.

No other book to my knowledge covers this field. There are general histories of China: Jacques Gernet's *Le Monde Chinois*. There are histories of particular aspects of China's relationship with the outside world: Joseph Needham's famous *Science and Civilization in China* on science and technology; Edward H. Schafer's *The Golden Peaches of Samarkand* on the T'ang; John K. Fairbank and colleagues' *The Chinese World Order* on diplomacy; and Louis Dermigny's *La Chine et L'Occident, Le Commerce à Canton au XVIIIe siècle 1719–1833* on the key period of the Enlightenment. There are pioneer studies of the emerging world system: Donald F. Lach's *Asia in the Making of Europe*; Immanuel Wallerstein's *The Modern World System: Capitalist Agriculture and The Origins of the European World Economy in the Sixteenth Century*; Jean Baechler's *The Origins of Capitalism*; not to speak of Teilhard de Chardin's speculations, hard to escape from when once absorbed. What there is not is a synoptic history of China's relationship to the rest of the world and its contribution to whatever world institutions there may be. This book attempts to fill that gap.

Each chapter follows the same pattern. First, a period of Chinese history will be analysed in order to compare China to the other leading centres of civilization at that time. Second, the avenues of contact between China and those centres will be explored: routes, embassies, commerce, missions, pilgrimages, espionage, hearsay and rumour. Third, what travelled along these avenues will be considered: people, goods, techniques, ideas, values, pathologies, institutions and myths. Finally, the contribution of these interchanges to various kinds of|world|institution'−ecological, political, cultural, technological − amounting in total to an emerging world system, will be examined. A picture of China in world history will be painted, sketchy and idiosyncratic no doubt, but, it is hoped, illuminating.

A book like this necessarily uses and abuses the work of others. Since all thanks and apologies cannot be made I think it most courteous to make none, except to Professor Joseph Fletcher of Harvard who would have appreciated the need for both.

I would also like to thank Mr Desmond Brice, National Library, New Zealand, who compiled the index.

1 World Apart: China in Antiquity, 200 BC to 400 AD

This chapter concerns China's relationship to the outside world in the period of the Han dynasty, 206 BC to 220 AD, glancing at the pre-imperial past of the Chou and the Shang and the post-imperial future of the San-kuo and the Chin. Its argument is that though Han China shared in the common foundations of civilized humanity laid down in the early Pleistocene epoch and extended in the Neolithic, it built on them in such an original fashion and with such little contact with other centres of civilization as to constitute a world apart in a planet of separate worlds. Teilhard de Chardin saw history as spindle-shaped:[1] original unity, a southern hemisphere of divergence, an equator of transition, a northern hemisphere of convergence, ultimate unity. Our story begins at the moment of maximum divergence.

We start with the *dramatis personae*. Throughout we shall be concerned with four primary civilizations: East Asia, Western Eurasia, pre-Columbian America and Black Africa; four collectivities sufficiently homogenous within and heterogenous without, both in space and time, to be regarded as elementary cultural units. Each unit, no doubt, is subdivisable into more unified but less isolated subunits. Thus East Asia has a Chinese core and Inner Asian and South-east Asian peripheries. Western Eurasia falls naturally into the North, the Mediterranean, Greater Iran and India. Pre-Columbian America divides into the parallel high cultures of the Central American and Andean plateaux and the contrasting low cultures of the North American prairie and the Amazonian jungle. Black Africa is dichotomized by the equatorial forest into north and south, old and new, and is then redichotomized into sub-desert savannah and sub-jungle forest societies. Nevertheless, in spite of these subdivisions, each of these units has enough coherence and independence in space and time to constitute it as one of the basic elements of global history.

Two objections should be met. On the one hand, the unity of Western Eurasia requires justification. From the standpoint of European history, the concept of Western Eurasia is an illegitimate aggregation, a confusion of civilizations divided by language, script, religion and ethos. 'In the Mediterranean', wrote Werner Benndorf, 'there are people who write from left to right and people who write from right to left'.[2] An advantage of the Chinese standpoint, however, is to eclipse these differences and to throw into relief the essential unity of the West. Whatever the differences of technology, sociology, ideas and institutions between India, Greater Iran, the Mediterranean and the North, they are united by age as contrasted with the older Africa and the younger East Asia; by linguistic kinship in the Indo-European family; by alphabetical as opposed to logographical script; by the Dumezilian sociology of priest-king, war-chief and merchant-commoner; by the common intellectual *problematik* of the one and the many; and by the shared influence of Hellenism, Christianity and Islam. The true East does not begin at Suez but at Singapore, at the T'ien-shan rather than the Caucasus, and from one point of view, Calvin, St Thomas Aquinas, al-Ghazzali, Sankara and Tsong-kha-pa are simply permutations of a single position.

On the other hand, some defence is necessary for confounding the world of the Inner Asian steppe with East Asia. Nomadic pastoralism, with its unique emphasis on animals and mobility, was the last major divergence in human ecology; it produced an original and distinctive form of society, military and elitist, which for a time controlled half the world's horsepower; and when raised to the level of state organization in the Mongol conquests, it played a crucial role in the onset of world convergence. Yet these very factors, late appearance (around 800 BC), idiosyncratic character and early convergence, deny Inner Asia full elementary status. Nomadic pastoralism is best regarded not as a civilization but as a temporary specialist subculture. It then remains to decide under which other civilization to place it. Although the first nomad state, that of the Royal Scyths around 550 BC, was Iranian and centred on the Ukraine, because the origins of nomadic pastoralism as an ecosystem are further east among the reindeer-riding Uriyanghai of the Altai and because steppe nomadism played a larger part in Chinese history than European, we place Inner Asia on the periphery of the world of East Asia. Here its extensive military pastoralism contrasts with the intensive civilian agriculture of the Chinese core and parallels the naval elitism of the South-east Asian periphery.

Between the four primary civilizations a number of contrasts may be drawn. First, age. Black Africa, the cradle of humanity, is oldest, reckoning its years in millions. Pre-Columbian America, or Amerindia, is youngest, post-glacial only, counting in tens of thousands. Western Eurasia and East Asia on the other hand, the two children of Africa, stand in the middle with hundreds of thousands, though the West is much older than the East in terms of advanced neolithic civilization. Second, size of population. Since neolithic times, Black Africa had had the smallest population, less than one eighth of humanity, with Amerindia ahead with just over one eighth. Next is China which, with its underpopulated peripheries, has usually contained one quarter of mankind. Finally there is Western Eurasia, mankind's main body, with one half of global population. Third, structure. Western Eurasia with its four rival centres in unstable hierarchy is complex; East Asia with its single Chinese core and perpetual peripheries is simple. Pre-Columbian America with its dichotomy between highland high cultures and lowland low cultures was differentiated; Black Africa, despite its dichotomies of north and south, savannah and forest, was homogenous. Fourth, organization. Here one can contrast the strong organization of Western Eurasia and East Asia – their eternal empires, ecumenical religions, centuries-old kingdoms, ancient aristocracies – with the weak organization of Africa and America – their tribal fragmentation, linguistic chaos, unstable states and ephemeral leaderships. Within the category of weak organization, one can contrast pre-Columbian America which, despite an economy which had not mastered all the techniques of the neolithic revolution, produced two different, if still loose, hypertrophies of state power, Aztec and Inca, with Black Africa which, despite an advanced iron-age technology, produced a much lower level of state building. Tenochtitlan and Zimbabwe mock a purely materialistic view of history.[3]

These then are the four primary civilizations. Together with their common technological foundations, their shared situations, their occasional interconnections, they constituted the ancient world whose relationship to the China of the Han dynasty forms the subject of this chapter.

CHINA'S PLACE IN THE WORLD, 200 BC TO 400 AD

To understand China's relations with the other civilizations of antiquity one must first assess her place in the world at the time, that is, her relative standing and individual features, by comparing Han China with the classical Roman empire. Other comparisons could be made: with the early civilizations of Meso-America, with what little is known of Black Africa in antiquity, or more temptingly with Iran under the Parthians or the India of the Mauryas, Greeks and Kushans. None, however, offers so close a parallel with Han China as does the Roman empire. This section therefore examines first the similarities between Han China and the classical, pre-Constantinian Roman empire and second, the differences. The conclusion will be that the differences outweighed the similarities.

Similarities to Rome

These may be divided into origin, organization and outcome.

Origin
Both the Han and Roman empires began in the third century BC with the military expansion of conservative, relatively unideological aristocratic states on the western peripheries of their respective civilized zones. The Roman republic was not a full member of the Hellenistic world; the duchy of Ch'in was an outsider in the Chou confederacy. Both expansions were based on a combination of political stability, abundant rural manpower nourished by advanced agriculture, and disciplined infantry, which was pitted against political instability, artificial urban growth and over-specialized military technology. Both were directed first against mercantile

rivals: Carthage, the emporium of tin and silver in the West and Ch'i, the emporium of salt and iron in the East; and then against colonial frontiers: the Hellenistic east and Gaul, Ch'u and Wu-yueh. In both cases conquest was followed by civil war. It ended in the elimination of the aristocracies which had organized the expansion and the establishment of bureaucracies which disguised their novelty by archaizing their ideology and exaggerating their continuity. Thus the neotraditionalist refoundation of the republic by Augustus was paralleled by Han-Wu-ti' *feng* and *shan* sacrifices in imitation of the sage rulers of antiquity. In both cases the *novi homines* of the bureaucracy came to be supplied by men from the defeated but more educated east, freedmen, from Greece and scholars from Honan, through the patronage of aggressive and colourful empress-dowagers: Agrippina in the West, empress-dowager Teng in the East.

Organization

In terms of organization the Han and Roman empires had much in common, both problems and solutions. The Roman empire under Hadrian covered 1 763 000 square miles; the Han empire towards the end of the second century AD covered 1 532 000 square miles. Both faced similar problems of distance and time in administering an area the size of the United States with a technology in which nothing went faster than a horse. Both sought a solution in the cultural solidarity of elites: the spontaneous coordination produced by the shared values, institutions, vocabulary and reactions of, on the one hand, the classical *paedeia* and, on the other, the Confucian *wen-yen*. Both empires relied on this solidarity as their foundation, both built roads to foster it and facilitate military flexibility, and both constructed great walls to give that flexibility time to operate and to avoid the costly continuous mass mobilization which might destroy culturalism by militarism. In both empires, the dominant element of the army was the infantry; the dominant colour of the culture, literary, with poetry giving way to prose. In both the army was opposed by cavalry enemies, the Iranian cataphract and the Hsuing-nu light horseman, and in both the culture of the elite was challenged by barbarians, sectaries, soldiers and peasants in varying degrees of alienation from it. In both the challenge was for a long time contained by political skill, social flexibility, economic prosperity and cultural syncretism, underpinned by military effectiveness. When the system needed reconstruction, the Severi of 193–235, provincial lawyers turned soldiers, populists and patrons of exotic religions, were closely paralleled by Ts'ao Ts'ao and the Wei dynasty of 184–265, outsiders from a eunuch background, meritocrats, founders of military colonies, and friends of unorthodox, new-style philosophy.

Outcome

Despite reconstruction, by the Severi and the tetrarchy and by the Wei and the Chin, the long-term outcome was the same: the rise of barbarism and religion; the collapse of the too-costly superstructure in one half of the empire; its survival, reformed, in the other. Both the Roman and the Han empires collapsed in their north-western halves through a mixture of institutional hypertrophy, military pronuntiamentos, ecclesiastical non-cooperation and barbarian invasions. Both survived in slightly new forms in their south-eastern halves with a new capital and the establishment of a foreign, previously 'sectarian', ecumenical religion which gradually conquered the north-west as well. In the north-west, the leaders of the invading barbarian armies, often ex-imperial *foederati*, set up kingdoms but, except in the vicinity of the *limes*, there was no serious linguistic change. In both China and the West, society ruralized and centred itself upon self-contained aristocratic estates, lay and monastic which, with their immunities, vassals, retainers, 'guests' and servants, were more sociological than economic units. In both, a new superstructure, a medieval civilization with deeper roots and firmer foundations than its antique predecessor, was eventually constructed, but in neither was it built on the old plan or centred on the segment of the old system which had survived in the south-east. Neither Constantinople nor Nanking were to be a basis for the medieval world.

Differences from Rome

These may be grouped as contrasts of foundation, architectonics and decay which paralleled the similarities of origin, organization and outcome, qualified their genuineness and limited their significance.

Foundation

Although both Rome and China shared a basic technological foundation common to all four primary civilizations, their variants were sufficiently divergent to differentiate their societies sharply. This divergence may be seen in both physical and intellectual technology.

Physical technology. In all four primary civilizations arable farming was the basic ecosystem. It produced the majority of the calories consumed by human metabolism and its higher productivity per unit of land area made possible the increase in population with underlay the other achievements of ancient civilization. Between China and Rome, however, there were significant differences as to crops, milieu and methods of cultivation.

In the Roman west, the principal crop was wheat or its relatives barley and oats. In Han China, on the other hand, although wheat and rice were known, the principal crop was millet. Millet is a less palatable grain than wheat, but it had a higher productivity in pre-modern conditions in both quantity sown and area sown. Before the nineteenth century, the ratio of wheat harvested to wheat sown was seldom more than 6:1, while the rate for millet was 10:1. Similarly, while the average pre-modern yield of wheat was 6 quintals a hectare, that of millet was 12 quintals a hectare.

The original difference in productivity was compounded by the difference of natural milieu. In the Roman west, grain was grown on light downland soils which, to maintain their nitrogen content and hence fertility, required fallowing in alternate years. In China, on the other hand, grain was grown on the porous loess of the north-west hills which, because of its permeability by the chemicals of the air and subsoil, was self-renewing and did not require either fallowing or manuring. The amount of arable land under grain at any one time in China was thus double that in Rome.

This fundamental advantage of Chinese agriculture was underlined by von Richthofen, the first scientific investigator of China's ecology. Having observed that 'Loess yields crops without manuring', he continued:

> There are two causes which render it probable, that Loess, where it is normally and largely developed, cannot be exhausted. The first relates to the organic substances required by the vegetation. They are, chiefly, carbonic acid and ammoniac. It is probable, that the great porosity of the Loess, shared by no other kind of soil in an equal degree, renders it capable to absorb these gases from the air in an extraordinarily large proportion. The second refers to the inorganic substances. They are likely to be supplied by a process due to the same property of the Loess. In the absence of any planes of stratification, the rain-water descends far into the porous Loess, and meets with the humidity retained in its lower portions; and, in obedience to the well-known laws of the diffusion of liquids, the substances which are kept in solution below will be communicated to those portions of the water next to the surface, and be taken up by the vegetation, so far as required.[4]

Thanks to the loess therefore, Han China, unlike the Roman west, could in principle produce a crop from the same piece of land every year. Richthofen concluded by observing, 'The want of sufficient quantity of rain will, therefore, be doubly injurious for the Loess-regions, and, as a rule very good crops change with very bad ones, years of plenty with such of famine.' But in artificial irrigation, too, China enjoyed a lead.

In 1957 in his book *Oriental Despotism*, Karl A. Wittfogel propounded his famous theory of China as a hydraulic society, which has given rise to so much controversy.[5] Among the controversialists, Ho Ping-ti in particular has shown that Wittfogel's connection of the characteristic features of Chinese politics and society with large-scale macrohydraulic agriculture cannot be sustained; that China was in fact the last of the four primary civilizations to use irrigation whether large-scale or small; and that millet was adopted as the basic crop precisely because its drought-resistant qualities made it especially suitable to the dry farming of the loessland hillsides.[6] Nevertheless, whatever the original characteristics of

Chinese farming, by the Han period, a higher percentage of its arable acreage was irrigated than in the Roman west, and a larger proportion of the irrigation was by large-scale macrohydraulic means than elsewhere. Except in Egypt, and K. Baer has argued that even here the irrigation system should be regarded as microhydraulic,[7] and possibly in Sassanid Mesopotamia, the West had nothing to compare to the Cheng Kuo irrigation canal, the Kuan-hsien diversion and interior delta system, the Ch'ang-an to Yellow River canal or Shao Hsin-ch'en's works in Nan-yang prefecture – all of which date from the Ch'in or Han periods. The combined effects of these works, together with emperor Han Wu-ti's careful control of the Yellow River so graphically described in *Shih-chi*, may have been to double again the yield of grain as a result of higher water inputs. If so, and if this advantage be added to those of millet yields and the absence of fallowing, then average Chinese grain yields would have been eight times those of the Roman west. The two societies had different nutritional bases.

A corollary of this greater intensity of Chinese grain farming was a difference in the role of animal husbandry between China and the Roman west. The difference was not as pronounced as it was later to become, but already the two societies were oriented in different directions. Because of the self-renewal of the loess, Chinese arable farming did not require animals for manure; because it did not need to lie fallow there were no unsown fields free for temporary stocking; and because farms could be smaller thanks to the higher grain yields, there was less marginal land for permanent pasture and less need for ploughing animals. Thus, though China and Europe shared the same domestic animals – cows, horses, sheep, goats, pigs – and, as we shall see, China in antiquity used the horse more efficiently than did the West, in China animals were ancillary while in Europe they were essential. True, in antiquity, animals, in particular horses, were much fewer in Europe than they subsequently became (why could Pheidippides not find a mount between Athens and Sparta?), while the opposite was true in China, but already the Chinese farmer was oriented to pure arablism in contrast to the European farmer who was oriented to a mixture of arablism and pastoralism.

This difference, in turn, contributed to others: different attitudes to space (the pastoralist can never have too much of it); to mobility (the pastoralist has both ends and means for it); to energy (the pastoralist will be lavish with it so long as it is non-human); to nomadic pastoralism (the mixed farmer can compromise, the pure arablist cannot); to food (the pastoralist will structure his meal round a main course of meat where the arablist will blend a collection of vegetable dishes); and even to human relations generally (the pastoralist is a herder whereas the arablist is a grower). In *Pilgrim's Regress*, C.S. Lewis called the Jews the 'shepherd people':[8] it would be an appropriate name for all westerners. Chinese regalia never included the sword. Even more significant is that Chinese official insignia never included the shepherd's crook, the pastoral staff.

Chinese agriculture was further differentiated from Roman by China's superiority in metallurgy in antiquity, particularly iron. Needham has shown that while the West could not liquify and cast iron until the fourteenth century AD, so that all ancient and medieval iron in the West was low-carbon wrought iron, China produced cast-iron hoes, ploughshares, picks, axes and swords from the fourth century BC. This metallurgical superiority affected both agriculture and war. The Chinese arable farmer, in addition to his other advantages, had more and better iron implements than his Roman counterpart. If China clung to infantry where Constantinople switched to cavalry, it was partly because the Chinese footsoldier was better armed and was better able to cope with his equestrian opponent than the Roman legionary. For example, it is doubtful if Roman artisans could have produced the precision-made bronze trigger mechanism required for the Chinese cross-bow. Consequently the Han never suffered a Carrhae or an Adrianople. The capacity to cast iron, in turn, raised the level of steel production both in quantity and quality. Wrought iron is low in carbon, cast iron is high in carbon, and steel lies in between. For pre-modern siderurgy it was easier to decarbonize than recarbonize. So, by the Han period, the Chinese, starting with cast iron, could produce considerable quantities of good steel by what was, in essence, the Bessemer process of oxygenation, i.e. liquifying the iron while simultaneously blowing away part of the carbon; while the West, starting with wrought iron, could only produce limited amounts of poor steel by heating the iron in charcoal. The Damascus and Toledo blades, which were later to so impress the Crusaders, were the products of transplanted Chinese technology and when Pliny the Younger spoke admiringly of Seric iron, he was probably thinking of Chinese steel.

Intellectual technology. All four primary civilizations shared the primary human tool of articulate speech. Western Eurasia, East Asia, and Amerindia all possessed the basic tool for higher organization: a system of writing. In China and the West, but not in Amerindia, writing was sufficiently old and diffused to constitute the necessary vehicle for education: a literary tradition. As between China and the West, however, there was significant differences in all three intellectual techniques; speech, writing and literary tradition.

Languages, one might assume are born equal. Each can express the full range of human consciousness and each is completely translatable into every other: as Leonardo Bruni put it: 'Nothing is said in Greek that cannot be said in Latin'.[9] All languages are equal vehicles of speech and writing, prose and poetry, even though one may think, with Robert Frost, that poetry is what gets lost in translation. The Chomskyan hypothesis of a single transformational grammar or syntactic structure governing all languages supports the assumption of linguistic equivalence. Yet, it may be argued, at a more superficial level, languages are not equal and the inequality may have implications for the thought expressed in them. In particular one may consider whether or not the different sound/meaning ratio in Chinese as compared to the Indo-European languages influenced thought patterns in China and the West. Chinese, it has been said 'is exceptionally rich in homophones', or, to put it another way, it operates with a 'poverty of sounds'.[10] Thus modern mandarin uses only 1280 sounds to express what must be presumed to be the same gamut of meaning as the phoneme-rich Indo-European languages. Although archaic and ancient Chinese, the languages of Confucius and the middle ages, may have had a wider phonological range than mandarin, economy in phonemes seems to be an original and basic characteristic of Chinese speech. The effect has been a wider indeterminacy of meaning *vis-à-vis* sound, a greater dependence on context and audience to establish signification, and a bias in favour of nuance, indirection, allusion and paradigm, as compared to the cruder, more direct, less allusive, more syntagmatic languages of the West. The medium does not prescribe the content of the message. It may be that nothing is said in Chinese that cannot be said in English, and vice versa: but it does determine the level of articulation, the degree of thematization, the place on the implicit/explicit scale. In this sense, the Chinese language with its peculiar sound/meaning ratio was an invitation both to the collective introversion which Jung found characteristic of the eastern mind and to the protocol thinking which Granet ascribed to the Chinese.

The Chinese script, through its partial independence of sound, worked in the same direction. The Chinese characters, *tzu*, are often described as non-phonetic, pictographic or ideographic. In fact, the Chinese script as it has existed since the Shang dynasty is not unrelated to sound and most contemporary Chinese characters are logographs, i.e. representations of words rather than things or ideas. Nevertheless the Chinese script is not as *closely* related to sound as are alphabetical scripts; it represents words but not the permutable sound-elements of words. The partial independence of sound had advantages. By its transcendence of variations in pronunciation, the *tzu* unified China's space and time: a man from Peking could correspond with a man from Canton even if their dialects were mutually unintelligible; and an old Chou text was in principle no harder to read than a new Han one. Further, although not wholly non-phonic like the Indian numerals, the *tzu* could be used by people like the Japanese, the Khitan, the Jurched and the Tanguts whose languages were unrelated to Chinese.

The Chinese script thus laid the foundation not only for China as an empire, but also for East Asia as a cultural unity. Moreover, the disadvantage often urged against the *tzu*, that they are an obstacle to mass literacy, is not true. While Chinese children take longer to acquire minimum literacy than European children, literacy rates in China were higher than in Europe until the eighteenth century, and Tokugawa Japan possibly had the highest literacy rates of any pre-modern country. What is true, however, is that the Chinese script affected the kind of literacy acquired. Neologism was harder in East Asia than in the West: it was harder for the individual to acquire new words and for the community to invent them, or for either to borrow them from foreigners. Where the alphabet gave an open literacy extraverted to novelty, the *tzu* gave a closed literacy introverted to its own prototypes. Signification, already depotentiated by the sound/meaning ratio, was further beclouded by the accommodating but unresponsive script. The alphabet was an arithmetic tailored exactly to sound and significance; the *tzu* were an algebra which could mean everything or nothing. Once again the medium smothered the message.

By the beginning of the Christian era, both China and the West possessed a body of literature and a tradition of study which was, on one hand, a vehicle of education and, on the other, both a means and end of government. Both the Han and the Roman empires, as we saw above, were founded upon a *paedeia*. The character of the *paedeias*, however, were different. The Chinese tradition was paradigmatic, introverted to concepts, ethical; the Western tradition was syntagmatic, extraverted to things, metaphysical. In both cultures there was a certain transition from mythology to philosophy, but it had been made to different degrees and in opposite directions. In Greece the concrete mythology of Homer and Hesiod was overlaid by the equally concrete pre-Socratic cosmologies, and both gods and cosmologies were eventually subsumed in the mathematical *Dieu cosmique* of orthodox Platonism or the transcendent *Dieu inconnu* of gnosticism. Concrete paradigm was replaced by concrete syntagmata and then by abstract syntagmata. There was a complete transition from mythology to philosophy. In China, *per contra*, the concrete mythology of the Shang and the early Chou was dissolved by, on the one hand, historicization (conversion of gods to heroes and dynastic founders, an inverse Euhemerism) and, on the other, ritualization (absorption of myth in liturgy), leaving only abstractions like *t'ien, tao* and *te* behind. Paradigm was reinforced by theoretical abstraction and practical concreteness and philosophy's problem was not the structure of the cosmos but the method of elucidating the paradigms. There was only a partial transition from mythology to philosophy.

The Chinese *paideia*, more than the Western, was centred on form rather than content. It was a communications system rather than a body of doctrine. The *Shih-ching* provided the model for poetry, the *Shu-ching* for prose, and poetry was preferred to prose as being more highly formalized. In both China and the West, the past was a prototype for the present, but where Alexander the Great used the model of Achilles to assert his personality and break continuity, the Han emperors used the model of the sage-emperors to conceal theirs and buttress it. History was understood not, as in Thucydides, as tragedy or pathology, but, as in the *Ch'un-ch'iu*, as annals where morality taught by example. In the *Li-chi*, ethics were reduced to protocol and the *I-ching* provided not an actual cosmology but a repository of concepts for all possible cosmologies.

Similarly, Confucius (author of *Lun-yu*) and Lao-tzu (author of *Tao-te ching*) had no doctrine to teach, no wisdom to impart. They were concerned not to advance views, but to define the conditions for any views: linguistic reform in the one case, the recognition of the inadequacy of language in the other. They defined the conditions for debate, not as a modern philosopher to clear the ground for argument, but because for them to settle the medium was to settle the message: the categories of thought are thought, thought and reality are isomorphic, and all thought needs are the proper paradigms, the little red book of reality. This tradition was in marked contrast with that of the West where, whether in Indian cosmology, Zoroastrian ethical prophecy, Greek empiricism and logic, or Old Testament theocentrism, there was a recognition of the duality of paradigm and syntagma and the primacy of the latter. In this major intellectual contrast with China, all the minor contrasts within the West – the one and the many, metaphysics and ethics, rationalism and religion, science and intentionality analysis – were swallowed up.

Architectonics
In addition to the contrast of physical and intellectual foundations between China and the West, there was also a contrast

in architectonics. The social and political structures erected on the foundations differed in ground plan, spatial relations and decor.

Ground plans. The Roman empire was laid out like an ampitheatre around the arena of the Mediterranean. Rome itself was the imperial box, the older coastal provinces were the stalls, the new inland *limes* provinces were the heavily buttressed upper circle. The internal differentiation was between, on the one hand, upper and lower, *limes* and city, and on the other, sun and shade, the old urbanization of the east, the new urbanization of the west. The Han empire, *per contra*, was laid out like a wheel. The region of the two imperial capitals, Ch'ang-an and Lo-yang, formed the hub; the converging valleys of the Wei, the Fen, the Ching, the Lo, the Han and the Huang-ho formed the spokes. The internal differentiation was between centre and circumference, capital and provinces. Both empires in antiquity were centrally planned, but Rome in a series of concentric circles, China in a series of radiating lines. The Roman empire was the work of a city state which sought to stabilize its dominion by universalizing cities, city life, institutions and values. It tended therefore to homogenization, a general rise in the level of urbanization, a Conrad Hilton civilization of everywhere-similar fora, basilicas, theatres, baths, circuses and insulae. The Chinese empire, on the other hand, was the work of a bureaucratic territorial state which sought to stabilize its dominion by monopolizing for the court capital resources, amenities, protection and prestige. It tended therefore to heterogenization, to a fall in the general level of urbanization following the unification of the empire and a growing disparity between the lifestyles of court and country. Both empires lived by and for cultural glamour and conspicuous consumption but in the one case they were diffused, in the other concentrated.

Spatial relations. A comparison of the extent and character of the communications systems of the two areas suggests that Han China was less integrated than the Roman empire. According to Needham, the Roman empire under Hadrian covered 1 763 000 square miles and had 48 500 miles of road,

an average of 27.5 miles of road per 1000 square miles of
territory. Han China, on the other hand, covered 1 532 000
square miles and had 22 000 miles of road, an average of
only 14.35 miles of road per 1000 square miles of territory.[11]
Moreover, while for Han China, roads were the essence of
the communications system, for Rome they were only an
adjunct to the Mediterranean whose sea lanes will have at
least doubled the total length of routes. Needham suggests
that the greater use of rivers and canals for transportation
in China as compared to Europe counterbalanced the advantage of the Mediterranean. This may be true for the later
periods of Chinese history, the T'ang and the Sung, for example, when the Grand Canal had been completed, but it is
doubtful for the Han. Neither the Yellow River nor its
tributaries, in whose valleys Chinese civilization was then
centred, are good for navigation and most Han hydraulic
activity was for irrigation, not communication. Like the
Achaemenid empire, Han China was a road state on a plateau,
and this in itself ensured inferiority in spatial integration to
a Mediterranean empire, since in pre-modern conditions land
transport was twenty to forty times more expensive than water
transport. Moreover, the loess limited the utility of the roads
by its vertical cleavage, crevassing and occlusion of adjacent
valleys. Teilhard de Chardin vividly describes this terrain: 'an
unbelievable network of fissures with vertical walls, in the
midst of which one feels as lost and paralysed as in the middle
of the trees of a forest or the waves of the sea'.[12] Needham
seems to imply that Han China and Rome were not dissimilar
in spatial relations; to me, the evidence suggests that they
were strikingly different.

Decor.   Even allowing for accidents of survival, it is difficult
not to conclude from the archaeological remains that Han
China was a less splendid society than Imperial Rome. The
Great Wall no doubt is a stupendous monument, though most
of its imposing appearance dates from Ming rather than Han
times, but it stands by itself, and though Chinese cities had
impressive walls, they did not contain the monumental public
buildings of the Classical West – the ampitheatres, aqueducts,
arches, basilicas, baths, circuses, theatres and temples. Rome

was a federation of city states, Han China was a swollen court; but in addition, the difference between their towns was rooted in different options for building materials and different conceptions of what a house was for. The fundamental options of Rome and, following her, Europe generally, were for stone, diffusion of heat by hypocausts or multiple fireplaces, and durability. A house was a capital investment, perhaps the prototype of all fixed capital investment, an assertion of culture in the face of nature. The fundamental Chinese options, on the other hand, were for wood, concentration of heat at the *k'ang* or heated divan, and repairability. A house was a charge on income, an extension of consumer non-durables, an adaptation of culture to nature. In the West, buildings were in principle winter palaces, exclusions of weather, permanent embodiments of hearth and family. In China, buildings were in principle summer houses, modifications of weather, makeshift additions to the real home which was the loess cave or the family tomb. The one option produced monumentality and splendour, the other convenience and harmony.[13]

This contrast particularly struck European travellers in the seventeenth century. Thus the Portuguese Jesuit Semedo explained that 'the houses where they inhabit are not so sumptuous and lasting as ours'; Athanasius Kircher, the learned collator of all the information about China available in Europe in the 1660s observed: 'As for the buildings within the walls, those of private persons are not stately, they having more regard to their conveniency than splendour or ornament.' The Italian layman Gemelli wrote from Nanchang, 'it is vain to look for stately structures here or in other parts of China; for as the cities here are all built by one model, so all the houses are flat, low, and made of brick and mud, there being very few of stone'; while the Tyrolese Jesuit Martino Martina stated, 'les maisons ne sont pas magnifiques; mais elles sont plus commodes et plus nettes que les notres'.[14]

Decay
Finally, besides these contrasts of foundations and architectonics, there was a contrast between the two empires in the pattern of their decay. Although there were superficial similarities between the fall of the Roman empire and the

fall of the Han empire, there were more profound differences which in the end made the two episodes more unlike than like: differences in health, pathology and prognosis.

The body politic of the Han was healthier than that of the Roman empire. With its superior physical technology in arable farming and metallurgy and its lower degreee of urbanization, intercommunication and luxury building, the Han world did not suffer from irremediable contradictions between superstructure and base, state and society. Frictions there were, no doubt, but they were adjustable without cataclysm. In the Roman body politic, on the other hand, with its more primitive physical technology yet more grandiose and more parasitic sociology, there were such contradictions, especially after the Illyrian emperors, in response to the military mutinies and barbarian invasions of the mid-third century, doubled the army and multiplied fortifications without sufficient provision for increased agricultural productivity behind the front. The huge carapace of the Roman *limes* imposed a burden on the organism it shielded that was far heavier than the Han protectorate garrisons in Central Asia. The Great Wall is impressive, but with Han Wu-ti's forward policy, it ceased to be a frontier and Han China was not a *limes* society with its attendant costs and dangers.

Both the Han and the Roman empires were the work of elites – educated, civilian and urban. Both coexisted with and were threatened by non-elites: barbarians beyond the frontier, sectaries outside the *paideia*, soldiers separated from the civilian community, and peasants below the level of urbanization. There were genuine parallels between the Huns and the Hsiung-nu, between African Christianity and the Five Pecks of Rice movement in Szechwan, between the military emperors and Chinese third-century warlords, between the Bagaudae and the Red Eyebrows. The difference, however, was that, while in the West these non-elites brought about the downfall of the empire (or at least its contraction to the southern Balkans and Anatolia), in China they did not. The pathologies were different.

There were two Roman empires not one. The first, the classical empire of the Julio-Claudians, Flavians and Antonines, was constructed as a pan-Mediterranean mosaic of *kulturstadts*. It was overthrown in the third century either, on Rostovtzev's social interpretation, by depressed peasants acting through military pronunciamentos or, in a more institutional view, by alienated soldiers of the *limes* acting through their ambitious commanders. The second empire, the *restitutio orbis* of the Illyrian, Constantinian and Theodosian emperors, was reconstructed, behind massive defences, as an hierarchy of field armies and imperial capitals. It was overthrown in the west by the combined, though contrary, action of the barbarian soldiers absorbed into its *limes* and the Christian culture which, until too late, refused to assimilate them. In the east, it was restricted to the southern Balkans and Anatolia by the sudden appearance of militant sectaries who united and projected against it a hitherto harmless subculture of camelmen. All four non-elites – barbarians, sectaries, soldiers and peasants – played some part in the fall of the Roman empire: it was a social revolution.[15]

In China on the other hand, under the Han and its successor states down to 400 AD, the San-kuo and the Chin, pathology came from within the elite. It came from the aristocracy of great families, the equivalent, *mutatis mutandis* of the senatorial aristocracy of the Western empire or the *pronoia*-holding magnates of medieval Byzantium. These people, the Ma, the Tou, the Liang, the Wang, the Ssu-ma, who as a Chin catchphrase put it 'share the world', were not primarily a landed aristocracy though they owned estates and, especially, the newly invented watermill. Rather their substance consisted in men: *k'o*, literally guests, that is clients, retainers, tenants, servants and slaves. For their *k'o*, as evidence of their power and prestige, patrons sought exemption from tax lists and muster rolls and thus weakened the fiscal and military foundations of the central government. The Han empire rested on a base of tax-paying and conscription-bearing free farmers. A vicious circle began: the more privileges for *k'o*, the greater the fiscal and draft pressures on the remaining free farmers, the greater the temptation to escape such freedom by commendation and an increase in the number of *k'o*. The Han empire died slowly by financial and military asphyxiation.

The rise of the great families began in the reign of Han Wu-ti who allowed society to solidify in return for unchallenged political power. Checked momentarily at the beginning of the Christian era by the usurper emperor Wang Mang who attempted to nationalize the land, the great families consolidated their position under the restored Eastern Han. The court tried to control them by successively promoting as counterweights, consort families, eunuchs and the literati meritocracy, but the cure was worse than the disease. It produced only an exacerbated, four-cornered factionalism in which the Han emperors first became puppets and then were swept away together. The San-kuo, or three kingdoms, which succeeded the Han in the third century, each represented an element of this factionalism. Wei in north China was based on eunuch militarism, Wu in the Yangtze delta represented the colonial and commercial tradition of the consort families, while Shu in Szechwan, legitimist and classical, looked back to the older patricians. The meritocracy, the losers, could only seek momentary patrons or retreat into religion. All three states, tended towards a common patronal-aristocratic social structure, which by 300 AD dominated all China.

In the fall of the Han the non-elites played only a subsidiary role. Ts'ao Ts'ao, the effective founder of Wei, was a politician rather than a warlord, more like Caesar Borgia than Maximinus Thrax; the Yellow Turbans, often described as a peasant revolt, were in reality managed by members of the gentry; and the Taoist religious communities under similar management never achieved the importance of the church under Gallienus and Diocletian. Barbarians were more noticeable, especially after 300, but even here, China, having no *limes* to provide a reservoir, experienced even less of a *Volkerwanderungen* than Europe. There was no permanent linguistic change along the Great Wall as there was along the Danube, Rhine and *Litus Saxonicum*, and the short-lived barbarian dynasties were the work of *condottieri* who were quickly absorbed into the on-going aristocratic structure of society. The fall of the Han did not involve a social revolution.[16]

In combination, the differences in health and pathology produced a different prognosis. The fall of the Roman empire was a true general crisis involving the relations of state and society, superstructure and base, culture and nature. Once fallen, it was going to be difficult to re-erect, as Justinian, Charlemagne and Frederick II variously discovered. The heirs of the non-elites, the manorial aristocracy, the monasticized church, the embryonic emporia, had been fundamentally de-imperialized and de-classicized. In neither its classical nor its late antique form could the empire expect revival. Increasingly it became a myth, its only future a renaissance, a resurrection after the spirit not the flesh. The fall of the Han empire, on the other hand, was not a general crisis, only a shift within the elite from political power to social power, from bureaucracy to aristocracy, from central to local patronage, from abstract social order to concrete inter-subjectivity. The imperatives which had led to the creation of the empire in the first place, the need of the elite for a central point of cultural activity to combat the suffocating provincialism of China, still existed. It only needed a measure of political and institutional creativity, to recombine what had proved dissociable, *imperium* and aristocracy, for the empire to be restored in a new and improved form. Restoration was not a myth or an aspiration, but a political programme and the resurrection would be physical.

Han China and the Roman West had both similarities and dissimilarities, but the latter were more significant than the former. The Chinese empire, with its superior physical technology, its half-mythic mentality, less pretentious sociology and more compromisable conflicts, was a different organism from the Roman empire with its shaky physical foundations, its powerful intellectuality, its over-ambitious structure and its liability to fracture. This disparity between the two island civilizations created the possibility of fruitful contact between them.

AVENUES OF CONTACT, 200 BC TO 400 AD

Until the Great Discoveries, there were four avenues of contact between China and Europe: the northern land route, the central land route, the southern sea route, and the far southern sea route. All functioned in antiquity; none provided more than tangential or episodic relations. The same may be said of China's marginal contacts with Black Africa and pre-Columbian America.

The central land route

The most famous of the traditional avenues of contact was
the central land route: the classical silk road, more accurately
a network of alternative roads, from north-west China
through the oases of the two Turkestans and northern Persia
to the ports of Syria and the Black Sea. The picture of the
silk road as a major Eurasian intercontinental link channelling
silk in one direction and precious metals, stuccoes and glass
in the other, derives from two men: Richthofen, the greatest
modern geographer of China, and Aurel Stein, the greatest
modern archaeologist of Central Asia. In his *Letters* to the
Shanghai chamber of commerce, 1870–72, which formed the
prolegomena to his three-volume *China: Ergebnisse eigner
Reisen und darauf gegründeter Studien, 1877–1885*, Richthofen
surveyed the trade routes converging at Sian:

> Since time immemorial, commerce has found out the
> natural road from Lan-chau-fu to Su-chau, and its further
> continuation and bifurcation. Along the Nan-lu the fame
> of the Tsin dynasty spread to the Persians and the Romans.
> Fourteen centuries afterwards Marco Polo travelled on it
> to Lan-chau-fu, to go thence by Ning-hai-fu and Kwei-hua-
> ching to the residence of Kublai-Khan. The Chinese
> Emperors were, at an early period of history, awake to the
> importance of the possession of these channels of interna-
> tional traffic, because it gave them the dominion of Central
> Asia.[17]

In his *On Ancient Central Asian Tracks*, a summary of his life's
work published in 1933, Stein wrote in a chapter entitled
'Chinese expansion into Central Asia and the contact of civilizations':

> In the interest of the development of China's internal
> resources it was very important to use the newly opened
> route for direct access to fresh markets for China's indust-
> rial products, and in particular for the most valuable among
> them, its silk textiles. There is in fact ample evidence in
> the Chinese records to show that the great westward move
> initiated by the Emperor Wu-ti was meant to serve economic

considerations connected with trade quite as much as political aims.[18]

Whether the flag followed trade as in Richthofen or trade the flag as in Stein, the concept of the silk road as founded by Chinese imperialism, developed by Roman luxury and sustained by Central Asian enterprise, won much support. In 1895 Chavannes in his introduction to his translation of the *Shih-chi*, provided the basic information from the Chinese end on which Stein drew. A catena of classical quotations: Lucan's story of Cleopatra's see-through dress of silk, Seneca's denunciation of similar dresses at Rome, Pliny's assertion that the eastern trade drained a hundred million sesterces a year, Ptolemy's account from Marinus of Tyre of Maes Titianos's expedition to the Seres, Pausanias' near correct description of the technology of silk, all supplied the Western background. Philologists were disposed by Stein's discovery of manuscripts in little or unknown languages such as Sogdian, Kuchean, Agnean and Khotanese to believe in a civilization of Central Asian city states supported by international trade. Archaeology, at Tunhuang, Niya, Samarkand, Ay Khanoum (Alexandria on the Oxus), Surkh Kotal, Taxila and Palmyra, found the silk road a convenient framework within which to operate. Zoology invoked a powerful trade route using hybrids to explain the retreat of the Bactrian two-hump camel before its one-hump Arabian rival on the Iranian plateau.

Nevertheless, while the existence of the silk road is not in doubt, there are reasons for thinking its economic importance has been exaggerated. First, Braudel, not an undervaluer of 'ports, routes et traffics', has warned against over-estimation of the quantitative significance of any pre-modern trade. In the seventeenth century, the Baltic grain trade, one of the prime components of intra-European commerce and a basis of the greatness of Amsterdam, supplied only 1 or 2 per cent of the grain consumed in the Mediterranean. Second, as noted above, in pre-modern conditions the average cost of transport by land was twenty to forty times as expensive as transport by water. Traffic would prefer a water route to a land route if one was available, which in this case it was. Third, the silk road, because of its terrain, its protection costs and its vulnerability to taxation at every oasis, was expensive even for a land route. Maes Titianos' expedition sounds more like an oil search than a business trip. Fourth, while silk had a success of novelty at Rome and writers commented on it, the pattern of Roman spending went more for luxury foodstuffs than textiles. According to M.I. Finley, the absence of large-scale textile production for the market was a feature of the ancient economy.[19] Even allowing that Pliny's hundred million sesterces were more than rhetoric, they would amount to no more than 2 per cent of a reasonable estimate of the gross national product of the Roman world. Fifth, when at other times the silk road was operating strongly, it brought in its wake plague, endemic in northern Central Asia, to both the Mediterranean and China. The best opinion of medical historians is that plague was unknown in the Mediterranean till the plague of Justinian in 541 and in China until the plague of the Empress Wu in 682.

The real significance of the silk road was cultural rather than commercial. Its true sponsors were Hellenism, Chinese curiosity, Buddhism and Christianity.

The antecedents of the silk road are to be found in the plans of Alexander the Great. Whether those plans were based on Tarn's inspired ecumenism, Lane Fox's lived epic, or Badian's military improvisation, Bactria held a pivotal place in them, as evidenced by Alexander's marriage to Roxana and his foundation there of numerous Alexandrias. Bactria was to be the pivot of Hellenism in the east. A land of city states, the home of the great horse and cataphract cavalry, Iranian without being Persian, it was ideal for Alexander's synthesis. The Greeks in Bactria and India may not have fulfilled all Alexander's hopes, but they achieved a considerable degree of Hellenization and their cultural ripples went far. Euthydemus I, c.210–190 BC, tried to make contact with China (the word Seres, from the Chinese *ssu* = silk, the regular Western term for China, first occurs in a work of Apollodorus of Artemita, quoted by Strabo, describing Euthydemus' activities), and his grandsons Euthydemus, Pantaleon and Agathocles succeeded, if, as seems probable, the cupro-nickel for their coinage came from Yunnan.

The actual beginning of the silk road, however, was due to Chinese curiosity about the outside world. It began with Han Wu-ti's flurry of diplomatic activity following the return in

126 BC of Chang Ch'ien's mission to Central Asia. The aim
of the mission had been military allies against the Hsiung-nu,
but the motive behind the subsequent embassies and the construction of a fortified road from Tun-huang across the desert
of Lop-nor to Karashahr was cultural. Han Wu-ti and his
successors wanted a window to the west to combat the isolation
which constantly threatened China with provinciality.

As cultural claustrophobia was the perpetual danger of
Chinese society, so the provision of cultural glamour was the
permanent function of the Chinese state.[20] The Han in particular, as plebeian upstarts, sought to strengthen their legitimacy by associating it with the dominant intellectual trend
of the day, the internationalist philosophy of Tsou Yen. Transmitted from the Ch'in via Han Wen-ti's chancellor Chang
Ts'ang and the circle of the prince of Huai-nan, this
philosophy taught that China was not the centre of the world,
that it was only one of a number of continents, and that as
knowledge was in principle global, China must make contact
with the outside world. When therefore Han Wu-ti learnt
from Chang Ch'ien that there was indeed, as Tsou Yen had
conjectured, a civilized world outside China, he hastened to
contact it by dispatching lavishly equipped embassies bearing
silk to Bactria, Parthia, Mesopotamia, India and possibly Syria
and Egypt, by constructing two monstrous exit roads north-
west and south-west, and by entertaining foreign return
embassies with banquets, gifts, tours round China and atten-
dance on imperial progress. Tax-payers might complain, Confucian moralists might remonstrate, but as Ssu-ma Hsiang-ju,
the emperor's court poet (and also his roads commissioner)
who hymned his boxing of the compass in his extravaganza
the *Mighty One*, put it: 'The proof that our ruler has received
the mandate of heaven lies in this very undertaking to the
west'.[21]

If the silk road was opened by Han Wu-ti's cultural diplomacy, it was consolidated and institutionalized by Buddhist
missionary activity. When Chinese Buddhist pilgrims give us
our first travelogues of the silk road, what is described is a
world of monasteries, relic shrines and pagodas maintained
by a pyramid of local royal patrons culminating in the
supreme patron, the *cakravartin*, the Kushan king. Thus Fa-
hsien, who was in Central Asia at the turn of the fourth and

fifth centuries, mentions 4000 monks at Karashahr, fourteen large monasteries at Khotan, 1000 monks at Kargalik, a pagoda for one of Buddha's teeth at Kashgar, a 400-foot pagoda at Peshawar built by Kanishka – the most famous of the Kushan kings – and also at Peshawar a monastery for 700 monks which preserved Buddha's alms bowl. Other major Buddhist centres were Turfan, an important source of texts and translations, Kucha, the headquarters of Hinayana in Central Asia and, above all, Bamiyan, a Kushan capital and the exemplar of the gigantic religious statuary copied in China. Buddhist pilgrimage provided a motive for travel, Buddhist institutions provided an infrastructure of guest houses, letters of recommendation and information facilities for travellers; and Buddhist piety promoted traffic by its demand for stucco Saint-Sulpicerie, incense and devotional scrolls. The chronology of 'export Buddhism', both Hinayana and Mahayana, and its expansion into Central Asia is not yet established. The beginnings of Bamiyan, however, may be associated with Kanishka in 'the twenties or thirties of the second century AD';[22] 'the first datable trace of Buddhism at Khotan is the famous Kharosthi manuscript of a Prakrit version of the *Dharmapada*. . . which seems to date from the second century AD',[23] and Kucha produced a Buddhist monk, Po Yen, who went to China in 258.[24] It may be supposed that the tolerant Kushans gave particular support to Buddhism because, more than Zoroastrianism, Hinduism and Hellenism which they also protected, it was not bound to a national culture but would absorb Hellenistic sculpture, Indian painting and Iranian imagery, while retaining its own identity. The Buddhist element of the silk road, like the Chinese, developed under cultural imperatives.

A third factor in the development of the silk road was Christian missionary activity which after 400 was to reach China and introduce the technology of silk to the West. Christian evangelization to the east began as early as to the west. It was for a long time more successful and it is only less well-known because it was conducted by the Judaeo-Christian and Aramaic rather than the Gentile and Greek half of the church.

The apostles Jude, Thomas and Bartholomew preached in the half-Jewish, Roman client kingdoms of Osrhoene and

Adiabene and established Christian communities, particularly at Edessa, which looked back to them and James, first bishop of Jerusalem, as their founders. At the end of the second century, as the exclusive Hellenism of the Antonines rose to climax, non-Hellenic Christianity expanded in compensation. Osroene became the first Christian state under Abgar IX, the number of bishops, and hence Christian communities, in Adiabene increased from one to more than twenty between 200 and 224, and new Christian nuclei appeared in Media, Parthia and Bactria. Philip the Arab, perhaps the first emperor personally a Christian, was a native of Osrhoene, and Paul of Samosata, first political bishop and exponent of the half-Jewish adoptionist heresy, was the relative and intimate counsellor of the Philosemite Queen Zenobia of Palmyra, co-ruler of the east under Claudius Gothicus. In 224 came the great disaster for eastern Christianity, the Sassanid revolution, which imposed the harsh anti-Western Zoroastrian orthodoxy of the Persian plateau on the Shah's semitic subjects in Babylonia and those he conquered from the Romans in Mesopotamia. After his victory over Valerian in 258, Shapur I deported the Christian communities of Mesopotamia to Iran to safeguard his frontiers, and Shapur II martyred three successive archbishops of Seleucia-Ctesiphon.

Eastern Christianity, however, survived and even expanded in its new home. From being a refuge from the implicitly persecuting Hellenism of the Roman empire, it became a refuge from the explicitly persecuting Zoroastrianism of the Sassanids. From being based on the non-Persian caravan cities of the west, it became based on the non-Persian, though still Iranian, caravan cities of the east in Khorasan, Ariana and Transoxania. When the tolerant Shah Yazdgard the Sinner allowed Archbishop Maruta of Maipherqat to reconstitute the church of the east by a council at Seleucia-Ctesiphon in 410, forty bishops attended; and more attended a second council in 424. The list of sees is a map of the western silk road: Seleucia, Rai, Seistan, Herat, Merv. Like Buddhism in the east with its monasteries, so Christianity in the west with its bishoprics (for Mesopotamian Christianity was originally hostile to monasticism), provided an infrastructure for circulation which could serve commerce, but whose prime purpose was cultural.

The southern sea route

More important economically than the silk road and in its western half, at least, carrying a greater volume of silk, was the southern sea route: a succession of sea lanes extending from Canton and Hanoi via the Malay Peninsula, Ceylon, the coasts of Coromandel and Malabar to the Persian gulf, the Red Sea and Egypt. The remote origin of northern Indian Ocean navigation has a pedigree which includes Queen Hatshepsut's expedition to Punt c.1495 BC, the commercial ventures from Elath organized by Solomon and Hiram of Tyre, the subsequent Tyrian trading network described meticulously but obscurely by Ezekiel in Chapter 27, of his book in the Old Testament, and the naval operations of Scylax of Caryanda under Darius the Great and Nearchos the Cretan under Alexander the Great; but its real beginning was the voyage of Eudoxus of Cyzicus from Egypt to India in the reign of Ptolemy VIII Euergetes II, 145 to 116 BC.

The Ptolemies were losing out in the Mediterranean to Rome and losing touch with the land route to the east in Syria. It is not surprising that Ptolemy VIII, one of the most intelligent of the later Lagids, sought compensation by opening a window to the south by sea. Besides Posidonius' account of Eudoxus' voyage, we have Agatharchides' reference in the next reign to the cosmopolitanism of Socotra and the report that, after Actium, Cleopatra considered sailing to India to found a new kingdom. As part of the Alexander–Dionysus myth, India played a considerable role in the cultural imagery of Ptolemaic Alexandria. At the same time, Ptolemy VIII's contemporary Han Wu-ti was developing the sea route from the Chinese end. His eunuchs used native shipping to go, certainly, to the Malay Peninsula, possibly to Bengal, armed with silks to purchase, among other things, glass, probably from Alexandria. Wang Mang, Cleopatra's contemporary, sent an embassy to Bengal by sea with the aim of obtaining a rhinoceros. With the Greeks and the Chinese active, the Indians soon took up their natural role as middlemen. In the *Milindapanha*, usually dated to the second or third century AD, but referring to an earlier period, Nagasena compares the *arhat* to the rich shipowner who having paid his port dues crosses the high seas to Bengal, Takola in the Malay Peninsula and China in one direction, and to Alexandria in the other. Ceylon too, which figures so prominently in Ptolemy's world map and which was so prosperous in the early centuries AD, was also involved in the route.

The scale of the traffic was considerable, Strabo was told that 120 ships sailed annually to India from Myos Hormos, the Egyptian port on the Red Sea. *The Periplus of the Erythracan Sea*, the first-century AD Greek description of the western half of the Indian Ocean networks, has an account of the ports of Malabar which were traded in by 'Greek ships from Egypt': 'The ships which frequent these ports are of a large size on account of the great amount and bulkiness of the pepper and betel of which their lading consists, while another commodity available was fine silk'.[25]

The Chinese sources likewise indicate a considerable volume of shipping. A third-century text, the *Nan-chou i-wu chih* ('Strange Things of the South') speaks of foreign, possibly Indian, vessels in the South China Sea, capable of carrying 600 to 700 people and 260 tons of cargo. The report of the Chinese ambassador to Cambodia in 260, K'ang T'ai, referred to 'great junks' with seven sails, belonging to a Malayan or Indonesian state, which voyaged from the Far East to the Roman empire.[26] A seventh-century text, the *Liang-shu*, describes one of the Cambodian satellite cities on the Malay Peninsula in the period after K'ang T'ai's visit:

> The eastern frontier of Tun-Sun is in communication with Tong-king, the western with India and Parthia. . . At this mart east and west meet together so that daily there are innumerable people there. Precious goods and rare merchandise – there is nothing which is not there.[27]

Fa-hsien, the Buddhist pilgrim who went to India by land via the silk road in 399, returned to China by sea. He had no difficulty in finding 'a large merchant-vessel on which there were over two hundred souls' to take him from Ceylon to Java, and a similar ship to carry him on to Canton.[28] From both east and west, the picture is of a regular, well-established traffic, in particular areas on some scale, using the best shipping of the day.

Nevertheless, the intercontinental component of this traffic was limited. Few ships travelled all the way across the Indian

Ocean and few travellers went from Alexandria to Canton, or vice versa, by a relay of ships. The *Periplus* describes the south-west monsoon route direct from Berbera to Bombay and Malabar and the dates for catching the north-east monsoon on the return; but the greater part of the book is concerned with the inshore route along the coasts of Arabia and Persia, a route of *cabotage* for localized imports and exports. Similarly, though the *Han-shu* describes routes from the Malay Peninsula across the bay of Bengal and back, the *Liang-shu* states, 'The gulf of Siam is of great extent and ocean-going junks have not yet crossed it direct'.[29] Coastal traffic short-distance was the rule, oceanic traffic long-distance the exception.

It was the same with people. Propertius has a poem about a girl at Rome whose husband had been twice to Bactria and had 'been seen by the mailed horsemen of China';[30] but the Han court were surprised when the An-tun embassy, probably a group of Greek merchants claiming authorization from Marcus Aurelius, arrived at Hanoi in 166. Similarly, K'ang T'ai knew of a Chinese merchant, Chia Hsiang-li who traded to and from India, but most Chinese merchants stopped at the barrier of the Malay Peninsula, which was where the knowledge of the *Periplus* gave out too. The *Periplus* was pessimistic about contact with China; 'to penetrate into China is not an easy undertaking and but few merchants come from it, and that rarely'.[31] Seneca referred to the Chinese as 'a people unknown even to trade',[32] known therefore only by their products transmitted by intermediaries. So while the southern sea route carried more traffic than the silk road, it was not much stronger as a link between the closed worlds of East Asia and Western Eurasia.

The far southern sea route

By contrast, the third route linking East and West, the far southern sea route, from the spice islands of Indonesia via the Cocos Islands and the Chagos archipelago to Madagascar and Zanzibar and thence to Somalia and the Red Sea, or alternatively direct from Timor to Madagascar and East Africa along the imaginary coast of Ptolemy's southern continent, was exclusively intercontinental. The existence of this route (which is also called the cinnamon route or the route of the raftmen) in classical times has been argued powerfully by J. Innes Miller.[33]

Cinnamon has probably been known in the Mediterranean since the second millennium BC. Herodotus describes it as being used in mummification and Ezekiel mentions it as one of the commodities handled by the Tyrian trading network. Classical authors are unanimous in regarding it as a product of Africa and it was not handled by the routes described in the *Periplus* except in so far as it was injected into them at Opone (Mogadishu) and Mosullan (Berbera) from the East African coast. In fact, however, in classical times, cinnamon was only produced in southern China, and northern Southeast Asia, its later centre of production in Ceylon not then having been developed. A passage in Pliny, whose significance J. Innes Miller was the first to appreciate, unlocks the mystery. Pliny explains that cinnamon was brought to Africa by 'merchant-sailors' who 'bring it over vast seas on rafts which have no rudders to steer them, or oars to push or pull them, or sails or other aids to navigation, but instead only the spirit of man and human courage', taking 'almost five years' over a round trip.[36] These raftmen Dr Miller understands to be Indonesians from Java and points east, using double outrigger craft and taking advantage of the south equatorial current, which would indeed carry them, without further navigational force, to East Africa and Madagascar, which thus became the curious Afro-Indonesian community, the world's first transoceanic colony, that it remains today. The history of this route clearly depends on the chronology of cinnamon and the outrigger, (also those of South-east Asian bananas and taro in Africa), but it may well be the oldest of the routes. However, as regards volume and, despite the high cost of the cinnamon, value of traffic, the use of this route must always have been limited.

The northern land route

The fourth route between East and West, the northern land route, from the Zungharian gate across the Kazakh and Kipchaq steppes to the Black Sea, was little used in antiquity. Its

existence may be inferred from Herodotus' account of the
Scyths and the peoples to their east which was based on the
information of the wandering shamans, Abaris the Hyperbo-
rean and Aristeas of Proconnesus, and from Chang Ch'ien's
report on the two nomadic countries to the north-west of
Transoxania, K'ang-chu or the Kazakh steppe and Yen-ts'ai
or the steppe to the north of the Caspian. According to the
court poet Ssu-ma Hsiang-ju, K'ang-chu sent ambassadors to
the Han, and the *Shih-chi* states that Chinese ambassadors
were sent to Yen-ts'ai. Similarly the Greek city states to the
north of the Black Sea – Tyras, Olbia, Chersonesus,
Theodosia, Panticopaeum, Tanais and Phanagoria, 'the hem
of Greece sewn onto the fields of the barbarians',[37] – were in
limited touch with the adjacent steppe peoples. However, the
sketchiness of the information available to both East and West
indicates that not much traffic travelled this route. Its significance was not that of an avenue of intercontinental contact,
though some silk and ginger may have been carried, but
rather a point of diffusion to both East and West of commodities and cultural goods from the Balkash–Baikal region,
notably gold and the hallucinogenic mushroom.

American contact

China's link to Black Africa in antiquity has already been
dealt with in what was said above about the route of the
raftmen, but something needs to be added about Chinese
contact with pre-Columbian America. The first writer to
argue that America must have been peopled by land from
Asia was the Spanish Jesuit José de Acosta in his *Historia
natural y moral de las Indias* published in Seville in 1590. Here
he considered and rejected both the theory of Atlantic origin
put forward by his contemporary rival, Philip II's librarian
Benito Arias Montano, and theories of accidental or deliberate voyaging across the Pacific: accidental, on the grounds
that it would hardly explain the fauna of America; deliberate,
on the grounds of its impossibility without the compass. The
theory that Meso-America derived from China by sea was,
however, revived by the Tyrolean Jesuit Martino Martini in
his *Sinicae Historiae Decas Prima* of 1658. It was accepted by
his fellow Jesuit Athanasius Kircher, a radical cultural dif-

fusionist and one of the earliest theorists of ocean currents, and in the eighteenth century it gave rise to a controversy between the speculative orientalist Joseph de Guignes, who supported it on the basis of passages in the *Liang-shu*, and the sceptical, sinologue Jesuit, Antoine Gaubil. Gaubil won on points and no definite evidence of Chinese voyaging across the Pacific before the nineteenth century has yet been found.

Indeed, the Chinese were conscious of the difference between their western and eastern contacts. As the Chin scholar Chang Hua wrote at the end of the third century, 'the ambassador of the Han, Chang Ch'ien won through across the western seas to reach Ta Ch'in (the Roman empire). . . but the eastern ocean is yet more vast, and we know of no one who has crossed it'.[38] Yet, as Needham points out, the exploratory expeditions to the east under the Ch'in and early Han recorded in the *Shih-chi*; the later voyages to Japan, possibly Kamchatka and even the Aleutians; the existence, known to the Chinese from the first centuries BC, of the Kurosiwo current and the north Pacific drift, plus the possibly Asian origins of American rafts, Inca cotton and Amerindian hookworms; and parallels at least in art and architecture all make early Sino-American contact by sea possible, even likely and further evidence must be awaited. However the import of this must not be exaggerated since the wind and current systems of the north Pacific make it unlikely that any Chinese travellers returned to the east from the New World. Columbus may not have been Chinese, but, as Chaunu has said, the significance of Columbus was not that he went, but that he came back.

INTERCHANGES, 200 BC TO 400 AD

We must now turn to see what travelled along these avenues of contact: people, flora and fauna, commodities, techniques and ideas. Surprisingly, given the tenuous nature of the links between East and West it was the intellectual interchanges which were the most notable in antiquity.

People

Few people travelled between China and the West in antiquity and fewer still between China and Black Africa or China and pre-Columbian America. Of those who did – the merchants, the diplomatic agents, the missionaries – most were transitory visitors who founded no permanent community of their compatriots. Four possible cases, three in one direction and one in the other, should be mentioned to underline their rarity and doubtfulness.

The first case is that of the supposed Roman military settlement in Kansu. A passage in the *Han-shu* describes how in 36 BC, following the siege of a city in eastern Transoxania, the Chinese captured 145 soldiers who practised a curious 'fishscale formation' military drill.[39] Homer H. Dubs argued that the 'fishscale formation' was the *testudo*, the Roman technique of interlocked shields, and that the soldiers were legionaries captured by the Parthians at the battle of Carrhae in 54 BC, stationed on the eastern frontier as was often done by the Parthians with prisoners of war, and now captured by the Chinese. Dubs went on to argue that the Han in turn settled their prisoners as a military colony in Kansu, at a place named Li-chien, this being one of the Chinese names for the West (A-*li-chien*-chi-chia = Alexandria), which Wang Mang renamed Chieh-lu which meant 'prisoners captured in the storming of a city'. Needham concludes, 'The evidence points, therefore, to a settlement of the remaining Romans as a military colony on the Old Silk Road, where they married Chinese women and spent the rest of their days'.[40]

The second case is that of the town of Khara-khoja in the Turfan oasis which has the local names of Apsus and Dakianus. A. von Le Coq thought that Apsus was a version of Ephesus and Dakianus a version of Decius, Roman emperor 249–251. One might guess that the name was given to the town by Roman soldiers captured by the Persians in 258 along with Decius' successor Valerian and, like their forerunners at Carrhae, transplanted and settled in the East. Another explanation would be that the Dakianans were Christians from Ephesus, refugees from Decius' persecution, though in that case it would have been others, not themselves, who gave them and their town its name. Ephesus was well known in the third century as a centre of intransigent, anti-*paedeia* Christianity. Maybe the Dakianans were Montanists.

The third case is that of the Jewish community at Kaifeng rediscovered by the West in the seventeenth century by Matteo

Ricci. Antoine Gaubil, who investigated its origins at a time when there was more evidence than now, believed that the Jews had come to China in a series of waves, of which the first two had been in the late Chou and in the reign of Han Ming-ti 58–75. His evidence, admittedly, was shaky: basically the tradition of the community as expressed in later inscriptions and oral testimony. But a migration following the fall of Jerusalem, at a time when the routes were open, is not impossible or implausible, though one may guess it was originally to Ch'ang-an or Lo-yang rather than Kaifeng.

Finally, in the opposite direction, there is the case of the ancient Armenian families who claim Chinese ancestry: the Orbelian who also use the name Cenbakurian, and the Mamigonian. Pelliot believed that Cenbakurian was derived from the Persian Cin-faghfur, 'the son of heaven of China', *faghfur* or *baghpur* being the normal Iranian titles for the Chinese emperor, subsequently transliterated in Latin as Pacorus, though not all Pacori are references to the *t'ien-tzu*. For the Mamigonian, Moses of Chorene, variously dated to the fifth or eighth centuries AD, tells us that they were descended from a Chinese prince who went into exile first in Persia and then in Armenia, two hundred years before his time. Either date is plausible from the point of view of political disorder in China. Armenia was in a favourable position for contact with China. It was the forward point of eastern Christianity, the second Christian state after Osrhoene, on the flank of the silk road and able to use the Caspian. The Chinese, like the Armenians, were on poor terms with the Parthian rulers of Iran, and it may be that in the case of the Cenbakurian, some Chinese diplomatic mission (we know there was a Parthian mission to China in 101) in difficulties at Ctesiphon, took refuge in Armenia and, as civilized men in a barbarous upland, remained to intermarry with its aristocracy and give them the name of their sovereign.

Flora and fauna

In later chapters this category will include not only plants and animals, but also other living things such as insects and the whole range of microorganisms. In antiquity, however, biological interchange between East and West was confined to plants and animals. As regards plants, the Mediterranean world received the peach and the apricot from China in the classical period, the first via the Persians, the second via the Armenians. Similarly, India received the peach under the Kushan empire where it was known as *cinani*, thus indicating its Chinese origin. Pears are mentioned in Homer, so they may be presumed indigenous to the Mediterranean, but India first knew them as *cinarajaputra* 'fruit of the king of China' in the Kushan period. Peaches, apricots and pears were the produce of north China and will have travelled by the silk road; the fruit of south China, oranges and lemons did not arrive until later. In the opposite direction, it was by the silk road that China drew its plant imports of this period: grapes, pomegranates, walnuts and alfalfa (lucerne). Grapes were introduced soon after Chang Ch'ien's expedition. They never held the same position in China as in Europe – Chinese and European tastes in drink diverged – but they enjoyed considerable support from the xenophile Han Wu-ti. Ssu-ma Ch'ien tells us that 'the lands on all sides of the emperor's summer palaces and pleasure towers were planted with grapes and alfalfa as far as the eye could see'.[41] Pomegranates are first mentioned in China under the Western Chin, 265–317, and walnuts under the Eastern Chin, 317–420.

Han Wu-ti's interest in alfalfa related to horses. It was part of the attempt, long persisted in by him and emperors of subsequent dynasties but ultimately unsuccessful, to introduce to China the great horse of the Iranians. In antiquity there were two types of horses: the *tarpan* or pony, the domesticated version of the only surviving wild horse *Equus przewalskii*, found from the British Isles to Manchuria, but bred on the largest scale by the nomadic pastoralists of the steppe; and the *cherpadh* or *arghumaq* which was selectively bred in Transoxania and possibly Thrace by sedentary peoples from horse strains distantly related to Grevy's zebra. The great horse, bred as an aristocrat in a stud, raised on alfalfa and ridden by the expert, professional armoured knight, was the Iranian antidote to the steppe pony, bred and raised in egalitarian profusion on the open range and ridden by men born in the saddle and naturally skilled in the use of the bow. Like the Shah, but unlike the Roman emperor, Han Wu-ti had steppe enemies. He therefore eagerly grasped at the Iranian antidote as soon as he heard of it from Chang Ch'ien. But the 'heavenly horses' proved elusive. Though China occupied the original breeding grounds when Han Wu-ti's brother-in-law, Li Kuang-li, conquered Ferghana on the second attempt in 101 BC, the difficulties of breeding in the warm Chinese climate prevented acclimatization in China proper. The great horse remained a prized import. The only Western animal successfully acclimatized under the Han was the donkey, introduced to north China from the Middle East by the trail bosses of the silk road. The West imported no animals from China in antiquity.[42]

Commodities

The commodities exchanged between East and West in classical times fell into a pattern of long-distance international trade in textiles, minerals and spices, which lasted until it was broken by the Dutch in the seventeenth century.

The two textiles which travelled were Chinese silk and Alexandrian linen. Although there are possible references to silk in Isaiah, Ezekiel, Herodotus and Aristotle, it was not until the late republic that the Roman world became familiar with it, and not until the late empire that it was received in quantity. Florus says that the first silks the Romans saw were the Parthian banners at the battle of Carrhae in 53 BC, and Lucan and Seneca regarded silk as an expensive exotic. By the end of the fourth century, however, Ammianus Marcellinus could say that all classes at Rome were wearing it, and at Constantinople St John Chrysostom could exclaim, 'what number of women now wear silken apparel but are indeed naked of the garments of virtue', while in another homily he tells us that silks are no longer costly.[43] Already there was a difference in the Chinese and Roman use of silk, in their underlying consumer preferences. The Chinese, with their preference for light housing, heavy clothes and concentrated warmth, used silk for brocade, a heavy textile, while the Romans, with their preference for heavy housing, light clothes and diffused warmth, used it for gauze, a light textile. The word gauze derives from Gaza and Lucan (*De Bello Civili*, x, 141–3) describes how Chinese textiles were unpicked and rewoven to Western tastes by Egyptian craftsmen to produce the Sidonian weave which so upset his uncle Seneca:

> I see silken clothes, if you can call them clothes at all, that in no degree afford protection either to the body or to the modesty of the wearer, and clad in which no woman could honestly swear she is not naked. These are imported at great expense from nations unknown even to commerce in order that our married women may not be able to show more of their persons to their paramours in a bedroom than they do on the street.[44]

The Roman textiles which reached China are entangled with the term *byssus* and the story of the water sheep. The *Hou Han-shu*, written about 450, states, 'Further, they [the people of Ta Ch'in, the Roman empire] have a fine cloth said to originate from the down of a water-sheep'.[45] This cloth has been assumed to be the *byssus* of classical texts and variously identified with cotton, a mixture of cotton and linen, or a curious textile spun from the threads of marine molluscs. The principal export textile of Egypt, however, was linen (it was a state monopoly in Ptolemaic times) and the *Periplus* records exports to Barbaricon of 'clothing, plain and in considerable quantity' and to Barygaza of 'cloth, plain and mixed, of all sorts'.[46] Most likely the *Hou Han-shu's* fine cloth was high grade linen, fine having the sense of heavy, i.e. some kind of damask, not so different from the heavier Chinese brocades. The Chinese bought what was similar to their own products, the Romans what was different. Here again is a fundamental contrast of consumer preference.

Trade in textiles between East and West in classical times was never large. Trade in minerals was smaller. However the West received a number of Chinese cast-iron or steel objects, Pliny's much admired Seric iron; jade, which is noted as an export from Barbaricon by the *Periplus*; and cupro-nickel, *paktung*, if indeed that is whence the Graeco-Bactrian kings obtained the metal for their coinage. Similarly, China may have received its first brass from Persia – an important stimulant to aurifictive alchemy; it probably received substantial quantities of precious metals from the Roman world – Roman coins for the period 14 to 275 have been found in Shansi; and it certainly received Egyptian silicon and gypsum in the form of Alexandria glass and plaster. Glass was one of the few branches of physical technology where the West was ahead of China and the *Hou Han-shu* noted with some surprise that in the palace of the Roman emperor 'the pillars of the halls are made of crystal and so are the dishes on which food is served'.[47] Of these mineral exchanges, the most significant was plaster: the Alexandrian stuccos and terracottas which were the indispensable vehicle for the iconography of the new religion of Mahayana Buddhism, in the long run the more dynamic form of export Buddhism. Without plaster Mahayana could not have projected its new objects of devotion, the *bodhisattvas*.

The spice trade in antiquity meant different things in West and East. For the Romans, particularly from the time of Augustus, it meant condiments and food preservatives directed to the sense of taste, though frankincense was subsidiarily important. For the Chinese, particularly from the time of Buddhism, it meant aromatics directed to the sense of smell, though pepper was subsidiarily important. What the Romans obtained from the Chinese world was cinnamon from south China, cloves from Ternate and Tidore, nutmeg from the Bandas – the three most expensive and aristocratic of spices – and ginger from Chekiang, another luxury food. The intercontinental trade therefore was of interest to them and both the *Periplus* and Pliny pay it considerable attention. What the Chinese obtained from the West was frankincense from the Hadramaut, myrrh from Somalia, storax from Asia Minor, bedellium or gum guggul from the Punjab, putchuk or costus root from Kashmir, and anise from the Mediterranean, all, except for anise which was soon replaced by superior Chinese aniseed from Kwangsi, secondary spices supplementary to the prime indigenous aromatic garoo or aloeswood from Champa. The intercontinental trade therefore was of little interest to them, the *Hou Han-shu* only referring to it *en passant*. As with textiles the foreign was used to reinforce the native rather than replace it.

Techniques

The technological exchanges between East and West in antiquity illustrate the principle that invention is not the same as development and that development may be more important than invention. One of the glories of pre-modern Chinese technology was its ability to cast iron long before the West could, and its consequent capacity to produce more steel by better methods. Yet the earliest known working of iron was not in China but in Asia Minor where a cuneiform text of 1275 BC of Hattusili III king of the Hittites refers to iron being made. The first reference to iron in China is in 513 BC and the maritime kingdom of Wu seems to have been the main centre for its production in association with salt boiling, so it is hard not to think that the original stimulus came from the West. Similarly, one of the glories of pre-modern Western technology was alphabetical script, and the consequent capacity for an open literacy extraverted to new words, foreign terms and fresh universes of discourse. Yet Edwin G. Pulleyblank has argued that the prototype for the Phoenician alphabet, the ancestor of all other Western alphabets, was the set of Chinese characters known as the heavenly stems and earth branches which today are a cycle of calendrical signs, but in the second millennium BC were an alphabet of initial and final consonants used in a compound script together with pictographs, ideographs and logographs. China therefore invented the principle of the phonetic alphabet, but did not develop it, and in fact eliminated it in her mature script. The West, on the other hand, did not invent the principle, but developed it, by eliminating all other elements in script and by adding the Greek invention of the representation of vowels.

The same disjunction of invention and development occurs in the history of the light horsedrawn war chariot – the weapon of Rameses II, Boadicea, Ben Hur and the Byzantine circus factions.

In the history of the draft horse, there is a discontinuity between the heavy horse cart, the new version of the oxcart, found in Mesopotomia in the third millennium BC and in the Kazakh steppe in the second millennium, used primarily for transportation, and the light horse chariot which came into use for hunting, war and high-speed travel, right across Eurasia from the seventeenth century BC onwards. The new vehicles were not only lighter and more specialized in use, but they had two spoked wheels instead of four solid ones and their draft animal was always the horse, generally a pair of horses, never the ox, onager or mule. War chariots required a specialized technology to build and operate. They were the product of palace workshops and the weapon of court aristocracy for whom war was a militarized hunt – between equals in ritual combat, or between unequals in relentless slaughter. Since the complex of chariot, palace and warrior aristocracy is not found in the steppe by Soviet archaeology and since the earliest mention of light war chariots in the West associates them with the Kassites and the Mitanni, people with at least Indo-European leadership, it may be supposed that the new chariot was invented by the Indo-Europeans as they left the steppe and entered the sedentary world as an army. The most likely place is the Merv-Herat region, a known area of early Indo-European penetration, a central point for the rapid diffusion of the chariot east and west, and a locality where Bactrian camels were probably already harnessed to light vehicles. Further, in 1275 BC, Hattusili III wrote to the Kassite ruler of Babylon asking for large horses for his chariots as his own horses were small. This use of the great horse suggests a central Asian origin for the chariot and it may be that it was the Kassites who introduced the great horse from Ferghana to Nisaea. From Merv-Herat the light chariot spread to China. The closeness in dates, the structural similarity between the chariot of the Shang dynasty and the Indo-European chariot, and the absence of a previous history of the draft horse in China, make independent invention unlikely.

Once invented and borrowed, however, the chariot was developed into a superior machine by the Chinese. First, they invented the *quadriga*. The earliest Indo-European war chariots were drawn by two horses only, as is made plain by Rameses II's account of the battle of Kadesh. The four-horse chariot is not definitely found in the West until the reign of Tiglath-Pileser III, 744–727 BC. In China, on the other hand, the four is taken for granted in the *Shih-ching* which dates back to 1000 BC. Second, probably as a consequence of the greater speed and better lock of the *quadriga*, the Chinese improved the wheels of the chariot, making them larger, giving them more spokes and, for additional strength, inclining them onto the hub instead of setting them straight, what is known as 'dishing'. This invention too was transmitted west in an attenuated form during the Assyrian new empire. Third, in the fourth century BC, the Chinese substituted for the unsatisfactory yoke and throat harness derived from the ox, which half-strangled the horse and reduced its tractive power to a third or quarter of its potential, the specifically equine shafts and breast-strap harness which is the precursor of the modern shafts and collar harness. At a blow the Chinese doubled or trebled their horsepower. Although China had fewer horses than the West, she utilized them more effectively. Her chariots were larger and faster and their use in war lasted half a millennium longer than in the West. The *Hou Han-shu* notes smaller chariots as one of the distinguishing marks of the Roman world, for, unlike the *quadriga* and the dished wheel, shafts and breast-strap harness were not borrowed by the West until after 400 AD.

Ideas

Thought, it has been argued, does not transplant easily because its meaning depends on context. Nevertheless, method can travel as well as discovery, individual ideas can detach themselves from their systems, and systems can create the contexts they require. Intellectual monads are seldom windowless. These principles are exemplified in the three fields of intellectual interchange between East and West in antiquity: music, alchemy and Buddhism.

One of the by-products of the structuralist revolution in social anthropology has been to underline the importance of music in intellectual history. Music, Lévi-Strauss has said, along with natural language, myth and mathematics, is one of the four fields to which structural analysis can and should be applied. It has been suggested that the dance is older than speech and that music is mankind's most primitive communications system. A comparison of different musical traditions is therefore a part of the history of civilizations.

The first serious Western student of Chinese music was the

French Jesuit Joseph Amiot, whose *De la Musique des Chinois* was published in Paris in 1780 in *Memoires concernant les Chinois*, Vol. VI. Amiot believed that the Chinese scale was based on the same principles as that of Pythagoras; he accepted the traditional very early date for its discovery in China, so he argued that the Western musical tradition was fundamentally derived from that of China. Chavannes, on the other hand, writing in 1895, took a modern critical view of traditional Chinese chronology, had available no musical text earlier than the *Huai-nan-tzu* of c.120 BC, and argued that the Chinese musical tradition was fundamentally derived from the West through the wave of Hellenism accompanying Alexander's conquests. However, both Amiot and Chavannes were mistaken in believing that the principles of the Chinese and Western gamuts were identical: they were only similar in that both started with the progression ½, ⅔, ¾ relating to octave, fifth and fourth. Their subsequent development was based on different principles: by subdivision of the octave and tetrachord in the West, and by expansion through an alternating series of fourths and fifths from a given fundamental in China. Nevertheless, the origin of the common starting point, the fundamental insight that musical scales can be mathematized, remains a problem. Needham supposes Babylon: the idea then moving east and west to be developed in different ways by Ling Lun and Pythagoras. Since in our schema Babylon is the West, Chavannes would in essence be justified against Amiot though in a more limited way than he supposed. What moved was not a musical tradition, but a principle, a heuristic structure, by which a number of different *eurekas* might be generated. Furthermore, as both Aristoxenus of Tarentum and Ssu-ma Ch'ien were quick to see, it was only a subsidiary principle: mathematization was the autopsy of music rather than its genesis.

The second field of intellectual exchange between East and West in antiquity was alchemy. Here one finds an illustration of the principle that individual ideas can detach themselves from their original systems and recombine with other systems. In antiquity and down to the seventeenth century, alchemy was more than a foredoomed, pre-chemical attempt to turn base metals into gold. It was a philosophy and technology of nature, in the East complete in itself, in the West part of a wider metaphysic, Aristotelian, Christian or both. Thus in China, the home of the first alchemical synthesis, the alchemy of the *Pao-pu-tzu* of Ko Hung (c.300 AD) aimed not only at aurifiction (the imitation of gold) and aurifaction (the making of gold) but also at macrobiotics (the extension and intensification of life) either by the elixir, the external drug of immortality, or by the *enchymoma*, the internally secreted panacea. Similarly, in post-Renaissance Europe, the home of the second alchemical synthesis, what is aimed at, for example in the *Rosarium Philosophorum* (c.1550) is not merely the philosophers' stone 'gold, silver, jewellery, all medicaments great and small', but 'the empress of all honour', the hermaphrodic symbol of psychological totality, the superordinate self.[48]

Needham has shown that alchemy began in China. References to an elixir (*pu-ssu chih yao*, lit. 'drug of no death') and to the art of immortality (*pu-ssu chih tao*, lit. 'way of no death') are found in the *Han-fei-tzu* of the third century BC and remarks in the *Shih-chi* and *Han-shu* indicate that such ideas had been current since 400. Systematic alchemy, i.e. the combination of aurifiction, aurifaction and macrobiotics, is attested by the *Shih-chi* and *Han-shu* stories of the alchemical magicians at the courts of Ch'in Shih Huang-ti (221–210 BC), Han Wu-ti (140–87 BC) and Han Hsuan-ti (73–48 BC). Under the usurper emperor Wang Mang (9–23 AD) alchemy was practically an orthodoxy of state, considerable resources being devoted to the manufacture of drugs and the amassing of gold. In the West, on the other hand, the first alchemical writings were those of the Pseudo-Democritus, datable at earliest to the end of the last century BC, iatrochemistry began only with John of Rupescissa (fl.1325–50), and the full mixture of aurifiction, aurifaction, and macrobiotics is not found until the time of Paracelsus in the sixteenth century.

Although alchemy originated in China, its development there may have been stimulated by detached techniques or ideas from quite different systems in the West. First, the probably Persian invention of brass may have been the original stimulus to both aurifiction and aurifaction: to aurifiction if the experimenter knew about the cupellation test for real gold; to aurifaction if he did not, or chose to ignore it. Next, the medical and psychotropic aspect of alchemy may have arisen through contact with the world of shamanism in south Siberia which used fungal hallucinogens, especially the juice of the fly agaric, and hallucinogenic smokes, notably hemp, to induce paranormal states of mind. Finally, acquaintance with arsenic, common to most of early civilized Eurasia but most developed in India, may have helped to bring together the metallurgical and medical halves of alchemy. Added in small quantities, arsenic turns copper golden; taken in small doses, arsenic acts as an appetite stimulant, an aphrodisiac and a skin tonic. To early investigators, arsenic must have seemed a vertiable philosopher's stone, which confirmed the alchemists' association of physical gold and biological health. The prototypes for alchemy may thus have come from outside the first alchemical system.

To this early eastward movement of ideas there corresponded a later westward movement of ideas detached from systematic Chinese alchemy. In Roman Alexandria, alchemy took two forms. There was the purely chemical aurifictive alchemy of a number of third-century papyri. There was the largely mystical aurifactive alchemy of the *Corpus Alchemicum Graecum*: the Pseudo-Democritus and his successors Maria Prophetissa and Zosimus of Panopolis. Both probably derived from Chinese alchemy via Persian intermediaries (Pseudo-Democritus cites Ostanes the Mede as his teacher), but they derived from different parts of it, which it united, but which they held in separation not understanding the original unity of *physica* and *mystica*. Both agreed, moreover, in overlooking the medical side of Chinese alchemy. Parts travelled but not the whole. To Iran, *per contra*, what travelled was not any of the parts, but the whole. Nathan Sivin has argued that the unifying idea of systematic Chinese alchemy was control of time: its acceleration to produce gold, its deceleration to produce incorruptibility. This notion of time as ontologically ultimate was the doctrine of the Zoroastrian heresy of Zervanism which flourished in the third and fourth centuries, especially under Shapur I and Yazdgard the Sinner, replacing the orthodox Mazdean dualism of Ohrmazd and Ahriman with the monism of Zurvan, cosmic time. Zurvan was an imperfect, unconscious divinity, containing both good and evil and in need of redemption: a view of the Godhead similar to that of the ancient gnostic Valentinus and the modern alchemist

C.G. Jung. Zervanism in Iran was associated with Greek philosophy and Indian science but, as far as we know, it had no connection with aurifiction, aurifaction or macrobiotics. It simply took the coping stone of the Chinese system and made it the foundtion of its own. That the two systems were different may be seen from the fact that while Chinese alchemy was highly manipulative, Iranian Zervanism was rigidly deterministic.[49]

The third exchange of ideas between East and West in antiquity, the transplantation of Buddhism from the Kushan empire to China, illustrates how a doctrine born in one milieu can take root in another and create afresh conditions for its propagation. Buddhism first came to China in strength in the second century. It came in both its Hinayana and Mahayana forms, exemplified by the two most famous early missionaries, the Hinayanist Parthian prince An Shih-kao (fl.148–168) and the Mahayanist Kushan pundit Lokaksema (fl.168–188). Neither form was tailored to the Chinese situation, yet both were able to find footholds in it and it was the more alien of the two, Mahayana, which eventually triumphed and imposed its own *problematik*.

Hinayana was dualist. There was *samsara* and *nirvana*, the cosmos and the anti-cosmos. What linked them was the *dharmas*, the momentary elements of experience, neither being nor non-being, which underlay both the illusion of *samsara* and the reality of *nirvana*. Hinayana was illuminist, it believed in the possibility of liberation, it was a religion of experience. In all these points except the last, Hinayana was antipathetic to the contemporary Chinese outlook with its naturalistic monism, its indifference to the problem of appearance and reality, its this-worldy practicality. Yet through this one point of psychotropic experience, Hinayana in its *dhyana* or yogic form could graft itself on to Taoist alchemical macrobiotics. What the Taoist adept claimed to effect by chemotherapy – by mushrooms, incenses and mineral elixirs – the *dhyana* master offered more certainly by psychotherapy – by meditation, autohypnotism and induced trance. As the psychotherapy was more advanced than the chemotherapy, impressive results were achieved and a hearing was gained for the underlying metaphysic. From *dhyana* one could move to *abhidharma*, Hinayana scholasticism.

Mahayana, on the other hand, was non-dualist. It subjected the concepts of *samsara* and *nirvana* to a rigorous logical critique and found both wanting: all the *dharmas* were *sunya*, empty, that is meaningless, non-computable and antinomous. Mahayana was intellectualist: it denied even the conceptual possibility of liberation, it affirmed the identity of *samsara* and *nirvana* on the score of their mutual indiscernability, and it offered not experience but insight, in the form not of a solution but of a dissolution of the problem, liberation from liberation. This critical negativism, 'all dialectic and no doctrine',[50] was even more alien to contemporary Chinese thought than Hinayana. The Chinese had no concept of critical philosophy, little logic, and possessed epistemologies which did not distinguish between *noema* and *noesis*, content and method. They regarded the Mahayana as simply a cosmology preaching a negative absolute. Yet this misunderstanding allowed Mahayana to graft itself on to the Confucian gnosticism known as *hsuan-hsueh*, the school of the mystery or dark learning as Zurcher calls it, whose doctrine of a metacategorical *wu* or nothingness, in reality closer to the Hinayana experience of *nirvana*, bore a superficial similarity to the Mahayana concept of *sunyata*, emptiness or the surdity of *all* the *dharmas*. By the end of the fourth century, however, Chinese Buddhists were beginning to see that there was something they did not understand and began to seek not only the authentic Mahayana but also the *problematik* which underlay it. Thus Seng-chao, 374–414, originally a Confucian gnostic, through contact with the Central Asian Mahayana missionary Kumarajiva, finally reached in his essay *Pan-jo wu-chih lun* ('Prajna is not Knowledge') the distinction between cognitional theory and cosmology which had so long eluded Chinese thought. Seng-chao was the first person to have mastered branches of both East Asian and Western thought. His was the first international mind.

WORLD INSTITUTIONS, 200 BC TO 400 AD

The subject of this book is not merely China's standing, contacts and interchanges with the rest of the world, but also the contribution of these things to the emergence of world institutions, in the sense of systems of various degrees of articulation covering all four primary civilizations at least in outline. Such institutions can be envisaged at every level of analysis: political, social and intellectual. If there has never been a world state, there have been states which operated so widely as to be recognized as world powers, international agencies such as the Red Cross, the Postal Union and the World Health Organization, generally accepted diplomatic procedures, common political techniques and global strategic perspectives. If there has never been a single world social order, there have been world markets, inclusive conjunctures, recognized gold standards, institutions such as Lloyd's society of underwriters, the Baltic exchange or the multinational oil companies. Though states have been divided, there have been dynastic alliances, international sets, cosmopolitan families, grand tours and *weltburgertum*. Just as the industrial revolution created a world investment bank of material technologies, so modern communications produced a biological common market in flora and fauna, bacteria and viruses. If there has never been human intellectual uniformity, except of the most primitive kind established by common brain and language structures, there have been republics of letters, worlds of learning, international art markets, invisible museums and conservatories, cultural Meccas and religious internationals.

Such bodies may be termed world institutions and we may begin by considering the extent to which they existed in antiquity. At the political level the case is not worth arguing: if the Han and Roman empires were more unlike than like, how much more these two and the states of Amerindia and Black Africa. The social level, however, needs closer examination.

Here it is best to start with ecology, the biological common market, because, of all the world systems, it was the most independent of conscious contact. Birds fly, animals move, currents and winds are factors in plant diffusion, so that such a system might have existed, even if China and the West were not aware of each other or of Africa or America. It has been suggested for example that peanuts and maize first travelled to East Asia from America not in post-Columbian times by human intervention but in prehistoric times by accidental voyaging. Conversely an East Asian origin has been postulated for American hookworms and Inca cotton. Was there then a common human ecology in antiquity?

In all four primary civilizations, the principal source of food was vegetable: antiquity was a world of carbohydrates; this had been the meaning of the neolithic revolution. In each, however, it was a different plant with its own technology: in the West, wheat and its relatives were *extensively* cultivated in symbiosis with animals; in China, millet was *intensively* cultivated without animals; in America, maize, which required little labour or public organization; in Africa, yams, which required much of both. Many plants remained on their original continents: maize, sweet potatoes, peanuts, Irish potatoes, manioc, cocoa, pimento, avocados, tomatoes, and tobacco in America; the eucalyptus and wattles in Australia; soya beans, tea, oranges, lemons and a vast range of garden flowers such as rhododendron, azalea, camellia, wisteria, hydrangea, magnolia and chrysanthemum in East Asia; the olive, opium, the pistachio and indigo in the West. Domestic animals were similarly restricted: the horse and camel were unknown in America and virtually unknown in Black Africa; the llama and turkey were unknown outside America; the yak outside East Asia. Although many diseases caused by microorganisms were common to neolithic humanity, such as malaria, tuberculosis and tetanus, some in antiquity were localized: plague in High Asia, syphilis in its more virulent forms in America, yellow fever and sleeping sickness in Africa. Smallpox was unknown in America and Africa, and was not certainly known in China until the third century when Ko Hung thought it was introduced from the Hsuing-nu. China had diseases probably of microbial origin apparently unknown elsewhere: for example, the curious *yang-mao wen* or sheep's wool fever.[51] The human ecological situation in antiquity was thus of considerable diversity.

The stock of technology with which the primary civilizations confronted their environments in antiquity was likewise diverse. All of them obtained food from agriculture, but the material of the implements used differed. China could both work and cast iron, the West and Africa could only work it, America was ignorant of it. Everywhere men lived in houses, but shelter was provided characteristically by stone in the

West, by wood in China, by adobe in America and by thatch in Africa. Everyone was clothed, but textiles differed: wool and linen in the West; hemp and silk in China; cotton, maguey bark and llama wool in America; grasscloth in Africa. Food, shelter and clothing, the basic human needs, were all differently satisfied.

More fundamentally, though all four primary civilizations used the five eotechnic sources of energy – wood, animals, water, wind and human muscle – they used them in different proportions. Even in antiquity China was short of wood. In historic times the loess plateau was never well timbered and the Chinese preference for wood as a building material tended to exhaust what there was. Accordingly China was the first civilization to use coal as a substitute for wood, though in the Han period not on any scale. In the use of animal energy the West with its mixed farming was probably already ahead of China and both were definitely ahead of Black Africa or Amerindia. As regards water power, although both China and the West possessed the water wheel, China with its canals and irrigation devices was certainly the premier user in antiquity. Wittfogel's hydraulic theory is questionable, Han China's hydraulic pre-eminence is not. Wind power, however, was pre-eminently Indo-Iranian. The windmill had not journeyed far from its presumed home in Seistan and the coasts of India and Ceylon were the leading area for the development of maritime sails in antiquity and possibly carried a greater volume of shipping than the Mediterranean. Human muscle, of course, was everywhere a major source of energy, but there is reason for thinking that in China the working day was longer and holidays fewer than in the other primary civilizations. As between the civilizations, both the quantity and the kind of energy expended varied considerably. The West was lazy and luxurious, China ascetic, Africa unambitious, Amerindia idle but extravagant.

Turning from technology to economy proper, there is little in antiquity which can be called a world, or even inter-continental market, even in the most likely field, the circulation of gold. True, the *auri sacra fames* may be found in all four primary civilizations, though in varying degrees. Possibly, in the ancient Old World there was a mainstream of gold, from Siberia to the Roman empire and thence via the spice and silk trades to India and China, fed by sidestreams from the Sudan and Zimbabwe. Further, it has been suggested that the acceleration of this circuit by Wang Mang's nationalization of gold in 6 AD led to a flight of bullion from the Roman world and prompted Tiberius' curtailment of the silk trade, and that its later disruption by the Huns was a factor in Indian expansion into South-east Asia in search of compensation. Neither suggestion is convincing. If Chinese holders of gold did not wish to exchange it for Wang Mang's copper, why should holders of gold farther west? If India was really short of gold in late antiquity, why are there not more signs of Indian activity on the East African coast where there were better sources of gold than in South-east Asia? The existence of an international bullion market in antiquity in any strong sense remains to be proved. In China the ratio of gold to silver was 1:5, whereas in the West it was 1:10. Silver was less used in Han China than gold, whereas in the West, until the introduction of the gold *solidus* by Constantine, it was the prime currency. China too made greater use of commodity money – grain and silk – than the West. The picture is of two independent monetary worlds with only tangential contact.

Finally, at the intellectual level, too, one is sceptical of any genuine world system in antiquity. No doubt all four primary civilizations possessed mythologies expressing a similar under-lying *mythologique*: a variously coded set of fundamental polarities 'good for thinking'. Only in China and the West, however, was the transition from mythology to philosophy made and, even there, to different degrees and in opposing ways. Chinese thought in antiquity, whether Confucian or Taoist, was half mythological: paradigmatic, concerned with the categories of thought, verbal or non-verbal Western thought in antiquity, whether Greek or Indian, was wholly liberated from myth: syntagmatic, concerned with the categories of reality, one or many. Even within the West there were intellectual watertight compartments. Festugière is scep-tical of any non-Greek influence on the apparently oriental revelation of Hermes Trismegistus, arguments for a Platonic influence on the *Avatamsaka-sutra* have never been convincing, and Dumézil can make a list of the contrasting qualities of Roman and Indian thought. Scraps of musical theory, scraps of alchemy travelled, but always to be incorporated into contrasting systems. Only Buddhism succeeded in creating something like a world institution. By 400 a thin film of monasteries, shrines, translation centres, sutras, Gandharan style artifacts, Central Asian missionaries, Chinese pilgrims and students joined the civilizations of the West and East Asia. If de Guignes' interpretation of the Fu-sang passage in the *Liang-shu* be accepted, Buddhist missionary activity was about to reach America and it may already have reached Black Africa via Madagascar and the East African coast. Buddhism was the only world conqueror of antiquity.

The clearest expression of this conquest was Kumarajiva's Chinese translation of the *Mahaprajnaparamitasastra*.[52] Kumarajiva himself, 344–413, was an international man. Born and educated in Kucha as a Hinayanist, he travelled and studied in Kashmir and Kashgar and was converted to Mahayana in Yarkand. Having returned to Kucha and taught there some years, he was brought to Ch'ang-an in 401 by the Later Ch'in Emperor Yao Hsing, Seng-chao being his leading disciple. The *Mahaprajnaparamitasastra*, the chief of a number of texts he translated and expounded, was a highly Indian, and therefore Western, work in outlook; indeed it contains almost racist passages which imply that Buddhism can hardly exist outside India, though it also shows some awareness of Chinese alchemy. In its own country the *Mahaprajnaparamitasastra* was not much appreciated (it has only survived in the Chinese version) probably because it modified the central tenet of its own Madhyamika school; but in China it became the *Summa Theologica* for four centuries of Buddhism. Ascribed to Nagarjuna and in form a commentary on a Mahayana pseudo-sutra, in fact the author was probably a Kashmiri scholastic and his book was a systematic exposition of how the doctrines of Hinayana *abhidharma*, especially as embodied in the *Jnanaprasthana* of Katyayaniputra the famous Sarvastivadin metaphysician, are transformed if the Mahayana standpoint of double vacuity in its Madhyamikan form is adopted. Simultaneously, Madhyamika itself was reinterpreted more self-consistently to arrive at an absolute, an open surdity rather than Nagarjuna's closed antinomy. That such a work could become the intellectual basis of Chinese Buddhism is testimony to the genuineness of China's conversion and to the reality of the link between civilizations. Here, if anywhere, was the beginnings of a world institution. But the Buddhist phenomenon was the exception in what was still fundamentally a disunity of worlds apart.

2 World Centre: China in Late Antiquity, 400 to 1000

This chapter concerns China's relationship to the outside world in the period of the T'ang dynasty 618 to 907, more particularly the period of the 'Golden' T'ang down to the great rebellion of An Lu-shan in 755, though sidelong glances will be taken at the periods of the Northern Wei and Sui which preceded and of the 'Silver' T'ang, Five Dynasties and early Sung which followed. Its argument is that in this period, which we will call late antiquity, the separate worlds of classical antiquity were drawn into a new unity, thanks to the magnetic pre-eminence of T'ang China – political, social, economic, and intellectual – and to the acquisitive cosmopolitanism of the T'ang court. For a brief moment under emperor Hsüan-tsung, 712–756, China was genuinely the centre of the world, the heir and supplanter of the Buddhist world institution. The new secular synthesis, however, was precocious, rarefied and fragile, and collapsed when the rebellion of An Lu-shan destroyed the extravagent imperial court which supported it. [1]

CHINA'S PLACE IN THE WORLD, 400 TO 1000

Between 400 and 750 China's place in the world was transformed. From being a provincial version of one of the Hellenistic kingdoms, with impressive technology, no doubt, but overall landlocked, static, bucolic and philistine, China became a metropolis, the most advanced society in the world, outgoing, dynamic, urbane and aesthetic. From being unknown, isolated and idiosyncratic, China became a cynosure, the centre of a world, and an admired model. This transformation came about through long-term trends or conjunctures either unique to China, experienced differently by China, or avoided by China. The result was that by the eighth century, the structure of the T'ang empire compared favourably with that of its nearest analogue in the West, the later Roman empire of Justinian.[2]

Conjunctures

Conjunctures unique to China

These comprised the revival of empire and the progress of capitalism.

The most obvious contrast between the histories of Europe and China in late antiquity and the dark ages was that, whereas in Europe the classical empire was never fully revived after its fall in the West, in China it was revived first by the Sui, 589–618, and then by the T'ang. At the outset of European post-antiquity, there was a discontinuity; at the outset of Chinese post-antiquity, a continuity. To this major watershed between 400 and 600 were related subsequent ones: the dominance of society in medieval Europe, the dominance of the state in medieval China; the tendency to expansion in pre-modern Europe, to implosion in pre-modern China; the preference for theology and science in the West, for magic and technology in the East. Indeed the eventual development of world institutions centred on Europe was related to the rejection of empire in the dark ages since the autonomy such institutions require is found most easily outside an imperial state. Imperial bureaucracy has institutional spin-offs, but the growth of global functional specializations is not one of them.

The contrast was not only between China and Europe. In the Middle East, though the imperial state of the Achaemenids was briefly recreated by the Abbasids, by 900 Islamic empire had given way to Islamic community, an *Islam des patries*, and was not restored even by the Ottomans. In India, the Guptas, whose era ended in 370, were the last Hindu imperial dynasty, and Harsha who died in 647 was the last native emperor until the originally only semi-Indian Moghuls. India like Christendom was a community rather than an empire. Only in the eastern Mediterranean where Basil II Bulgaroktonos carried the Byzantine empire to new heights, did bureaucratic empire survive outside China in the Old World around 1000.

Behind the subsidiary reasons for the contrast – the lesser
weight of the Han empire, the more superficial character of
the revolution which overthrew it, the greater skill and institutional creativity of the dynasties which followed it – lay a main
reason in Chinese culture. Because of the isolation of China
behind deserts, mountains and jungles, without neighbours,
and with its back to a dead ocean, a higher proportion than
in the West of the ruling class had an interest in an imperial
state as the purveyor of culture and the countervailant to
provinciality. In China's circumstances community was no substitute for empire. Only an imperial court could command
the resources necessary to draw out China's cultural potential
or open her windows to a wider world. The empire was both
stage and impresario of liturgies which would not be performed in other theatres. As the first emperor of the Sung
dynasty commented when it was suggested to him that the
state of Nan T'ang in the Lower Yangtze should be allowed
to remain an independent satellite: 'What crime have the
people of Kiangnan committed that they should be separated
from the empire?'[3] Once restored for mainly cultural reasons,
the empire brought other benefits: peace over wide areas,
security from foreign invasion, an open structure of society,
a high level of consumer spending. These in turn opened
the way to the second conjuncture which was unique to China:
the progress of capitalism.

Late antiquity, or the dark ages, was everywhere the seed-
time of capitalism. In Byzantium there was a revolution in
conceptualization. The Christian charity, first of the Cappado-
cian bishops starting with Basil, then of the Syrian monks
starting with Simeon, broke down the classical concept of
society as constituted by degrees of social distance and in
particular urban social distance, and substituted a less imbedded, more purely economic categorization which transcended
town and country. Economic poverty and wealth replaced
social, the *chora* acquired institutions of its own against the
polis and, conceptually at least, space was left for an autonomous sphere of the economic, the field of an unlimited
capitalism. In Western Europe on the other hand there was
a drastic clearing of the ground. The limited municipal and
military capitalism of antiquity was removed by the decay of
imperial consumption, the ruralization of society to manor

and monastery, and by the effects of Moslem conquest on sea lanes and coastal cities. The acommercial, non-imperial society of the Benedictine centuries, however, afforded institutional space for the implantation of a new emporial order, a more radical capitalism than that of antiquity, once the seeds stored in Constantinople and the Moslem cities of north Africa, or secreted within its own cells, were scattered. Western Europe between 400 and 1000 was storm-wracked and uncultivated but not barren. In Islam, *per contra*, there was hothouse growth to premature harvest. The dethesaurization attendant on conquest, the extravagance of *nouveaux riches* shaikhs, the jerry-building of cities, the new lingua franca, the sudden common market from Spain to Transoxania, all stimulated the capitalism of antiquity without altering its nature or counting the cost. Behind the splendid façade of the Abbasid cities, there was rural impoverishment and depopulation, exhaustion of energy resources particularly timber, and technical, institutional and intellectual stagnation. There had been a bumper crop, but it left the soil exhausted and not enough was put aside for seed.

China combined elements of all three scenarios. The capitalism of the Han empire, based on poorer communications serving few cities, was even more limited than that of the ancient West. There was already room for development, a disequilibrium between China and the outside world. In this field ready for sowing, the seeds of capitalism were scattered by Buddhist monasticism, the world institution of the age. Buddhism came to the successor states of the Han from areas more commercialized than China: north-west India, the Kushan corridor between the silk road and the southern sea route; Coromandel and Ceylon, the eastern pivot of the sea lanes. Monks were vowed to poverty, but monasticism brought in its *vinaya*, or rule, essential capitalist institutions previously unknown to China: the prototype of the permanent, non-kinship association; the specific practices of the auction, compound interest, equitable mortgage and the money club. The Buddhist monastery, unlike the Benedictine, was a capitalist institution. Under the Plantagenets 15 000 monks owned between a quarter and a third of the lands, rents and dues of England. Under the T'ang, 350,000 monks owned only 4 per cent of the cultivated area of China. The monasteries' major sources of income were lending in money or grain, royalties from hydraulic flour mills and oil presses, and gifts from the faithful. For example, at the Ching-tu monastery near Tun-huang, a house of 50–70 monks, grain receipts as harvest or rent from land came to only 23 per cent of the total, as against 45 per cent from interest on loans and 32 per cent from gifts.[4]

Beyond capitalist institutions, Buddhist monasticism, particularly of the Mahayana variety, implanted the notion of capital itself. The infinite merits of the bodhisattva constantly laid out in unlimited liability for others and as a challenge to emulation could easily be secularized as the multiplication of wealth by investment and circulation. Some monasteries operated kinds of 'telethons': permanent festivals of mass, competitive giving and charitable outpouring, *wu-chin tsang* or inexhaustible treasuries, which eventually had to be checked by the state because of the monetary disorder they threatened. Finally, both by their teaching and by their own outlay on lavish buildings, temple furnishing, *saint-sulpicerie*, incense, precious ornaments and books, the Buddhist monasteries encouraged spending and circulation. In a pre-modern economy where there is unused capacity and a tendency to the immobilization of wealth, consumptivity is a more significant variable than productivity. Hyperconsumption can kill a pre-modern economy by disinvestment – the Baroque Mediterranean is an example of this – but if there are hidden resources it can be a stimulant. China thus had the right environment, seed and climate for an unparalleled progress of capitalism in late antiquity. Unlike Byzantium its growth was more than conceptual; unlike Western Europe, it was palpable; unlike Islam, it was permanent. The imperial cities of Ch'ang-an and Loyang were reinforced by a new set of commercial cities: Liang-chou and Tun-huang by land, Yang-chou and Canton by water.

Conjunctures experienced differently
Conjunctures which China experienced differently from Europe comprise fluctuation and spatial expansion.

The evidence of Alpine glaciers, Greenland ice cores and American tree rings indicates that during the period 400 to 750 the earth underwent a climatic fluctuation in the direction of greater cold and wet. The mechanism behind this and subsequent similar fluctuations in the thirteenth and seventeenth centuries was probably, in the northern hemisphere, a more southerly track and weaker strength on the part of the prevailing westerly winds of the temperate zone. Although the facts of East Asian climatic history are even less established than those of European, evidence such as the records of cherry blossom time at Kyoto suggest similar conditions in the east as in the west. For example, the Japanese monk Ennin described forests, luxuriant vegetation, pools, damp grottoes and, most significant, glaciers in the region of Mount Wu-t'ai in Shansi where, in the warmer and dryer conditions of the last hundred years, none have been reported by modern travellers. Although both China and Europe shared the same climatic fluctuation, they experienced it differently. For Europe, whose grain crop, particularly in the north whence European recovery was to spring, was constantly threatened by too much moisture, the climatic fluctuation was a disaster coming on top of other disasters and contributing to them. For example the progress of the plague epidemic between 541 and 767 may have been assisted by the increased humidity which favours the multiplication of fleas. For China, on the other hand, whose grain crops, both millet and rice, particularly in the north-west, were constantly threatened by too little moisture, the climatic fluctuation was a blessing. It made possible the last great age of the *kuan-chung* aristocracy and the final use of Ch'ang-an as capital. Without this capital and that class, T'ang China would not have been possible. The deeper penetration of the monsoon made large-scale hydraulics less necessary: irrigation could be safely abandoned to local authorities and the central government avoided a potent source of friction and over-extension. China thus had good weather from 400 to 750; Europe, except possibly in the Levant, had bad.

Between 400 and 750, both Europe and China underwent spatial expansions, notable increases in the area over which civilization was exercised, but they were in different directions and on different time scales. In Europe expansion was to the north: into the Alps, to Germany, to Ireland, along the Baltic, across the North Sea. It involved essentially the clearing of forest, a protracted operation. Although the move to the

richer soils of the northern European plain brought a greater
use of three-field rotations instead of two and hence a 50 per
cent increase in productivity, there was no improvement in
the crops themselves. Indeed, the north may have raised more
barley, oats and rye, and less wheat than the south. The impact
of the new northern cereals on the European economy was
slow to emerge. It was not until the sixteenth century that a
major waterborne traffic carried four million hundredweight
of grain from the Baltic to the Mediterranean.

In China, on the other hand, expansion was to the south:
into the Yangtze delta, to Kiangsi and Chekiang, along the
coast of Fukien, around the Po-yang lake. It involved essentially the draining of marshes, something which had to be
done quickly or not at all. Not only were the southern soils
richer because more irrigated, but the move south meant an
improvement in crop, from wheat or millet to rice. The yield
per acre of rice was twice that of wheat and double-cropping
could make it four times. The impact of the new southern
cereals on the Chinese economy was quick to emerge. The
grain surplus of the Lower Yangtze was the basis, first, for
the state of Wu from 222 to 280 and, then, for the southern
dynasties of Eastern Chin, Liu Sung, Southern Ch'i, Liang
and Ch'en between 317 and 589. Although China was not
reunified by the south at the political level, the southern
kingdoms enriched Chinese society by their Buddhism,
maritime trade and more sophisticated legal systems, and
contributed to the T'ang synthesis. The building of the Grand
Canal by the Sui emperor Yang-ti between 604 and 610 from
Hang-chou via Yang-chou to Lo-yang and Ch'ang-an placed
the grain surplus of the south at the disposal of the north.
By the 730s, after a reconstruction by Hsüan-tsung's minister
P'ei Yao-ch'ing, the canal carried 3 300 000 hundredweight
of grain to the imperial capitals, and by the eleventh century
this figure had increased to 8 480 000 hundredweight.
China's *drang nach suden* in late antiquity was more like
Europe's Atlantic explosion in the sixteenth century than her
slow drive north in the dark ages. In Braudel's words about
America, the south enabled China 'to live above its means,
to invest beyond its savings'.[5] Here was another source of
China's rise to superiority in late antiquity.

Conjunctures avoided

Conjunctures that were avoided by China were the plague and barbarian invasion.

Plague was a major factor shaping Europe in late antiquity.[6] It appeared in 541 during the reign of Justinian at Pelusium in Egypt and continued its assaults in a series of twenty pulsations at roughly ten-year intervals right into the 760s. These pulsations, due most likely to the action of the sunspot cycle on the population of the wild rodents who are the reservoir of plague, fell, according to their geographical incidence, into four groups: initial, early, middle and late. The initial pulsation of 541 to 544, as is usual with the beginning of a plague series, was violent and widespread. Outbreaks are reported from Spain to Azerbaijan: in Egypt, Syria, Thrace, Illyria, Italy, Tunisia and the Rhone Valley. At Constantinople, Evagrius reported 800,000 victims, a third or even half the city's population. The early pulsations which followed, numbers two to five, 558 to 591, particularly affected the western Mediterranean: northern Italy, the Rhone Valley and Catalonia. In the middle pulsations, numbers six to thirteen, 599 to 700, the emphasis shifted to the east: Mesopotamia, Constantinople, Alexandria, Antioch. The final pulsations, numbers fourteen to twenty, 704 to 767, swung west again, but to a different rim of the Mediterranean: southern Italy, Sicily and perhaps Tunisia.

The effect on Europe, which only ceased when the rise of Islam cut the Mediterranean trade routes and circulation fell below a critical minimum, was profound. Justinian's failure to complete the restoration of the classical empire, at least around the rim of the Mediterranean, was influenced by the fiscal and manpower losses of the furious onset of the plague series. His successors' difficulties in the Balkans, Italy and North Africa with the invasions of the Slavs, Lombards and Berbers may be related to the demographic voids produced by the early pulsations. The shift to the east in the middle pulsations prepared the way for the Arab invasions and the inability of either Roman Syria and Egypt or Sassanid Persia to withstand them. Similarly the failure of the Christian far west, Sicily, Tunisia and Spain – to which Constans II moved his headquarters – to hold, may partly be ascribed to the final pulsations. The whole series deeply affected the psychology of Christian late antiquity. The final discredit of pagan therapeutic sanctuaries, the grim Augustinian and iconoclast orthodoxies of west and east, the belief that the world was nearing its end, all owed something to the panic of the plague centuries. Similarly Gregory the Great's half-successful attempt to stem the panic, by his *Morals on Job*, his introduction of litanies, his resistance to millenarism, increased his and the papacy's prestige.

In China, on the other hand, there was none of this. Protected by the aridity of the Gobi, the aversion of the flea for horses and camels, better clothing and more washing, China experienced plague only marginally. Ko Hung describes what may be plague as a disease of the newly opened south: a possible indication that the Indo-Chinese reservoir of plague, the home of *Yersinia pestis orientalis*, and the source of outbreaks in Kwangtung in the nineteenth century, was already established. However, the T'ang Chinese had no specific name for plague, though an epidemic with a particularly high mortality in Ch'ang-an and Lo-yang in the winter of 682–683 has been regarded as the deadly pneumonic form of the disease. In general China avoided the flail of Justinian, Gregory the Great and the Omayyads.

Because she avoided the plague, China also avoided barbarization in late antiquity. Although both Europe and China experienced the irruption of barbarian armies, the *Heerenwanderungen* of what were essentially armed immigration companies, China avoided the more genuine *Völkerwanderungen*, the massive invasions of the Anglo-Saxons, Franks, Slavs and Arabs, which altered the linguistic map of Europe along the full length of the Roman *limes* from the Saxon shore to the Syrian desert. *Völkerwanderungen*, the conversion of the *limes* from an instrument of civilization to an instrument of barbarization, had serious consequences in Europe. Not so much in the north where the Franks and Anglo-Saxons were soon recovered for Romanitas, though in its ecclesiastical rather than imperial form, as in the Mediterranean. The submersion of Roman Illyria and Thrace by the Slavs de-Latinized eastern orthodoxy and forced it into a policy of Hellenization at home and vernacularization abroad (the development of Slavonic liturgies) which drove a wedge between it and the Latin west.

Similarly the submersion of Greek Syria and Egypt by Semitic speakers before and after Muhammed, de-Hellenized eastern heterodoxy and made Monophysitism into what it had never been before, and only reluctantly became: a Semitic religion. Again, the Moslem conquest of north Africa removed the eastern emperor's last sizable piece of Latinity, while the Moslem invasions of Sicily and southern Italy removed the natural area of Graeco-Latin cooperation. The basis of western antiquity since the time of Caesar had been a Latin state, whether at Rome or Constantinople, protecting a Greek society. The Slavs and the Arabs changed this: the state was no longer Latin, society was no longer Greek. Instead there was a Greek empire in the east and a Latin society in the west. Reconstruction on the old basis was impossible and Christendom was forced into a long march towards a new political form.

In China, on the other hand, there was none of this. There were no demographic voids caused by plague to be filled by migrants. There were no *limes* to accumulate non-Chinese speaking population. Islam, supreme throughout the region where the pack camel was a cheaper form of transport than the cart, reached a frontier in Kansu where it met carts pulled by a superior Chinese harness. China was not subject to barbarization in late antiquity. There were no cultural obstacles to the restoration of imperial unity: indeed, as we have seen, culture was the prime incentive to restoration. The only problems were political: the incorporation of the barbarian military leaders into the ruling class, which was accomplished under the Northern Wei; the reintegration of the society-oriented colonial aristocracy of the south under the leadership of the state-oriented court aristocracy of the north, which was accomplished under the Sui; and the provision of all three aristocracies – barbarian, northern and southern, military, court and colonial – with a cultural focus, which was accomplished under the T'ang.

Conjuncture therefore – avoided, differently experienced and shared – benefited China and aided her rulers in their reconstruction of their world. While western Europe sank into the atony of the dark ages, while the eastern Roman empire hardened into the sclerosis of Byzantium, while the Middle East enjoyed or suffered the meteoric career of early

Islam, while India turned away from empire and ocean to ruralized, Brahminical clericalism, China rose to new heights of political and social structure under the T'ang.

Structures

A comparison of the T'ang empire under Hsüan-tsung (712–756) with its nearest contemporary analogue, the Roman empire of Justinian (527-565) completes the survey of how China stood in the world of late antiquity. As with the Han and classical Roman empires, there were similarities and differences, with the second preponderating over the first, but this time the comparison is to the advantage of China.

Similarities in state and society

Similarities between Justinian's empire and Hsüan-tsung's existed at the levels of both state and society. With regard to the state, the imperial institution itself, *first*, both empires were the product of self-consciously conservative *restitutio orbis*. Thus the T'ang empire, the work of the traditionalist *kuan-chung* aristocracy of the north-west, was centred in the old Western Han capital of Ch'ang-an and saw itself as the revival of that empire. The fall of its predecessor, the Sui, an otherwise highly competent dynasty, was largely due to emperor Yang-ti's appearance of removing the capital to Yang-chou and of abandoning the military *kuan-chung* ethos. Similarly, the Constantinian empire of the new Rome (which was also a new Troy, a return to the origins) complete with senate and seven hills did not see itself as Byzantine. On the contrary, it was a reassertion of Romanitas by the Latin military aristocracy of Illyria and later by Latinized Slavs such as Justinian himself and Belisarius, against the Greek east of Alexandria and Antioch. Chalcedon was a Latin church council.[7]

Second, both empires ruled through an expert civilian bureaucracy and a new articulation of law. At Constantinople, there was a greater differentiation of civil and military hierarchies than there had been at Rome; the great officers of state such as the praetorian prefect and the *magister officiorum* were eclipsed in the consistory by their technical assistants the *logothetes*; and a mass of imperial constitutions and jurisconsults' opinions were consolidated and rationalized in the

Codex and the Digest. At Ch'ang-an, the household government of the Han inner court or *nei-t'ing* was replaced under the T'ang by the more bureaucratic regime of the three secretariats or *san-sheng*; within the *san-sheng*, the under-secretaries *(chung-shu she-jen)* and review officials *(chi-shih-chung)* came to have more power than the secretary of state or the chancellor; and the code was strengthened, Confucianized and humanized under the influence of the jurisconsult P'ei Cheng (510–588), the Chinese Tribonian, legal adviser successively to the southern Liang, the northern Chou and the Sui.[8]

Third, in both empires the army was increasingly based on heavy cavalry, modelled ultimately, on the cataphracts of the Iranians. Although the Roman legions had had a cavalry component since the time of Gallienus (his father Valerian, a civilian, had been defeated and captured by the Persians), it was not until the reign of Justinian that heavy cavalry became the predominant arm and not until the time of the Heraclians that it was fully institutionalized by the creation of *themes*: army corps districts of soldier settlers endowed with land sufficient to support large horses. In China conversion to heavy cavalry was begun by the western Chin, completed by the northern Wei and institutionalized in the *fu-ping* system of privileged draft established by their successor state western Wei in 550 and extended by the T'ang. In the border regions *t'un-t'ien* or military agricultural colonies, were established to maintain the frontier patrols; in Chinese Central Asia an elaborate *ma-cheng*, or horse administration, operated studs and pastures to provide remounts for the army and postal service; and Chinese diplomats sought to import superior animals from beyond the frontiers of the empire.[9]

Fourth, to a greater extent than their classical predecessors, both empires supplemented force with diplomacy and established 'commonwealths', systems of satellites with themselves at the centre. In the West, Olympiodorus of Thebes (d.425) is regarded as the first great diplomat of antiquity. Justinian was an organizer of *détente* as well as of victory and Menander the Protector declared that 'without war, by his prudence alone he would have destroyed the barbarians had he lived long enough'.[10] St Constantine Cyril, who had participated in embassies to the Arabs and the Khazars, inaugurated the Byzantine system of religious satellites with his mission to

Moravia in 863, and Constantine Porphyrogenitus' *De Administrando Imperio* is the first treatise on *Weltpolitik*. In China too, the T'ang had their *Weltpolitik*. T'ai-tsung married one of his daughters to the king of Tibet and sent two embassies to Emperor Harsha in India. Kao-tsung supported Peroz, son of the last Sassanid emperor, Yazdgard III, against the Arabs. Su-tsung obtained military help from the Arabs and the Uighurs against the rebellion of An Lu-shan. Te-tsung collaborated with Haroun al-Rashid against the Tibetans.

Similar parallels existed with regard to society. *First*, both empires functioned through a new, monumental urbanism. Despite the destruction of many of the smaller Antonine cities by the military anarchy and barbarian invasions of the third century, the later Roman empire was still an urban society, as witness both archaeology and the testimony of contemporaries, Ausonius' *Ordo Nobilium Urbium* for example. The cities, however, were no longer local centres of classical culture maintained by and for cultivated oligarchies. They were imperial cities: capitals, such as Trier the arms factory, London the granary, Ravenna the naval base, Constantinople all three rolled into one; patriarchates such as the new *Roma Christiana* of the basilicas, the new Alexandria of the pharaoh-pope; pilgrimage centres such as Jerusalem rebuilt by Constantine to house the body of his God as Constantinople was to house his own. The T'ang empire was likewise an urban society, more so than the Han. That the T'ang state was more firmly based than those of previous dynasties was both the result and the cause of urban development. The T'ang empire operated in and through cities, and the towns that were developed were characteristically mandarin cities: capitals like Ch'ang-an and Lo-yang; regional centres like Chengtu and Wei; state emporia like Yang-chou the headquarters of the salt administration; frontier checkpoints like Liang-chou or Tun-huang. Axially planned from the palace or *yamen*, strictly zoned within, and segretated from outside by massive walls, the mandarin city was the expression of a state which perfectly canalized the forces of its society.

Second, both empires rested upon a new articulation of rural life. In the later Roman empire, this was done through villas and parishes in Gaul; the *themes* in the Balkans and Anatolia; shrine communities in north Africa, monastic villages in Syria and Egypt; new rural bosses, 'patrons', in the Roman east generally. In China it was done through local power, the villages from which the so-called 'choronymic' aristocracy took their names; through private estates, villas in effect, monastic and lay; but mainly through the *chün-t'ien* system, that state's scheme of land allocation through the district magistrate and village headmen. In both cases the result was that the countryside, the classical *chora*, for the first time acquired institutions of its own and ceased to be simply an exploited appendage of the town.

Third, in both empires in late antiquity, partly as a result of this rural institutionalization, there was a wider diffusion of literate culture. In the West, thanks to the imperial tax collector and the Christian bishop, Latin and Greek, the languages of culture, spread at the expense of the pre-classical languages – Celtic, Illyrian, Berber and the dialects of Anatolia – which in this period declined to become mere local patois. In China, likewise, mandarin advanced at the expense of the other dialects of Chinese and spread to Korea and Japan. The multiplication, under the auspices of imperially supported Buddhism, of village associations, *i-hui* or *she-hui*, brought a wider participation in culture than had been achieved by the pre-Buddhist classical religion of clans and collectivities. In particular, the institution of the *chai* or maigre feast, the Buddhist *agape*, brought a cross-class sense of solidarity and a certain osmosis between high and low cultures to the villages. Both Christianity and Buddhism at this stage were theological religions and popularized theology meant minimum literacy, more books, new thought structures.

Fourth, both societies in late antiquity saw a significant increase in maritime activity. In the West, there was the channel fleet of Carausius, the new *limes* of the Saxon shore; the imperial dockyard of Ravenna; the new Merovingian ports of Dorestad and Quentowic; the Byzantine import from the Black Sea of grain, fish, salt and gold; the naval *themes* of Cephalonia, Nikopolis, Dyrrachium, the Cybyrrhaeots, the Aegean and Samos; late Sassanid and early Moslem Persian Gulf commerce from Ubullah and Siraf; the maritime kingdom of Axum in Abyssinia; the argosies from Ceylon which traded to China; and the thalassocracy of the Cholas in the Tamil Nadu. In the East, there was the imperial grain fleet on the Grand Canal; increased private shipping on the Yangtze; the Korean maritime complex of the north-east seas; Japanese voyages to China; a considerable volume of shipping round the mouth of the Yangtze; the emporium of Canton; and the Sumatran thalassocracy of Srivijaya. This nautical pre-revolution of late antiquity, though subsequently overlaid by Moslem, Carolingian and Mongol continentalization, laid the foundations for the thirteenth-century maritime revolution and for its greater successor, the oceanic revolution of early modernity.

Differences in state and society

To each similarity in state and society, however, there corresponded a more significant difference, in every case to China's advantage. With regard to the state, *first*, though both empires were the product of self-conscious *restitutio orbis*, the extent of restoration was much greater in China than in Europe. Justinian's empire never included the extra Mediterranean provinces of classical Rome, still less, except marginally in the Black Sea, new areas coming into civilization such as Ireland, Germany, Sudan or Abyssinia. Its population was at most 25 million and its revenue 30 million cwt of grain equivalent. Hsüan-tsung's empire, on the other hand, included all the provinces of the Han empire except for north Korea, as well as new provinces in the lands opened up in the south. Its population was at least 50 million, possibly 75 million if full account is taken of the southern population, and its revenue was 60 million cwt of grain equivalent. The T'ang empire was a unique political entity in its world. The caliphate might have a wider theoretical jurisdiction, but the population under its effective rule was only 20 million and its revenue only 35 million cwt of grain equivalent.

Second, though both empires ruled through an expert civilian bureaucracy and a new articulation of law, the T'ang bureaucracy was uniquely rationalized through recruitment by competitive examinations and control by superior personnel management techniques, and the T'ang state achieved higher levels of law and order, more power over its subjects. T'ang government was more meritocratic, more intelligent, more effective than any other in its world.

Third, although in both empires the army was increasingly based on heavy cavalry, China possessed more military horses than east Rome thanks to its readier access to the Inner Asian source of supply. According to Agathias, Justinian's main field army, the *comitatenses*, numbered 150 000 men; of these half may have been cavalry, mounted on barbary roans from north Africa and 'capital horses' from Thrace: a horsepower reserve of perhaps a quarter of a million. The Northern Wei, on the other hand, a dynasty with close contacts with the nomads, had a horsepower reserve of two million. After the heavy losses of the Sui, T'ang T'ai-tsung built up his studs to 700 000 and in 725 Hsüan-tsung possessed 400 000 military horses. China's capacity to breed good horses might be less than the West's (though thanks to the colder climate it may have been greater under the T'ang than later), but she had greater ability to import; both great horses from Ferghana and ponies from Mongolia. The figurines of T'ang horses and horsemen in the museums, the importance of the theme of the horse in Li Po's poetry, the significance of remount control in the manoeuvres leading up to An Lu-shan's rebellion, all reflect the uniquely equestrian character of the T'ang state.

Fourth, while both empires to a greater extent than their classical predecessors supplemented force with diplomacy and established 'commonwealths' of satellites with themselves as centre, T'ang diplomacy was more sustained and the T'ang commonwealth farther flung, particularly in a maritime direction. With embassies coming from Korea, Japan and Indonesia, the T'ang was the first continental empire to organize an adjacent maritime space, a satellite system better articulated than the Byzantine Black Sea, the Merovingian North Sea, or the Celtic Sea of the Irish monks.

It was the same with regard to society. *First*, while both empires functioned through a new monumental urbanism, that of the T'ang was more massive and presented a greater discontinuity with the classical past. The first Rome had urbanized its society and, while the second had its own urbanization, it is questionable whether the new cities compensated for the losses of the third-century anti-urban revolution. The Han, on the other hand, had de-urbanized their society, so that there can be no doubt that the T'ang and their predecessors increased the overall level of urbanization. Ch'ang-an with a population of two million was twice the size of Constantinople. Its walled area, 30 square miles, was more than six times the 4.63 square miles within the Theodosian walls, though admittedly this does not take account of Galata, Pera and Scutari. Urbanization was no longer concentrated at the imperial capitals. There were twenty-six cities in T'ang China with a population of over half a million. With a fifth of the population living in towns, T'ang China was the most urbanized society of its day.

Second, while both empires rested upon a new articulation of rural life, the *chün-t'ien* system with its periodical allocation and redistribution of land, its coordination of landholding and tax responsibility, was more radical, less decentralizing and more beneficial to the state than anything in the West. It solved the problem of aristocratic exemption, peasant commendation, tax evasion and consequent fiscal anaemia which had been largely responsible for the fall of the Han. By its allocation of land to farmers, it provided an assured basis of taxation, by its periodic resumptions it extended bureaucratic control, and by its toleration of marginal private plots, orchards and pleasure gardens, it gave private enterprise room to grow. Except for the system of Ptolemaic Egypt, which it resembled in its combination of public and private elements, the *chün-tien* system (made administratively possible by urbanization and bureaucratization) was the most ambitious pre-modern scheme of land control. It maximized the advantages China already enjoyed in the field of agricultural technology and provided the framework for others she was acquiring: bigger farms, the substitution of wheat for millet, the plough for the hoe, more water mills, closer integration of arable farming and silk production.[11]

Third, while in both empires in late antiquity there was a wider diffusion of literate culture, the process went further in China because of the inventions of paper and printing and was of greater significance because the previous cultural level was lower. Quantitatively literacy rates in China probably reached 15–20 per cent under the T'ang compared to 10 per cent at most in the West. Qualitatively, though both Christianity and Buddhism revolutionized intellectual horizons by introducing new analytical concepts, the Buddhist intellectual revolution was in a sense the greater since it brought with it the notion of critical, self-reflective thought itself, previously unknown in China. Not only was Chinese thought liberated from its preoccupation with prescriptive paradigm but, thanks to the *Mahaprajnaparamitasastra*, it leap-frogged over Greek and Indian cosmology to reach a critical philosophy hardly surpassed in the West till Descartes.

Fourth, while both societies in late antiquity saw an increase in maritime activity, Chinese ships were larger and there were more of them. The largest Byzantine vessel was the *dromon*, a single-masted bireme, 150 by 24 feet, with 25 oars a side and a tonnage of 300; the largest fleet, that of Leo VI against the Moslems in Crete in 910, consisted of 122 *dromon* and 250 *pamphyla*, lighter transport galleys. In T'ang China, there were Kiangsu traders, multi-masted junks, up to 170 feet in length and with a tonnage of 600, operating from the Lower Yangtze, and the imperial grain transport fleet numbered several thousand vessels: standard grain junks, 80 feet by 15, with a tonnage of 200. Thanks to the Grand Canal – that artificial Nile from Hang-chou to Ch'ang-an built by the Sui, reorganized by P'ei Yao-ch'ing in the 730s and further reorganised by Liu Yen between 760 and 779 – a higher percentage of China's commerce was waterborne and a higher percentage of China's production was commercialized than anywhere else in the world of late antiquity. The Chinese economy had taken a great leap forward out of the immobility of the Han.

Supported by these advantages of conjuncture and structure, and conducted by a series of capable and long-lived rulers, the heirs of several centuries' successful experimentation in institutional innovation, T'ang China enjoyed a pre-eminence in the world which was to haunt the Chinese mind long after it had ceased to exist. For three centuries, while Byzantium blossomed and atrophied, Western Europe and India suffered dark ages, and the Middle East received the mixed blessing of Islam, China really was the middle kingdom, the lucky country of late antiquity. As a result, her contacts with the rest of the world multiplied, more travelled, and she herself became a world institution.

AVENUES OF CONTACT, 400 TO 1000

Under the T'ang, as under the Han, there were four avenues
of contact between China and the outside world: the central
land route, the southern sea route, the far southern sea route
and the northern land route. Under the T'ang, however, all
four routes acquired a new degree of organization. It is now
possible to speak of institutions of contact as well as avenues.
In particular, on all four routes, there developed a new kind
of specialized mercantile community. These communities
were rudimentary and fragile; they were itinerant with halting
places rather than homes; they consisted of outsiders, expat-
riates, resident aliens, and members of minorities both religious and secular. Nevertheless, by their relative permanence,
their solidarities, their active ferment, they gave the routes a
firmer foundation and shifted their spectrum from culture
towards commerce. A capitalism of mobile ghettos, the communities, ethnic in form but international in operation, were
the *Gemeinschaft* pre-figuration of the regulated companies
of the true *Gesellschaft* capitalism of the middle ages. In
antiquity capitalism had been unspecialized: the necessary
but unacknowledged activity of people who regarded themselves as primarily notables, mandarins or monks. Now for
the first time, it became professionalized, albeit at a humble
level and on the margin of society.[12]

The central land route

For the first time a contemporary document gives quantitative
information about the people operating this route. An
account of the Northern Wei capital of Lo-yang around 528
by Yang Hsüan-chih describes the different zones, appointed
for various activities, in the hierarchically designed imperial
city. In the south 'to the east of the imperial thoroughfare,
there are the four aliens' hostels; to the west of it are the four
aliens' wards'. Aliens were divided according to the direction
from which they had come: north, south, east and west. On
arrival they were accommodated in one of the four hostels
and after three years were given houses in one of the four
wards. Thus 'the aliens of the west who have chosen to become

loyal subjects are housed first at Yen-tzu hostel and then Mu-i ward'. Yang Hsüan-chih explained:

> None of those innumerable states and cities west of the Pamirs to as far west as the Roman empire (Ta Ch'in) have failed voluntarily to send their people to pay homage. It may indeed be said that the alien merchants who rush here every day to trade represent practically all nationalities of the world. Those aliens who love the land and culture of China and hence have settled here are too numerous to reckon. Consequently aliens who have been naturalized exceed ten thousand households.

If this figure refers to the four aliens' wards and if they were about equal, then the population of the Mu-i ward for westerners would have been 2500 households or 12 500 people: a not implausible figure for a community which will have grown larger in the days of the T'ang. The foreigners were prosperous:

> Their stately houses are neatly clustered together, and the tidily arranged and well-shaded lanes and alleys are lined with Japanese pagoda trees and willows. Rare commodities and articles from the world over are all to be found here. They have established a separate market here south of the river Lo, which is called the Worldwide (Ssu-t'ung) market.[13]

The two communities which operated the central land route in late antiquity were the Sogdians and the Syrians. As this was predominantly an Iranian route, both came appropriately from the extremities of the Sassanid empire: the Sogdians from Transoxania, the Syrians from northern Mesopotamia.

The homeland of the Sogdians is revealed both by archaeology and by Chinese travelogues. Excavations on the Afrasiab site at Samarkand show a large city with a wall 10½ kilometres in circumference, ruled by a cultivated, literate aristocracy which appreciated painting. The Chinese ambassador Wei Tse who visited the area between 605 and 617 stated:

> The people of the kingdom of K'an (Samarkand) are skilful traders. As soon as a boy reaches the age of five he is instructed how to read and write. When he can read he is

sent to study commerce. The majority of the inhabitants consider the pursuit of profit an excellent career.[14]

The Buddhist philosopher–pilgrim Hsüan-tsang, who was in Samarkand in the 630s, observed that its citizens 'were a real example to their neighbours in their observation of the laws of morality and decency'.[15] At home, the Sogdians, or at least their leadership, were Zoroastrians, though they seem to have sat lightly to the new orthodoxy being proclaimed on the plateau of Fars. Abroad, the emigrant communities of Turfan, Tun-huang and Ch'ang-an supported Buddhism, Nestorianism and especially Manichaeism, that deliberately ecumenical religion of the caravan routes, which had come to them from Mesopotamia and which they diffused to Central Asia, where it found a second home among the Uighurs when its first had been uprooted by Zoroastrian and then Moslem orthodoxy.

With its internationalism, its loose organization of half-believing aristocratic patrons, hard-core *perfecti* and half-practising hearers, and its emphasis on scripture and doctrine rather than fixed ecclesiastical institution, Manichaeism was well suited to be the ideology of a mercantile community, cosmopolitan and civilized, but insecure, displaced and rootless. Like all gnosticisms, Manichaeism was a religion of alienation and nostalgia whose redeemer was a stranger God worshipped by metics in other men's lands. Sogdians were often in this position. They were involved in the silk trade to the west and the bullion trade to the east, though their original acceptability everywhere probably derived from their access to, and expertise with, the great horses of Ferghana which every aristocrat of late antiquity wanted. Sogdians were soldiers as well as traders, as was An Lu-shan, T'ang marshal and greatest of Chinese rebels, whose Chinese name transliterates the Sogdian Rokhshan, a masculine form of the more familiar Roxana, and, as perhaps was Maniakh, 'chief of the people of Sogdiana', presumably a Manichee and ambassador of the *yabghu* of the western Turks, Istämi, to Justin II in 567.

If the Sogdian community was part of the wider, and not exclusively Sogdian, Manichaean diaspora, the Syrian community and its religious expression, the Nestorian church, was part of the wider, and not exclusively Nestorian, Syrian diaspora. Syria in late antiquity was larger than the modern republic. It covered in addition Lebanon, Palestine, Transjordan, southern Turkey and northern Mesopotamia. A Seleucid creation as Roman Egypt was a Ptolemaic, Syria contrasted with Egypt by size, lack of political unity (parts of Syria were frequently not in the Roman empire at all), intenser regionalisms, and absence of religious consensus. In the Christological disputes of the fifth century, Edessa was Nestorian, Antioch, perhaps as a result of plague and Semitic immigration, was Monophysite, while Jerusalem, the new pilgrimage city, was intransigently Chalcedonian. Nevertheless there was a minimum sense of community and all three Christianities shared in devotion to St Sergius at Resafa and to Simeon Stylites at Kalat Seman. A unity of fragments, however, rather than, as Egypt was, an organic unity, Syria in late antiquity was a land of losers, the diversity of its portfolio simply multiplying its risks. From a peak in the third century under the half-Syrian dynasty of the Severi, Syria suffered a series of disasters: the unsuccessful but destructive invasion of Shapur I; the destruction of Palmyra by Aurelian; the demotion of Antioch by the creation of Constantinople as the capital of the east; the failure of Arianism, the Antiochene intellectuals' heresy; the more successful invasion of Shapur II which separated east Syria from west; the renewed failure of Antiochene theology at the councils of Ephesus I and Constantinople II; the Antioch earthquake of 526 followed shortly by the onset of the plague series; the incursions of Chosroes I and II; the Moslem conquest; and the splendid but parasitic rule of the Omayyads.

These events and the de-urbanization they initiated – Syria lost as many towns as north Africa or Britain – produced emigration. The losers became the diaspora. Abroad, however, the Syrians, thanks to their urban, polyglot background and religious versatility, were highly successful. From their western headquarters at Marseille they handled the import of eastern goods into Western Europe during the Merovingian period. In seventh-century Rome three popes were of Syrian origin: John V, 685–686; St Sergius, 687–701; and Sisinnius 708. Their half-Monophysite piety introduced the *Agnus Dei* into the liturgy and feasts of Our Lady into the calendar. Theodore of Tarsus, Archbishop of Canterbury

668–690 and second founder of the church in England, was a Greek-speaking Syrian. In Persia Chosroes I used Nestorian Syrian bureaucrats in his reconstruction of the Sassanid empire, while Chosroes II's favourite wife, Shiren, was a Monophysite and his finance minister, Yazden of Kevhuk, a Nestorian. Under the caliphate, the Nestorian patriarch, Timothy I, was an influential friend of Harun-al-Rashid and the polymath al-Jahiz who died in 868/9 reported that the Nestorian business community was expanding in wealth and standing.

Further east, the Mar Sargis (Ma Ch'ing-hsiang, St Sergius) family moved from Khorasan to Kansu in 578 and the Sian stone inscribed in Chinese and Syriac, discovered in 1625, gives the history of the Nestorian mission to China organized by patriarch Yeshuyat II, from Bishop Reuben in 635 to Bishop Adam in 781. Its most notable member was Bishop Cyriacus who arrived in China in 732 in the train of an Omayyad embassy and who remained to become a figure in the intellectual life of the capital as the author of a number of apologies for Christianity. The T'ang court was receptive to the *Ta Ch'in Ching-chiao* (lit. 'Luminous Religion of the West', perhaps a loose translation of 'Roman Catholic faith'), as Nestorianism was called, both on account of its cosmopolitan, Persian flavour and as a counterweight to the over-mighty Buddhism of its subjects. Kuo Tzu-i, the imperial commander-in-chief against An Lu-shan, was at least a Christian sympathizer and his chief-of-staff I-ssu (Jesus) who paid for the Sian stone, was a Nestorian from Balkh. Sogdian and Syrian fought each other in China as they competed along the trade routes of Central Asia. If the Sogdians owed their original acceptability to their association with the great horse of Ferghana, then the Syrians may have owed theirs to their association with new breeds of one-hump camels, hybrid or hardy, which, as Bulliet has shown, replaced the two-hump Bactrian camel on the caravan routes of western Asia in this period.[16]

The southern sea route

Although the central land route, thanks to the Sogdian and Syrian communities, the improved camels and better cavalry protection, carried more traffic in the days of the T'ang than it had in those of the Han, it was still less important quantitatively than the southern sea route. The Western colony at Lo-yang under the Northern Wei numbered about 12 500, a figure which possibly reached 25 000 at Ch'ang-an under the T'ang. Abu Zayd of Siraf, however, tells us that at Canton, the eastern terminus of the sea route, on the eve of its capture by the rebel Huang Ch'ao in 878, there were 120 000 foreign residents: Moslems, Christians, Jews and Zoroastrians. A century before, the Buddhist monk Chien-chen described the port with its 'argosies of the Brahmans, the Persians and the Malays, their number beyond reckoning, all laden with aromatics, drugs and rare and precious things, their cargoes heaped up like hills'.[17] Similarly, the T'ang poet Chang Chi, addressing a friend leaving for a post in Canton, wrote of 'the babble of barbarian voices in the night market' – that is, in the unsupervised trade area in the port suburb outside the walls.[18]

The trade of Ceylon, the central pivot of the sea route, is likewise described in glowing terms, by Cosmas Indicopleustes, the Nestorian, probably Syrian, ex-merchant and monk, who wrote his *Christian Topography* in Alexandria around 547. The island, he says:

'is much frequented by ships from all parts of India and from Persia and Ethiopia, and it likewise sends out many of its own. And from the remotest countries, I mean Tzinista and other trading places, it receives silk, aloes, cloves, sandalwood and other products, and these again are passed on to marts on this side. . . and the island receives imports from all these marts which we have mentioned and passes them on to the remoter ports, while at the same time, exporting its own produce in both directions. . . Ceylon is a great seat of commerce.[19]

Although the southern sea route was highly international and according to Chinese sources the largest ships came from Ceylon, the most prominent mercantile community came from the Persian Gulf: Muscat the port of Oman, Siraf the port of Shiraz and Isfahan, and Ubullah the port of Basra, all three serving ultimately whatever was capital of Mesopotamia, Ctesiphon, Baghdad or Samarra. Persian Gulf navigation, in itself of considerable antiquity, expanded with the shift in the centre of gravity of the Sassanid empire from

Fars to Mesopotamia in the reign of Chosroes I. At this period the mercantile community was Nestorian, co-religionists of the Syrians along the central land route, though of Persian ethnic origin. Cosmas Indicopleustes, who had been a pupil of the Nestorian patriarch Mar Aba before his elevation to the primacy, has much information about the Nestorian sea world. Ceylon, he says 'has also a church of Persian Christians who have settled there, and a Presbyter who is appointed from Persia, and a Deacon and a complete ecclesiastical ritual'. Further north, 'in the country called Male [Malabar] where the pepper grows, there is also a church, and at another place called Calliana [Kalyana, near Bombay] there is moreover a bishop who is appointed from Persia'. To the west, at Socotra, still Greek-speaking having been settled from Ptolemaic Egypt, 'there are clergy who receive their ordination in Persia, and are sent on to the island, and there is also a multitude of Christians'.[20] Nestorianism, unlike Manichaeism, operated on both the land and sea routes. Its Judaic interpretation of Christianity shared with Manichaeism an intense scripturalism (the leading Nestorian doctor, Theodore of Mopsuestia, was a biblical interpreter *par excellence*); both were religions of books and literacy, but Christian faith regulated by bishops may have provided a more open basis for a community than Manichaean *gnosis* guided by *perfecti*.

With the coming of Islam, navigation in the Indian Ocean expanded, the opposite of trends in the Mediterranean. Even under the Omayyads who ruled from Syria, Mesopotamia was an important province of the caliphate and in the Indian Ocean, unlike the Mediterranean, Moslems faced no hostile sea power. It was with the move of the caliphate from Damascus to Baghdad, however, that Persian navigation reached its climax. At the founding of Baghdad in 762, Caliph al-Mansur declared: 'We have the Tigris to put us in touch with lands as far as China, and bring us all that the seas yield as well as the foods of Mesopotamia and Armenia'.[21] By this stage, the mercantile community was mainly Moslem. Masudi, writing in 943 about the entrepot of Kalah, probably a port on the Tenasserim coast, said: 'Today this town is the general rendezvous of the Moslem ships of Siraf and Oman where they meet the ships of China'.[22] Ethnically, however, Persians still predominated. Persian was the lingua franca of the southern sea route; the Chinese commonly referred to Po-ssu ships; the names of the leaders of the Nestorian emigration to India in 840, Mar Sapor and Mar Peroz, were Persian; and one of the foreign communities at Canton were Shiites. Just as the central land route east of the Oxus was dominated by Sogdians from north-east Iran, so the southern sea route east of Ormuz was dominated by Persians from south-west Iran. Both dominations reflected the importance of Iran, first under the later Sassanids and then under the early Abbasids, in the contact between East and West in late antiquity. The T'ang emperors were Philoaryans, devotees of polo and the chase, just as the Abbasid caliphs were Sinophiles, connoisseurs of silk and porcelain, as witness the vast number of Chinese shards at the site of Siraf. On both routes culture stilll predominated but trade had expanded.

The northern land route

In addition to the expanded activity of the central land route under the leadership of the Sogdians and Syrians, the southern sea route also faced increased competition from the northern land route under the leadership of another ethnic mercantile community, the Radhanite Jews. The meaning of the term Radhanite, *al-Radhaniyah*, has given rise to much dispute. Its *locus classicus* is a passage in the *Kitab al Masalik w'al Mamalik* (Book of Roads and Provinces) of Abu al-Qasim ibn Khurdadhbih, written about 845. Here Ibn Khurdadhbih described a group of Jewish merchants who, he says, traded from the south of France to China. Their primary languages were Arabic and Greek, but they also spoke Frankish, Slavonic, Spanish and Persian. Their market was the Abbasid caliphate. From the West they imported eunuchs, girl slaves, brocades, furs and swords; from the East, musk, aloes, cinnamon, camphor and medicinal plants; and among their trading stations were Damascus, Oman, places in India and the Crimea. It has been supposed that the term Radhanite derives from Rhodanus, the Rhone, since in the time of Gregory of Tours there was an important Jewish colony at Clermont-Ferrand. Alternatively, Radhanite could have been derived from the Persian town of al-Raiy near modern Teheran where there had been a Jewish settlement since the time of the *Book of*

Tobit around 200 BC. Most likely, however, in accordance with the mobile character of such mercantile communities, Radhanite did not have so precise a spatial connotation but was simply the same as Rabbanite. That is, it referred to the orthodox Rabbinical Jews officially recognized by the government of the caliph, as opposed to the heretical Karaite Jews who rejected both the *Resh Galutha*, the exilarch, nominated by the caliph and the authority of the rabbis generally. The Radhanites then were the collaborators: those who accepted and exploited the position of associate conquerors offered to them by the Moslems. For the Moslem invasions could be seen as a Jewish counter-revolution against the intolerant orthodoxies of Christianity and Zoroastrianism; Moslems, too, were children of Abraham; and it was perhaps not only by Christians that the Dome of the Rock was seen as a new Temple.

The secession of the Karaites from the Rabbanites, which deeply divided world Jewry for the next two centuries, took place in 760, not long after the foundation of the Abbasid caliphate. This date therefore gives a *terminus a quo* for the term Radhanite which would not have preceded the schism. Of course the Jewish diaspora and, to a lesser extent, Jewish involvement in international trade were much older than this, but the Abbasid revolution expanded both. Indeed the Karaite secession with its scriptural fundamentalism was in part a protest against the Arabizing liberalism which the patronage of the Abbasids threatened to bring to the *geonim*, the rabbinical doctors. Ibn Khurdadhbih's remark about the languages of the Radhanites is significant here. They were the Jews who took up the opportunities of the Abbasid peace.

For the Abbasid period, when loot gave way to production and trade, was the first age of peace in the history of Islam. It was an era of heightened consumption by Iranized court aristocracies who required the services of mercantile, or potentially mercantile, communities like the Jews. It was also the time when the defects of early Islamic society became apparent. Early Islamic society was anthropophagous. By its polygamy which lowered the birth rate; by its land system which produced chronic *anachoresis*; by its massive but parasitic urbanization which raised the death rate; by its militarism and mobility which did the same, early Islamic society dissipated its human resources for pleasure, work or war. Consequently it was a tolerant society religiously: the toleration of demographic deficiency. Beyond toleration, it was an immigrant society: the forced immigration of slavery. The Abbasids needed girls for their harems, boys for their armies, eunuchs for their households. As their urbanization, fleets, brick kilns, sugar mills, steel furnaces, dissipated their timber reserves, they also needed wood. As the climate grew colder and the centre of Islam shifted from mild-wintered Syria and Iraq to the plateaux of Iran and Central Asia, they began to want furs. All these things could be procured from the north by the Jews who could travel easily between Islam and Christendom or Slavdom.

Thus the Radhanites had their eunuch factories at Khwarazm and Verdun; their fur-processing centres at Khiva, Tabriz and Saragossa; their collecting points for both commodities at Kiev, Nijni-Novgorod, Kazan and Itil; their transit stations from Poland and Prague across Europe to their customers in Moslem Spain. Originally the axis of Radhanite trade was north and south: Tabriz and Itil were the head offices, the Caspian the highway and Baghdad the outlet. Later, Russian competition (the Varangians were another international mercantile cum warrior community), the Islamic common market from Spain to Sinkiang, and the exigencies of the traffic itself, realigned the axis west and east, so that by the middle of the eighth century, the Radhanites operated, as Ibn Khurdadhbih says, from China to the south of France. Except at Canton, there is a gap in the history of the Jews in China from the Han to the Sung, perhaps because of the rebellion of An Lu-shan which occurred at the same time as the Radhanite efflorescence, but there is little reason to doubt their presence on the land routes. Aurel Stein found a Persian business letter in Hebrew script dated 708 at Dandan-uiliq in Chinese Turkestan, while Pelliot discovered an eighth-century sheet of passages from the Psalms and Prophets at Tun-huang. Ibn al-Nadim at the end of the tenth century reported that Chinese was understood in Khazaria and that the Philosemite court there used Chinese etiquette. Chinese silk reached Sweden, Chinese rice was cultivated in the Volga delta, and the Viking name for lands to the south-east was Serkland, the land of silk. Thanks to the

Radhanites and their converts, the Khazars, the northern land route was better articulated than it had been in antiquity.

The far southern sea route

Finally there is the cinnamon route of Pliny's raftmen to consider. Here too, though the evidence for late antiquity is even more exiguous than that for antiquity, there is reason to believe in increased activity, at any rate for a time, under the guidance of an ethnic mercantile community, the Afro-Indonesians of the East African coast. Cosmas Indicopleustes, like Pliny, regarded cinnamon as an African product. Ibn Khurdadhbih, on the other hand, knew it as one of the products handled by the Radhanites, presumably in their maritime branch operating from Oman to Canton. Here is prima facie evidence of a switch in the route followed by cinnamon between 547 and 845. Another indication of a relaxation of contacts between Indonesia and East Africa is that the multi-masted outrigger galleons shown on the Borobudur reliefs, unlike the earlier outrigger vessels of Indonesia, never found a place in the Madagascan shipping complex.

Indonesian connection, which at the Indonesian end may be associated with the rise of Srivijaya, since the closest affiliation of Malagasy is with Borneo, was preceded by a rise. Cosmas Indicopleustes regarded the line Ethiopia, Barbaria, Zingium, that is Eritrea, Somaliland and the East African coast (Zingium being based on the same word which lies behind *Zanj*, Azania, Tanzania, Zanzibar, etc.) as one of the major articulations of his highly structural universe, and the Red Sea, i.e. north–south navigation, as one of the four navigable gulfs of the world before the unnavigable ocean was reached. Raymond K. Kent believes that Madagascar was not the base for Afro-Indonesian activity, but a refuge for it when the advance of the Bantu (and one might add, the rise of Srivijaya back home) made the mainland too difficult for it.[23] Afro-Indonesian enterprise did not advance from Madagascar: it retreated to it, in Kent's estimate, by the tenth century. Such a manoeuvre, however, followed by the survival of the community, the imposition of its language and the eventual development of impressive political structures, argues a considerable degree of organization beforehand. The Afro-Indonesians had no technical advantage over the Bantus: iron was only introduced to Madagascar in the eleventh century and, as we have seen, Madagascan shipping, like so much of the society of the Great Island, remained archaic. Tenth-century Madagascar was like twentieth-century Taiwan. Its leadership must have enjoyed an antecedent period of success. That period can only have been in the early part of late antiquity before the coming of the Bantu, before the rise of Srivija, that is, between 400 and 700. The locus of the leadership will have been the Tanzanian coast, the *Zanj* coast *par excellence*. This was the natural landfall for anyone riding the south equatorial current on a raft, well north of the Mozambique current which must have been known to the Afro-Indonesians, as it was to Cosmas Indicopleustes, as the irretrievable path to interminable ocean.

On all four avenues of contact the distinguishing feature of late antiquity was the emergence, in the interstices or on the margin of the great empires, of mobile ethnic groups – Sogdians, Syrians, Nestorian Persians, Varangians, Radhanite Jews and Afro-Indonesians – who figure variously as merchants, mercenaries and missionaries. Most of these groups had existed before and their emergence in late antiquity as conductors of international contact was due to changes in their milieu rather than in themselves. Nevertheless these communities were a new phenomenon, different from the unspecialized, intermittent and non-thematized commerce of the *polis* or the palace. They represented a new, more mobilized differentiation of the economic out of the non-economic 'imbedded' society of antiquity. Their ethnic composition and ideological commitment were unstable and their real homes were not their cities but their markets. From the cross-pollination cast by this *Gemeinschaft* capitalism, in the one area where bureaucracy did not stifle it and where there was no existing undergrowth to compete with, was eventually to grow the *Gesellschaft* capitalism of the European middle ages. In the meantime it served to underpin an increased volume of interchange between China and the outside world.

INTERCHANGES, 400 TO 1000

The pattern of interchange between China and the West in late antiquity reflected the contrast in their general evolution. For China, late antiquity was no dark age but a restoration. As an active, dynamic society T'ang China was eager to import and the flow of imports increased significantly. However, with the exception of cotton which took several centuries to make an impact, none of the imports was structurally significant. All were decoration to a building complete. For the West, *per contra*, late antiquity was an eclipse. As a society disorganized and falling behind, the West had much to learn from China and the flow of imports increased significantly. Moreover, some of these imports were of considerable structural significance. Within the West, too, there was a clear trichotomy between a Europe which received, an India which gave, and an Islam which, broadly, did neither. For northern Europe, sunk in rurality with the fall of the western empire and cut off from the sea by Moslem naval primacy, these were centuries of monastic hibernation, while in the Mediterranean the embattled Byzantium of the Iconoclasts had little to offer the outside world except Greek fire and its own example of militancy. Islam, on the other hand, was too mature in itself to need imports and too backward *vis-à-vis* T'ang China to offer exports. Based on an heroic simplification of ideology and institutions, Islamic society, the last of the classical empires of conquest, early on achieved a balance and a perfection to which little could be added. By the same token, this society of *souqs* and desert palaces, *sharia* and Bedouin, however effective, offered little to the sophisticates of T'ang; less indeed than its Sassanid predecessor.

India, however, was different. Although the Indian imperial state, the cumulative work of the Mauryas, Bactrian Greeks, Kushans and Guptas, had been in decline since the Hunnish invasions of the fifth and sixth centuries, Harsha's revival on a more seigneurial basis being only a Martinmas summer, Indian society, despite a decline in maritime trade, remained brilliant, dynamic, and a magnet to the rest of the world. If Pran Nath's estimate of 100 to 140 million is correct,[24] then India, with double the population of Europe and China, half of civilized humanity in fact, was a demographic community of a different order from anything in the rest of the world.

India was fed by the best food – rice; she was clothed by the best textile – cotton; and she went to war on the most powerful animal – the elephant. Beyond necessities, India used widely before anyone else the two initial foods of affluence: chicken and sugar. Although India in late antiquity had lower rates of literacy than China because she had neither paper nor printing, her level of numeracy was higher because of her superior mathematical notation. The first example occurs on an inscription in Gujerat dated to 595; it was first noted in the Roman world by the Jacobite bishop Severus Sebokht who died in 667; and the first European instance is Spanish and dated to 976. Indian philosophy as developed by the Buddhist scholastics of the Madhyamika and Vijnanavada schools – Nagarjuna, Aryadeva, Bhavaviveka, Candrakirti in the first; Asanga, Vasubandhu, Dignaga and Dharmakirti in the second – reached a more advanced level of intellectuality than anywhere else in the world at that time. A critical philosophy, it moved from the object of knowledge to its subject, from cosmology to cognitional theory, to anticipate elements of the Cartesian *cogito*. In particular, the Madhyamika emphasized, indeed exaggerated, the function of what Bernard J.F. Lonergan has called inverse insight, while the Vijnanavada developed the method he calls the reversal of counter-positions.

Indian civilization was in full expansion in late antiquity. While Hinduism, Vaisnavite and Saivite, monist and less than monist, was being adumbrated at home, Buddhism was exported abroad. A Greater India was established in Southeast Asia, both peninsular and insular, more by cultural imitation than by trade or emigration. Not only Ceylon, Burma, Cambodia, Sumatra and Java, but China itself might be regarded as part of this Greater India. Emperor Sui Wen-ti, the reunifier of the empire and the patron of Buddhism, was happy to be thought a second Asoka, and the Sung scholar Shen Kua thought the caste-like social structure of the T'ang, so different from that of his own time, to be of Indian origin. India was the only part of the outside world that Chinese in the T'ang period regularly visited, the only part whose balance of interchange with China was not negative.

People

In late antiquity more foreigners came to China for permanent residence than Chinese went permanently to foreign parts. Chinese went abroad temporarily: as soldiers, like Kao Hsien-chih who led T'ang armies to victory over the Tibetans across the Hindu Kush, and to defeat by the Arabs on the Talas river; as diplomats, as Sung Yun, representative of the Northern Wei Empress Hu to the court of Gandhara in 518, or Wang Hsüan-ts'e, ambassador of T'ang T'ai-tsung to the court of Magadha in 643 and 647; as Buddhist 'pilgrims', that is research students, like Fa-hsien the *vinaya* expert, Hsüan-tsang the Vijnanavadin doctor of philosophy, I-ching another *vinaya* man, or the 150 monks sent west by Sung T'ai-tsu in 960 in search of the law; as secular students, like the nameless Chinese medical student who, Abul Faraj al-Nadim tells us, studied under Rhazes and astonished him by his shorthand copying of Galen. Those who stayed permanently did so unwillingly: Princess Wen-ch'eng whom T'ai-tsung sent to marry and civilize the aggressive Tibetan king Srong-bTsan-sGam-po in 641; the Buddhist pilgrim Hsüan-chao who, on his second visit to India, found his return blocked by the military activity of the Arabs and Tibetans and died there around 681; humbler figures, the painters Fan Shu and Liu Tz'u, the weavers Yüeh Huan and Lü Li, unhappy prisoners of the battle of the Talas river, who, their companion Tu Huan who was released and returned to China reported, were retained by their captors to ply their trades and introduce their technologies into Mesopotamia. These, however, were the exceptions: the intention was to return to the middle, flowery kingdom which no T'ang Chinese need doubt was the best place in the world, and most travellers accomplished it.

Foreigners, *per contra*, came to China permanently in considerable numbers, generally by their own will and at every level of society. At the top were princes, scholars and ecclesiastics: Peroz and Narses the Sassanid old and young pretenders exiled by the advance of the Arabs; Arjuna king of Tirabhoukti and pretender to the throne of India brought back less voluntarily by the imperious high commissioner

Wang Hsüan-ts'e in 648; Anne of Kabudhan, the dancing girl from Tashkent who became a concubine of emperor Hsüan-tsung and a princess; the physician Narayanasvamin who perhaps introduced mineral acids to China; the Khotanese philologist Siksananda brought to Ch'ang-an by Empress Wu, that famous termagant and bluestocking, to translate the *Avatamsaka-sutra*; the three Indian families of astronomers, the Kasyapa, Gautama and Kumara; *dhyana* master Buddhabhadra from Kashmir; Sanghadeva, another Kashmiri, who translated the *Jnanaprasthana* of Katyayaniputra into Chinese; Paramartha who introduced the Vijnanavada to China; the Singhalese Amoghavajra who brought the Tantrayana; the three Nestorian bishops from Syria, Reuben, Cyriacus and Adam; 'the Great Musha' the Manichaean *perfectus*, sent by the king of Tukhara in 719.

In the middle there were entertainers such as the hypnotist sent by a western nation in the seventh century; the dancers from Chach; 'the western twirling girls' from Samarkand; the Indian acrobats who came to Ch'ang-an in 646; the contortionist who arrived from Tukhara in 719; or the large numbers of musicians from Kucha, the oriental Coblenz of the Sassanids' exile; artisans such as the Syrian glass workers introduced by the Sogdians; soldiers such as the Arabs sent by Caliph al-Mansur to help Emperor Su-tsung recover his throne from An Lu-shan; merchants such as the Uighur usurers who fleeced the young blades of the imperial capital.

At the bottom there were the servants: grooms, stable boys and camel drivers from Central Asia; Annamite ladies' maids; and household slaves – *Kurung* from Greater India, Slavs and Turks from the Jewish-Moslem slave centre of Khwarazm, Negritos from Melanesia, Negroes from the *Zanj* coast of East Africa brought by the far southern sea route of the Indonesians. Like all dynamic societies, T'ang China operated by brain drain. Many of its leading figures were of foreign origin. Thus An Lu-shan was of Sogdian origin; so was Fa-tsang, the doctor of the Hua-yen school of Buddhist scholasticism; Kao Hsien-chih was of Korean origin; Ko-shu Han, another general, was a Turk; Li Po, greatest of T'ang lyricists, was born in Afghanistan; while Yen Li-pen, greatest painter of the early T'ang, was likewise of Central Asian descent. Emperor T'ai-tsung himself, the founder of the dynasty's tradition of cosmopolitanism, had two and possibly four of his nearest maternal ancestors non-Chinese, probably Turkish.

Flora and fauna

The exchanges of living things in late antiquity were few but significant. The West received the plague bacillus and the Seville orange. China received cotton and sugar.

When plague first appeared in the West at Pelusium in 541, contemporaries associated it with Ethiopia, i.e. the upper Nile and the Horn of Africa. Modern scholars have therefore derived it from the reservoir of plague which exists today in the rodents of the eastern Congo and Great Lakes regions of central Africa. Monophysite missions to the Sudan, increased trans-Saharan contacts as a result of the introduction of variants of the north Arabian camel saddle, and possibly the activities of the Afro-Indonesians from the *Zanj* coast, could be supposed as intermediary factors.

However, it is not certain that the central African plague reservoir existed in late antiquity; the scarcity of fleas in the tropics presents a difficulty about transmission; and this route was not, in later times when the reservoir certainly existed, a common highway for plague. Further, the evidence of contemporaries may be no more than a literary souvenir of Thucydides who attributed an Egyptian origin to his plague of Athens, which may not have been true plague. Again, although the first pulsation of the series began in Egypt, most of the subsequent pulsations began in Constantinople, Antioch or Mesopotamia. On the principle of Occam's razor, it is best to suppose that the Inner Asian plague reservoir was still the only one in late antiquity and that the plague of Justinian derived from it as a result of the increased traffic along the central land route. If silk worms could survive the long journey by camel, as we shall see they did, why not infected fleas in a bundle of silks? One recalls that the Marseille plague of 1720 was caused by a single infected cargo of cotton from Smyrna. A less likely explanation would be to suppose the Indo-Chinese reservoir already in existence and active and to postulate a similar transmission to the Persian

Gulf and the Red Sea via the southern sea route. In either case the comparative shortness of the plague of Justinian series as compared to the later Black Death series would be due to the failure of the plague bacillus to establish a secondary reservoir among the rodents of Kurdistan. The fact that the plague series ended around 750, when the central land route was hit by the rebellion of An Lu-shan but when the southern sea route was still in full prosperity, is a further argument for an Inner Asian origin. For it was not only isolated western Europe and beleaguered Byzantium which discarded the unwelcome gift from the marmots of High Asia, but the Islamic common market as well. Just as its arrival marked the end of late antiquity in the West, so its departure marked the brief revival of the Carolingians, the Isaurians and the Abbasids.

If the significance of plague was immediate, profound, but transitory, the significance of the Seville orange, the other European import from East Asia in late antiquity was delayed, superficial in itself, but permanent and, in combination with other imports, not without importance. Reacting against the notion of a perennial Mediterranean, Lucien Febvre pointed to what are now regarded as typically Mediterranean flora which were unknown to classical antiquity: oranges and lemons from China; tomatoes, maize, potatoes, tobacco, pimento, cactus from America; eucalypts from Australia; cypresses from Persia; rice and sugar from India. Citrus fruit were the earliest element of the new Mediterranean ecology which appeared between antiquity and modernity, and the Seville orange, the bitter *Citrus aurantium*, used today for marmalade and as graft stock for other oranges, was the first widely used citrus fruit. The new Mediterranean ecology, significantly an addition of luxuries rather than a transformation of necessities, was a factor in the revival of the Mediterranean after the dark ages, first in the medieval communes and then in the sixteenth-century empires. Oranges not only joined the Chinese peach and apricot in diversifying Mediterranean fruit farming, but also were an anti-scorbutic, a long-term factor improving the health of Europeans and a foundation of their oceanic supremacy. Where the plague was an avalanche, the orange was part of a glacier, which in the long run would move more earth.

The introduction during the T'ang period of cotton to Kwangtung and sugar to Szechwan should be seen as part of another slow development of long-term significance: the spread of these Indian crops across the world to become everywhere key elements in the textile and food industries. Although historians of the industrial revolution have limited the sway of King Cotton, they have to allow that cotton was the first fibre to be subject to true industrialization (factory organization, steam power, coal fuel) and that before synthetics it was the number one source of world textiles. Similarly, sugar played a notable role in the genesis of the modern economy. The sugar plantation was both an object and an instrument of European colonial expansion on both sides of the Atlantic; the sugar mill, denounced by the Portuguese Jesuit Antonio Vieira in the seventeenth century as dark and satanic, was one of the ancestors of the industrial factory; and the consumption of sugar, first of comestible luxuries, is a prime index of the modest consumer affluence which was both cause and effect of the industrial revolution.

The first steps of cotton and sugar outside India are therefore matters of moment. Cotton was the staple textile of the Harappa people of the Indus valley civilization; it is mentioned in the Rig-Veda; and its technology in India is described by Herodotus. By the time of the *Periplus*, cotton was a major Egyptian import from India; it may have been cultivated in Egypt in late Christian times; and it was certainly cultivated there under the Omayyad and Abbasid caliphates. The European word fustian, meaning a mixed cloth of linen and cotton, is derived from Fustat, the Arab capital of Egypt from 641 until the foundation of Cairo by the Fatimids in 969. Cotton, known under both its Sanskrit and Persian names, became an import to China from India in the third century AD by both the land and the sea routes. Under the T'ang, cottons were imported from both Turfan and Ceylon. The first definite reference to cotton manufacture in China, in the Canton region and probably based on local production, comes in a poem of the ninth century.

Sugar was first cultivated outside India in Persia in the fifth century. It was introduced to Egypt in the seventh century and to Spain in the eighth, and first appeared in the rest of medieval Europe as a Venetian import from Egypt. In the seventh century, Emperor T'ai-tsung sent a mission to Magadha to learn the secret of its manufacture. The industry came to be centred in Szechwan, in the districts of the T'o valley, in particular Nei-chiang. Sugar was associated with Buddhism: a monk introduced the technique of refining to Szechwan, and the attraction of Buddhist doctrine was compared to that of sugar cane. Sugar, however, never exercised the leading role in the Chinese economy that it did in the European. Marco Polo observed it growing in the Min Valley in Fukien in some abundance, but he regarded the refining technique as only recently introduced from Egypt. The industry never achieved a more than local importance. Cotton, *per contra*, did achieve national importance, but slowly, not until Ming times. Marco Polo treats it as a major product only of the Chien-ning region of Fukien. One can only suppose that silk was a more formidable competitor to it than wool in the West. The relative failure of sugar in China is more puzzling. As with the somewhat parallel case of grape wine, Chinese taste seems simply not to have been attracted by this kind of modest luxury.

Commodities

As in classical antiquity, so in late antiquity, the chief commodities traded were textiles, minerals, and spices. The only changes were in the locus and level of consumption: a shift eastward in the main centres of Western spending, and an increase in the scale of Chinese spending thanks to the greater prosperity of the T'ang compared to the Han.

Although China in this period lost her absolute monopoly of silk production, she remained by far and away the greatest producer. Indeed with the destruction of the Alexandrian linen industry by the Arabs, China's pre-eminence in high grade textiles was greater than ever. Except for some cottons, Persian carpets and Indian indigo (more a cosmetic than a dyestuff), she was the exporter, the rest of the world the grateful customer. The shift from Rome to Constantinople and the stabilization of the eastern empire probably increased the European demand for Chinese silks, as the shift from Damascus to Baghdad and the stabilization of the caliphate increased that of Islam. Cosmas Indicopleustes regarded the

silk trade as a regular one with the central land route supplying more than the southern sea route because of its shortness.
The chief testimony to it is archaeological: silks found in
Sinkiang, particularly at Turfan and Niya, whose designs indicate production for the export market. The designs – paired
birds, vines, wine jars, wine drinkers – are Sassanid in character, though Omayyad or Abbasid in date, and reflect the Iranian imprint on early Moslem secular culture. Byzantine and
Frankish taste at this period were also under Iranian influence, as may be seen from the Vatican Annunciation textile
and the even more Sassanid relic cloth of St Aman in the
cathedral of Toul. The actual silk, however, was probably
Chinese.

The mineral product which travelled in greatest quantity
in late antiquity was Chinese porcelain. Porcelain was an
invention of the T'ang, evidence of a new luxury and a new
craftsmanship just as Meissen, Sèvres and Wedgwood were
to be in eighteenth-century Europe, and until the eighteenth
century, the Chinese ceramics industry enjoyed a monopoly.
Porcelain was highly appreciated by the consumerist aristocracy of the Moslem world and numerous shards of T'ang
ware have been recovered from the sites of Siraf, Samarra
and Fustat. In the opposite direction, fewer goods travelled
and quality replaced quantity: amber from Persia and from
the Baltic, perhaps brought by the Radhanites via Khwarazm;
red coral, 'veritable métal precieux' as Braudel calls it, [25]
fished in the Byzantine far west in the waters of Tunisia, Sicily
and Sardinia and used in China for the official buttons of
high officials; and realgar, arsenic disulphide from Persia,
required as superior to the local product by Chinese
alchemists for aurifaction, for the treatment of skin diseases
and as an ingredient for the manufacture of elixirs.

The international spice trade saw two changes in late
antiquity. On the one hand, the western European market
temporarily contracted. These were the centuries of Pirenne's
'great disappearances': of the decay of what was left of the
Roman commercial networks operated by the Syrians; of the
ruralization of northern European life round manor and
monastery. On the other hand, the Chinese market expanded
and diversified. Buddhism increased the consumption of
aromatics where the replacement of paganism by Christianity

in the West reduced it. Much of the increased demand was met from within East Asia, particularly Champa the supplier of garoo or aloes wood, but there was some importation of Indian or southern Indonesian sandalwood.

At the same time, changes in the Chinese diet initiated a Western-style trade in condiments and food preservatives, notably pepper. Before late antiquity Chinese cuisine had been closer to what today would be thought Japanese: lightly cooked, lightly flavoured. Under Indian influence spices gradually came in. The Buddhist pilgrim I-ching who had been to India stated: 'In China, people of the present time eat fish and vegetables mostly uncooked; no Indians do this. All vegetables are to be well cooked and to be eaten after mixing with the asafoetida, clarified butter, oil or any spice.'[26] Another T'ang writer, talking of pepper 'which comes from the country of Magadha', said 'men of our time always use it when they make "Western plate" meat dishes'.[27] Through this cultural shift from the raw to the cooked, the Chinese spice trade acquired a new dimension in the T'ang period, just as the Western spice trade lost one. Acquisition and loss, however, were not on all fours. The contraction of the European spice trade was an anomaly: it ran counter to the underlying tendency of the European economy towards greater consumption of meat and had therefore, sooner or later, to be reversed. The diversification of the Chinese spice trade was the removal of an anomaly: it only redressed the previous overemphasis on spices serving the sense of smell, and it might therefore not be maintained. In the long run, pepper, like sugar, was to be more important for Europe than China, and China was to find her own substitutes for it.

Techniques

Four major techniques were exchanged between East and West in late antiquity. Silk, stirrups and harness, and paper were received by the West, and an improved technology of glass was received by China. Not only did the West import more from China than vice versa, but she was more deeply affected by her imports.

The familiar story of the transmission of the secret of silk to the Byzantine empire by itinerant monks in the reign of

Justinian raises as many problems as it solves. First, the two ancient authorities do not agree. Procopius says that the monks were Indians and that they brought the silkworm eggs from Serinda (which of course cannot be assumed to be Sir Aurel Stein's Serindia), while Theophanes says that the person was a Persian and that he brought the eggs from the land of the Seres. Hudson's solution, that the monks were Nestorian Persians who went to Indo-China having previously been to India, is neat but unconvincing. Second, there are technical problems. *Bombyx mori* would have to adapt itself to the black mulberry instead of the white and one is surprised that enough leaves were immediately available to supply the enormous number required; and silkworms are notoriously liable to disease. Procopius' date for the arrival of the secret is 552, yet before he died in 565, Theophanes tells us, Justinian was able to send the Turks specimens of Byzantine silks. Third, even assuming that the monks were Nestorians and that a planned programme of industrial espionage and acclimatization could be organized through them, there is the problem of fitting this programme into the pattern of Justinian's generally unfriendly relations with the church of the east culminating in the condemnation of the three Nestorian doctors at Constantinople II in 553. Most of these problems, however, may be solved in the context of the Syrian diaspora and of the western policy of the reforming Nestorian patriarch Mar Aba, 540–552, the teacher of Cosmas Indicopleustes. The Syrians were already silk merchants and it would have been a natural step for them to become silk producers, especially as the *T'ang-shu* hints that the technology of silk had been transplanted from China to Khotan in the fifth century. It only required mercantilism on the part of the emperor (or possibly, as Robert Graves guessed, on the part of the empress) and ecumenism on the part of the patriarch, to set events in motion.

If the secret of silk was the work of the Syrian diaspora, it was a princely gift which deeply affected subsequent European history. True, it did not make Europe independent of foreign supplies. Down to modern times, Europe has needed to import: from Persia, which received the secret of silk shortly after the Byzantine empire; from Bengal, to which the technology of silk was transmitted from China via the

Burma road in the early middle ages; and from China itself whence the best raw silk and the finest silks came until the nineteenth century. Nevertheless the ability to produce raw silk locally was a safety net to the successive centres of the European silk industry: Constantinople, Naples and Lucca, Lyon, Spitalfields and Macclesfield. It was part of the new Mediterranean ecology. Silk, particularly black velvet produced at Lucca, sold by the Genoese at Lyon and sought after in Paris, was the outstanding luxury textile of early modernity, and it was from a widening taste for luxury that the industrial revolution grew. Silk was the first European textile to adopt powered factory technology: first at Bologna, then in Venetia and Piedmont, finally in Derbyshire; and the semi-industrial *molino bolognese* (ultimately itself of Chinese origin as we shall see in the next chapter) was the model for the fully industrial cotton and woollen mills of Manchester and Leeds. The secret of silk, only a scratch at the time, a stimulant to the *gynaecaea*, an irritant to the middleman, conveyed a powerful virus.

Hardly less powerful and faster acting were stirrups and efficient equine harness. From the evidence of tomb statuettes, stirrups are known to have been used in China in the Chin period, 265 to 420. Their development by the basically anti-equestrian Chinese was probably a response to increased pressure from barbarian mounted *foederati* at this time. In the West, though there is a tradition that stirrups were used by Belisarius, and the thrust of his military reforms towards heavy cavalry would seem to require them, there is no definite evidence of stirrups till the Isaurians. As the Chinese sources record Byzantine embassies for this period, presumably seeking alliance against the Moslems, it may be that, while the envoys did not get what they wanted, at any rate until Kao Hsien-chih's unhappy venture in 751, they did learn about a small but crucial piece of technology which allowed them to make better use of their cavalry. The combination of stirrups, large horses, lances and armoured knights, used first by the Isaurians and then by the Carolingians, coincided with the turn of the tide of the Moslem invasions. No doubt there were other reasons, in particular changes in leadership in both halves of Christendom, but the new Christian application of horsepower against the Moslem camelry was probably decisive. The alliance forged in the dark ages between the European aristocracy and the large horse was to stand Europe in good stead in the even darker days of the Mongol invasions and led eventually to Europe's acquiring a crushing world superiority in horsepower.

Efficient equine harness took longer to make its impact. Its history in Europe is complicated by the fact that it may have had an African as well as a Chinese source. Throughout Western antiquity the prevailing equine harness was the inefficient yoke, throat and girth arrangement borrowed from the ox. In China, from the third century BC, horses were harnessed by a shafts and breast-strap arrangement more suited to their anatomy, and from the fifth century AD, by the even more suitable shafts and collar arrangement. In Needham's view, the breast-strap harness was not known in Europe until the sixth century, possibly not until the eighth, while the collar harness is not represented in art until Frankish miniatures of the tenth century. Bulliet, however, has pointed out that in reliefs from Lepcis Magna, datable to between the second and fourth centuries, camels are represented harnessed to ploughs by a whipple-tree and withers'-strap, i.e. the same principle of pulling from the sides as in the breast-strap and collar arrangements. Modern harness therefore originated in Europe not with the horse but with the camel and there are philological grounds for thinking that its subsequent application to horses was in southern Europe derived from a north Africa source. The Chinese source operative in northern Europe, however, was more significant because it was there that the horse first replaced the ox as the ploughing animal and the light Mediterranean scratch plough was replaced by the heavier *carruca* which was more suitable for the rich, damp, recently deforested wealden soils. These results, it is true, were slow in coming. The Bayeux tapestry provides the first certain evidence of horse, *carruca* and modern harness, and the combination may not have been common till the Cistercian agricultural offensive of the following century. Nevertheless in the long run, the cart horse, *carruca* and collar harness combination was to be of even more importance in European history than the war horse, lance and stirrups combination. As the second armed the state, the first armed society.

With its simpler technology, the history of paper is more straightforward. It was invented, according to the *Shih-shih* (Beginning of All Affairs) of the Sui mathematician, Liu Hsiao-sun, by the eunuch Ts'ai Lun early in the second century AD. With demand from renascent bureaucracy and supply assured by the textile industry, its use steadily increased in China. The documents collected by Sir Aurel Stein for the Han period are written on wood, those for the T'ang period are written on paper. Paper indeed was probably a precondition of the revival of empire in China.

As a result of contact with the Chinese in Sinkiang, paper manufacture passed to pre-Islamic Samarkand where its high quality was noted by the Moslems in 704. The technique was introduced to Islam, however, not by the Sogdians, but by Chinese technicians, no doubt part of Kao Hsien-chih's staff, captured at the battle of the Talas river in 751. Harun al-Rashid established a paper mill at Baghdad, and the earliest surviving Moslem paper manuscript, the *Gharib al-Hadith* of Abu-Ubayd al-Qasim, in Leiden University library, is dated 866. The Archduke Rainer collection illustrates the change from papyrus to paper in Egypt. All thirty-six manuscripts from 719 to 815 are papyrus, between 816 and 912, there are ninety-six papyrus to twenty-four paper, one document apologising for its use of papyrus; and between 913 and 1009, there are nine papyrus and seventy-seven paper. From Egypt paper manufacture spread to Moslem Sicily and Spain and thence to Christendom. Paper was described by Peter the Venerable and the first Christian paper mill is reported from the French Pyrenees in 1157. A deed of Roger II of Sicily dated to 1109 is the first surviving Christian paper document. Sicily was the most bureaucratic of the early European monarchies, the protagonist of empire and hence the enemy of the imperial papacy and its allies, the Italian city states, but in the long run they were the beneficiaries of paper. The Avignonese papacy with its throngs of litigants, its bulls, briefs, faculties, dispensations and indulgences, is inconceivable without paper. In China, paper was the ally of bureaucracy. In Europe it came too late for this. Politics were already set in another mould and paper served to bureaucratize the clerical, municipal and, later, royal enemies of imperial monarchy.

China's only major technological import from the West in late antiquity was in the field of glass technology. Late Chou and Han China possessed the elements of glass-making, but they were not well developed. Most of the glass objects recovered are either imports or such things as beads, of a humble character technically. China did not possess the capacity to make coloured, translucent glass like that of Syria or Alexandria, and according to the *Pei-shih*, it was this which was introduced by people from *Yüeh-chih* (i.e. the former Kushan empire) in the reign of the first Northern Wei emperor, T'ai Wu-ti, 424–452. These people were probably Sogdians since the ruins of glass workshops have been found at the Sogdian site of Pyandjikent near Kokand, which is known to have been in touch with China because of the Chinese coin finds there. Glass was appreciated under the T'ang: the opaque form was regarded as an artificial jade, while the translucent form was both imported, from Sogdiana and Syria, and after 424, copied.

Yet advanced glass technology in China never became the basis of a major industry as it did in the West. In Europe, the glass industry supplied tableware and window cover, and its successive headquarters at Murano, L 'Altare, St Gobain and St Helens were prototypes of factory organization and industrial chemistry. In China, the superlative ceramics industry supplied tableware and the paper industry supplied window cover, and the glass industry, though technically sophisticated (both the microscope and the telescope were invented simultaneously in Europe and China) remained a backwater. One reason was the precocious development of porcelain. Another was fuel. Glass required immense quantities of wood. It may therefore have been a victim, first, of the chronic timber shortage of north China and, later, of the acute timber famine of the whole of China whose serious effects on Chinese attitudes to energy we shall note again. Like wine under the Han, like sugar under the T'ang, glass, welcome in times of affluence, was cut back in more straitened circumstances. There was no Chinese Chartres.

Ideas

Despite its better organized avenues of contact, the world of late antiquity was not propitious to the exchange of ideas. It was the period when the religious frontiers of the Old World were drawn, when ecumenisms regionalized, and regionalisms reasserted themselves. In the West orthodoxies were triumphant. Western Europe saw the victory of Augustinian institutionalism over semi-Pelagian mysticism and the extraversion of Benedictine spirituality to missionary activity by Gregory the Great and to liturgy by Cluny. The Byzantine sense of being the beleaguered people of God expressed itself alternatively in the militant, rationalized imperial piety of the iconoclasts and in the equally militant unrationalized monastic piety of the iconodules. In Islam, the half-believing Omayyads were replaced by the committed Abbasids and within Sunnism, Hanbalite fundamentalism rejected both Mutazili rationalism and Sufi mysticism. Even tolerant India saw the rise of a new Hindu orthodoxy between 400 and 1000: the inflexible *advaita* metaphysics of Sankara and the aggressive revivalisms of Vishnu and Siva. Everywhere embattled communities used orthodoxies as shibboleths and safeguards.

In these circumstances, the only ideas which may have travelled west in late antiquity were some further notions of Chinese alchemy, possibly introduced through the Arab alchemist Geber, 721–813, who had opportunities for contact with China and whose thought shows Chinese influence. In Islam and India, as later in Christendom, alchemy served as an anti-orthodox intellectual underground. In China, until the great persecutions of 845 there was no victory of orthodoxy and the T'ang court welcomed exotic ideas: Central Asian music, Persian secular culture, and above all, Indian Buddhism, the first Westernization of China. What there was, however, was increasing intellectual maturity and self-sufficiency which reduced the need for cultural imports: a different process from that in the West, but producing the same results. Most notably, Indian Buddhism in China was checked by the rise of an original Chinese Buddhism.

The history of Buddhism in China in late antiquity falls into three periods each dominated by two rival sects. In the first, the age of Indian scholasticism, 400 to 600, Indian influence was paramount, not only in doctrine but more importantly in *problematik*. It was through Indian Buddhist critical metaphysics, first grasped in its entirety by Seng-chao, that Chinese thought moved from constituent reason to deliberative reason, from mythology to philosophy, from paradigm to syntagma, from form, medium and method to content, message and conclusion. This decisive breakthrough was accomplished between 400 and 600. The Chinese absorbed the two leading Indian scholasticisms: the Madhyamika, the middle school of Nagarjuna, which taught a critical doctrine of absolute logical agnosticism; and the Vijnanavada, the school of consciousness only, of Asanga and Vasubandhu, which opposed to it a metacritical doctrine of the necessary knowledge of mental activity. These two schools, introduced respectively by Kumarajiva and Paramartha, dominated Buddhism in China down to the end of the sixth century. Their greatest Chinese exponents were the Madhyamikan Chi-tsang, 549–623, the descendant of a Persian trader who had settled at Nanking, and the Vijnanavadin Hsüan-tsang, 596–664, purely Chinese but pilgrim, explorer and diplomat.

In the second period, the age of Chinese Buddhist scholasticism 600 to 800, Buddhist philosophy in China, while continuing to take Indian texts as its starting point (though often texts not much regarded in India) went beyond the Madhyamika and the Vijnanavada. The new T'ion-t'ai and Hua-yen schools were specifically Chinese – not because they Sinified Buddhism or expressed some perennial Chinese mentality but because they were original and born in China. The hallmark of Chinese Buddhist scholasticism was its paratheism. It rejected Madhyamikan logical agnosticism and advanced beyond the Vijnanavadin self-knowing mind, to affirm an absolute. The T'ien-t'ai school founded by Chih-i, 'the orchid of the spring', affirmed the coexistence of absolute mind and being as its intention, and canonized the Lotus sutra, the *saddharmapundarikasutra* as the exoteric expression of this abstract doctrine. The Hua-yen school of Fa-tsang, 'the chrysanthemum of the autumn', reinterpreted mind and its intention as relation rather than substance and affirmed a universe which could be known as a relative absolute of objective relations, a pre-established harmony. It substituted the esoteric Flower Garland sutra, the *Avatamsakasutra* (in Chinese, Hua-yen) for the Lotus as the highest revelation of Buddhism. T'ien-t'ai and Hua-yen were developments of an Indian debate, but neither existed as a school in India and both represented a line of development which had been explicitly rejected by the founders of Indian Mahayana. Chinese Buddhism had come of age.

In the third period, the age of Chinese Buddhist anti-scholasticism, 800 to 1000, Chinese Buddhism, though moving in the same direction as Indian, rejected the specific Indian solutions in favour of new developments of its own. In both India and China there was an anti-intellectual reaction against the scholasticism of Madhyamika, Vijnanavada, T'ien-t'ai and Hua-yen. In India, this reaction took three forms: in north-west India and the Deccan, the so-called Hindu revival, i.e. the new emotional religions of Vishnu and Siva; in Ceylon and Burma, a reversion to Hinayana illuminism; and in Bengal, under the Palas, Tantrayana, a new, non-verbal, liturgical Buddhism emphasising *mudra* (gesture), *mandala* (symbol) and *mantra* (formula). Neither the new Hinduism nor the new Hinayana found a foothold in China, and although the Tantrayana was introduced, its cycle of favour was brief and limited to the late T'ang court, whose separation from the provinces and fall, it hastened. Instead, anti-intellectualism took three different forms in China, which thereafter became the standard types of Buddhism there. These were Ching-t'u or Pure Land, an exoteric, scriptural, evangelical pietism; Ch'an (Zen) or Meditation, an esoteric, anti-scriptural, contemplative spirituality; and the cult of Maitreya, a millenarism alternatively exoteric and esoteric with scriptures of its own, often influenced by Manichaeism.

Although two out of the three scriptures emphasized by Ching-t'u had Sanskrit originals and its litany-like invocation of Buddha's name *(nien-fo)* may have had an Indian prototype, Ching-t'u did not exist as a popular lay movement in India as it did in China. Similarly, Ch'an claimed to reproduce a secret doctrine transmitted from the Buddha through successive Indian patriarchs and then brought to China by the Persian master Bodhidharma, but when Indian monks learnt of the Chinese doctrine at the Council of Lhasa in 792 they rejected it. The true founders of Zen were the Chinese monk, Hui-ning, and his combative disciple Shen-hui. The Maitreyan scriptures were likewise mostly Chinese in origin. Tibet became the frontier between Indian and Chinese Buddhism. In the high land of monk and nomad, Indian doctrines continued to flourish: Tantrism, Vijnanavada, Madhyamika, and neither Ching-t'u nor Ch'an nor Maitreya millenarism established themselves. In China, contrariwise, Indian influence on Buddhism after 800 was never more than tangential. In

Japan, Tantrayana (Japanese Shingon, Chinese Chen-yen) was
more influential for longer, but there too Ching-t'u and Zen,
together with the Nichiren sect, a highly idiosyncratic version
of T'ien-t'ai, eventually triumphed. In the last resort, despite
the liberalism of the T'ang, East Asia was not immune to the
victory of orthodoxies and the closing of ideological frontiers.
Further, Buddhism itself was ceasing to be the world institution it had been.

WORLD INSTITUTIONS, 400 TO 1000

Despite its ideological divisions, the world of late antiquity
was more unified than the world of classical antiquity. In
classical antiquity the only approximation to a world institution was the Buddhist international, which spanned India,
eastern Iran and China and was probably probing Africa and
America, and the only, highly tenuous, links were intellectual.
In late antiquity the links passed from the intellectual to the
social band of the spectrum. Rice, the wonder food of India,
was now also a major crop in Iraq, Egypt and Sicily, in the
East African islands and in the Volga delta. Cotton, the wonder fabric of India, was now present also, in East Asia, Meso-
America and Africa. The new unity of late antiquity was most
manifest, however, in the realm of aristocratic luxuries: silk,
spices, aromatics, sugar, glass, porcelain, heavy horses, hawks,
polo and chess. By origin the lifestyle to which these appurte-
nances belonged was Iranian, put together at the court of
Chosroes II, Parwiz – feckless ruler but matchless paradigm
– at Ctesiphon, copied by T'ang T'ai-tsung at Ch'ang-an,
bequeathed to Harun al-Rashid at Baghdad and commemo-
rated for posterity by Firdousi in his *Shahnameh*, which became
the instrument for its revival in the days of the Timurids.
   If the new unity rested on Indian and Iranian pillars, the
keystone was Chinese. The T'ang court itself was the new
world institution of late antiquity. All Chinese dynasties aimed
to provide cultural glamour for their subjects: that was their
primary *raison d'être*. The T'ang alone aimed to provide cosmopolitan glamour, and not for their own subjects only. They
were the most outward looking of all Chinese dynasties, the
least xenophobic, and the most receptive to foreign influence.

China was the middle kingdom, not in the later exclusive sense of having nothing to learn from the rest of the world, but in the inclusive sense of being able to learn anything. In 872, Emperor I-tsung showed the Arab traveller Ibn Wahab of Basra scrolls containing pictures of Moses, Jesus, Muhammed and Buddha and summaries of their teaching, commenting courteously and broadmindedly on each. It is difficult to imagine any other ruler of the ninth century, or a ruler of any other Chinese dynasty, doing the same. It was under the T'ang that the sinocentric view of the world, to which later Chinese clung with such tenacity and unrealism, most corresponded with reality. Sinocentrism was not only the rationalization of a fact of space, that in East Asia China really was the uniquely civilized superstate surrounded by relatively uncultivated satellites, but also of a fact of time, the age of T'ang cosmopolitanism. China had become the centre of the Buddhist world. The T'ang emperors, though secular in their tastes, Taoist in their house religion, Erastian in their politics, even Christian in their personal preference, consciously used Buddhism to enhance their world role. The richest monasteries, the most profound theologians, the most lavish royal patronage, were now to be found in China rather than India. China was the magnet which moved world trade, which set Koreans, Sogdians, Persians and Radhanites in motion with its silks and porcelain. The T'ang court boxed the compass with its diplomacy, receiving missions from Japan and Java, Tibet and Turkestan, Sogdia and Ceylon, Baghdad and Byzantium. T'ang geographers described the east coast of Africa and sought to discover what might lie beyond the Kurosiwo current.

The clearest surviving literary expression of T'ang China as a world institution is Ennin's diary, *The Record of a Pilgrimage to China in Search of the Law*, written in the middle of the ninth century. Ennin was a Japanese Buddhist monk of the T'ien-t'ai school, eventually its head in Japan, who went to China between 838 and 847, for the purpose of studying the new Tantrayana doctrines, which on his return he synthesized with those of T'ien-t'ai. His diary describes his experiences, gives an incomparable account of the splendours of T'ang China, and covers a crucial episode in its downfall, the great persecution of Buddhism and other foreign religions in 845. He visited Yang-chou, the major emporium near the intersection of the Grand Canal and the Yangtze, Wu-t'ai-shan the Buddhist pilgrimage centre in Shansi, and Ch'ang-an the imperial capital. In Ch'ang-an Ennin associated with a group of monks which included men from northern and southern India, Ceylon, Kucha and Korea; he wrote his own diary in Chinese, the language of civilization; and the Tantric doctrine he learnt and transmitted to Japan was essentially Indian. He witnessed the return to Ch'ang-an of a T'ang princess who had been sent to marry the Manichaean king of the Uighurs and returned home to Japan on a Korean ship. Ennin's China was not the whole of T'ang cosmopolitanism – as a religious, he had little contact with its secular court culture – but he is a vivid witness to its Buddhist foundations.

Another aspect of T'ang cosmopolitanism is revealed in the relations of Ch'ang-an and Constantinople. The *Chiu T'ang-shu* records four embassies from the eastern Roman empire: in 643, 667, 701 and 719. These missions are not mentioned in any Western source, possibly because they were initiatives of a frontier official rather than of the central government. There is little doubt of their existence since they fit into an intelligible pattern of Byzantine *ostpolitik* and T'ang *westpolitik*.

The pattern began in 568 with the dispatch of an embassy by the *yabghu* of the Western Turks, Istämi, to Emperor Justin II, which proposed economic cooperation in the silk trade to avoid Sassanid middlemen and perhaps military cooperation against the Shah as well. For eight years *pourparlers* were pursued, seven Byzantine embassies went to Lake Balkash, and a Turko–Byzantine entente seemed a possibility. Then in 576, Istämi's successor, Tardu, known as Bilga-kaghan, broke off negotiations on the grounds of Byzantine friendship with his enemies, the Avars, former suzerains and hoped-for vassals, by then in the Ukraine and eastern Balkans. In 598, Tardu resumed negotiations by writing to the Emperor Maurice: he described the diplomatic situation in his part of the world and in particular stressed the power of Taugast, the Toba Wei empire of China; but no agreement, commercial or military was reached. The exchanges, however, recorded by Menander the Protector and Theophylact Simocatta, opened Byzantine eyes to the possibility of allies in further Asia against nearer enemies if circumstances warranted.

The following century, circumstances did warrant. First, the Avars proved unreliable allies. In 626 they brought the empire to one of its most dangerous hours by combining with the Slavs and Sassanids to besiege Constantinople. Emperor Heraclius, however, was equal to the crisis. He dispatched one Andrew to the Khazar king, a vassal of the Turks; Khazar units joined his counter-attack into northern Iran; and the Khazar alliance remained a constant of Roman diplomacy down to the time of Constantine Porphyrogenitus. Then, after 632, came the Moslem invasions. With the fall of Alexandria and Ctesiphon in 642, it is not surprising that someone in the Byzantine high command thought of looking for allies further east. The Chinese recorded his name as P'o-to'li, which might transliterate patriarch or patrician, one of the regents for Constans II who was only 13. Emperor T'ai-tsung, however, was currently more concerned with India than with Iran: the first mission of Wang Hsüan-ts'e to Harsha was dispatched in 643; and the Roman embassy obtained nothing more than confirmation that China was the greatest power in further Asia. In 667, Constans II, or one of his ministers, tried again. Circumstances were now even worse. The Arabs had become a seapower and the emperor was in Italy considering moving the capital back westwards. The T'ang, however, were even less receptive. The literati government of Empress Wu, hostile to continental adventures which would have to be conducted by aristocratic generals, was caught up in a naval war against Korea. Furthermore, the Sassanid prince, Peroz, the leader of the anti-Moslem resistance, was losing ground in Tukhara and had to take refuge in Ch'ang-an in 674. The Heraclians, therefore, received no help from China against the first onrush of Islam, though the T'ang were aware of the first Moslem siege of Constantinople between 671 and 678 by the Caliph Muawiyah.

The third Roman embassy, that of 701, took place in the reign of Justinian II, or more exactly during his exile in the Crimea during a usurpation. Justinian II was a man of expedients. In the Crimea, he married the sister of the Khazar khan and he eventually recovered his throne through an alliance with the pagan Bulgars. An embassy from him to China would be in character and it would explain its absence from the Byzantine records and the puzzlement of the Chinese as to who exactly had sent it. Justinian may have been prompted by a report of the counter-offensive which Empress Wu allowed Narses son of Peroz to make at the end of the seventh century.

The last Roman embassy, that of 719, falls early in the reign of Leo III, the Isaurian, the founder of the Iconoclast dynasty and the reviver of Byzantine military power after the confused reign of Justinian II. This visit was only a year after the second Moslem siege of Constantinople, a major crisis in imperial, indeed European history. The emperor could not be sure the Moslems would not come again and we know he was interested in *ostpolitik* since, in 733, he married his heir, the future Constantine V Copronymus, to the daughter of the Khazar khan, thus resuming the initiative of Justinian II. The embassy to China, however, again arrived at an unfortunate time. Emperor Hsüan-tsung was under the influence of literati ministers trained under Empress Wu. In 719 requests for aid against the Arabs from Maimargh, Bokhara and Samarkand were turned down and in 732 an embassy was received from the caliphate.

The Roman demarche, however, may not have been without effect. In 726 the aristocratic party more favourable to continental adventures returned to power under a new and energetic prime minister, Li Lin-fu. A forward policy was resumed in Central Asia, perhaps urged on by the Nestorian bishop Cyriacus who came to China with the caliphal embassy of 732 and stayed to become a considerable figure at Hsüan-tsung's court. In 744, Chinese authority was reasserted in the Lake Balkash area; in 747 and 749, the Chinese viceroy of Central Asia, Kao Hsien-chih, crossed the Hindu-kush via the Baroghil and Darkot passes to take the Tibetans, the allies of the Arabs, in the rear at Gilgit; and in 750, his flank safeguarded, Kao advanced into Transoxania against the still precariously established Abbasids. The T'ang marshal, however, had overestimated his strength. At the battle of the Talas River in July 751, Chinese power, so long sought as an ally, proved a paper tiger.

The defeat of Kao Hsien-chih was only an incident which if times had been other might have prompted reinforcements and a vigorous Chinese counter-offensive. But in the political circumstances of the 750s it set in train the course of events which was to destroy the T'ang court as a world institution and to wreck the international order based on aristocratic Iranian culture of which it was the expression and centre. In 752 the masterful Li Lin-fu died, leaving a legacy of provincial discontent, especially in Hopei, against the lavish cosmopolitan court at Ch'ang-an that he had provided for Emperor Hsüan- tsung and his famous consort Yang Kuei-fei, the Pompadour of China. His successor, Yang Kuo-chung, the consort's cousin, lacked his aura and skill, and in December 755 Hopei revolted under the leadership of the huge, overweight, diabetic marshal An Lu-shan, a Sogdian from Samarkand and a military rival of Kao Hsien-chih. The ageing Emperor Hsüan-tsung fled to Szechwan, his bodyguard mutinied and insisted on the lives of Yang Kuei-fei and Yang Kuo-chung, his son Su-tsung declared him deposed, and the golden age of T'ang dissolved.

Order was at length restored. An Lu-shan, an unlikely leader for puritan provincialism, having served Hopei's turn, was murdered in January 757. With the aid of Uighur allies and with the chief-of-staff, a Nestorian from Balkh, Su-tsung recovered his capital in November. But the old cosmopolitanism was never restored. To obtain Uighur and later Abbasid assistance, Su-tsung mortgaged the Chinese empire in Central Asia, which because of provincial hostility to its expense was anyway more a liability than an asset. In the silver age of T'ang from 755 to 906, though elements of the *ancien régime* survived to be observed by Ennin, China turned in upon herself and relaxed her links with the outside world. The embassies fell off; the Byzantines went no further than Khazaria; the Japanese stopped coming after 838; relations with the Abbasids did not proceed. In 760 there was a massacre of foreign merchants at Yang-chou. In 779 Uighurs at Ch'ang-an were forbidden to wear Chinese dress. In 845 there was a general proscription of all foreign religions including Buddhism, later repealed, it is true, but its effects were never undone.

Foreign trade declined. The Tibetans occupied the Kansu corridor. Between 870 and 880 Basra and Ubullah, home ports for Persian navigators were sacked by the mutinous slaves of the *Zanj* rebellion. In 879 Canton was likewise sacked by the Huang Ch'ao rebels, another mobile, anti-aristocratic revolution of destruction. Finally in 977, Siraf, the greatest of the Persian ports, was destroyed by an earthquake and not rebuilt, doubtless because a shrunken trade and a reduced caliphate would not support it. With the battle of the Talas River (an outcome of *weltpolitik*), the rebellion of An Lu-shan (a protest against its costs), and the persecutions of 845 (a rejection of its ideological basis), a whole international order foundered. By 1000 AD the brilliant cosmopolitanism of the T'ang court was no more and the world of late antiquity, temporarily unified by it, dissolved once more into worlds driven yet further apart by triumphant orthodoxies.

3 World Axis: China in the Middle Ages, 1000 to 1350

In the history of China's relationship to the outside world, the period of the middle ages, 1000 to 1350 – in China the periods of the Sung and Yüan dynasties – was doubly important. First, in the outside world in the sense of the other primary civilizations, 1000 to 1350 saw the emergence in Latin Christendom of a unique, radically new form of society which was eventually to make western Europe and its prolongation in America, the centre of the world. No doubt such a future was unimaginable in 1350. Western Europe was still the least civilized of the four regions of Western Eurasia and Western Eurasia as a whole was still less civilized than East Asia. No doubt much progress was still needed, whereas instead of advancing, in the fourteenth century Latin Christendom suffered disasters unparalleled since the ninth century. Nevertheless, take any of the major elements of European predominance – territorial states, capitalist cities, supranational church, parliamentary government, the conjugal family, a high level of education – and one finds its origin in the middle ages. An outer part of China's environment had therefore undergone a major mutation.

Second, in the outside world in the sense of an envelope of rudimentary world institutions, the middle ages saw a unification of disease patterns and an integration of geographical information which, unlike the ephemeral Buddhist international or T'ang cosmopolitanism, were to remain permanent elements of a thickening world system. Unperceived by the Chinese, what Joseph Fletcher has called the interlocking of histories had begun. The primary agent was the Mongolian explosion, the conquests of Chinggis and his successors, whose beginning and culmination was China. It was an East Asian microorganism which initiated the unification of disease patterns, and the revelation of Cathay was the major item incorporated into European geography. Despite the brilliant civilization of the Sung, China had ceased to be the centre of the world in the middle ages. She had slipped into being the axis round which others turned.

CHINA'S PLACE IN THE WORLD, 1000 to 1350

Between 1000 and 1350 China's place in the world was transformed by profound changes both in itself and in its nearest competitor, the community of Latin Christendom. The China which Marco Polo saw was different from that seen by Ennin: different in ecology, topography, sociology and intellect. Similarly the Christendom from which he came and which read his book when he returned was different from that ruled by emperor Justinian: different in ecology, topography, sociology and intellect, but more radically, in institutions. In China bureaucratic empire had simply shifted its foundations, recast its structure, redefined its functions. In Europe, bureaucratic empire had gone. In its place was a community of a bureaucratic church, aristocratic monarchies and commercial republics – institutions new not so much in themselves as in the way they combined and the milieu they produced.

The result was a paradox. Superficially and in the short run, the gap between China and Europe had widened to China's advantage. Marco Polo was astonished by the wealth and sophistication of thirteenth century China, as are modern scholars and connoisseurs. Contemporaries were reluctant to believe him or his successors, John of Cori, Odoric of Pordenone and John of Marignolli, and in Sir John Mandeville turned science fact back into science fiction. Who can blame them when Venice, Europe's biggest city, had a population of 160 000, while China's, Hangchow, had a population of six million?[1] However, profoundly and in the long run, the gap between China and Europe had narrowed to Europe's advantage. For all its manifest splendours, Sung China was a cut flower civilization, separated from its roots in Buddhist transcendentality and T'ang comprehensiveness, too divided socially, and lacking confidence to resist the Mongol invader.[2] For all its manifest backwardness, Latin Christendom had laid institutional foundations from which to deter the Mongols, survive the fourteenth century and borrow much from China to build the Renaissance. In time, it was not what Marco Polo saw that was to matter, but that it was he, citizen of Venice, legate of the Pope, best-selling author in French, who did the seeing.

Changes in China

The beginning of Sung China is to be found in the measures of the silver age T'ang emperors to defeat An Lu-shan and restore the empire to viability: Su-tsung's evacuation of Inner Asia to the Moslems and Uighurs, not to be reoccupied by Chinese armies till the nineteenth century; the tacit abandonment by Tai-tsung's minister Liu Yen of the *chün-t'ien* system and the replacement of state-controlled landholding by the salt monopoly as the principal source of government revenue; Te-tsung's compromise with the provincial *literati*, the power behind An Lu-shan and the support of the *chieh-tu-shih*, or regional commanders, who, whether for or against the T'ang court, were the major factors in politics after 755; Wu-tsung's temporary but decisive breach with the Buddhist international in 845; and Hsien-tsung's reassertion of imperial power on these bases in the early ninth century.

When the T'ang court finally collapsed at the end of the ninth century with the anti-metropolitan rebellion of Huang Ch'ao and the breakdown of the mechanisms hitherto successfully used to control the *chieh-tu-shih*, these measures – isolationism, a free land market, symbiosis with trade, coexistence with the *literati*, anti-Buddhism – survived it. They were continued and developed by the Five Dynasties and Ten States, 907 to 960, one of the periods of interdynastic disorder in Chinese history which have often been remarkably creative in institutional terms.[3] Their institutions – the military secretariat (*shu-mi-yüan*) and three financial offices (*san-ssu*) of Later Liang; the emperor's personal army (*shih-wei ch'in-ch ün*) of Later T'ang; the expanded Yangtze salt trade of Nan-T'ang; the urban dynamism of Wu-yüeh, Min and Southern Han, city states of the south-east – became the basis for the Sung founded by the two Chao brothers, Sung T'ai-tsu and T'ai-tsung, two desk generals turned board chairmen, who gaze at us from their official portraits as intelligent, shrewd and unflappable as Harley Street doctors.

After T'ai-tsu and T'ai-tsung came the five good emperors: Chen-tsung the Taoist, 997–1022, who introduced to the Yangtze the quick maturing rice of Champa which allowed a double harvest; Jen-tsung, 1022–63, whose minister, Fan Chung-yen, the first of the Sung reformers, devised the in-depth defence system of fortified cities against Inner Asian cavalry; Ying-tsung, 1063-67, high minded and Confucian; Shen-tsung, 1067-85, the patron of the second great Sung reforming minister, the etatist promoter of *laissez-faire* Wang An-shih; Che-tsung, 1085–1101, who was first served by the conservative panjandrum Ssu-ma Kuang but later became the patron of the third and greatest of the reforming minis-ters, Ts'ai Ching. These were the Antonines of China, good because they fulfilled the first duty of Confucian kingship, to consent to be advised by those qualified by education to give advice: the *shih-ta-fu*, the scholar officials – men such as Ou-yang Hsiu, the theorist of Confucian constitutionalism; Su Tung-p'o poet and bureaucrat; the polymath Shen Kua – the *bienpensant* Wykehamists of the Confucian world.

The first half of the Sung period was the golden age of the *shih-ta-fu*, the carriers of traditional Chinese culture, who now for the first time came to dominate Chinese society. Its climax was the reign of Hui-tsung, 1101–26, the founder of the palace art collection and himself no mean painter, who, after a brief flirtation with the conservatives, until 1125 main-tained in office the reformer Ts'ai Ching, the exponent of business confidence and Keynesian stimulants. Hui-tsung's reign, however, ended in double disaster, internal and exter-nal. The internal, and lesser, disaster was the rebellion of the Manichaean ex varnish merchant, Fang La, in Chekiang bet-ween 1120 and 1122. Basically, it was a protest of the rich tax-paying south-east against the costs of the military–bureaucratic complex in the north. In itself, without much organization or purpose beyond plunder, the rebellion was not serious, but it required 150 000 crack troops under the grand eunuch T'ung Kuan to suppress, and the suppression involved so much destruction that tax-paying capacity was reduced and business confidence ruptured.

The external, and greater, disaster was the fall of Kaifeng, the imperial capital, to the Jurched in 1126. Its remote cause was Su-tsung's evacuation of Inner Asia in 756 which left a vacuum which was eventually filled by new, better organized, more aggressive barbarian states based on the *ordo* or horde: the cohesive detribalized military machine which was the medieval equivalent of the modern totalitarian party.[4] More immediately, however, the fall of Kaifeng was due to miscalculation and mishap. The previous century the Sung had fought the Liao or Khitan *ordo* state to a standstill, thanks to the in-depth defence system devised by Fan Chung-yen, though they had failed to recover the line of the Great Wall lost during the weakness of the Five Dynasties. Early in the twelfth century an opportunity occurred for recovering it. In 1114 the Jurched, that is, the north Manchurian vassals of the Khitan, revolted. In 1117 they established their own *ordo* state and took the dynastic title of Chin, meaning gold, partly because north Manchuria was a gold area and partly in defiance of Liao which in Khitan meant iron. By 1120 it was clear that the partition of Manchuria which was at first contemplated was not going to work and that gold and iron must fight to the finish.

At this point the Sung government intervened. It allied with Chin against Liao in return for a promise of the Peking area and the line of the wall. The intervention, however, miscarried. The Sung failed to capture Yen-ching, the present Peking, perhaps because of the diversion of troops to Fang La's rebellion. They had to send for the help of their Chin allies who had overthrown Liao and who occupied the city early in 1123. Bitter renegotiations for a new partition were pursued and eventually concluded, but in 1124 the former Liao governor of Yung-p'ing to the north of Peking, which in the final agreement was assigned to Chin, refused to submit to the Jurched and offered allegiance to Sung. The Sung government, eager to regain the wall, unwisely accepted and war inevitably followed. In 1125 the Chin besieged Kaifeng and extracted a huge danegeld. The following year war resumed. Kaifeng was once more besieged and the Chin demanded an even larger danegeld. For twenty-three days, the Sung government struggled to find the money. It even appealed to the public, an unprecedented move, and it was said that 'even the pockets of prostitutes and entertainers were emptied to meet the demand'.[5] All to no avail: with business confidence gone and the south so devastated by the suppression of Fang La's rebellion, the money could not be found. At the end of the twenty-three days, the Chin took the city by assault and carried off the unfortunate Hui-tsung, who had already abdicated, to die in Manchuria in 1135.

The fall of Kaifeng, a city of certainly one and possibly four million, was a disaster for civilization and the forerunner of more widespread disasters a century later under the Mongols. Yet at the time it made surprisingly little difference to China or the Sung. A Chao prince escaped to the south to become emperor Kao-tsung, 1127–63, founder of the later or southern Sung. A new headquarters was established at the old provincial city of Wu-yüeh, the modern Hangchow, which was optimistically renamed Hsing-tsai or temporary capital, Marco Polo's Quinsai. A famous river admiral, Han Shih-chung, reconstructed the in-depth defence system to include a navy so that the frontier against the Chin was stabilized along the Yangtze and its northern tributaries. Behind the new great wall, as a Sung finance minister termed it, China's progress indeed accelerated, since the militarized north had been something of a burden on the economic south. Under a new series of self-effacing emperors, a second collection of masterful prime ministers took the lead in a realigned system of factional politics: Ch'in Kuei 1130–55, Han T'o-chou 1195–1207, Shih Mi-yüan 1207–33, Chia Ssu-tao 1259–75. Under their leadership, the Sung state, still based on isolationism, a free land market, symbiosis with trade, coexistence with the *literati*, and anti-Buddhism, gave China a prosperity unparalleled elsewhere or in her own history until the nineteenth century. Quinsai was the largest city in the world, China was the most urbanized and urbane society, and the Chinese enjoyed the highest standards of living, including significantly the highest rates of literacy. It was as if America having lost New York to the Russians reconstructed itself west of the Mississippi on the basis of California and Los Angeles.[6]

The China which Marco Polo saw was still essentially southern Sung China, since in the south the Mongol conquest was effected with much less destruction than in the north. It was, however, very different from T'ang China, in some ways an un-Chinese China.

In the first place, the ecology had changed. In T'ang times, the primary foodstuff had been millet or wheat and rice was only a subsidiary. Now rice was primary, its productivity multiplied by the introduction of fast-maturing Champa strains by Emperor Chen-tsung. More cereal was consumed per capita and of a different kind. All Chinese now enjoyed three meals a day. Protein consumption had also increased. Chinese agriculture in the north never made much provision for animals. In the south there were more pigs and poultry. Marco Polo was struck by the quantity of pepper consumed in Quinsai, a good index of meat-eating since in pre-modern conditions pepper was a preservative rather than a condiment. Likewsie Ibn Battuta noted the abundance of poultry – hens, ducks and geese – in the inns along the routes of China. Southern agriculture was more intensive than northern and had less pasture, but it had perfected the technique of what might be called refuse pastoralism: the feeding of pigs and poultry on scraps. Another protein source more available in the south than the north was fish, from the sea, rivers and fishponds. Food generally was more plentiful and diversified. The 'best fed mass population in world history to that time' is Michael Freeman's comment on the Sung, while in the restaurants of the capital to which even the emperor might send out, gourmets could choose between northern, southern and Szechwanese cuisines.[7] Also more plentiful in the south was wood. Sung China was more lavish with it than T'ang, so much so that, by the end of the dynasty, the nearer hills of the Nan-shan had been denuded and wood had to be imported from Japan. In cereals, protein and energy, Sung China enjoyed higher standards and was more consumerist in outlook than T'ang China. Marco Polo's Quinsai was not only a super-Venice, an enlarged emporium, it was also a super-Sybaris, the forerunner of the Baroque consumer cities of the European Renaissance.

In the second place, the topography had changed. T'ang China had been the country of the yellow dissected plateau of the north-west, *kuan-chung*, the land within the passes. Late Sung China was the country of the green deposited alluvium of the south-east, Kiang-nan, the land south of the river. Foreigners were struck by the importance of water, the quantity of ships. John of Cori, Dominican archbishop of Sultaniah who wrote a compendium on China, noted that 'there be many great rivers, and great sheets of water throughout the empire; insomuch that a good half of the realm and its territory is water'.[8] The Yangtze now became the chief artery rather than the Grand Canal. Marco Polo wrote of it that 'the amount of shipping it carries and the bulk of merchandise that merchants transport by it, upstream and down is so inconceivable that no one in the world who had not seen it with his own eyes could possibly credit it'.[9] Ibn Battuta compared China to Egypt:

> This river runs through the heart of China for a distance of six months' journey, reaching at last Sin-ul-sin. It is bordered throughout with villages, cultivated plains, orchards and markets, just like the Nile in Egypt; but this country is still more flourishing, and there are on the banks a great number of hydraulic wheels.[10]

Sung cities were intimately related to water, Hangchow and Soochow in particular. Su Tung-p'o spoke of the western lake at Hangchow as 'the eyes and eyebrows of a face',[11] while a map of Soochow carved on stone in 1229 shows it so criss-crossed with canals that Marco Polo might be pardoned for thinking that the city contained 6000 bridges. Water played an important part in counter-siegecraft, the *pièce de résistance* of Sung tactics, and the successful Chinese strategic defence for nearly 150 years against first the Jurched and then the Mongols was based on river power.

In the third place, the sociology had changed. For all its recruitment of commoners to the bureaucracy through the examination system, T'ang society was aristocratic, dominated by a versatile but perduring hereditary ruling class, the *kuan-chung* aristocracy which by skilfully shifting its basis from local patronage to social exclusiveness and court politics, maintained its pre-eminence for half a millenium and more.[12] For all its new monumental urbanization, the fiscality of T'ang China remained rural. Of 60 million taels revenue in the reign of emperor Hsüan-tsung, 59 million came from farmers and farming and only 1 million at most from commerce. For all its impregnation with capitalist institutions and notions derived from Buddhism, T'ang society retained strong pre-capitalist elements. Trade in grain and cloth was handled directly by the government; urban markets were strictly con-

trolled; cities were the home of bureaucracy or the play-
ground of aristocracy rather than commercial premises; and
until after the rebellion of An Lu-shan most merchants were
foreign.

Sung China was different. Meritocracy predominated over
aristocracy. Though the new *literati* were in no sense a middle
class and faked genealogies to link themselves to the great
families of the past, the old caste-like society of the T'ang
based on pretension and pedigree had gone. In the examination lists of 1148 and 1256, for which there is relatively complete information, over 50 per cent of the successful doctoral
candidates had no father, paternal grandfather or paternal
great-grandfather in the bureaucracy. Trade predominated
over agriculture in finance. Of 120 million taels revenue in
the reign of Hui-tsung, 40 million came from the salt
monopoly, and over 10 million from the liquor monopoly. In
the reign of Qubilai's successor Temur Oljeitu, the salt
monopoly provided half the total revenue of 200 million taels,
and in the 1320s it is said to have produced 80 per cent of
perhaps 450 million taels. Capitalism had made remarkable
progress. The state was now in partnership with the merchants; zoning restrictions in town planning were lifted; business was now predominantly Chinese. We hear not only of
supercargoes, sleeping partners and investors, but also of
joint stock companies, *lien-ts'ai ho-pen*. Private shipbuilding
equalled or exceeded that of the state and overseas trade, in
particular, was private rather than public. Marco Polo tells us
that the Sung emperor used to entertain 'the wealthy indus-
trialists of the city of Quinsai' in his palace, something which
would have astonished any T'ang ruler.[13]

In the fourth place, intellect had changed. Whatever the
reservations of the emperors, their counterbalancing with
indigenous Taoism and exotic Nestorianism, their devotion
to Iranian secular culture, T'ang China had been a Buddhist
country: the Buddhist international sublated into the Chinese
imperial system. The effect of Buddhism had been to project
China from myth to philosophy, indeed to leapfrog from
infracognitional paradigm over pre-critical cosmology and
metaphysics to critical cognitional theory and supracogni-
tional mysticism. By Sung times, however, Buddhism in China
had been defeated: internally by its own flight into

irrationalism in Tantrism, millenarism, Pure Land and Zen; externally by the rise of the various varieties of Neo-Confucianism. It had been reduced to a subculture, mainly of the Yangtze valley, not negligible, but no longer dominant.

Under the Sung, Chinese thought retreated from cognitional theory and mysticism towards cosmology. The effects were twofold. On the positive side, there was a greater confidence in the possibility of knowledge within nature, as for example in the work of Shen Kua, and a greater differentiation of what Bernard J.F. Lonergan has called the scholarly and artistic realms of meaning. Here one thinks of the Sung historians, Ssu-ma Kuang's *Tzu-chih t'ung-chien* and the Ma Tuan-lin's *Wen-hsien t'ung-kao* in particular, and the landscapists: Li Ch'eng, Fan K'uan and Kuo Hsi before the disaster of 1126; Ma Yüan and Hsia Kuei after it; not forgetting the sensibility of the incomparable Sung celadons. On the negative side, there was an abandonment of the critical approach and a conscious restriction of horizons from the absolute to the relative; a shift from theory to practice, metaphysics to morality; and a long-term regression from philosophy to myth, so that Confucianism lost its intellectual dynamism and ended as the communications system of the upper class. All the great Neo-Confucians were ethicists rather than metaphysicians: a reversion to pre-critical cosmology appears in Chou Tsun-i and Chang Tsai; the flight from syntagma to paradigm is illustrated by Shao Yung and the new interest in the *I-ching*, that perfect set of cosmic categories.

This double movement, an increased differentiation of consciousness combined with a diminished grasp of method, a combination found later in the European Renaissance where scholarship and art were juxtaposed with Platonic magic and Biblical fundamentalism, left algebra the most lively part of the Sung intellectual scene. This was not an accident. Algebra was legitimately concerned with paradigm rather than syntagma, it could avoid cognitional theory by keeping within the practical algorithmic tradition of non-axiomatization, and, until Goedel, it could think of itself as a closed deductive system, or at least advancing towards such. Sung China was supreme in algebra, but, compared to T'ang China, weak in metaphysics.[14]

Changes in Europe

A similar analysis in terms of ecology, topography, sociology and intellect may be made of the Europe from which Marco Polo came. It had changed profoundly since the days of Emperor Justinian. From a Byzantine point of view it was an un-European Europe.

Europe, too, was changed in ecology, though less dramatically than China. Europe had nothing to compare to the Chinese switch from millet or wheat to rice, but she had added to the largely arable-only agriculture of the Mediterranean *ager* based on the scratch plough drawn by oxen, the more balanced arable–pastoral agriculture of the northern *ager/saltus* based on the heavy plough and the horse. This development in the eleventh and twelfth centuries produced a per capita improvement in cereals, protein, textile materials and energy, though less than the corresponding Chinese move.

Europe, too had changed in topography, but inversely to China. If China had moved its centre of gravity from north-west to south-east, Europe had moved its from south-east to north-west: from Alexandria, Rome and Constantinople to Venice, Avignon and Paris. If China had maritimized by moving from dry *kuan-chung* to wet Kiangnan, Europe had continentalized by moving from the coastal plains of the Mediterranean, now left as malarial, to the inland plains of Champagne, Castile and midland England. Despite the progress of the Italian maritime republics, European shipping was at a lower volume than it had been in the days of the imperial *annona* and the great galleys of Venice were actually smaller than the *dromon* of tenth-century Byzantium. By the weight of its population non-maritime France dominated the continent.

Europe, too, had changed its sociology, though less straightforwardly than China. Society in China had changed from aristocratic, rural and pre-capitalist under the T'ang, to meritocratic, urban and capitalist under the Sung. In Europe, however, *trecento* society was less meritocratic, more aristocratic than early Byzantine except in the church; the city population was smaller than in the best days of the later

Roman empire; and the percentage of goods traded, though higher than in late antiquity because of the rise of the textile trade, remained low. Nevertheless, despite this unfavourable milieu which was aggravated by an archaising cult of aristocratic chivalry in the fourteenth century, capitalism was more deeply rooted in European society than Chinese. Meritocracy, however, until the Renaissance, was much weaker.

In Europe, too, intellect had changed, but in contrary fashion to China. In China culture had advanced, method had retreated. In Europe it was the other way round. The classical *paedeia* no longer possessed the field. It had retreated to the shrunken city state of Constantinople or to the households of a few enlightened ecclesiastics and nobles whose little renaissances did not yet amount to a Great Renaissance. Except for Italian, the vernacular languages of Europe were not yet capable of carrying literature and humane letters were at a greater discount in the thirteenth century than the twelfth. What possessed the field was the new method of scholasticism – the recurrent operations of *lectio* and *quaestio, videtur quod non, sed contra est, respondeo dicendum quod* – which were applied to create *summas*, systems, not only in theology, but also in canon law, exchequer administration, common law, grammar, letter writing. It was a technical, professional method, barbarous in language no doubt, the work of *obscuri viri* rather than Ciceros, and overly reliant on deductive logic, but genuinely scientific in its drive to investigate, criticize and synthesize. Until checked in the fourteenth century by the Scotist demand for deductive self-sufficiency, scholasticism, from Abelard to Aquinas, was intellectually liberating, just as Neo-Confucianism after Chu Hsi was, in the long run, intellectually stultifying. Weak in particular sciences, Latin Christendom was strong in the metaphysical roots of scientific enquiry.

Although Latin Christendom may thus be analysed in terms similar to those applied to Sung China, such an analysis misses its real originality. This originality lay in its institutional milieu: the combination of no bureaucratic empire, a bureaucratic church, aristocratic monarchies and commercial republics.

The basic characteristic of medieval Latin Christendom was negative: the absence of bureaucratic empire.[15] This was the *causa removens prohibens* underlying everything else. It allowed

Western Europe to constitute for the first time in human history, a large-scale, enduring, ordered pluralism. Hitherto, since the development of organized states in the ancient Near East, the alternatives had seemed to be empire or anarchy, monolithic order or pluralistic disorder. Pluralism might exist *de facto*, as it existed in India from Harsha to the Delhi sultanate, in China under the *Nan-pei ch'ao*, in the post-Abbasid *Islam des patries*, but it lacked legitimacy and stability and was regarded as abnormal. The only *de jure* pluralisms before medieval Europe had been Classical Greece and the Hellenistic kingdoms, and both had been brief in life and ended in imperial unifications. In western Europe empire died in the dark ages and despite Carolingians, Ottonians, Hohenstaufens, Habsburgs and Bonapartes, never revived. Europe did not lack the imperial urge, but the three social forces, the church, the aristocracy and the merchants, which in China were harnessed to empire, in Europe rejected it, initially and decisively in the investiture controversy and in the papal campaigns against Frederick Barbarossa and Frederick of Hohenstaufen. Nevertheless, although the absence of empire was a necessary element of Europe's originality, because it permitted the fuller growth of other institutions, it is not a full account of it. Of equal significance, and more unique, were three positive factors shaping the European institutional milieu.

In the first place, thanks to the papacy, a clearer distinction was drawn in Europe than elsewhere between church and state, spiritual and temporal, sacred and secular, intellect and power, private and public. By this distinction the totalitarianism inherent in the *polis*, the Byzantine identification of church and empire, the Moslem interpretation of the people of God as the *umma* or the community, the sacred society of Hinduism, the Chinese union of *chiao* and *cheng*, teaching and ruling, was excluded until the rise of the secular totalitarianisms of the twentieth century. Medieval Europeans were the first to grasp and practice the wisdom that philosophers ought not to be kings nor kings, philosophers. In itself the medieval papacy was not unique. Benjamin of Tudela compared the Abbasid caliphate to it; Marco Polo saw the similarity of the Nestorian catholicate; Odoric of Pordenone called the abbot of Sa-skya the pope of the idolaters.

But it represented what W. Ullmann has called the hierocratic theme in an unusually pure form so that the papacy avoided territoralization, pseudo-heredity or becoming another's puppet. The move from Rome to Avignon, sometimes represented as the capture of the papacy by France, was not really an aberration. In the circumstances it was a prudent rejection of Italianization and the preservation of a proper balance between *urbs* and *orbs*.[16] Similarly, the religious orders which were the papacy's best support intellectually and politically were not unique institutions. They may be paralleled by the Buddhist *sangha*, Islamic *tariqats*, and especially by the monastic federations of Tibet. But few religious orders outside Latin Christendom had a foundation document so sane as the rule of St Benedict or an organizational structure so rational as the *Carta Charitatis*.

In the second place, thanks to the plurality of stable aristocratic monarchies in a context of cultural unity under the church, Europe more than elsewhere was accustomed to limited war between states and limited state power inside them. Complete elimination of opponents – the Saxon aristocracy after Hastings, the Hohenstaufen after Benevento and Tagliagozzo – was uncommon. So also was the complete disappearance of political entities: the middle kingdom of Lotharingia being likewise exceptional. Violence, internal and external, was limited and subject to law. In particular, the problem of succession which in other parts of the world put everything up for grabs – even institutionally as in the 'sanguinary tanistry' of nomadic Inner Asia and its derivatives – in Europe was solved by a characteristic extension of private family law into the public domain. Yet no more than ecclesiastical theocracies were aristocratic monarchies unique to Europe. Richard I's kingdom had much in common with Saladin's. Tunisia, Algeria and Morocco have as long pedigrees as Sicily, Castile and Portugal. Korea is older than England, Vietnam as old as Sweden. The kingdoms of the Deccan have had long runs of independence. In none of these areas, however, did aristocratic monarchy produce constitutionalism within, a concert of nations without. Two factors were crucial. First, the church, a more institutional form of cultural unity than Islam, Hinduism or Confucianism, was quick to arbitrate, so that, as in thirteenth-century England, a baron's war was succeeded by a legate's peace. Second, law – canon law everywhere, civil law on the continent, common law in England – which became the principle of European institutions rather than custom, virtue or utility. In the days of Justinian and P'ei Cheng there had been little to choose between law in the West and in China. By the time of St Raymond, Azo of Bologna and Bracton, Europe had acquired a legal sophistication quite unmatched in China and relatively unmatched in Islam.

In the third place, thanks to commercial republics in a non-imperial context of cultural unity and aristocratic *rechtstaaten*, the economy in Europe was more autonomous institutionally with respect to non-economic factors than elsewhere. Just as church and state were distinguished by papacy, religious orders and canon law, just as governments and community were distinguished by a strong sense of law international and private, so economy and sociology were distinguished by *emporia*, charters, guilds and *jus mercatorum*. Despite its low quantitative level, and irrespective of differences within it between market economy and command economy, i.e. free enterprise and *etatisme*, the European economy was less 'embedded' than economies elsewhere, to use Karl Polanyi's useful distinction between embedded and disembedded economies. The roots of this autonomy of the economic went back to Evelyne Patlagean's revolution in societal conceptualization in late antiquity, but *de facto* Jean Baechler is surely right to connect it with the *tabula rasa* of the dark ages. The total collapse of commerce meant that its revival was unrooted in the existing structures of society and was from the start extramural, alien, extraterritorial and autonomous. Because there was an existing order, i.e. the worlds of the church and the aristocratic monarchies, commercial communities were free to concentrate on business and were eventually able, when the outside world became sufficiently intelligent, to dispense with politics altogether and become pure *emporia* like fifteenth-century Antwerp. The medieval commercial republics were not like ancient city states (only rarely were they their successors like Marseille), their purpose was not politics but business, though they might develop, as in the case of Venice, the most sophisticated political institutions (more sophisticated than those of classical antiquity) to forward this. *Navigare necesse est vivere non necesse* could never have been the motto of a *polis*, but it was the implicit motto of every medieval *emporium*. Venetian political genius was in fact rather exceptional among medieval commercial republics. More typical was the Genoese combination of political incompetence (too-frequent revolutions) with economic creativity (the company, marine insurance, oceanic voyages), the reluctance of the Flemish communes to become city states, or the rather chequered political career of the Hanseatic league.

Emporia, like papacy, religious orders and aristocratic kingdoms, were not unique to medieval Europe. They had their prototype in Ptolemaic Alexandria and remoter ancestors perhaps in Tyre and Carthage (was Hannibal's mistake to try to turn an *emporium* into a *polis*?). They had their parallels elsewhere too. In Islam, there was Aden, Ormuz, Malacca and Algiers by sea; Mecca, Tabriz, Ghadames and Kokand by land. In the Indian world, there was Surat, Srivijaya and Macassar. In East Asia, there was Canton and Zayton by sea; riverports like Chinkiang, Yangchow and Hankow; Ninghsia, Tunhuang and Sining by land. What distinguished the European *emporia* from the junk ports and caravan cities was their institutional relationship to the other entities on the scene, the church and the monarchies; their economic autonomy yet depoliticization and lack of ideological alienation. An expression of this relationship was the precocious European development of banking in the sense of loans to the state and church. At the time of their spectacular bankruptcy in 1346, the Bardi, the Peruzzi and the Acciaiuoli were known as 'the columns of Christendom'. No other society would have seen its great merchants in this light. *Gesellschaft* capitalism had succeeded *Gemeinschaft*. Extramural the merchant might be, but he had gained the right of incorporation.

The results of the changes

In the late Sung-Yüan period Chinese civilization reached one of its three peaks. In respect of urbanization, relatively free government, command of the sea in peace and war, aesthetic taste, and approximation to modern science, it was superior to the golden T'ang before and the mid-Ch'ing afterwards. In comparison with its contemporaries in India, Islam and eastern Christendom, Sung China certainly had the advantage.

Northern India, the site of the ancient Indian empires, had been devastated successively by Mahmud of Ghazna (998–1030), Muhammed of Ghor (1173–1206), the Chaghatai khans of Turkestan, by the greatest, but most disastrous, of the slave sultans of Delhi, Muhammed ibn Tughluq (1325–51), and finally by Tamerlane. Southern India, not subject to Moslem invasion until the reign of Muhammed ibn Tughluq – and even then able to rally under the state of Vijayanagar – was more prosperous. It saw the flourishing first of the Vaishna-vite culture of the dualist metaphysicians, Ramanuja and Madhva, and then of the Saivite ascetic reaction of the Saiva Siddhanta; but except in these specialist fields there was little to compare with China. The world of Islam, following the social and intellectual convulsions of Shiism and Sufism, was under Turkish leadership, safe, conservative, till the Mongols appeared, militarily effective, but uncreative. Ibn Battuta was as admiring of China as Marco Polo: 'the best cultivated land in the world'; 'nowhere in the world are there to be found people richer than the Chinese'; 'porcelain in China is of about the same value as earthenware with us, or even less'.[17] Like medieval northern India, eastern Christendom suffered a series of disasters in the middle ages. The military over-extension of the Macedonian emperors turned into the bureaucratic feudalism of the Comnenians, Anatolia was lost to the Seljuks, naval supremacy to the Italians, and Constantinople itself to the Crusaders. The Ottoman society of counter-crusaders fastened its hold on Bursa and Adrianople. Against these disasters, the continued expansion of orthodoxy in Slavdom and the substitution by the Palaeologan city state of a spiritual empire based on the Hesychast international were inadequate compensation. Constantinople might still be splendid but it was no rival to Hangchow.

In comparison with Latin Christendom, however, the standing of Sung China was less clear. China since Hsüan-tsung had made more manifest progress than Europe since Justinian, but Europe had advanced more in the means of progress. China was richer in present civilization, but Europe, thanks to its new institutional foundations was richer in the

China in World History

possibilities of future civilization. China, *per contra*, by giving up T'ang cosmopolitanism, by relegating Buddhist thought and institutions to second place, had pulled up some of its roots of greatness. A live bush in spring green confronted a dying tree in autumnal gold.

The thirteenth century was axial for the relations of China and the outside world. The dynamism of Europe which then first emerged was eventually to remodel the world and impose it on China. Before that could happen Europe needed to build on her institutional foundations with fresh weapons, technologies, institutions and ideals. These elements would best come from a society already at a higher level of progress. Such a society was available in late Sung China. Whether its resources would be used depended on the further availability of suitable avenues of contact.

AVENUES OF CONTACT, 1000 to 1350

In the middle ages the avenues of contact did not increase in number. In fact they were effectively reduced to three as the far southern sea route lost the cinnamon trade to Ceylon and the southern sea route. After a period of reduced traffic following the decline of the Abbasid caliphate and the destruction of Siraf, the three routes which continued in operation were reanimated by movements associated with three pieces of transport technology: the Islamic camel, the Sung junk and the Mongolian pony. These movements must be outlined before the history of the routes is examined.

The Islamic camel

Early Islam lived in symbiosis with the camel. The herded camel supplying milk, wool and meat was the basis of Arab bedouin nomadic pastoralism. The pack camel, operated first with the simple behind-the-hump south Arabian saddle, and later with the more advanced over-the-hump north Arabian saddle, was essential in the incense trade organized by the caravan cities: Petra, Palmyra, Damascus, Gerra, Medina and Mecca. The sudden and unexpected lateral unification by the *umma* of the networks of traders, trail bosses, protectors and breeders vertically appended to these cities, was the foundation of the initial Islamic empire. It was in the area from Morocco to the Jaxartes, where the camel had already replaced the cart as the cheapest and most efficient form of transport, that the foundation was built on most rapidly, completely and permanently. Within that area the dominance of the camel over the cart shaped Islamic urban topography into its pattern of narrow streets and bazaars inside the city and directed Islamic public works toward caravanserais and bridges beyond it. Moreover, Islam did not merely utilize a pre-existing camel system. It expanded it into Spain, the Balkans and India, and eastwards, by making better use of the Bactrian camel, towards China.

Although never bred in such numbers as its Arabian cousin, and never a key element of Inner Asian nomadic pastoralism, the Bactrian camel had long been used as both a pack and draft animal, as witness the well known T'ang figurines. Nevertheless, down to the middle ages, the camel did not hold the dominant role in transport east of the Pamirs that it held west of them and came to hold later in Chinese Central Asia. For example in the second expedition of Li Kuang-li to Ferghana in 102 BC, the principal part in transportation was played by 100 000 oxen; donkeys, mules and camels together only amounted to several 10 000. The records of the T'ang *ma-cheng* at Turfan, recovered by Sir Aurel Stein, make little reference to camels, in contrast with the later Ch'ing *ma-cheng* in the same area which was much concerned with them. Camels do not figure in the pastoral activities of Buddhist monasteries at Turfan and Tunhuang in the way horses and sheep do. The T'ang court received camels as tribute and bred some itself in Kansu, but the tributaries were far to the west and the numbers bred were not large. The impression is that in the T'ang period the camel was not crucial in transportation across the Gobi. If this was so, it would explain why the Islamic wave reached a temporary high tide on the frontiers of Chinese Central Asia.

By the Sung period, however, the picture was changing. The Khitan kingdom of Liao, the first of the *ordo* states in north China, received considerable tribute of camels: from Hsi-Hsia, the Tibetan *ordo* state based on present-day Ninghsia; from miscellaneous Tangut tribes, probably the

Tsaidam, an important breeding area in modern times; from the Tsu-pu, an eastern Mongol confederation; and from other Mongols in the Barga. Marco Polo describes the 'innumerable camels' bringing supplies to Qubilai's new year feast and, *à propos* of patridges, he says that they are brought to the khan in 'camel-loads' as if camels were the obvious means of transport.[18]

There are only hints as to the mechanism of this change. First, in the Liao kingdom, camels were associated with the Uighurs, formerly a nomadic, pastoral people, but at this time masters of the sedentary caravan city of Turfan, which was in touch with the Islamic west. Second, the technique later generally used on the Central Asian routes of heavy loads, short stages and feeding the camels both by grazing and nose-bags was associated with the sedentarists rather than with the nomads who used a different technique of light loads, forced marches and working the animals to exhaustion. Third, sometime between T'ang and Ch'ing, a new pack saddle was introduced for the Bactrian camel: a fixed frame going round the humps, rather than the load being stowed between them with flaps to protect the flanks; thus, larger and heavier loads could be carried.

The origin of this new saddle is of some significance for the history of the camel in Central Asia. André Haudricourt, largely on linguistic grounds, thinks that the camel saddle was derived from the ox yoke and was later used round horses' necks to become the modern horse collar. This would mean that the camel saddle was invented before 851, the first definite date for the collar harness. Bulliet, on the other hand, supposes that the influence was in the opposite direction: from the horse to the camel, which would fit in better with the chronology here being proposed. It may be, however, that the camel development was independent of that both of the horse and the ox and that the modern Bactrian saddle derives from Bulliet's north Arabian saddle, which also goes over the hump and involves rigid poles. The new saddle would then be of Islamic provenance, the product of competition between the camel and the hitherto superior Kansu cart, Islam thus laying down a camel cushion over which it was to advance into the borderlands of north-west China. The cart, of course, resisted and even in the nineteenth century Tso Tsung-t'ang had difficulty in persuading the Chinese military authorities of the superiority of camels. From the middle ages, however, there were more Bactrian camels bred by specialists such as the Kirghiz and the Mongols of the Tsaidam, which carried heavier loads and were operated by sedentary experts. These facts, however they are dated, facilitated contact between East and West along both the central and northern land routes.

The Sung junk

Another new factor in the contact between China and the outside world in the middle ages was the rise of Chinese maritime shipping. Foreigners were struck by the importance of water and the quantity of river shipping inside the Chinese empire. They were also impressed by the quantity of maritime shipping outside the empire which was in fact of greater importance, then, than before or afterwards in Chinese history. Marco Polo declared that Zayton was 'one of the two ports in the world with the biggest flow of merchandise'.[19] (One wonders which was the other: Aden perhaps, or Alexandria, or Venice itself?). Odoric of Pordenone described Canton: 'This city hath shipping so great and vast in amount that to some it would seem well nigh incredible. Indeed all Italy hath not the amount of craft that this one city hath'.[20] Ibn Battuta wrote of the port of Zayton that it was 'one of the largest in the world – no, I am wrong, it *is* the largest of all ports. I saw about 100 large Junks with small vessels unnumerable'.[21]

How much of this shipping was Chinese? Marco Polo's remark about Foochow being 'much frequented by ships from India' and his account of Zayton as 'a great resort of ships and merchandise from India' might suggest that much of it was still foreign: Indonesian, Singhalese, Persian.[22] However, Polo also speaks of 'the ships in which merchants voyage to and from India', while Ibn Battuta found fifteen Chinese ships on the Malabar coast and stated categorically that 'people sail on the China seas only in Chinese ships', ships 'nowhere made except in the city of Zayton in China or at Canton'.[23] Polo's 'ships from India' were probably Chinese

East Indiamen and it seems certain that a substantial proportion, much higher than in T'ang times, of the shipping at Canton, Zayton and Foochow was actually Chinese.

This conclusion, that much of the shipping in the eastern seas was Chinese, is reinforced by the fact that foreigners were impressed by the quality as well as the quantity of shipping, and drew attention to features characteristic of Chinese ships and, as far as we know, at that time unique to them. Thus Marco Polo describes the use of four or even six masts each with multiple sails, watertight compartments, caulking with tung oil and lime, repair at sea by doubling, and in general contrasts the seaworthiness of Chinese ships with the unseaworthiness of the Moslem vessels putting out of Ormuz. Ibn Battuta adds to the description, mat-and-batten fabric for sails, the lug sail form of fore and aft rig, and the *yuloh* or fishtail stern sweep. The superiority of Chinese ships over those of other civilizations was recognized as late as the mid-fifteenth century by the Florentine traveller Nicolo de Conti: 'They doe make bigger shippes than we doe, that is to say, of 2000 tons, with five sayles, and so many mastes.'[24] Chinese ships went certainly as far as Malabar, probably as far as the Persian Gulf (though Arab chroniclers' references to 'China ships' have the same ambiguity as Marco Polo's 'ships from India'), and maybe as far as the East African coast. The chronology of the Sung junk, like that of the Islamic camel, awaits clarification. Most likely its rise should be dated to the period following the fall of Kaifeng to the Jurched in 1126 and the subsequent great leap forward of the southern provinces. The result was that by the thirteenth century, the possibilities for exchange between East and West along the southern sea route were greatly expanded.

The Mongolian pony

A third new factor in East–West contact in the middle ages was the Chinggisid unification of the horsepower of the Central Eurasian steppe. Just as Muhammed and his successors unified the camel networks of Arabia and the caravan cities of the Fertile Crescent and used them to overrun the whole area where the camel could replace the cart, so Chinggis and his successors unified the pony resources of Mongolia and

Kazakhstan and used them to overrun the whole area where light cavalry was superior to heavy cavalry or infantry. Just as the early caliphate controlled perhaps four-fifths of the world's camel population, so the early *gaghanate* controlled perhaps half the world's horse population. The resulting *pax Mongolica* was a major factor in increasing traffic along the two northern land routes.

The Mongolian explosion has been variously explained: by Chinggis' genius (in fact he seems to have been highly competent rather than brilliant as a soldier); as a lived version of heroic epic (an interesting parallel to Robin Lane-Fox's thesis about Alexander the Great, the more so since the Alexander romance was known in Inner Asia in Chinggis' time via a Sogdian translation); as response to climatic change; and in terms of steppe sociology and institutions.

The climatic explanations are at once most attractive and least coherent. The earliest of them, Ellsworth Huntington's, saw Inner Asian history as a series of nomadic pulsations, the Mongolian explosion being the greatest, caused by drought which reduced pasture and extruded population. The climatic facts, however, are against this theory. The periods of greatest nomad activity, notably 400+, 1200+, 1600+, were wet and cold rather than warm and dry, though there is some difference among climatic historians about the situation around 1200: it may have been warm but not dry. Even if the facts were as Huntington supposed them, it is not clear why they should have produced movement east, west and south towards deserts rather than north where pasture conditions would have been improved by the drying out of marshland and forest. Some further non-climatic factor is required to explain this.

Later versions of the climatic explanation have adopted the alternative hypothesis of colder and wetter weather coincident with steppe pushes, but there is no agreement on the mechanism involved. Did the new weather injure nomadic pastoralism by being cold, by extending the fatal refreeze phenomenon known as *dzud* which prevented animals weakened by winter from getting at spring grass? Or did it benefit nomadic pastoralism by being wet, by encouraging grass, thus increasing the number of animals? In other words, did steppe society turn aggressive because it was diseased or because it was healthy? Again, all climatic theories are faced with the double difficulty that while the Chinggisid explosion was unprecedented in steppe history in its scale, and so is not comparable to Attila or the Turks before or Galdan afterward, it was preceded by the little explosions of the Liao, the Hsi-Hsia, the Chin and the Qara-Khitay which fall in a different period of climatic history. Finally, the climatic explanations violate Le Roy Ladurie's principle that climatic changes intensify but do not initiate conjunctures.

More convincing are the explanations in terms of steppe sociology and institutions, particularly the concept of the *ordo* state developed by K.A. Wittfogel. Any explanation of the Mongolian explosion must take account of the fact that, although the possibility of the mobilization of crushingly superior horsepower in central Eurasia had existed since the first millenium BC – it was indeed envisaged by Jeremiah and Habakkuk and became part of the eschatological scenario – it did not actually happen until the thirteenth century when Ibn al-Athir diagnosed it as the greatest calamity that had ever befallen mankind. Steppe society was not inherently aggressive. The nomad, it is true, was a natural cavalryman. Life on the steppe, especially political life, was violent, migration cycles conflicted and the organized collective hunts loved by idle, nomad males, were war games as well. No doubt the nomads would take what they wanted from the sedentary world by raid if they could not obtain it satisfactorily by trade: the so-called trade/raid syndrome. But these things were quite different from the systematic assault on the sedentary world launched by Chinggis, Ögödei and Möngke. Indeed the Mongol empire ran counter to them and sapped their roots as the ordinary herdsman eventually found out. Between militarized steppe society and the Mongolian explosion, there is a gap, just as there is between diffused anti-semitism and the Holocaust, or between repression of superstition and the witchcraze of the sixteenth century.

The bridge can only be institutional. In the Mongolian explosion, the crucial new factor was the *ordo*: the system of restructuring tribes into decimal units whose top level of leadership was organized on bureaucratic lines. The *ordo* introduced discipline into the steppe: tactical discipline to win battles, strategic discipline to win campaigns, political discipline to win wars, social discipline to maintain an on-going ruling institution. Thus, where Sui Yang-ti noted of the Turks that 'their troops were not drawn up in orderly ranks', John of Pian di Carpine thought discipline precisely the Mongols' strong point. 'Our armies ought to be marshal-led after the order of the Tartars, and under the same rigorous laws of war.'[25]

Like the party state of the twentieth century, the medieval *ordo* state was in itself relatively simple, in the long run perhaps too simple. What was difficult was application – the appropriate circumstances, techniques and personnel – so it is not surprising that it took some time from its invention in the tenth century under the Khitan to reach a fully mature form under the Chinggisids. *Ordo* states were not necessarily pastoral nomadic or necessarily aggressive: Chin was not the first, and Hsi-Hsia was not the second; but combined with the nomadic pastoral military potential, the *ordo* created the possibility of sustained aggression. It then only needed an outstanding khan, a tradition of heroic epic and perhaps a psychological conversion – a kind of collective extraversion of shamanistic ecstasy – to set up the Chinggisid scenario. Once launched, massive organized pony power would give military supremacy over a wide area. The availability of remounts made possible campaigns of movement, battles of attrition, wars of terror, which the sedentary world, internally divided, suspicious of its own rulers and half-hearted about fighting, could not withstand. Thanks to the Mongolian pony, mobilized and organized by the *ordo* and projected forth by Chinggisid leadership, ideology and psychology, a large part of Eurasia was united in the common disaster of the Mongolian explosion, the common doubtful blessing of the *pax Mongolica*. Unity even of this kind, however, facilitated intercommunication.

In late antiquity a certain level of contact between East and West had been maintained through the international merchant communities: the Sogdians, the Syrians, the Nestorian Persians and the Radhanite Jews. In the early middle ages these communities were disrupted by the universal rise of orthodoxy, Christian, Islamic and Confucian, and the universal decline of empire, Carolingian, Byzantine, Abbasid, Hindu and T'ang. The result was that the early middle ages were a low point for relations between China and the outside world. The avenues of contact became blocked, communication dwindled to a trickle. Then as successively came the Islamic camel, the Sung junk and the Mongolian pony, the channels were decongested, traffic moved again, and between 1250 and 1350 relations soared to a new high. *Apertura*, however, did not last. The *pax Mongolica* collapsed, orthodoxy, Christian, Islamic and Confucian re-emerged, pogroms were resumed against Jews, Nestorians and Manichees, the Black Death shattered demography and morale, and the frontiers once more closed. Until then however there was an intercommunication optimum.

The central land route

The evidence about the central land route in the early middle ages is fragmentary. This, combined with the fact that, with the ending of the Chinese monopoly, the mere presence of silk west of the Pamirs is not evidence of trade with China, makes one sceptical of claims, generally founded on Moslem rhetoric about the prosperity of Transoxania and Khorasan on the eve of the Mongol invasion, to any considerable volume of traffic.

Between 981 and 984 a Sung ambassador, Wang Yen-te visited the Uighur kingdom of Turfan. He found it a civilized place, Buddhist and Manichaean, practicing irrigated agriculture (possibly using the Iranian *kariz* or underground water conduit), growing cotton and raising horses. The archaeological finds of Grünwedel and Le Coq likewise suggest a cultivated lay society preserving in a provincial environment the secular, cosmopolitan and aesthetic traditions of the T'ang. The Uighurs sent embassies east to both Liao and Sung and in the west, the Uighur king, the Idikut, intervened with the caliph al-Muqtadir on behalf of the Manichees of Khorasan. Juvaini, the Moslem apologist of collaboration with the Mongols, regarded the Uighurs as determined enemies of Islam, rivals for the favour of the conqueror. Ex nomads themselves the Uighurs diffused sedentary culture to the nomads. Mongolian script is borrowed from the Uighurs who took it from the Sogdians together with Manichaeism, the Sogdians having it from the Syrians. The Mongolian word *nom*, meaning book, derives from the Greek *nomos* by the same route. It is possible that the *ordo* too in its origins was Uighur and certainly Uighurs were the clerks of the early Mongolian empire. Nevertheless, despite their international contacts and modest prosperity, too much should not be built on the Uighurs. Their resonance was limited and most of their trade was intra-regional.

The same was also true of Samarkand and the now Islamized Sogdians. In the tenth century an anonymous Moslem author wrote 'Samarkand is a large flourishing town. It is a place where traders gather from all corners of the world.'[26] In the eleventh century, the famous vizier Nizam-al-Mulk in his treatise on government the *Siyasatnamah* describes a number of trade routes centring on Samarkand, while Ibn Kallikan the biographer of the Seljuk sultan Malikshah tells how the king once paid a boatman on the Oxus with a cheque on a bank in Antioch. In the twelfth century, the *Chahar Maqala* of Nidhami-i-Arudi of Samarkand (d. 1161) mentions that a single caravan there might consist of thousands of camels, while Wu-ku-sun Chang-tuan, an unofficial Chinese agent of Inner Asian origin whose travels were recorded by the Chin scholar Liu Ch'i in his *Pei-shih-chi* of 1221, adds the important detail that the camels were one-humped, i.e. Arabian or hybrid, thus showing the city's integration into the Islamic caravan network. Jewish trade, too, was still considerable. Benjamin of Tudela, the wandering rabbi in search of a refuge from the growing anti-semitism of Europe, wrote in his *Itinerary* , 1165–73: 'Thence it is five days to Samarkand, which is the great city on the confines of Persia. In it live some 50 000 Israelites and R. Obadiah the Nais is their appointed head. Among them are wise and very rich men.'[27] That Samarkand was a place of commercial importance, a true *emporium*, is clear. Whether it formed a link in a chain linking East and West to any significant degree is not established.

For the period 1250 to 1350, the evidence for a real international trade route becomes more convincing. The Polos themselves twice travelled through Central Asia. Despite the recent devastation by the Mongols, Bokhara and Samarkand are both described as 'large and splendid' cities, and Bokhara, which the elder Polos visited, as 'the finest city in all Persia'.[28]

Marco, who went via Balkh and Badakhshan, did not visit
Transoxania, but he commented on the Tarim basin that 'this
country is the starting point from which many merchants set
out to market their wares all over the world'.[29] Odoric of
Pordenone went to China by the southern sea route, but he
observed of Tabriz, the western terminus of the silk road,
that it was a city 'better for merchandise than any other which
at this day existeth in the world'.[30]

Juvaini, however, is the best witness to the huge spending
spree released in the wake of the Mongolian explosion by its
nouveau riche beneficiaries.[31] He writes of Ögödei:

> When he seated himself upon the throne of kingship and
> the fame of his kindness and generosity was spread
> throughout the world, merchants began to come to his
> court from every side, and whatever goods they had
> brought, whether good or bad, he would command them
> to be bought at the full price.[32]

Ögödei initiated the policy of supporting the *ortaq* or commercial partnerships who supplied the Mongol court with consumer goods and in return farmed its taxes. The *ortaq*, at
first mainly Christian or Manichee Uighurs, later Moslems
from Transoxania, were an important element in the Mongols'
exploitation of their conquests. They were the agents of a
profitable, predatory, palace capitalism. Ögödei's successor
Güyüg continued the same policy:

> Merchants had hastened to the presence of Guyuk Khan
> from all parts of the world and having concluded very large
> deals had been paid by drafts on the lands of the east and
> west (i.e. north China and Transoxania). . . . And after his
> death, his wives, sons and nephews concluded deals on a
> still greater scale than during his lifetime and wrote drafts
> in the same way. And crowds of other merchants came one
> after the other and carried out transactions with them.[33]

One is in the world of the oil sheikhs. No wonder that Juvaini
believed that Bokhara was more prosperous than before the
Mongol invasion:

> Today no town in the countries of Islam will bear compari-
> son with Bokhara in the thronging of its creatures, the

multitude of movable and immovable wealth, the concourse of savants, the flourishing of science and the students thereof and the establishment of pious endowments.[34]

The southern sea route

Whatever efflorescence the central land route experienced as a result of the parvenu extravagance of the Chinggisids, the greater part of the traffic between East and West, in the middle ages as earlier, went by the southern sea route. Till the thirteenth century, however, traffic was fairly restricted.

In China, the elimination of the mercantile city states of Wu-yüeh, Min and Han, by the Sung empire and its early absorption in continental wars against the Liao and Hsi-Hsia temporarily reduced maritime activity. Kaifeng, the new capital, though large and splendid, was after all a canal city. Though the Sung established a *shih-po-ssu* (maritime trade bureau) at Canton where the T'ang had had a similar agency, it was not until the twelfth century that the institution was extended to Swatow, Zayton, Hangchow, Ning-po and Tsingtao. In Islam, the axis of trade shifted from the Persian Gulf to the Red Sea: negatively because of the *Zanj* rebellion at Basra, 868–883, the Qarmatian piratical revolutionary state in the gulf in the tenth and eleventh centuries, and the destruction of Siraf by earthquake in 977; positively because of the foundation of Cairo and the rebuilding of Alexandria by the Fatimids, the least destructive economically of the major Islamic dynasties. Benjamin of Tudela was impressed by Alexandria: 'a commercial market for all nations. . . merchants of India bring thither all kinds of spices'.[35] Ashtor has shown that in the eleventh century there was a considerable exodus of merchants and craftsmen from the Persian Gulf to Egypt. Nevertheless, whatever the enthusiasms of Arab travellers and geographers, the hard facts of the papyri for this period and of the Cairo geniza documents indicate a mostly localized trade. Similarly the rubbish dump at Fustat, the biggest shard collection in the world, shows a falling off in northern Sung fragments compared to Wu-tai and T'ang.

With the thirteenth century, there is evidence for an expanding intercontinental trade. From the Chinese end there is the *Chu-Fan chih* (Treatise on the Various Barbarians)

of Chao Ju-kua, superintendent of customs at Zayton, dated
to 1225.[36] Chao's treatise is divided into two parts: an account
of the countries of the south seas; and the sources of the
principal imports to China. In the first part, Srivijaya is noted
as the *emporium* for products of the Islamic world, Malabar
is described as exporting cotton in return for silk and porcelain, and there are convincing sketches of Cairo, Baghdad
and even Sicily (Ssu-chia li-ye) with Mount Etna. In the second
part, frankincense is traced to the Hadramaut, myrrh to
Somalia, gardenias to Isfahan and Khwarazm, oak galls to
Mosul, pearls to the Persian Gulf, ivory to Aden and ambergris to the western sea of the Arabs, i.e. the south-west Indian
Ocean. Most of these commodities were luxuries, small in
quantity, but pepper, essential for meat preservation, and
traced to Java, Sumatra and Coromandel, was not. With
changes in Chinese taste and diet the pepper trade was now
the *primum mobile* in the East as in the West. In China, it was
in the sphere of private enterprise, there never being a pepper
administration on the model of the salt administration.

From the European end, there is Marco Polo who came
home via the southern sea route. He was impressed by the
Chinese pepper trade: 'I assure you that for one spice ship
that goes to Alexandria or elsewhere to pick up pepper for
export to Christendom, Zaiton is visited by a hundred.'[37]
Across the Indian Ocean, trade was large, international and
Chinese. Of Quilon in Malabar he notes: 'Merchants come
here from Manzi [i.e. the former southern Sung empire] and
Arabia and the Levant and ply a thriving trade; for they
bring various products from their own countries by sea and
export others in return.'[38] Further north at Ely near the modern Cananore he says, 'ships from Manzi and elsewhere come
here in summer, load in four to eight days, and leave as soon
as they can, because there is no port and it is very hazardous
to linger here'.[39] Concluding his account of Malabar he comments: 'You must know that ships come here from very many
parts, notably from the great province of Manzi, and goods
are exported to many parts. Those that go to Aden are carried
thence to Alexandria.'[40]

The rubbish dump at Fustat has quantities of southern
Sung and Yüan shards and Yüan fragments have been found
on the East African coast and as far inland as Zimbabwe.
Marco Polo says that:

Aden itself is the port to which all the ships from India come with their merchandise. It is a great resort of merchants. . . Aden is also the starting point for many merchant ships sailing to the Indies. . . the sultan of Aden derives a very large revenue from the heavy duties he levies from the merchants coming and going in his country. Indeed, thanks to these, he is one of the richest rulers in the world.[41]

The Mamluks were the Mongols' worst enemy, yet at the same time their best customer. By Polo's time the Persian Gulf was reviving. Of Ormuz he writes:

Merchants come here by ship from India, bringing all sorts of spices and precious stones and pearls and cloths of silk and of gold and elephants' tusks and many other wares. In this city they sell them to others, who distribute them to various customers through the length and breadth of the world. It is a great centre of commerce.[42]

Unlike the hot-house caravan trade of the central land route, the maritime trade of the southern sea route was firmly founded in a stable market: the high consumption of meat in the Yangtze provinces of China and in north-west Europe, which underlay the demand for pepper, since Ashtor's figures suggest that Islam was already past its best figures for mutton consumption and that the Mamluks bought pepper for others rather than for themselves.[43] The world described by Chao Ju-kua, its patterns, commodities, even with fluctuations, and its general levels, was to continue till the eighteenth century.

The northern land route

Just as the *Zanj*, the Qarmatians and the destruction of Siraf disrupted the Persian Gulf outlet of the southern sea route, so the raids of the Pechenegs and the conquest of Khazaria by the Russian prince Sviatoslav in 964 disrupted the Don outlet of the northern land route. The Pechenegs who became the predominant force on the Kipchaq steppe till the end of the eleventh century, were described by the German missionary St Bruno of Querfurt, who visited them unavailingly in 1008, as 'omnium paganorum crudelissimi'.[44] Their successors, the Cumans or Polovtsy, were little better and in 1200 the Byzantine government was glad to have the assistance of the Russian prince Roman of Galicia against a threatened Cuman invasion. Both the Russian principalities and the Magyar kingdom, itself an ex nomad state, suffered much from Cuman attacks, and Byzantine control over the Crimea and the ecclesiastical province of Gothia beyond it became shadowy. Such contact with Inner Asia as Constantinople had in the early middle ages was maintained via the southern outlet of the northern land route through Georgia and the territory of the Christian Alans, or via the Trebizond exit of the central land route. Benjamin of Tudela claimed that 'wealth like that of Constantinople is not to be found in the whole world',[45] but not much of it will have come from further Asia across the steppe.

The situation improved when, as a result of the fourth crusade, Italian shipping penetrated the Black Sea and treaty ports were established on the northern shore: Soldaia in 1205 and Tana in 1322, by Venice, and Caffa in 1262 by Genoa. Although the local trade in wine, salt, grain, fish and slaves was always the more important, there was significant intercontinental trade in silk, spices and pearls, particularly after the establishment of Mongol rule along the whole route. Ibn Battuta regarded Soldaia, the elder Polos' starting place, as one of the five biggest ports in the world, and Tana which the Venetians established to pre-empt the competition of Caffa was an issue in the Venetian–Genoese wars of 1350 and 1376. Beyond the Crimea, the chief *emporia* of the northern land route were Khiva or Urgench which Ibn Battuta described as 'the largest, greatest, most beautiful and most important city of the Turks'; Almaliq the northern capital of the Chaghatai khanate, an important Christian missionary centre; and Bishbaliq the Uighur city near the modern Urumchi which the Korean world map of Yi Hoe and Kwon Kun shows as being as large as Tabriz.[46]

This route was used by the Franciscan missionaries: John of Pian di Carpine; William of Rubruck; John of Montecorvino's successor, Nicholas, who died at Almaliq; John of Marignolli. It was also a trade route. The Florentine Francesco Balducci Pegolotti in his handbook for commercial travellers, *La Practica della Mercatura*, described its stages and commodities around 1340. Linen could be sold at Urgench for silver ingots which in China could be exchanged for paper currency with which to buy silk. Pegolotti claimed that 'the road which you travel from Tana to Cathay is perfectly safe whether by day or by night according to what the merchants say who have used it', but he had not been to Cathay himself and some of his optimism should be discounted as brokers' sales talk.[47] Nonetheless, the northern land route under the Golden Horde carried sufficient traffic for Tamerlane to wish to destroy it when he tried to monopolize trade for the central land route; John of Montecorvino thought it a better, because quicker, route to Cathay than the southern sea route he himself travelled; and Ibn Battuta found Chinese goods readily available in the bazaar at Sarai. Probably in its heyday it carried a volume of traffic second only to the southern sea route. It benefited both from the *pax Mongolica*, better and longer maintained by the Golden Horde than by any other of the Chinggisid successor states, and from the improvements in Bactrian camel caravaning.

The far southern sea route

During the middle ages the route of the raftmen lost its *raison d'être* and virtually ceased to exist. For Marco Polo, cinnamon was a product of south-west China and southern India. It was no longer associated with Africa and was carried west along with all other spices on the southern sea route. Chinese contact with Africa as measured by the shards on the *Zanj* coast, the new information in the *Chu-fan chih* (for example, a possible mention of Mount Kilimanjaro), and the fact mentioned by Marco Polo that Qubilai sent two embassies to East Africa, certainly increased during the Sung and Yüan periods, but the concentration of shards, especially heavy in Somalia, indicates that the means of access was Aden and the southern sea route. Conversely, nothing in Madagascar indicates continued contact with the Indonesian homeland, while within Indonesia there was a shift in commerce from Bali and the south to Srivijaya and the north, with a resulting growth in Islamization. In Madagascar, if Islam came, it came from the north-west not from the north-east. The increasing rejection by geographers, Moslem and Christian, of Ptolemy's belief that the Indian Ocean was a landlocked *mare clausum* has usually been taken to suggest greater knowledge of southern

Africa, but it may also have been due to lesser knowledge of northern Australia, its probable original basis. The Moslem geographer al-Idrisi, writing around 1154, knew of the former far southern connection, because he says that Zabag (Srivijaya) and *Zanj* (East Africa) understand each other's languages. Other Moslem authors used the term Wak-Wak indiscriminately of Indonesia and Madagascar. The old route however had really passed into history. The junk and the dhow had superseded the outrigger canoe.

Down to 1350 contact between East Asia and the West increased on all avenues of contact except the far southern sea route. For the first time, thanks to the Sung junk and the clear predominance of the southern sea route, trade not culture was the major component of the contact, even though diplomacy and religion still had considerable roles. As Olschki was the first to observe, Marco Polo the leading witness to the increase of trade, was not himself a merchant, but, on the outward journey, a papal legate and on the return journey, a Chinese imperial commissioner.[48] Ibn Battuta likewise was able to travel because he was a skilled Moslem canonist. Without religion and diplomacy we should not have evidence about trade, but the misreading of Marco Polo as a merchant, though erroneous, is not misplaced, in that the volume of trade had increased.

INTERCHANGES, 1000 TO 1350

The pattern of exchange between China and the outside world in the middle ages looked forward as well as back. Concentrated in the short period of the *apertura* produced by the Mongolian explosion, the exchange looked back to what had already happened: China's immense progress, material and cultural, from T'ang to Sung; the stagnation of Islam under its new Turkish leadership; the decline of India now divided between Moslem and Hindu; the opening of Africa by Moslem slave trading; the rise of backward but institutionally talented Latin Christendom. Because of these earlier developments, except in people, the movement of interchange went west rather than east. India now had little to offer China, except the Vaishnavite culture of the south which was largely inaccessible to outsiders, and lacked the ability to learn from her. Turkish Islam, as in late antiquity Arab and Iranian Islam, gave little to China and borrowed little from her, though that little perhaps was its salvation from the Mongols. Africa, a fringe of Islamic *emporia* drawing gold and slaves from the new Bantu states of the interior, took Chinese consumer goods, silks and celadons, but little else, and gave nothing except perhaps cobalt from the mines of Katanga for blue porcelain glaze.

Latin Christendom, on the other hand, while, as a still primitive peninsula had little to give, took not only consumer goods but also capital goods: techniques, processes, institutions, ideas and horizons. This receptivity, or rather acquisitiveness, reflected the fact that Europe had advanced not in progress but in the means of progress. Her choice therefore looked forward as well as back. The items taken from China became key elements in what may be called the fourteenth-century revolution: Europe's creative response to the disaster produced by the most immediately significant of the imports from East Asia, plague. Plague might have ruined western Europe and did produce a century of depression and dislocation. But thanks to its institutions, reinforced from China, Europe could recast itself and emerge enriched and mint-new; whereas China, having taken only people and not their ideas, institutions and techniques, could only resolder her metal into a simulacrum of its former glory.

People

The Mongolian explosion caused, for pre-modernity, an immense displacement of people. It was an age of refugees, slaves, deportees and adventurers, and the greater part of this displacement was from west to east. At the beginning of their conquests the Mongols adopted a deliberate policy of deporting skilled craftsmen and technicians to Karakorum. Möngke, with his policy so much praised by Juvaini of making the *pax Mongolica* tolerable to the sedentary populations, abandoned deportation in favour of state *karkhane* or sweated workshops in the craftsmen and technicians' home towns. Emigration however to Karakorum and Khanbalik continued, and at the courts of all the Mongol rulers there was a floating foreign population. John of Pian di Carpine was much assisted by the Russian goldsmith Cosmas at the court of Güyüg, to whose enthronement had come the king of Georgia, the sultan of Konia and the brother of the emir of Aleppo. William of Rubruck, likewise, at the court of Möngke was assisted by an unnamed Hungarian boy and by the Parisian goldsmith William Boucher who married a Hungarian. William mentions at Karakorum, Basil 'the son of an Englishman' and 'a vast multitude of Hungarians, Alans, Ruthenians, or Russians and Georgians and Armenians, who had not received the sacrament since they were taken prisoner'.[49] Indeed William's whole mission, which was not diplomatic but pastoral, was designed to minister to such people. Marco Polo refers to a German, perhaps really an Alan, mangonel expert at the siege of Siang-yang, and he himself served the *qaghan* as an intelligence officer, salt official and diplomatic agent. John of Montecorvino received money, with which he bought the land for his first church, from an Italian merchant in Peking, Peter of Lucolongo. *A propos* of Hangchow, Odoric of Pordenone observes that in Venice that are 'people in plenty who have been there', while Andrew of Perugia, bishop of Zayton, and John of Marignolli refer to a Genoese community at the great seaport.[50] In 1951 the tomb was discovered in Yangchow of an Italian girl, Catherine Vilioni who had died there in 1342.

Moslems from Cental Asia no doubt were more numerous than Franks. They dominated the *ortaq*, the banking partnerships which organized the economic exploitation of the empire for the Mongol aristocracy. One, Ahmad, became a much disliked finance minister under Qubilai. Another, Said Ajall Shams al-Din, perhaps a Bokharan, was governor of Yunnan, supervising the construction of the Kunming reservoirs and helping to create the Chinese-speaking Moslem community in the province, the Panthays, who remained powerful there until the nineteenth-century rebellion of Sultan Suleiman (Tu Wen-hsiu) led to their virtual extermination. The early history of the other Chinese-speaking Moslem community, the Tungans of Shensi-Kansu, is obscure, but most likely it too originated in the Yüan period with immigrants from the West. Foreign travellers have often been struck by the unChinese appearance of the Moslem population in Lanchow. Probably more non-Chinese came into China under the Yüan dynasty than in any other period of Chinese history till the nineteenth century.

Two groups, brought together by John of Montecorvino, first archbishop of Khanbalik, call for mention: the Alans and the Franciscans. The Alans were a nomadic people of Iranian language whose pasture was the upper Terek valley north of the main Caucasus divide. They were early associated with the Georgians in their intra-montane basin south of the divide, and through them were converted to eastern orthodox Christianity in the tenth century and became valued military auxiliaries of the Byzantine empire. The Alans came into contact with the Mongols in 1220 during Subotei's blitzkrieg round the Caspian in pursuit of the shah, but they were only incorporated into the Mongol federation in 1239 by Möngke when he was acting as representative of the house of Tolui in the pan-*ulus* campaign against the West under Batu. It was probably Möngke who first took Alan military units to China, when he became *qaghan* in 1251 and went to war, not very successfully, with the Sung empire in 1253. Qubilai inherited the Alans from his brother in 1260 and they may have been reinforced from time to time in accordance with the alliance between the houses of Tolui and Jochi. At any rate, the Alans continued to be a valued component of the Yüan army down to the reign of Toghon Temür and the end of the dynasty in China.

Their value lay in their part in the obscure but crucial military revolution whereby, after the Mongolian explosion, heavy cavalry mounted on large horses again became superior to light cavalry mounted on ponies. From the time of Qaidu's rebellion, really the secession of the outer steppe, the Yüan emperors lost control of Mongolian pony power and were thrown back on the traditional Chinese horse policy of heavy cavalry based on imports. The Alans were traditionally Iranian heavy horsemen, like their cousins the Massagetae of Khwarazm and Ferghana. That they were still so in the fourteenth century is proved by the fact that the Alan embassy to Pope Benedict XII in 1335, which prompted John of Marignolli's mission, asked for, and via John obtained, large horses. Toghon Temür was so pleased that he had one of the horses painted by Chou Lang with an accompanying ode by Ou-yang

Hsüan. The Alans therefore were at the intersection of the Yüan withdrawal from the steppe and the more general revival of heavy cavalry.[51]

The Marignolli mission, requested by the Alans and warmly welcomed by the emperor, was the climax of medieval Franciscan activity in China: the story of the three Johns.[52] It began in 1245 with the dispatch by Pope Innocent IV from the first Council of Lyon of John of Pian di Carpine, a personal disciple of St Francis, on a fact-finding mission to the Mongols, who in 1241 invaded Poland and Hungary, penetrating to the Adriatic. This invasion had been observed and chronicled by another Franciscan, Jordan of Giano, the provincial of Bohemia, with whom John had been in touch when he had been provincial of Saxony. The first John therefore was an experienced man of 60 when he set out along the northern land route to the court of Güyüg. His report, the *Historia Mongolorum* was not encouraging. It recognized that the Mongol empire was an aggressive military state of a new kind which was unlikely, despite the Nestorianism of Güyüg's ministers, to prove the Christian counter-reformation in Asia for which the Prester John legend hoped. It was John's report which led the papacy to reject any alliance with the Mongols against the Mamluks in the 1250s. Nevertheless, John also recognized the plasticity of Mongol policy, that the situation should be watched, that opportunities for diplomacy might occur. This second strand of John's report led Gregory X, Tedaldo Visconti the former legate in Outremer, to back the Polos, and Nicholas IV, a former Franciscan general, to respond to the Nestorian mission of Rabban Sauma, sent by the Il-khan Arghun to Rome in 1287, by sending John of Montecorvino, who was in Italy as envoy of Hethum II of Armenia, direct to Peking.

In Peking the second John found the situation favourable. The Alans, eastern orthodox, were under pressure from the Nestorians to convert, perhaps because relations between the houses of Tolui and Jochi were no longer as close as they had been. They were reluctant to do so and the Yüan government itself wanted to maintain its universal character by increasing contact with the West, especially as Alan heavy cavalry was a factor in the struggle for Caucasia developing between the Il-khanate and the Golden Horde. The Alans therefore were allowed, perhaps even encouraged, to convert to Catholicism. On his side, John would have been able to point to the union of the churches recently concluded in 1274 at the second Council of Lyon. Soon he could claim 10 000 converts and Clement V created him first archbishop of Khanbalik, sending other Franciscans to be his suffragans at Zayton and elsewhere. John of Montecorvino died in 1328. When his successor failed to arrive, the Alans with imperial support, asked for another, plus horses, and Benedict XII in 1339 dispatched the Florentine John of Marignolli to Peking. Toghon Temür would have liked the third John to have remained himself as archbishop, or for the pope to have sent someone else of cardinalatial rank. John, however, refused, perhaps because he perceived the Yüan regime in China was tottering, and returned to Avignon in 1353. While he had been away, the Black Death had struck Europe: within a year two-thirds of the Franciscan order were dead. Although popes continued to appoint archbishops of Khanbalik for over a century, none of them actually reached Peking. One at least perhaps tried. Alexander of Caffa was captured by the Turks in 1475 and remained five years in captivity before returning to Italy. By this time the Alans had long disappeared from China, though Chinese emperors were still interested in large horses.

Of movement in the opposite direction, from East to West, the nearest equivalent of the Alans and Franciscans was what may be called the Chinese brains-trust of the Il-khan Hülegü. In his account of the pan-Mongol expedition of 1253 organized by Möngke to eliminate the Assassins (the justification of Mongol rule in the eyes of Sunnis) and conquer the caliphate (the scandal which Juvaini avoids writing about), Juvaini tells us that the *qaghan* 'sent to Khitai to fetch mangonel experts and naphtha-throwers; and they brought from Khitai 1000 households (*khana*) of Khitayan mangonel-men, who with a stone missile would convert the eye of a needle into a passage for a camel'.[53] Most likely these Chinese artillery-men and chemical warfare personnel will have remained with Hülegü after the fall of Baghdad in 1258, since the siege of the Mamluk cities of Syria and Egypt was anticipated. Even when the death of Möngke, the battle of Ain Jalut and the beginning of trouble with the Golden Horde on the northern frontier ended these hopes, the Il-khanate continued to use

Chinese experts such as Fu Meng-chi at the astronomical observatory at Maraghah, or the Sino–Uighur monk, Mark of Peking, who was Catholicos of the east as Yahballaha III from 1280 to 1317. It also admired Chinese painting as is clear from the illustrations to Rashid al-Din al-Hamdani's *Jami al-Tawarikh*, and sought Yüan princesses as brides for its rulers, as we know from Marco Polo. The Sino–Iranian culture patronized by the Timurids, the Ottomans and the Saffavids was the revival of what had been begun in Tabriz and Sultaniah in the early fourteenth century, particularly under the Il-khan Oljeitu, 1304–16.

Flora and fauna

The exchanges of the middle ages duplicated those of late antiquity. The West again received the plague bacillus, this time for a much longer stay, and the Seville orange was reinforced by the sweet orange. China received a further injection of cotton and her own indigenous *kao-liang* was reinforced by foreign sorghum.

The sweet orange, *Citrus sinensis*, the ancestor of Valencia and navel oranges as produced by Jaffa, Florida, California and the Riverina, arrived in Europe in the fourteenth century, probably via the southern sea route, perhaps from the Genoese community at Zayton. As with the Seville orange, its significance was as part of the regeneration of the Mediterranean landscape between antiquity and the Renaissance. Today the sweet orange is the largest part of all citrus production. In 1350 its significance was marginal except as a symptom of European consumptivity, penchant for sweetness, and readiness to try the exotic.

More immediately important was the reintroduction of plague. Jean-Noel Biraben has established the stages by which it took place. At the beginning of the fourteenth century, the chief, perhaps only, reservoir of *Yersinia pestis* was in the wild rodents of High Asia, especially the tarabagan or marmot, *Arctomys bobac*, in whom plague existed for long periods in a latent form. From this reservoir, under the imperatives of rodent demography controlled, it seems, by the sunspot cycle, colder and wetter climatic conditions favourable to fleas, and more human circulation thanks to the Mongolian explosion which broke the barrier around the reservoirs afforded by the dislike of fleas for the smell of horses and sheep, *Yersinia pestis* in the 1330s overflowed. It overflowed *either* by the movement of fleas from wild rodents to domestic rodents to humans and to other humans, *or* by direct inhalation through the air from wild rodents to humans to other humans; or by some combination of the two routes. If entry was by the skin the result was bubonic plague; if by the mouth or nose, the even deadlier pneumonic plague.

The first indication of the overflow is the Nestorian tombstone inscriptions in the Semirechie, investigated by D.A. Chwolson, which record people dying of plague in 1338 and 1339. Independently, it is known that there was an epidemic in the Moghulistan half of the Chaghatai khanate at this date and Biraben suggests that the shift in leadership within Moghulistan from the Nestorian north to the Islamic south was one of the first results of the epidemic. Next, combining the testimonies of the Spanish Moslem Ibn Hatimah and the Englishman Geoffrey Baker, there is reason to believe that plague reached Samarkand in 1341. Certainly it was at Tabriz and Astrakhan in 1346, and New Sarai and Tana in 1347. At this time Janibeg, khan of the Golden Horde, was besieging the Genoese treaty port of Caffa. He had catapulted over the walls (by Chinese mangonel experts?) the bodies of plague victims, guessing what Wu Lien-teh was to establish scientifically in 1911, that plague bacilli could survive in corpses for as long as six months.

Caffa did not fall, but this early piece of bacteriological warfare produced extraordinary results in other directions. Plague appeared in Pera, the Genoese quarter of Constantinople, in the middle of 1347. It soon spread to the rest of the city causing maximum deaths in November and December, the winter date indicating the pneumonic form of the disease. Twelve Genoese galley, returning from Constantinople, touched at Messina at the end of September, whence plague spread to Catania and in October to Syracuse, Sciacca, Trapani and Agrigento. Genoa refused to admit its own galley, so they went to Marseille where the first cases of plague appeared in November. By the end of the year plague had appeared at Alexandria, Corsica, Spoleto and Genoa, infected now from Sicily. On 13 January 1348 it was at Ragusa,

25 January Venice; in February, Lucca, Montpellier and Carcassonne; in April, Siena, Lyon and Toulouse; in May, Naples and Barcelona; in June, Gaza and Weymouth; in July, Damascus and Southampton; in August, Bristol, Gloucester and Aleppo; in September, London; and by the end of the year Rome, Styria, most of France and Tunis. In 1349 Germany was invaded, in 1350 Poland, in 1352 north-west Russia. This, of course, was only the beginning. Western Europe till the beginning of the eighteenth century, eastern Europe and the Near East till the middle of the nineteenth, were subject to the decennial assaults of *Yersinia pestis*.

Why did the plague of Janibeg last twice as long as the plague of Justinian? Neither episode was a true cycle in the sense of an endogenous sequence whose end was contained in its beginning. The hypothesis that infection gradually built up resistance to itself is unlikely because too few people survived infection; in the case of pneumonic plague, virtually none. Each episode had specific causes for beginning, continuing and ending. Three factors were involved in the long duration of the plague of Janibeg.

First, as a result of the Janibeg invasion, by a reversal of the overflow mechanisms from wild rodent to man outlined above, new, secondary wild rodent reservoirs of *Yersinia pestis* were established: notably in Kurdistan, but also in Central Africa and Indo-China, and later the south-western United States, south-west Africa and western Patagonia. Europe was no longer attacked simply or even primarily from Lake Baikal with which communication could easily be disrupted, but rather from the ports of the Levant, especially Smyrna. This is well documented in the last plagues of north-west Europe and the western Mediterranean, the plagues of Amsterdam and London in 1665 and of Marseille in 1720; but it may be presumed of earlier pulsations.

Second, the era of Janibeg's plague coincided with the spread, of *Rattus rattus*, the gregarious and human-loving black rat, perhaps as a result of urbanization. In the past the role of the black rat in the aetiology of plague has been exaggerated. Its fleas are not a necessary part of the chain of transmission even in bubonic plague. For example, in Marseille in 1720, *Yersinia pestis* went direct from the wild rodents of Kurdistan to humans via a bale of cotton, the resulting epidemic of bubonic plague being generated by inter-human movements of fleas without the mediation of domestic rodents. The presence of the black rat therefore, for example in York in the second century AD, cannot be taken as an indication of plague nor its absence as a contra-indication. The black rat acted as a local point of vulnerability, an additional and even more flea-ridden proletariat through which *Yersinia pestis* could gain access to the rest of cleaner humanity. In the cellars of every city of Europe plague had a ready-made beach-head.

Third, the plague of Janibeg appeared in a world where people moved more than in the days of Justinian. Then only the Rhone had been a trade route and a carrier of plague into the interior. Now every river carried traffic and the seas were fully utilized, so that plague spread in a twofold movement: along coasts, Mediterranean, Atlantic, North Sea, Baltic; and up rivers, Rhone, Garonne, Rhine, Elbe, Vistula, Dvina. Europe was no longer an atonic, rural immobility, but the area with the least embedded, most mobilized economy which would diffuse *Yersinia pestis* like any other commodity. Europe was no longer protected by its backwardness.

What is puzzling about the plague of Janibeg is not its beginning and continuing, but its end. Increasing resistance will not do as an explanation. Nor will the replacement of *Rattus rattus* by *Rattus Norwegicus*, since, apart from exaggerating the role of domestic rodents in the genesis of plague, the brown rat came too late (the end of the eighteenth century) and, although less gregarious and human-loving than its predecessor, is just as liable to plague and a better conservator of it. Also too late is *Yersinia pseudotuberculosis* because although, mediated to humans as a mild flu through domestic cats, it gives 100 per cent immunity against its cousin *Yersinia pestis*, its existence cannot be established before the late nineteenth century. The end of the plague of Janibeg must therefore be assigned to human action: government action – quarantines, isolation, destruction of infected clothes and bodies – and social action – better housing, the primary form of European high consumptivity, and higher standards of hygiene. It was a surprising triumph of pre-modern empiricism misled as much as encouraged by current reason. For what was required was not so much theories such as

Athanasius Kircher's 'fine, invisible boddikins' emerging from a *putredo animata*, as to recognize the link with the East and break it by a *cordon sanitaire* of sufficient amplitude.[54]

China's imports in the category of flora and fauna in the middle ages were more utilitarian than the sweet orange, less dramatic than plague. Indeed it is questionable whether cotton and sorghum should be considered as more than reintroductions. Cotton was grown and manufactured in Kwangtung in the nineth century and Ho Ping-ti finds traces of sorghum far back in Chinese prehistory. Nevertheless the middle ages saw a notable expansion in the cultivation of both crops due in part to foreign contact. Cotton in the Sung period advanced from Kwangtung to Fukien and Kiangsu to become the major textile of the Yangtze valley. At the same time it was introduced to north-west China from Turfan and Samarkand. In Shensi and Kansu, and by the middle of the thirteenth century Honan, cotton became an important crop and contributed to the revival of north China which was a feature of post Yüan history.

Sorghum made a similar contribution. *Kao-liang* or tall millet may have been cultivated by the Yang-shao culture of earliest neolithic China. However its main focus in antiquity was Ethiopia and before the Sung period it was known in China chiefly as a product of Szechwan, then a frontier province in touch with India and points beyond. In the Sung period and under the Mongols, *kao-liang* became more widely used, perhaps as a result of further contact with areas where it was a major crop. In China *kao-liang* eventually became the principal grain crop of the north-east and a prime instrument of Chinese colonization in Manchuria. Both cotton and *kao-liang* were plebeian products, congruent with the tendency of post-medieval China to a multiplication of peasant family units. Providers of minimum diet, minimum clothing, they were agents not of development but of indifferentiation.

Commodities

In the later Sung and Yüan, Chinese society reached a peak of consumerism which it never surpassed and perhaps never equalled. It was one of the aspects of China emphasised by Marco Polo and admired by Europeans who were themselves developing a taste for luxury, though at a lower economic level. Consumerism at both ends of the Eurasian continent increased the volume of intercontinental trade in textiles, minerals and spices, but with different results. China, the more mature economy, ran an adverse balance of trade with the outside world, leading to an outflow of precious metals and the beginnings of a negative attitude to foreign trade. Europe, with an economy less mature but more dynamic, ran a favourable balance of trade with the outside world, leading to an inflow of precious metals and the beginnings of a positive attitude towards foreign trade. For China, outside commodities were a source of impoverishment; for Europe a source of profit.

Although both Christendoms, Islam and India all now grew silk and manufactured silks, there was still a Western demand for Chinese silk and silks because of their superior quality at the highest level, their superior quantity at the lowest. In Latin Christendom the market for all kinds of textiles had widened. In classical and late antiquity, textiles, except for luxuries such as Alexandrian linen, Indian cottons and Chinese silks, had not been a major item of commerce. The principal fibre was flax, the primary textile was rough linen and the usual place of production and distribution was the home. Wool was a luxury since animals were few and, as in China and India with silk and hemp, arable farming provided both food and clothing.

In the middle ages, both place of production and distribution, and predominant fibre changed. The professional weaver in a town working wool for the market replaced the unprofessional farmer's wife in the homestead working flax for her family. Wool, produced in larger quantities by a more pastoral agriculture, ceased to be a luxury, and clothes hitherto a domestic commodity became a market commodity. Both changes expressed a greater interest in comfort and fashion which also affected the market for silk. Whereas antiquity was aware only of heavy Chinese brocades and damasks on the one hand and light Syrian gauzes and muslins on the other, the middle ages produced words for a whole range of intermediate or specialized forms: velvet, from the Latin *villus* shaggy haired; samite, hexamitos, six-ply, doubtless of Byzantine origin; satin, Chaucer's 'blak satyn de owter mere', perhaps from Zayton rather than the more obvious *seta*; organdie and organza, from Urgench the midway point of the northern land route; taffeta, from the Persian *taftah* meaning cloth; scarlet, originally a kind of cloth rather than colour, from the Persian *saqalat*, a rich cloth produced in Samarkand; chiffon from a French word meaning rags; tussore from the Chinese *t'u-ssu*, wild silk. This growing textile vocabulary reflected the diversification of the silk market even though words, goods and their origins did not always stand in a simple relationship to each other.

Unlike textiles which only travelled from East to West, minerals travelled in both directions. Apart from porcelain, China's most significant mineral export in the Sung-Yüan period was copper, in the form of the copper cash sent overseas in the course of foreign trade which became increasingly deficitary. Sung cash in considerable amounts have been recovered from Japan and the countries of the Nan-yang as well as Somalia and the coasts of Kenya and Tanzania. According to L.S. Yang, the Sung minted more copper than any other dynasty.[55] The main mining areas were Shao-chou in Kwangtung, T'an-chou in Hunan and Hsin-chou in Kiangsi, with Changsha the capital of Hunan, which in a census of 1075 figured as the largest city in the empire, as the headquarters of the industry. Copper was also imported for the mints from Japan and Korea, some of it to be exported back in the form of cash. Sung statesmen took a relatively liberal and unmercantilist view of metallic movements though from time to time there were attempts to check the outflow.

In the opposite direction, Europe, so long deficitary in relation to the outside world and a chronic sufferer from bullion anaemia, began to receive precious metals through its export of base iron, copper and tin. Venice in particular was deeply involved in exporting iron from Brescia, Friuli, Carinthia and the Upper Palatinate, to the Islamic world, especially Egypt. Whether any of this iron reached China is not clear. In the eleventh century China was the biggest producer of iron, 125 000 tons a year, perhaps double the European figure, and produced by more advanced technology – the blast furnace powered by coal. Demand, however, outran supply, particularly after the production area in west Shantung fell to the Jurched, and it is possible that some of the iron imported from Turkestan really came from the West. Shortage of iron was one of the weaknesses of the southern Sung state, just as it was of Islam *vis-à-vis* Latin Christendom.

Like textiles and minerals, the international spice trade expanded in the middle ages. After the insipid centuries of Pirenne's great disappearances, Europe returned to the market, and in a bigger way. Demand now came not only from the protein-poor Mediterranean but from the protein-rich north as well: France, England, Germany, Poland. Not only did Europe return hungrier for spices, but the changes produced by the Black Death – the switch to pastoralism, the increased consumption of meat, milk, butter and cheese, and the larger commerce in these commodities – enlarged demand yet again. China too experienced a shift to protein. Osmosis with successive barbarian invaders, the Khitan, Tangut, Jurched and Mongols, produced a greater readiness to eat butchers' meat and Mongolian and Korean barbecues became fashionable. In pre-modern conditions butchers' meat meant spices.

Despite the decline in Buddhism, the non-alimentary spice trade in incense and aromatic woods did not decrease. It had now become part of secular luxury. Similarly, the valetudinarian age of southern Sung saw an increase in medical or pseudo-medical imports such as rhinoceros horn from the East African coast and the Chinese pharmacopeia reached its maximum proportions. It was the spice trade in this wide sense which produced China's balance of payments deficit under the Sung, just as it was the base metal trade which produced Europe's surplus.

Techniques

In this category of interchange more than any other, movement was one way, from East to West, reflecting the disequilibrium between the maturity of China and the promise of Europe. Down the slope created by this disequilibrium moved a package of superior Chinese technology which, absorbed by the unique institutional milieu of Latin Christendom, was crucial in preparing for Europe's take-off in the Renaissance. This package may be seen as a constellation of five elements.

Nautical element

First, and most obvious in its contribution to Europe's take-off, there was a nautical element. During the middle ages Europe received from China the sternpost rudder, the magnetic compass, multiple masts with multiple sails, and the lug sail. Without these techniques Europe's oceanic explosion would have been impossible.[56]

An Eastern Han tomb ship model, discovered in Canton in 1958, established that the sternpost rudder was developed in China during the first two centuries AD, earlier ship models of the Warring States and western Han periods showing only steering oar rudders. In Europe, the sternpost rudder is first represented on fonts at Zedelghem and Winchester carved by craftsmen from Tournai around 1180. It is then found in an illustrated manuscript in Breslau dated to 1242 and in a stained glass window in Le Mans cathedral of similar date. Finally, it appears on numerous thirteenth-century city seals: Ipswich 1200, Elbing 1242, Wismar 1256, Stubbkjoeping and Harderwyk 1280, Damme 1309; at which last date it is also mentioned for the Mediterranean by Villani's chronicle. How the sternpost rudder travelled is not established. The southern sea route might seem most likely, and there is literary evidence for Arab use of an axial rudder in the Red Sea in the tenth century; but since the new rudder appeared first in Europe in northern rather than Mediterranean waters, Needham inclines to travel via the northern land route, part of which could involve shipping on rivers, lakes and the Caspian.

The route of the magnetic compass is even more obscure. It, too, was known in China in the first two centuries AD. In Europe the first mention of magnetic polarity was by Alexander Neckham, Austin canon and abbot of Cirencester, in his *De Naturis rerum* of 1180. In the middle of the thirteenth century the Parisian philosopher Peter of Maricourt, who taught Roger Bacon, described its use in a compass in his *Epistola de magnete* and, by the end of the century the use of a freely swinging magnetized needle attached to a compass card was coming into use in the Mediterranean with revolutionary effects on the pattern of navigation. Since Chu Yü in his *P'ing-chou K'o-t'an* of 1119 mentions the use of the magnetic compass by Chinese shipping between Canton and Sumatra, a southern sea route transmission through the Arabs as a result of contact at Srivijaya would seem most likely, but there is no proof as yet.

Marco Polo and Ibn Battuta make it clear that Chinese ships in their day commonly had at least three masts with at least three sails. Polo says of the Great Khan's fleet on which he travelled to Persia, 'he fitted out a fleet of fourteen ships, each of which had four masts and often carried as many as twelve sails'.[57] Later he describes the ships plying between China and India:

> They have one good sweep or helm which in the vulgar tongue is called a rudder. And four masts each with four sails, and they often add to them two masts more, which are raised and put away every time they wish, with two sails according to the state of the weather.[58]

Similarly, Ibn Battuta, having said that there are three kinds of Chinese ships, large, middling and small, states, 'A single one of the greater ships carries twelve sails and the smaller ones only three'.[59]

Multi-masted ships were old in China. They are referred to in a third-century AD text, the *Nan-chou i-wu-chih* (Strange Things of the South): 'The people beyond the barriers [beyond the Nan-Shan, i.e. Kwangtung and Tongking] according to the sizes of their ships sometimes rig as many as four sails, which they carry in a row from bow to stern.'[60] In medieval Europe, however, although three-masted vessels had existed under the classical Roman empire, the characteristic ships were *either*, in the Mediterranean, the round ship with two masts each carrying a single lateen sail; *or*, first in northern seas and only later in the Mediterranean, the cog with a single square sail. After 1300 when Chinese influence is already a possibility, a larger two-masted cog was developed, square-rigged on the main mast, lateen rigged on the mizzen; but it is not until the fifteenth century that there is definite evidence of three-masted European ships. Between the two-masted cogs and the three- or four-masted carracks and galleons, came Marco Polo's report and the Catalan map of 1375 and Fra Mauro's map of 1459, both of which show large multi-masted vessels as characteristic of Chinese waters. It is hard to resist Clowes' conclusion that the development in

Europe of the *nau redonda*, the three-masted ship with a variety of sails, the instrument of European naval supremacy, was made under Chinese influence transmitted along the southern sea route.

A fourth piece of nautical technology the germ of which reached Europe in the days of Marco Polo, though the fruit did not appear until the sixteenth century, was lug sails, the Chinese form of fore and aft rig. Fore and aft rig itself, whose advantage over square rig is the ability to sail much closer to .the wind, was probably developed in the last centuries BC by the Indonesians with their canted square sails. It reached the Mediterranean in its Islamic form of the lateen sail by 880 AD, when it is depicted in a Byzantine manuscript of the sermons of St Gregory Nazianzen. The Chinese lug sail, described by Ibn Battuta and fully developed by at least the thirteenth century, was a development out of the Indonesian canted square sail, perhaps via the Melanesian double-mast sprit sail. It did not appear in Europe until the sixteenth century. However, the place of its first appearance, the Adriatic, and the fact that the *trabaccolo* and the *braggozzi*, the luggers of Chioggia, have two Chinese features – absence of keel and huge rudders – suggest that experiments with lug sails may go back to the days when Venice was the diffusion point for information about China. At any rate, the knowledge that the Chinese, despite, as it must have seemed to a European, the size of their vessels, used fore and aft rather than square rig, will have encouraged those in Europe who were experimenting with a mixture of square and fore and aft rig on ever larger ships: experiments which eventually produced the characteristic mixed rigs of Renaissance carracks and galleons. This mixed rig was unChinese, but it would have never come into existence without Chinese influence.

Metallurgical element

Second, and in the long run more important in Europe's take-off, there was a metallurgical element. During the middle ages Europe received from China the blast furnace for the complete liquefaction and casting of iron. China had been able to cast iron since at least the fourth century BC and the Sung period was a high point in Chinese iron production and consumption. Iron was used in such quantities for pagodas, bridges, tiles, statues and anchors that it had to be imported despite home production being the largest in the world. In return China exported its technology. In Europe the first true blast furnaces, used for casting cannon, appeared in Liège and Styria around 1380. Water-wheels were used to operate bellows to raise sufficient heat to smelt iron in preparation for casting. In Germany the word *blahhaus* first appears in 1389. Carthusian monks in the isolation of their charterhouses were notable metallurgical pioneers. They had been experimenting since the twelfth century, but it was crucial information about Chinese processes, probably transmitted along the northern land route via those old metal-workers the Turks, which finally led to success. Under the impetus of this discovery, European iron production probably at least doubled between 1350 and 1500 to achieve, not yet parity with China, but at least production not far behind. It was a leap forward for Europe. Given sufficient fuel, and she was already experimenting with coal aware that the Chinese used it extensively, she had acquired in principle that capacity so to extend the production of iron as to make it the primary material instead of wood, which was the metallurgical half of the industrial revolution. Corollaries, such as the sedentariza-tion of the industry and the encouragement given to all kinds of mining in the later middle ages were also significant.

Mechanical element
Third, less radical a departure but an innovation from which revolutionary changes were to develop, there was a mechan-ical element. In the middle ages, from a Chinese prototype, Europe began to use waterpower in a primary process of a branch of the textile industry. In China a waterpowered machine for spinning hemp was described by Wang Chen in 1313 in his *Nung-shu* (Treatise on Agriculture). The actual machinery had been adapted from a device for reeling silk and it was used, Wang Chen tells us, 'in all parts of North China which manufacture hemp'.[61] Waterpower was then added and, Wang Chen continues, 'many of these machines have been installed in those places in the North China plain which are near to running water.'[62] Silk then borrowed water-power in return for its loan of machinery. A stone tablet in Szechwan of the Yüan period refers to 'water-wheels for hul-

ling and grinding rice and for spinning and weaving machinery, to the number of tens of thousands'.[63] The reference is
probably to silk filatures rather than hemp mills since silk is
a more characteristic product of the Chengtu plain, which is
being described, than hemp.

At any rate, in 1372 a Luccan introduced at Bologna a
hydraulic spinning, or more accurately reeling or 'throwing',
machine for silk. It was not plarticularly efficient in comparison with hand-spinning machines and it was not copied outside Bologna till 1538, but it was the prototype for all subsequent developments in powered textile machinery down to
Arkwright's substitution of steam for water as the prime
mover in 1790. Carlo Poni has shown that the *molino Bolognese*
was the model first for the improved mills in the Venetian,
Piedmontese and French Alps in the seventeenth and early
eighteenth centuries, then for the Lombe brothers' hydraulic
silk filature at Derby in 1718, and finally for Arkwright's waterpowered cotton spinning mill at Cromford in Derbyshire in
1771, the last step before the fully industrial steam mill of
1790.[64] Since 1372, therefore, Europe had possessed the principle of the textile half of the industrial revolution: the application of power to the primary processes of reeling or spinning. Since the Chinese and European prototypes are structurally similar, and since Italian silk buyers were in China in
the fourteenth century, it was from this source that the principle must have been drawn.

Chemical element
Fourth, revolutionary not in the economy but in politics, there
was a chemical element. In the middle ages Europe received
from China the secret of explosives. *Huo-yao*, fire drugs, were
the fruit of collaboration between Taoist alchemists and not
necessarily Taoist military engineers, especially those active
in China's series of defensive wars against the *ordo* states of
the north. A ninth-century Taoist text refers to the inflammat-
ory properties of a mixture of charcoal, saltpetre and sulphur.
The *Wu-ching tsung-yao*, a military encyclopaedia presented
to Emperor Jen-tsung in 1044, gives an exact formula for an
explosive composed of these substances and described its use
in grenades. The *Shou-ch'eng lu* (Record of the Defence of
Towns), a collection of military writings compiled around

1200, describes how between 1127 and 1132 Ch'en Kuei defended Te-an on the Han river against successive sieges by the Jurched with *huo-ch'iang*, fire lances, a primitive kind of explosive flamethrower. *Huo-tung*, bombards or short cannon, came later, but pictures dated to 1332 have survived. In Europe the first mention of explosives is in the *Opus Maius*, c. 1278, of the Franciscan Roger Bacon, a friend of Peter of Maricourt the European discoverer of magnetism and of William of Rubruck the missioner to the court of Möngke.

The first major engagement in Europe in which gunpowder played a part was the battle of Crécy in 1346 where Froissart describes the not very effective activities of the English *bombardiaux*. It was used more effectively the following year by Edward III in his siege of Calais, but artillery was not a major factor in war until the Hussite wars of the following century. Needham emphasises the role of gunpowder in the decline of castle-based feudalism. In fact gunpowder appeared during the decline of the medieval monarchies of France and England and the rise of bastard feudalism. No doubt, however, in the long run, by raising the cost of war, gunpowder helped to make territorial, even imperial, monarchy the predominant political form in Europe. Marine artillery was also an ingredient in European naval supremacy.

Horological element

Fifth, outwardly merely a convenience but revolutionary in its long-term impact on thought, there was a horological element. In the middle ages Europe received from China the device known as the escapement which is an essential component of clockwork. The earliest kind of clock, used in the classical empires of Rome and Han, was the hour glass or *clepsydra* in which water or sand runs freely. Its problem was that it was difficult to regulate, difficult indeed to establish its original correspondence with the apparent revolution of the heavens. The solution is the escapement which by interrupting the flow or turning wheel divides time into discrete units, which in turn permits of accurate adjustment. Its inventor was the Buddhist monk I-hsing who put one in a hydromechanical clock in 725 and it was common in China thereafter. A plan can be reconstructed of a huge astronomical hydro-mechanical clock with an escapement mechanism erected by the imperial astronomer Su Sung at Kaifeng between 1088 and 1092. In Europe the first modern clocks began appearing in the thirteenth century. Westminster Abbey is said to have had a clock in 1288, Canterbury Cathedral in 1292, St Albans Abbey in 1326. On the continent, the oldest surviving clock is that of Beauvais Cathedral, parts of which date back to 1325, and, in England, the clock in Salisbury Cathedral which dates from 1386. The particular kind of escapement used in these weight- or spring-driven clocks is different from that used by Su Sung in his hydro-mechanical clock, but the principle is the same.

The diffusion of clocks, soon wider than in China, had profound consequences. It produced a heightened awareness of time and of its quantitative, atomic character. A passage in the *Cloud of Unknowing*, c. 1370, reads 'there can be as many movements or desires of your will within the hour as there are atoms of time'.[65] The clock provided a new intellectual paradigm. In the writings of Nicholas of Oresme, who died in 1382, is first found the image of the world as a huge piece of clockwork. Determinism and automata and the reduction of the four Aristotelian causes to a single efficient cause defined in terms of push, as found in the writings of John Buridan (d. 1358) or Albert of Halberstadt (d. 1390), are cognate ideas. Nicholas of Oresme was the first post-classical thinker to reconsider heliocentrism. Perhaps more significantly his empiricism led him to pronounce the evidence insufficient to decide between it and geocentrism. He also anticipated Gresham's law. Applicable in many directions, the clock paradigm was a major factor in dissolving the scholastic synthesis into logic, mysticism and positivistic science.

Ideas

The middle ages were not propitious for the exchange of ideas. The Mongolian explosion intensified orthodoxy in Islam and China, also indirectly in Hindu India, and in Latin Christendom there was a counter-reformation in the thirteenth century as well as a *réforme Catholique*. Nevertheless, ideas, theoretical and practical, did cross from East to West through the distinction, made in Islam and more emphatically in Latin Christendom, between nature and supernature, reason and revelation. This distinction allowed orthodoxies rigid at one level to be flexible at another. It was the Western equivalent of the nineteenth-century Chinese formula: Chinese learning for the substance, Western learning for practical use.

On the theoretical side, the chief idea which travelled from East to West in the middle ages was a deeper understanding of Chinese alchemy: the realization that its primary purpose was medical rather than mineral, that aurifiction and aurifaction were less important than the elixir and the *enchymoma*. The full expression of this new understanding had to wait until the sixteenth century and Paracelsus, but the beginnings are in Albertus Magnus, Roger Bacon, the *Aurora Consurgens*, Arnold of Villanova, John of Ruperscissa the English Franciscan, and Petrus Bonus of Ferrara. In particular, the conjuncture in the sixth part of Bacon's *Opus Maius* of longevity theory, explosives and the transmutation of metals, seems too close to Chinese alchemy to be explained without influence from the East. A possible transmitter would be Islamic alchemy, in particular the Geberian corpus which was translated into Latin in the thirteenth century, but the authentic works of Geber, while they do show Chinese influence in their concept of sulphur and mercury as processes rather than substances, are metallurgical rather than medical. It may be that there was a direct influence via the Franciscan mission on the northern land route. The partial reception of alchemy in Europe was the more remarkable in that it ran counter to the development of positivistic science set off by the reception of clockwork. The resulting rivalry between alchemists and physicists, the images of the laboratory and the clock, was not to be resolved until the seventeenth century.

On the practical level, the chief ideas which travelled from East to West in the middle ages were the outlines at least of three institutions. First, implicit in the *Il Milione*, particularly in the famous descriptions of Quinsai and Zayton, is the notion of the royal *emporium*: the market town enlarged to the scale of a territorial state by princely patronage. With the exception of Ptolemaic Alexandria, the cities of Graeco–Roman antiquity had not been *emporia*. With the exception of pre-Comnenian Constantinople, the *emporia* of medieval Christendom had not been enlarged to the scale of a territorial state, but remained in the form of the classical city state. The sixteenth century, *per contra*, was an age of royal *emporia*: Antwerp, Seville, Lyon, the city of London, Leghorn. Amsterdam was exceptional in retaining the medieval city state form. Between the middle ages and the Renaissance had come the revelation of Quinsai and Zayton.

Second, although, in general, fourteenth-century Europe was not ready for the social technology of Chinese bureaucracy, it is possible that the development of government salt monopolies owed something to Chinese example. Thus there was a major reorganization and intensification of the Venetian salt monopoly in the interests of the merchant patriciate at the end of the thirteenth century. Again it seems too much of a coincidence that the reigns of King Charles I (1246–85) and King Robert (1309–43), the organizers of the Provençal gabelle – the Rhone salt division, the prototype for the rest of France – should come just as Europe was learning about the Chinese salt monopoly from Marco Polo and others. Limited local taxes on salt had existed in antiquity and in the earlier middle ages, but Provence–Sicily was the first large state to try to base its finances on them. Similarly the new Venetian organization was the first attempt in the West to make salt a basic component in a complex trading system.

Third, that Mamluk Egypt, unlike other parts of Turkish Islam, was able to withstand the Mongolian onslaught was due to its adoption of elements of the East Asian *ordo*. Although the Mamluks were neither nomads nor light cavalrymen, they adopted the bureaucratic organization of Chinggis Khan's *Yasa* as the basis of their state. This gave it solidity which allowed it to compete with the true *ordo* state of the Il-Khanate. Early Ottoman organization too was really a fusion of the *ordo* and the dervish underground resistance to it: nomad organization, sedentary ideology. Thus major economic, fiscal and political institutions of the post-Mongolian West had remote East Asian origins.

In retrospect, Europe's borrowings from China in the fourteenth century form a coherent whole. The first, plague, precipitated or at least intensified, the most acute general crisis since the end of late antiquity. At one level Latin Christendom reacted pathologically – pogroms, flagellants, *Fraticelli*, the Hundred Years War, civil war in England and Castile, social war in the free cities – but at another, with rationality. This rationality expressed itself in the new interest in education by people such as William of Wykeham and Gerson; in the restructuring of the family through late marriage and emphasis on conjugality; in the shift in diet to protein and in consumption generally to luxury. It also expressed itself in the things borrowed from China: luxuries like the sweet orange, varied silks, more spices, a constellation of technologies which foreshadowed revolutions in nautics, metallurgy, textiles, war and thought; a new vision of the future and an institution for fiscal mobilization. The fourteenth century was a Phase B in Francois Simiand's sense: a century of contraction – economic depression, political breakdown, intellectual oversight – on the surface; but underneath a renewing of capital for further expansion. Because it needed in part to borrow this capital, the fourteenth century, like the seventeenth though in a smaller compass, was an age of Sinophilia. More Europeans than ever before went to China and most of them, like Columbus, came back.

WORLD INSTITUTIONS, 1000 to 1350

If the middle ages marked a decisive stage in the development of Western Europe, the future centre of the modern world system, they were also highly significant in the development of the world institutions of which that system was to be composed. To indicate this significance the argument must be recapitulated and the notions of world institutions and world system developed.

The subject of this book is not merely China's horizontal relations with the outside world in the sense of other parts of the globe, the three other primary civilizations. It is also about China's vertical relation with the outside world in the sense of a superordinate set of factors operative in the world as a whole: world institutions. These institutions, if a mere aggregate, can be called a world network, but, if organized by a centre or centres, become a world system. On the one hand, there is a world of parts, a geosphere *des patries* of which China is one; on the other, there is the world as a whole, a geosphere *communitaire* which affects China and to which China contributes.

Since mankind has always been shaped by superordinate factors, one may speak of a prehistoric world network. Some such factors were physical: the planetary preconditions for life in general and human life in particular. Some were somatic: the biological characteristics which make *Homo sapiens* a single species and the genetic code which maintains them, the inborn cerebral aptitude for speech in particular. Others were psychological: the supposed universality of the Oedipus complex, the compensatory will to power, the individuation process, the *eros* of *logos*. Others again belonged to Karl Popper's World 3: language itself as opposed to somatic dispositions or words; Chomsky's linguistic constants, at least half a million years old; Lévi-Strauss' *mythologiques* probably as old as human occupation of America 30 000 years ago; the eotechnics of palaeolithic man, notably fire, cooking and housing; the technology of neolithic agriculture, arable and pastoral; the semi-universal spread of elite literacy, which, as Lévi-Strauss argued in *Tristes Tropiques*, did more than anything else to end prehistoric society. Without this enveloping network of superordinate factors, a network because lacking any organizing centre except its own orthogenesis, mankind would not exist. As Teilhard de Chardin put it, 'in each new phase of anthropogenesis, we shall find ourselves faced by the unimaginable reality of collective bonds'.[66]

Below the over-arching set of superordinate factors, there were other factors of diversification which by the time of classical antiquity had produced a maximum of differentiation within the body of mankind. If the physical preconditions for life and human life remained the same for all, biological foundations were diversified by group differentiations of skin pigmentation, blood groupings, possibly intelligence even in some sense, even if mankind never ramified nor developed true subspecies – ultimately, it would seem, because of institutions in Popper's World 3. Psychology, the medium through which World 3 interacts with the physical and somatic world shows little group diversification. Jung toyed with the notion of a differential racial psychology, an ethno-psychology as he called it, much to the scandal of *bien-pensants* who accused him of anti-semitism (an entirely unjust accusation as his letters from wartime Switzerland make clear), but though he retained its theoretical possibility he abandoned it as a practicable research programme.

Nevertheless, although the World 3 factors maintained human unity and prevented the ramification of *Homo sapiens* into subspecies, they were also the cause of considerable diversity within the prehistoric world network. Thus there was the diversity of languages; the linguistic constants were schematized in different ways particularly with respect to sound/sense ratio; the basic myths were put into a variety of codes, culinary, acoustic, astronomical and sexual and grouped round mutually exclusive epics, sacred books and revelations; the palaeolithic eotechnics of fire, cooking and housing were developed in the West from the cave towards the thermally homogeneous stone mansion, in the East from the treehouse towards the thermally heterogeneous wooden pavillion; the deposits of neolithic technology were variously cashed in wheat, millet, maize and yams and in different proportions of arable and pastoral; literacy dichotomized literate and non-literate, alphabetical and non-alphabetical. Human unity became the diversity of the four primary civilizations.

From classical antiquity, however, diversification was balanced by the development of a new set of world institutions which eventually became an organized totality, the modern world system as opposed to the prehistoric world network. The first two such institutions, perhaps not global in the strict sense but sufficiently far flung to be so regarded, were the Buddhist international and the T'ang *Weltreich*. Buddhism in its Mahayana form was the first true ecumenical religion. It had substantial communities in both Western Eurasia and East Asia and its missions may have touched both Africa and America. Its teaching of liberation, and liberation from liberation, was for all mankind. Similarly the T'ang court, which absorbed, sublated and emasculated Buddhism under the umbrella of its secular aristocratic culture, operated the first truly cosmopolitan empire. It drew substantial elements of its culture from Iran and India, had definite contact with the East African coast and possibly had resonances in Meso-America. It deliberately played an international role and tried to draw the best from everywhere to itself. However, both the Buddhist international and the T'ang *Weltreich* were ephermeral as world institutions. Both were victims of triumphant parochial orthodoxies. Both were repudiated by their provincial societies which espoused those orthodoxies. In 1000 AD the world seemed as divided as in 500 BC, the more so for the failure of two ecumenisms.

The significance of the middle ages in the history of the modern world system was that two world institutions, the microbian common market, as Emmanuel Le Roy Ladurie has called it, and the integration of geographical information, came into existence and remained permanent. In the formation of both these institutions, China played a key role. China's northern backyard was the source of plague, the principal factor in internationalizing disease and measures to combat it. China itself was the principal item of geographical knowledge which the West had to integrate in order to form a true geography. Moreover, in the event which initiated the convergence of histories by the unification of pathology and geography, the Mongolian explosion, China also played a crucial part as both starting point and finishing point. China was the axis of world history in the middle ages.

The history of plague in the West has already been outlined. It remains to consider its travels in other directions and its role in world history.

As a permanent guest of the tarbagans of Lake Baikal, *Yersinia pestis* was already a citizen of East Asia and did not need naturalization. However, in antiquity and late antiquity there were few signs of plague, bubonic or pneumonic in China proper. The middle kingdom was too well insulated by the aridity of the Gobi, the infrequency of contact across it and the aversion of fleas for horses and sheep. Did the increase in contact with the tarbagan areas which must have started with the Chin, if not with the Liao, lead to a wider diffusion of plague in China as it did in Central Asia?

Renaissance Europeans such as Mendoza, de Rhodes, Athanasius Kircher and Rodriguez the Interpreter believed that there was no plague in China, indeed regarded this as one of China's privileges, but as their knowledge was largely confined to the coast, their evidence cannot be accepted as conclusive. There is some evidence the other way. First, in the period 1300 to 1400, eleven serious outbreaks of epidemic disease are recorded in China, some of which at least are considered by Needham to have been plague. Second, an infection of plague would be a convenient way of accounting for the fall in Chinese population from as high as 150 million at the height of the Sung to as low as 60 million at the beginning of the Ming: a fall which must otherwise be attributed to the Mongolian explosion itself or attenuated by modifying the maximum and minimum of population to 100 and 80 millions. Third, in the local histories of Lu-an in Shansi and of Tientsin, under the date 1644, there are references to what certainly seems to be bubonic plague in the first case and pneumonic plague in the second. If there was plague then, there may have been earlier, for example in the massive and lethal epidemics of the 1580s. However, the Tientsin gazetteer refers to the 'peep sickness' (people died just from taking a peep at the sick – an all too accurate account of the contagion of pneumonic plague) as 'a strange disease' and 1644, of course, saw a new and unique link with Manchuria.[67] Chinese doctors were not as familiar with plague as their European *confrères*. The safest judgement must be that while the Mongolian explosion, possibly earlier and certainly later irruptions, may have diffused plague more widely in China, it did not do so to the same extent as in Western Eurasia. Early modern China was not under the shadow of the Black Death as Europe was.

As regards America, the usual date for the arrival of rats and plague is 1544–46, but if there is anything in the theory that the collapse of the Viking western settlement in Greenland was due to plague brought from Bergen, the disease may have been transmitted to the Eskimos and Indians of the mainland in the fourteenth century too. In Africa, the history of plague is even more obscure. Since it was there in East Africa when the Europeans arrived, it was probably brought there by the Arab navigators to the Zanj coast, Basra being a likely diffusion point south from the Near Eastern reservoir as Smyrna was to the west. It was from the Zanj coast that the modern reservoirs of the Great Lakes and Madagascar will have been established. Another point of diffusion, which produced the reservoirs of southern Tunisia and Mauritania was the Maghreb, Tlemcen in particular, which was seriously affected by plague in the fourteenth and fifteenth centuries. In both diffusions, the *haj* will have played a part, as it has continued to do until a recent date, and Biraben notes a plague reservoir just south of the Holy Cities. However, because of climatic and hygienic conditions, aridity

Sahara, nakedness south of it, none of these areas was as seriously affected as Latin Christendom. Slavonic Christendom, too, suffered less severely and this was one reason for the shift in the balance of power within Europe from west to east in the later middle ages.

Plague, the first element in the modern medical world, was an ecological disaster of the first magnitude. Biraben calculates that between 1350 and 1650 the effect of plague in Barcelona was to raise the death rate by 50 per cent from 40 per thousand to 60 per thousand. This may have been an extreme case, as the Catalans were in unusually close touch with the Levant, but in London between 1601 and 1680 plague deaths amounted to 17 per cent of the total and before 1630 to 23 per cent. More lethal in town than country, plague was a heavy drag on urban growth, especially as it struck particularly at women and children: presumably because they spent more time indoors in contact with each other and with the domestic rat population. While one should not regard the plague centuries as a period of unmitigated gloom, nor ascribe all the intellectual pessimisms of the day to its influence (any more than, later, to the sixteenth-century aggravation of syphilis), there can be no doubt that plague was a serious brake on the progress of civilization.

Yet not all effects of the plague were negative. First, the struggle against it by quarantine, conducted in Europe municipally in the fifteenth century, regionally in the sixteenth, nationally in the seventeenth century, led to international cooperation in preventive medicine. Quarantine was the basis of modern world health organizations. Another line of defence was isolation of infected areas, first successfully operated on an international scale against the Marseille oubreak of 1720. The struggle against plague also produced the first modern statistics. The eventually successful campaign against plague was an advertisement for practical reason, an ingredient in the propaganda of the Enlightenment, a boost for rationality.

Second, plague changed mentalities. In Europe, because of the sexist and ageist incidence of plague deaths, it was a factor in the valorization of women and children from the fourteenth century onwards which in turn revolutionized the family, education and rates of literacy. Europe was seized by panic at the loss of its womenfolk and the massacre of its innocents. In China, less severely affected, it was a factor in the valorization of natality – more children and younger marriage – which, while it may in the long run have had deleterious effects on Chinese civilization, was the basis for the achievements of the Ming and Ch'ing.

Third, it has been suggested that the disappearance of leprosy from Europe in the fourteenth and fifteenth century may have been connected with plague. There appears to be a three-cornered relationship of affinity, antagonism and immunity between the bacilli of leprosy, plague and tuberculosis, what the Chinese would have called a 'mutual conquest' (*hsiang-sheng*) order, so that in Europe there were successive ages of leprosy, plague and tuberculosis. In China, leprosy never reached the epidemic proportions it did in Europe (where leprosy prompted the first systematic establishment of hospitals by St Basil the Great), perhaps because of the earlier use of chaulmoogra oil; but tuberculosis was earlier established, possibly because of more massive towns and poorer housing. The history of tuberculosis in China, which goes back at least as far as the writings of Ko Hung in the fourth century AD, may prove the explanation of the limited history of plague there.

An integration of geographical information took place in both Europe and East Asia. It gave scholars, at least, for the first time a factual vision of the world as a whole.

On the one hand, Europeans now knew much about China if only they could bring themselves to believe it. They knew a little about Black Africa. They even knew something about America in the sense of Atlantic islands and land to the southwest of Greenland. The *Catalan Atlas* of 1375, prepared for Charles V of France by the Majorcan Jew Abraham Cresques, presents, thanks to the integration of the information of Marco Polo and his successors, an immense advance over any previous European map of East Asia. The French cardinal Pierre d' Ailly (1350–1420) in his influential *Imago Mundi* (a significant title) accepted the habitability of the tropic zones (a belief for which Pietro d'Abano in the early fourteenth century had already adduced Marco Polo's evidence), rejected (presumably on Moslem though possibly on Chinese information) the Indian Ocean as *mare clausum*, and suggested the feasibility (because of improvements in navigation largely of Chinese origin) of sailing west to reach India across the ocean.

On the other hand, the widening of East Asian horizons is revealed in the Korean world map of Yi Hoe and Kwon Kun of 1402, the *Hon-li Kangni Yoktae Kukto chi To* (Map of the Territories of the One World and the Capitals of the Countries in Successive Ages). As Needham says, 'one is astonished to see a very recognizable outline of the Mediterranean, with the Italian and Greek peninsulas, Sicily, Sardinia, the coasts of Palestine and Spain and a pagoda marking the position of the Pharos of Alexandria (A-la-sai-i) in the land of al-Misr (Mi-ssu, Egypt).'[68] Even more astonishing is the presence of the Chi-shan islands off the coast of Spain, which can only be the Azores, known to Europeans, as were the Canaries and Madeira, only since the middle of the fourteenth century. Thus East Asia was aware of European tentatives in the direction of America just as Marco Polo repeated Qubilai's propaganda for the conquest of Japan. The difference between East and West was not in the level of geographical information or the degree of its integration. It was in the use to which it was put. China, after a brief flurry of *weltpolitik* with the expeditions of Cheng Ho in the early Ming, settled back into myopic, solipsistic sinocentrism. Europe in the person of Christopher Columbus, in a paroxysm of Franciscan utopianism, set out for Cipangu and the land of the Great Khan. China was still in the mainstream of history, but it was now a passive axis rather than an active centre.

4 World Horizon: China in the Renaissance, 1350 to 1650

For a history of China focused on Chinese relations with the outside world, the age of the Renaissance must hold a position of exceptional importance. If the modern world system was born in the middle ages with the mutation of Latin Christendom, the Mongolian explosion and the unification of information and disease, it began to walk, indeed leap forward, with the oceanic revolution, the Iberian empires and the first sustained extra-European missionary activity. It is arguable that before Columbus, Magellan and St Francis Xavier, there was no true world history. Philip II was the first planetary ruler in the sense of possessing lands in all four primary civilizations: Europe and America, the Far East and Black Africa. His was the first empire on which the sun never set: he was the true *roi soleil* of the Egyptomanes. From the sixteenth century there was little doubt that there was going to be a world system or that Western Europe was going to be its centre, as new world institutions, of which the two first were the Atlantic economy of Seville and the Jesuit international, were cantilevered out from it.

In this world-building, the role of China under the Ming dynasty 1368–1644 was as a horizon, neither inside nor out. After an attempt by the early Ming to dominate the environment both by land and sea, the middle Ming opted out of it and withdrew within their frontiers. For most of the Renaissance, China was a world in itself, a monad as far as possible windowless. Yet if the Chinese, except for an elite, were not interested in the outside world, the outside world was certainly interested in China. It was to Cathay that Columbus sailed, the principal result of Magellan's voyage was the Sino–Spanish colony of Manila, and the China mission was the glory of the Jesuits. If mainland China's contact with the world being built by Europe was marginal, margins can domi-

173

nate and even distant horizons frame. Nominally a closed country, with an even more closed Confucian mind, China under the Ming was losing her autonomy and becoming dependent on a world system not of her making. By the middle of the seventeenth century, the Chinese economy was ebbing with the tide of the Atlantic, Chinese diplomacy and Chinese artillery were dependent on Jesuit expertise, and a Chinese emperor was about to study Euclid's *Elements*.

CHINA'S PLACE IN THE WORLD, 1350 to 1650

In the second half of the sixteenth century, four empires reached their apogee: the Ming under the Wan-li emperor (1573–1620) during the ministry of Chang Chü-cheng (1573–82); the Moghul, better described as later Timurid, under Akbar (1556–1605) during the ministry of Raja Todar Mal (1562–86); the Ottoman under Selim II (1566–74) during the ministry of Sokollu Mehmet Pasha (1565–79); and the Habsburg under Philip II (1556–98) during the ministry of Cardinal Granvelle (1579–86). This coincidence of imperial apogees and *ministériats* was not merely fortuitous. It was orchestrated by the common prosperity brought about by the second and greater expansionary period of the Atlantic economy of Seville. Yet behind the single rhythm were different local scores: the Ming restoration, the Islamic revival and the Christian Renaissance; and the parts in the concord were far from identical.

The Ming resoration

The Ming dynasty dated its accession to 1368 when Toghon Temür, the Yüan emperor who had received Marignolli, fled from Peking to Jehol. The fall of the Mongol *ordo* state had taken twenty years of blood and confusion. So long as the emperor maintained the masterful prime minister Toghto in office (1349–54), it did not look inevitable, despite a hydra-like undercrust of revolt in the semi-urban half-moon from Shantung to Chekiang circling the tax base of the empire, the lower Yangtze conurbation.[1]

By the middle of the fourteenth century, the Yüan empire had lost all connection with the steppe. The army was now composed of heavy Alan cavalry and the bureaucracy was heavily Confucianized. The regime was accepted by the leading classes of Chinese society: by the meritocracy because of the revival of the state examinations; by the non-scholar land-owners because of a fiscality of indirect taxation which spared them; and by the merchants because of their partnership in the state monopolies through which that fiscality operated. But if the classes accepted the Yüan the masses did not, the small towns in particular. The Mongol regime was the most expensive in Chinese history before the communists. Its revenue of maybe 300 million taels absorbed a third or a half of the gross national product. Its principal method of raising it, the salt monopoly, was regressive in its incidence and bore particularly heavily on hinterland market towns like Feng-yang the home of Chu Yüan-chang. In its origins, the revolt against the Mongol was a generalized anti-gabelle riot. Based on heterodox cults, *mafias*, smugglers and pirates, it developed to become a social as much as a political war in which the Mongols, so long as they looked like winning, were supported by the Chinese upper classes of the big cities. The Yüan government, however, was faction ridden: the Catholic Alans, we have seen, constituted one of these. After Toghto, the leader of the strongest faction which united Merkit aristocrats and Kiangsi meritocrats, fell from power in 1354, the regime degenerated into a typically late dynastic congerie of courtiers and *condottieri*, susceptible of dissolution by the rebels through divisive diplomacy and selective assault.

Chu Yüan-chang, the founder, as the Hung-wu emperor, of the Ming dynasty, was originally only one out of a number of claimants to power, a less likely man apparently than Chang Shih-ch'eng the Yangtze delta salt smuggler, Fang Kuo-chang the east Chekiang pirate, or Ch'en Yu-liang the Hu-kuang yamen clerk. He began as a wandering religious associated with several heterodox sects, and the name he chose for his dynasty, Ming, meaning light or enlightenment, mixed Manichaean connotations with Maitreyan millenarianism. From heterodox religious, it was an easy step to *mafia* boss and from there to guerrilla chief, social revolutionary and regional power-holder.

Chu owed his success superficially to his greater ability than his rivals to make the transition from primitive rebel to dynastic challenger, by incorporating enough educated personnel into his machine to give it organizational power without thereby losing popular support; more profoundly, since this is simply the formula for success in China, to the location of his base which gave him strategic advantages in applying it. Chu's headquarters was at Nanking, the naval hinge between the delta and the middle river and his patch was Anhwei and Kiangsi, the first semi-rural provinces beyond the heavily urbanized region of Kiangsu. As a river-and-lake lord, he was strategically placed to move freely against either the warlords to the west or the sealords to the east. Chu's success came in two moments: first, his naval victory over Ch'en Yu-liang in the battle for the Po-yang lake in the autumn of 1363, which by eliminating his enemies upstream enabled him to concentrate in 1366 on Chang Shih-ch'eng downstream; second, his diplomatic victory over the Yüan court by the schism he provoked between it and the leading *condottiere* of the north, Kökö Temür, which allowed him to take Peking in September 1368.

As it developed after 1368, the Ming empire was the product of two forces, the one gradually overtaking the other. On the one hand, there was the Ming state, authoritarian, populist, anti-capitalist and expansionist. Although Hung-wu proclaimed a restoration of traditional China after the Mongol interlude, neither he nor his dynasty ever lost entirely their radical un-Confucian antecedents. In their eyes the revolutions had been against not only the Mongol conquest, but also the corrupt southern Sung society which had led to it. Indeed, as time went on, the Ming shed their anti-Mongol animosities and saw themselves as the heirs of the Yüan within China and beyond. Even after he was established as legitimate emperor and had proscribed the heterodox sect from which he had started, Hung-wu disliked and distrusted the oligarchy of the delta conurbation, the base of the southern Sung and later of his rival Chang Shih-ch'eng. He placed his capital not at Hangchow or Soochow, bourgeois consumer cities, but at Nanking, an artificial dockyard town, and his son, the Yung-lo emperor, removed it from the Yangtze altogether to the half-barbarian military headquarters of the north, Peking.

Suspicion of the ruling class led to greater autocracy in the ruler and greater democratization of the civil service. In 1380 the office of the prime minister, which had been a centre of bureaucratic influence and a curb on the whims of the emperor, was abolished. Henceforward Hung-wu and his successors ruled through personal aides and palace eunuchs without organic connection with the bureaucracy. In his later years, Hung-wu was a veritable Stalin, cruel, suspicious and arbitrary. Great officers of state were publicly beaten in court or privately tortured to death. Yet there was method in this madness. Hung-wu realized that he could not change the basic class structure in China. He had to rule through the privileged educated elite. But he could ensure that this elite was not a closed oligarchy, that the career of mandarin was really open to the talents. Ho Ping-ti has shown that the early Ming was the era when the Chinese bureaucracy was most open and least oligarchic. Between 1368 and 1496 over half the degree-holders came from families without previous record of elite membership. With state schools in every magistracy, China was given an educational system which would have made every humanist in Europe envious.

Anti-oligarchic, Hung-wu was also anti-capitalist. Fiscality, at least halved to at most 100 million taels, was settled on the land rather than trade, and the salt monopoly, much curtailed, was tied to an uneconomic but convenient system of supplying grain to the northern military frontier. Much of the government's needs were supplied by command rather than the market. The population was conscripted into a triple caste system of peasants, artisans and soldiers under the ministries of finance, works and war, corresponding geographically to the countryside, the capitals and the frontier. The early Ming corporate state was economically active: millions of trees were planted, the grand canal was constructed, new cities were jerry-built. From this base, for a hundred years, the Ming emperors pursued an active, Yüan-like, foreign policy, sending armies to Lake Baikal, fleets to the Indian Ocean and ambassadors to Kyoto, Lhasa and Herat. China would once more be the centre of the world, as under the T'ang.

On the other hand, there was Ming society, anti-authoritarian, oligarchic, capitalist and pacifist; nostalgic for the halcyon days of the southern Sung. In the last resort Hung-wu and Yung-lo failed to impose their revolutionary vision. The underlying current of Chinese society, fed by so many institutions, was too strong for them. All they could do was to deflect it into alien channels. By the late sixteenth century, instead of autocracy and the career open to the talents, there was constitutionalism and increasing oligarchy; instead of a planned economy, vigorous capitalism; instead of aggressive, confident expansion, defensive, pusillanimous appeasement.

These changes came about by drift rather than decision, though the ministers who adjusted to it, the Yangs in the 1430s, Yen Sung in the middle of the sixteenth century, Chang Chü-cheng towards the end of it, were conscious midwives. In government, Hung-wu's personal aides turned into the grand secretaries (*ta-hsüeh shih*), permanent heads of a government office, the *nei-ko*, which went out of court to become the chief department of state. The palace eunuchs, the other agency of despotism, survived in situ, proliferating as a Gestapo without a Führer, a KGB without a Stalin, but in the process bureaucratized to become a counter civil service with a vested interest of its own with which deals could be struck. The censorate, originally a thought police, was captured by the bureaucracy and became a carping, impracticable, but negatively effective, organ of Confucian consensus. In society, the marginal advantages under conditions of intense educational competition of tutors, private libraries, family motivation and exclusive colleges allowed the Kiangsu-Chekiang oligarchy to manipulate the examination system so that, in the sixteenth century, the percentage of new families entering the elite by its means fell to below 25 per cent. By the seventeenth century, the liberal arts colleges, the *shu-yüan*, were claiming a constitutional right to advise the emperor, like that of the *parlements* in France and a kind of magistrates' freehold was being advocated.

In the economy the straitjacket of the corporate state only held for a few generations. Salt escaped from the trammels of the frontier grain system and by the end of the dynasty the government was forced to take the merchants back into more equal partnership. The land tax was, in effect, frozen and an unwise attempt to unfreeze it was a factor in the final alienation of public opinion from the dynasty. In foreign policy, naval aggression was abandoned in the 1430s, military aggression in the 1450s, and in the 1560s a military defence was given up in favour of diplomatic appeasement. When at the end of the century, in response to severe external threats, the dynasty remobilized, the resulting financial crisis was a factor in its demise. At every level the Ming state was thwarted by Ming society. Yet because the state continued to rule, society was fixated in sterile oppositionism, and the springs of Chinese creativity, already choked and desiccated in the transition from T'ang to Sung, were further dammed.

The Islamic revival

The world of Islam was the worst sufferer from the Mongolian explosion. Its Turkish leadership, its knightly armies, its half-nomadized political structures, its divided societies, had all been revealed as inadequate. Its central spiritual institution, the orthodox caliphate, had been destroyed. So had its central heterodox institution, the order of the Assassins. Three of its homelands, Transoxania, Persia and Mesopotamia, had been conquered and devastated, their ruling classes compelled to collaborate with non-Moslem regimes. In Anatolia, Syria and Egypt, long-suppressed Christian minorities only awaited the appearance of the Mongols to revolt. Despite Juvaini's special pleading, it was hard to see the hand of Allah in the Mongols. On top came the Black Death, less serious than in Europe but worse than in China. To these challenges Islam responded with remarkable vigour. The Christians were repressed, the conquerors were converted, the caliphate was re-established first in Cairo then in Constantinople, fresh styles of warfare were developed, new political institutions were borrowed from the enemy, and a more cohesive society was constituted. By the sixteenth century, the world of Islam re-emerged, larger, more aggressive and more alive culturally. The revival was based on two institutions: court renaissances and dervish reformations. In the west they combined to produce the Ottoman empire. In the east they conflicted to produce the history of the Timurids, first in Central Asia, then in India.[2]

The dervish orders or *tariqats*, existed before the Mongolian explosion. A cross between a Catholic order and a Free

Church denomination, they were based on a holy man *(pir)*, his disciples *(murid)*, lay associates and a special devotion *(dhikr)*. Within the legalistic community of Islam, they offered a more interior, experimental and personal religion and a quietistic refuge for fugitives from more explicitly anti-establishment movements, Mutazilite, Sufi and Shiite. Already, from the twelth century, dervishes, always strongly proselytizing, played a part in the Turkish conquest of Anatolia. It was, however, the Mongolian explosion which made the dervish orders the backbone of Islamic society. When Islamic governments were shattered, the caliphate destroyed, the leaders of the community forced into collaboration with predatory, half-infidel regimes, the dervish orders picked up the pieces. They reasserted Islamic values, relieved refugees, reactivated mosques, accompanied *hajjis*, established links with the craft guilds and inspired the *sarbadars*, or gibbet men, who resisted Mongol exactions, the *akhis*, or red guards, who went out to convert the infidel, and the *gazis* who went to fight him. As peace returned, as the *sarbadars*, *akhis* and *gazis* became valued allies in in-fighting, the orders acquired political influence, religious foundations *(waqf)* endowed with inalienable property and, through the *haj*, an interest in long-distance trade. From their convents and hospices the dervishes infiltrated the establishment, the *ulema* (law doctors) and *medrese* (higher colleges). By the fifteenth century, everywhere in Islam, the dervishes were a major force in politics and society.

There was, however, a fundamental difference between dervishism in eastern and western Islam. In the occupied east, because the *sadr*, the notables, the leaders of the establishment, had been forced into collaboration with the tolerant and intellectually curious Mongols and Islam itself was in danger, the dervish orders, the Naqshbandiyya among the sedentarists, the Yassawiyya among the nomads, were orthodox, conservative intellectually, rigorist and clerical, hostile to the secular poetry, painting, philosophy and science patronized by the *sadr* and their princes. In the unoccupied west, *per contra*, in Anatolia, Syria and Egypt where the infidel was a threat rather than a reality, it was the *sadr* who were orthodox, conservative, rigorist and clerical, and the dervishes, notably the Mevleviyya and the Bektashiyya, who were heterodox, liberal, anti-nomian and anti-clerical. This difference shaped the history of the Timurids and the Ottomans.

The Timurids, the civilized, pacific, successors of Tamerlane, sought to rationalize his robber empire by commercial diplomacy and cultural glamour. Their courts with their scriptoria, libraries, observatories, collections of porcelain, their imported astronomers, miniaturists and calligraphers, their resident poets, house philosophers and dynastic historians, were instruments of policy to induce a brain-drain to give them an Islamic monopoly of intelligence and talent. These Renaissance courts, of Shah Rukh and Husayn Baiqara in Herat, Ulugh-beg in Samarkand, Iskandar in Shiraz, were modelled on the ideal chivalresque society of the *Shahnameh*, itself a souvenir of the court of Chosroes Parwiz. They were disapproved of by the eastern dervishes for their cost, elitism, doubtful orthodoxy and secularity. Their opposition, muted at first because they preferred Tamerlane to his less-Islamized rivals, increased in virulence until, in the second half of the fifteenth century in the days of Khoja Ahrar, the Naqshbandi John Knox, the Timurids were faced with the alternatives of either becoming the puppets of the dervishes or abandoning Central Asia altogether to those who would. After some hesitation and much humiliation at the hands of Ahrar and his successors, the Timurids in the person of Babur gave up the struggle and moved their essentially transplantable system to India where, in a partly non-Islamic environment they might hope to be more successful.

In India the Moghul empire retained Timurid features: huge mobile camps, splendid but ephemeral palace cities, lavish cultural patronage. Even Akbar's *Din Illahi*, the imperial syncretism which has given rise to so much controversy, was really only the Timurid house religion run to seed in a hot climate. Yet even in India the Timurids could not escape the dervishes. A branch of the Naqshbandiyya, the disciples of Mawlana Khwajagi Amgangi, established themselves and became the cutting edge of Islam. Heads of a nominally-Moslem government, the Moghuls could not dispense with the Islamic proletariat and its dervish recruiting sergeants and were condemned to oscillate between defiance and capitulation, tolerant Akbar and Aurangzeb, the grim puritan fanatic of the next century, representing the two extremes.

The Ottomans played from the opposite position in a different game. They began, not as a renaissance court, but as the secular arm of a reformation. The reformation was that of the Mevleviyya and the Bektashiyya, the dervishes of the Anatolian and later Balkan religious frontier, the first small-town, the second rural, but both anti-dogmatic, syncretistic, mystical, evangelizing. The Ottomans organized from below a dervish party state complete with storm troops and cadres. They recruited from those dissatisfied with orthodoxies and oligarchies, Christian and Moslem, in particular the Bogomils of Bulgaria and Bosnia. The early Ottoman empire, like the Ming, was a meritocracy, an opportunity state. Its first capitals, Bursa and Adrianople, were not court cities like Samarkand and Herat, but military headquarters, temporary safehouses, like Alamut of the Assassins, or Yenan of the Chinese communists. The move to Constantinople, however, though at the time of its conquest no more than a grass-grown city state garrisoned by *condottieri*, brought changes. The Ottomans were now at the head of an empire and a more imperial ideology was needed. Having considered, so it is said, eastern orthodox Christianity, the Ottomans plumped for Timurid court culture, which was acceptable to their kind of dervish. A lavish building programme, financed by the surplus revenues of Egypt, transformed Constantinople into a super Samarkand, a huge collection of porcelain was accumulated, the astronomer Ali Kuşçu was enticed from the Zarafshan to the Bosphorus, Bellini was summoned to portray Mehmet II as a Renaissance prince, miniaturists were commissioned, Seyh Hamdullar initiated a distinctive Ottoman calligraphy.

Timurid court culture, however, did not last in Constantinople. If the dervishes accepted it, the Hanifite *ulema*, the law doctors, and even more the *softas*, the law students, some of whom belonged to the more fundamentalist Hanbalite school, did not. These canonists gained ever greater influence as the empire bureaucratized, established ever more religious foundations, acquired the orthodox caliphate, became the guardian of the Holy Places, and had to repress Shiite radicalism in eastern Anatolia. Timurid features disappeared. Beyazit II executed Ali Kuşçu's pupil Molla Lufti for polytheism and philosophy; the Galata observatory was destroyed by law students during a plague outbreak; the Seyh-ul-Islam decreed that libraries should not contain books on philosophy, astronomy or history; the *ulema* forbade the study of Persian. The older dervish orders who might have resisted had their links with the craft guilds attenuated and newer orders, such as the Naqshbandiyya from the east, were introduced to reinforce the conservative trend. By a different route the Ottomans reached the same destination as the Timurids under Aurangzeb: wooden orthodoxy maintained by the state. Liberalism, dervish or courtly, had lost; conservatism, canonist or dervish, had won.

The Christian Renaissance

Latin Christendom was spared the Mongolian explosion, but, worse than elsewhere, it suffered from the Black Death and its complications: war, revolution, class conflict, schism. Under these blows the European commonwealth fell to a low ebb. Its presidency, the papacy, dichotomized by its double vocation to *urbs* and *orbs*, split in two. Its three major territorial monarchies, England, France and Castile, the main centres of population, were reduced to aristocratic anarchy by war, foreign or civil. The commercial republics, whose capital financed both papacy and monarchies, were torn apart by the struggle of factions and classes. Yet by the last third of the fifteenth century, the worst was over and a new order was emerging, one segment of which was about to initiate what Pierre Chaunu has called 'L' explosion planetaire de l'Extreme-Occident chrétien'.[3]

The principal agent of this order was a new ruling institution, the Renaissance court, which in a short space of time, 1450 to 1500 rendered antiquated the three political forms of the middle ages, the household (royal or noble), the city state and the ecclesiastical palatinate. The Renaissance courts had three elements of novelty. They were bureaucratic: appointed councils and law, civil or common, replaced hereditary household officers and local custom. They were secular: though cardinals and bishops might be ministers, the rank and file of the administration were lawyers, noblesse de la robe, letrados, arts graduates, lay courtiers. They were large scale: their origin might be territorial, their outcome might be national, but their basis was dynastic and their ambition was imperial – an accumulation of principalities to constitute a new kind of Roman empire. Hitherto, bureaucracy had been clerical, as at Avignon, or if lay, as at Venice, small scale.

Secular territorial monarchy had not been bureaucratic. The limiting factor had been finance: how were officials to be paid? The basis of the Renaissance court was the earlier, papal discovery that bureaucracy could be made to pay for itself through its customers: by fees, commissions, presents, sweeteners and bribes. Thus, established officials could collect or at least farm taxes. Taxes could be used to hire more mercenaries, equip better artillery, fight longer wars than households, city states and palatinates could afford. Conquest or the end of internal franchises meant more customers for the bureaucracy, more taxes, further conquests, fewer franchises. An accelerating cycle of power extracting wealth supporting power was established and the Renaissance court could head towards its imperial ambitions limited only by its rivals, dynastic accident, and the capacity and willingness of the country to pay.

For beyond the court was the country. If the court had echoes of classical antiquity, China or even of the Timurids, the country was irreducibly European and medieval. Its institutions were those of the medieval milieu which the court subsumed but did not destroy. Indeed, it itself was shot through with aristocratic values, assumptions and ambitions. No Renaissance prince was as despotic as the Sultan or the Great Moghul: no Renaissance bureaucracy was as unchallenged from society as the Ming mandarinate or the Ottoman meritocracy. Beyond the court were institutions with lives of their own: parliaments, law courts, quarter-sessions, universities, inns of court; duchies, counties, manors, latifundia, *gutsherrschaften*; chartered municipalities, city companies, *consulados*, charitable trusts; abbeys, convents and confraternities – a largely private world of an institutional wealth and articulation unparalleled elsewhere. Though it resented the cost, complained of the methods and queried the centralization, the country was not in principle opposed to the court. On the contrary it owed its articulation in part to it. But on two occasions, crucial for European history, with tensions heightened by economic contraction, the country did strike at the court.

The first was the reformation in the mid-sixteenth century depression when a religious elite attacked not only the clerical court of Rome but also the secular courts which supported it. Not the Protestant reformation only, for in the old religion too, besides the anti-reformation of inquisition and index, there was, as Braudel saw, 'ce mouvement de fond, democratique et passioné qui soulevait la Contre-Reforme'.[4] Then, perhaps because the economic contraction was only a pause between two expansions, the conflict remained limited to the religious sphere. All parties except the unmentionable sects proclaimed their loyalty to social order and accused their enemies of endangering it. The second occasion was the great rebellion during the much more serious economic contraction of the seventeenth century. Here a wider range of issues were in dispute though, except at the extremes, both sides assumed an underlying complementarity and did not seek total victory. On both occasions the outcome varied regionally: the church was reformed, the church was not reformed, the church was half reformed; the country won, the court won, there was a compromise. But, except in the deep south where complete non-reformation of the church and complete victory of the court produced stupor and atrophy, the conflict was institutionally fecund: cheaper, more efficient government from the court, greater production and release of wealth from the country, less frictional procedures for adjusting their relationship. The contrast with the institutional arrest of China and Islam was striking.

The empire of Wan-li

With these contours established, we may now look at the China of the Wan-li emperor, its state, society and culture, and see how they stood in relation to the same elements in the empires of Akbar, Selim II and Philip II.

The Ming state under Wan-li had two outstanding characteristics: lightness and introversion. Since its foundation it had been a physiocracy in the sense of being based fiscally on the land. By the late sixteenth century, in the face of society's resistance to its domination, it had become a physiocracy in the sense of a state minimizing its activities. Though naturally the work of time, the single individual most responsible for this system of *laissez-faire* bureaucracy, liberty by negligence, was the grand secretary Chang Chü-cheng, the representative and moulder of a political generation.

Chang sought a midpoint between state and society, palace and bureaucracy; by bureaucratizing the grand secretariat, while maintaining good relations with the eunuchs; and by keeping the censorate and academics on a tight rein, while checking corruption and reducing taxation. In 1400 with a population of, at most, 100 million, the expenditure of the Ming state amounted to 100 million taels. In 1600, with a population of 150 million with a higher per capita income, expenditure had fallen to 50 million taels or less. The corporate state with its castes of soldiers, artisans and peasants was allowed to lapse and the private sector of the economy became larger than the public. China again experimented with capitalism. The corollary of fiscal physiocracy was diplomatic introversion – an isolationism which relied on detente rather than confrontation. Although this stance had been developing since the abandonment of maritime aggression after Cheng Ho's last voyage in 1433, its culmination was the decision by Chang Chü-cheng in 1571 to handle the new Inner Mongolian confederation of Altan Khan by appeasement rather than by force. The army which had earlier risen to over 3 million was reduced to 845 000 effectives and the high seas fleet had long since been allowed to crumble in the Nanking dockyard. The earliest European missionary observers of China agreed on her pacifism, military weakness and the feasibility of her conquest by Spain.[5]

During the Ming period, Chinese society acquired two characteristic features: economy in the use of energy and a family system based on early and almost universal marriage. Like all pre-modern societies, China used five major sources of energy: animals, wood, water, human muscle and wind, in roughly that order of importance. In China animal power had always been relatively less significant since Chinese intensive agriculture did not provide draft animals. Wood, however, was unusually significant because of the preference for it over stone in building and because of the development of shipping. The Sung had been lavish house and ship builders and the early Ming period with its rebuilding of cities and construction of a high seas fleet saw a large consumption of wood. By the middle Ming therefore, there were signs of an incipient timber famine.

This energy crisis was met not by searching out new sources of supply at possibly higher cost, but by a reduction in demand. The fleet was abandoned partly through shortages of masts; after a last paroxysm in the Wan-li reign palace requisitions for wood were drastically reduced; and the salt industry began to shift from wood-based boiling to solar evaporation. Attitudes to energy changed, expectations of consumption fell. Just as the state contracted its demand for taxes, so society contracted its demand for goods. At the same time, a cause perhaps, a significant change took place in the Chinese family system. The age of marriage for boys fell, the percentage of people marrying rose, nuclear families multiplied at the expense of extended families and the birth rate increased. The introduction of American food plants facilitated the provision of new farmlets, but the demand preceded the supply and was rooted in psychological changes: a preference for children over goods, perhaps as insurance against age, a greater push or pull from the family nest. China became increasingly a community of low-energy micro-units, farms and workshops – a pattern which has been regarded as typically Chinese but which in fact dates only from the sixteenth century.[6]

Chinese intellectual life also changed significantly in the sixteenth century. The loss of dynamism produced by the shift from Buddhism to Neo-Confucianism was intensified by the adoption within Confucianism of an inadequate cognitional theory so that the retreat from theory to practice, philosophy to myth accelerated. The person most responsible was the existential moralist Wang Yang-ming (1472–1529), whose views became fashionable around the mid-century during the ministry of Chang Chü-cheng's predecessor and patron Hsü Chieh. Wang initiated an emphasis on practice rather than theory which lasted as long as the empire and influenced the existentialist Marxism of Mao Tse-tung.

Sung Confucianism, the *li-hsüeh*, or school of reason, of Chu Hsi, had already restricted philosophy by abandoning mysticism and playing down cognitional theory. Wang, with the *hsin-hsüeh*, or school of the heart, repudiated discursive reason altogether in favour of intuition. For a trialism of *hsin*, *ch'i* and *li*, mind, matter and intelligibility, which made knowledge, and morality, a gradual process of learning, he substituted a monism of *hsin* which made both an instant commitment confirmed in action. Science and ethics became simply a matter of taking a look. In Wang's case it was an existential look, but the presupposition was taken over by Wang's critics, so that science and ethics became successively taking a historical look in the writings of Huang Tsung-hsi, taking a philological look in the school of Han learning, taking a materialist look in the thought of Wang Fu-chih, taking a sexual look in the thought of Tai Chin, taking a practical look in the *Ching-shih* school of statecraft, taking an esoteric look in the neo-New Text School. All Chinese philosophy after Wang Yang-ming was monist and simplistic. Since *Anschauung* was everything, cognition was a matter of acquiring the right paradigms rather than discovering the best theories; and in Chinese circumstances, the right paradigms were those of Confucian scholarship which became increasingly a self-justifying in-game of the governing class. Wang Yang-ming's particular *eureka*, the self-commiting existential mind, might be repudiated in the political changes at the end of the dynasty, but his heuristic method established itself all too successfully.

The empires of Akbar and Selim II

If the Ming state under Wan-li was light and introverted, the Moghul state was heavy and introverted; and the Ottoman state was light and extraverted.

Government in India was expensive. Todar Mal's land tax was assessed at one third of the average yield, a much higher percentage than attempted by any Chinese government until the communists. Aurangzeb was credited with a revenue at least twice that of his Chinese contemporary from a population smaller and less rich per capita. The main reason for this expense was the size of the army (said to have been over 4 million under Akbar), especially the number of retainers and servants with whom Indian military men felt it necessary to surround themselves. Possibly the use of elephants had something to do with this parade-ground concept of war: Jesuit sources tell us that Akbar maintained 50 000 of the great beasts. Nevertheless, despite this military establishment, the Moghul empire was not aggressive. Until the reign of

Shah Jahan no serious attempt was made to reconquer Central Asia. The conquest of the Deccan proceeded slowly and the Moghuls built no fleet so that coastal India remained independent. The army was really only used for suppressing revolts by sections of itself. The Moghul empire was angled inwards.

The Ottoman empire *per contra* was extraverted. Until the peace of Tsitva Torok in 1606, it never concluded a definite treaty with any of its enemies and was as much a movement as a state. Under the half-Russian Selim II it was angled east rather than west. Sokollu Mehmet, a former grand admiral, planned to project Ottoman naval power into the Caspian and Indian Oceans by Don and Suez canals to by-pass the heretical Safavids and link up with the orthodox Uzbeks, drive back the Russians to the north, the Portuguese to the south, and restore the prosperity of the continental trade routes under Ottoman protection. He did in fact conquer Cyprus to secure his communications with Egypt, reoccupy the Yemen, send a fleet to Sumatra, and commence hostilities against the Sophy in Caucasia, his son occupying Tiflis. Nevertheless, to support these conditions, the Ottomans maintained only a modest military establishment: 200 galleys, 50 000 sailors, 50 000 Janissaries, 100 000 spahis; 50 000 Crimean light horse – a total of a quarter of a million men to fight wars in three continents. Similarly, except in Egypt, Ottoman fiscality was not heavy. At the end of the sixteenth century, 10 million ducats a year were raised from some 20 million people, a rate of taxation half that of the Moghul empire. The reputation of the Ottomans for providing cheap government was a factor in their expansion.

Both Moghul and Ottoman society shared the Ming attitude to energy but diverged from Ming demography. As Maurice Lombard showed, shortage of wood, uncompensated by any other energy source, was a major factor in the early arrest of Islamic civilization. The Ottoman empire possessed in the Balkans the best timber reserves in Islam (reserves which had enabled Byzantium to survive so long), but they were difficult to exploit and their availability for house construction and shipbuilding was limited. Despite the yali along the Bosphorus, under the Ottoman reformation, Islam remained a civilization of scarcity and frugality. Though southern India contained considerable timber reserves, the Indo-Gangetic plain, the seat of the Moghul empire did not, and teak, although used in shipbuilding by the coastal powers, was not traded on a large scale till the nineteenth century. At the Moghul court, Timurid extravagance under Akbar gave way to dervish austerity under Aurangzeb.

Neither Ottoman nor Moghul society followed the Ming pattern of early marriage, high nuptiality, nuclear households and strong natality. Ottoman society was not natalist: polygamy, acceptance of contraception, tolerance of male homosexuality, considerable rural male celibacy, the *devşirme* system and eunuchs all militated against it. Households were nuclear but, as in Europe, marriage was elitist. There were large houses or *konaks* with children and servants, and cottages and crofts without. Moghul society in so far as it was Islamic shared these characteristics, though households were less nuclear and more extended. In so far as it was Hindu, there was early marriage at least for girls and high nuptiality, but unlike China, set in the framework of an extended family system. Natality was strong, but not so strong as in China. Indian agriculture was less affected by American food plants than Chinese, perhaps because the family system had not the same propensity to throw off new units. Indian demography, unlike Chinese, was not revolutionized till the coming of modern medicine under the British.

As under the Ming, so under the Ottomans and Moghuls, imperial greatness was accompanied by cultural decline. Institutionally the agents of that decline in Islam were the canonists in the west and the dervishes in the east. Intellectually, however, the mechanism remains to be explored. In China, Wang Yang-ming's existentialism initiated a flight from method to oracularity. Chinese culture was undermined by an inadequate cognitional theory. In Islam the order of causality was different. There was no revolution in cognitional theory. Indeed the attempt at such by Timurid astronomers and Mevlevi mystics was precisely what dervish and canonist orthodoxy rejected. Under Timurids and Ottomans, the cognitional system of Hanafism – the infallible, inspired Koran interpreted by tradition *(hadith)* and reason as voiced by the law doctors *(ulema)* – continued. This system, with its mixture of scriptural authority and expert interpretation, was not unlike that of European Protestantism, but it differed in the quality of the expertise, i.e. it was culture rather than method which made the difference. Whereas Protestant pundits brought to their scripture all the resources of Erasmian scholarship, the Islamic doctors, deprived of the Timurid Renaissance by dervishes and canonists, brought only traditional exegesis. Method requires a methodist. In China, it was the method which, thanks to Wang Yang-ming, became defective. In Islam, it was the methodist, thanks to his cultural asphyxiation by dervishes and canonists. In itself the Hanafite system was no more to blame for Islam's intellectual regress than Hooker's system should be praised for Anglicanism's intellectual progress. Each was made to work or not work by the level of culture. By the same token, Islam's intellectual malaise was less deep-rooted than China's. It was a disease of the artisan, not of the tool.

The empire of Philip II

Whereas the Ming state under Wan-li was light and introverted, the Habsburg state under Philip II was heavy and extraverted. When bureaucratic monarchy was first developed in Europe in the second half of the fifteenth century by the Dukes of Burgundy, Louis XI, the Catholic kings and Henry VII, its impact on society in terms of money, men and material was limited. This remained true even with the larger and more militarily active courts of Charles V, Francis I and Henry VIII and was the reason Charles V had to peregrinate round his domains raising taxes and supervising mobilizations. Following the state bankruptcies which led to the peace of Cateau-Cambrésis the situation, at least for Spain, changed. Philip II settled at the Escorial and systematically increased his revenues. By the end of his reign he was obtaining nearly 20 million ducats a year, quadruple his father's income, from 14 million Iberians and Italians.

Philip's income was unequally raised. Only two or three million ducats came from America and generally went straight to the Genoese bankers; Portugal, Aragon and the Italian provinces supplied six million, mostly spent for their own purposes; and over half the revenue, and the part immediately applicable to imperial purposes, came from the continental and not very well-endowed kingdom of Castile with a population of 8 million. Successive governments tried to remedy this situation by spreading the load, but the result was the revolt of the Netherlands, the secessions of Portugal and Catalonia, disorders in Naples and Sicily. Philip needed money. Where his father's empire was European, his was planetary. He had to provide an army and a fleet in the Mediterranean, an army in the Netherlands, two fleets in the Atlantic, ships in the Pacific, as well as providing for the Grenada revolt, the French civil war, and the long-delayed crisis in Germany. From the Portuguese crisis and the arrival of Cardinal Granvelle in 1579, the prudent king pursued aggressive policies on all fronts except in the Mediterranean. The result of the policy, continued in the next generation by the Count-Duke Olivares, was the ruin of Castile by fiscal overload. The economies of Burgos, Segovia, Medina del Campo, Seville and Grenada were drained to supply a temporary, unhealthy prosperity to the bureaucratic cities of Valladolid, Salamanca, Madrid and Toledo.

Whereas Chinese society under Wan-li was characterized by economy and early, almost universal marriage, European society under Philip II was characterized by extravagance and late, almost elitist marriage. Visitors to Valladolid, the effective capital of the Spanish empire for much of the sixteenth century, were struck by the standard of living: abundant food, magnificent clothes, rich furnishings, number of servants, frequency of festivals; an aristocratic ostentation which Bartolomé Bennassar calls 'le spectacle permanent'.[7] The sixteenth century was lavish in the use of wood. Jean Delumeau shows that Rome with a population of 100 000 consumed a million cubic metres of wood a year, a tenth of China's whole production in the first half of the twentieth century. Shortages were met, not as in China by restriction of demand, but by expansion of supply: afforestation which changed the characteristic trees of the Valladolid countryside from oaks to firs; imports from the Baltic which in the sixteenth century became what it has remained, Europe's forestry reserve; eventual mobilization of the resources of the Caribbean, New England and the teak forests of Asia. Underlying this extravagance in the use of energy, was a more general consumerist revolution, the spending spree of the Renaissance, which, while ruinous to the overloaded economies of the south, was a major factor in the growth of the European economy as a whole.

It was in the sixteenth century that the European family system – late marriage, high celibacy, nuclear households, flexible natality – rising since the fourteenth century, perhaps originating earlier, finally surfaced. Spain, like most of southern Europe, was tardy and half-hearted in its adoption. However, whereas in China the average age of marriage was late teens for boys early teens for girls, in Valladolid the corresponding figures were 23–25 for boys, 20 for girls. Marriage was a privilege: over half those born died unmarried. The average size of household was small: in the city, even allowing for big houses with servants, not much more than five; in the countryside, four or less. The Chinese family system diffused and dissipated resources. The European family system concentrated and multiplied them. It facilitated education, the accumulation of capital, conjugality rather than filiality, family planning. It made family life a luxury, part of the new consumerism. European society headed towards affluence, Chinese society towards subsistence. In Europe the aristocracy defined the style of life, in China the peasantry.

Whereas Chinese intellectual life retreated from philosophy to myth under the impoverishing influence of a monist cognitional theory, European intellectual life in the sixteenth century advanced from philosophy to science under the enriching influence of a number of new monist cognitional theories. In themselves the cognitional theories current in Renaissance Europe – Scotism, nominalism, humanist philology, Paracelsian alchemy, Galilean numerism, Baconian empiricism, Cartesian dualism – did not provide better models for science than Wang Yan-ming's intuitionism. Indeed they were all basically forms of it: simplifications of the complex process of knowing to a single act.

Yet their effect was different. Negatively, the hard shell of Aristotelian deductivism was broken by Renaissance magic: neo-Platonic, Egyptomane and Paracelsist. Positively, mechanist materialism and mathematicization led to quantitative abstraction, content enrichment, greater testability, the discovery of discovery. By themselves Renaissance cognitional theories might have produced no more than Confucian higher criticism, Taoist proto-science, I-ching numerology.

What made the difference was the starting point, the meta-Aristotelian scholasticism, which, when freed of its deductivist accretions, could be made the foundation of critical science. Just as the Renaissance court did not destroy the medieval country but raised it to a new level institutionally, so the new cognitional theories did not destroy medieval thought but raised it to a new level intellectually. As Karl Popper argues, the inception of science needs both dogma and criticism. Islam had the dogma but, thanks to the dervishes and canonists, no criticism. China had the criticism, but, thanks to the abandonment of Buddhist scholasticism, no dogma. Latin Christendom alone had both and hence made the crucial breakthrough into higher rationality.

China's place in the world changed radically between 1350 and 1650. Compared to the empires of Akbar and Selim II, that of Wan-li still held first place, but compared to the empire of Philip II, its position was more doubtful. Westerners were still impressed by China: the size of cities, the exploitation of water, the productivity of the soil, the refinements of life. But they no longer treated her with the kind of astonished awe Marco Polo had evinced. Still the largest state in population if no longer in area, its society the most literate, its economy still providing the highest per capita income, China's small political head, her proliferating body, the atrophy of her brain, rendered her increasingly dinosaur-like in a world of evolving mammals.

AVENUES OF CONTACT, 1350 TO 1650

In the age of the Renaissance the major innovation in the avenues of contact between China and the outside world was the addition by the Iberians of two new routes: the Cape route and the Pacific route. Next, the Dutch, the supplanters and heirs of the Iberians, gave a new meaning to the far southern sea route. Finally, all routes benefited to greater or less extent from the Iberian creation, in outline at least, of a world economy which by revolutionizing the time perspectives of business, extended the inducement to invest and multiplied the scale of global interchanges.

The central land route

Between 1350 and 1650 the central land route reached its apogee and went into decline. For the apogee, those most responsible were Tamerlane and his successors; for the decline, not, as is often supposed Vasco da Gama, or even, more plausibly, Legazpi and Urdaneta, but the Safavids. That, despite them, the route remained prosperous for so long was due, ultimately, to Columbus, and the Atlantic of Seville.

The Chaghatai khanate in which Tamerlane was born as Temür Barlas was a robber state unsatisfactory alike to sedentarists and nomads. Its military establishment, by the mid-fourteenth century a congerie of Turkish clans of whom the Barlas were one, disrupted oasis trade and steppe pastoralism by requisitions for increasingly unsuccessful looting expeditions against its neighbours and even its own subjects. Clan feuds aggravated by urban protests and nomad secessions fragmented society until in 1370 anarchy was arrested, it was expected temporarily, by a coalition of swordsmen and *sarbadars* led by Temür Barlas. Tamerlane realized that if his regime was to be less ephemeral than those of his predecessors, he must devise a system to satisfy the contradictory demands of the nomads for war, and of the sedentarists for peace. His solution was simple but effective: war abroad, peace at home, with the war serving the peace. Abroad, Tamerlane was a vandal, a destroyer of cities, a scourge of God. Remorseless looting expeditions were directed against the Golden Horde, the Mamluks, the sultanate of Delhi, with the aim of destroying the northern land route and, as far as possible without a navy, the southern sea route too. At the price of a general contraction of activity, trade was recanalized through the central land route to the advantage of the cities of Transoxania. At home, Tamerlane was a Maecenas, finding Samarkand in brick and leaving it in marble, rebuilding bazaars, and establishing welfare mosques to draw the sting of the Sufi orders and urban *mafias*. Conscious of the contradiction and calling himself the Lord of the Favourable Conjuncture, Tamerlane himself remained a nomad but with a portable bath, chess set and a collection of Chinese porcelain.

Tamerlane's success, continued by the Timurids by diplomatic rather than military means, was considerable. Ruy de Clavijo, ambassador of Henry III of Castile, the ruler who occupied Tetuan and supported the colonization of the Canaries, described Tabriz at the end of Tamerlane's wars: 'The city of Tabriz is very rich by reason of the great quantity of merchandise that passes through it every day. They say in former times it was more populous, but even now there are more than two hundred thousand inhabited houses'.[8] Samarkand, though smaller than Tabriz, impressed Clavijo as larger than Seville. Commerce was flourishing and the China trade was the richest. During Clavijo's stay a caravan of 800 camels arrived from Peking. Porcelain was used by the aristocracy who had Zayton silk tents in the camp city. Clavijo names musk, rhubarb and pearls among the imports from China. After Tamerlane's death in 1405, the fluctuations of the route can be inferred from the tribute missions to Peking which were both an occasion for trade and a reflection of it. Between 1405 and 1419 when Shah Rukh and the Yung-lo emperor were negotiating a *modus vivendi*, seven Timurid embassies went to Peking and six Ming embassies went to Samarkand or Herat. After relations had been stabilized on the basis of open trade routes and the sale of large horses to the Chinese, the Ming history noted between 1433 and 1500, embassies from Hami (a rising intermediary) more than every other year, and embassies from Turfan and Samarkand about one year in four. At the other end, the Venetian diplomat Josaphat Barbaro who went to Persia in 1471, noted at Shiraz the large number of merchants going to Samarkand to buy Chinese silks, rhubarb and porcelain.

In the sixteenth century, however, despite the inflation of all economies by the Spanish Atlantic system, activity along the central land route marked time or declined. The imperial statutes *(hui-tien)* of Wan-li of 1587 provided that embassies should come quinquennially from Hami, Turfan, Samarkand, Arabia (probably Syria) and the kingdom of Rum (the Ottoman empire) – in the case of the first three, a lower level of activity than had occurred between 1433 and 1500 – but the embassies actually recorded for the sixteenth century by the Ming history amounted only to Hami nineteen, Turfan twenty-four, Samarkand sixteen, Arabia thirteen, Rum six.

When Anthony Jenkinson visited Bokhara in 1558 as the representative of the Muscovy company, he found the city still an international emporium with traders from India, Persia, Balkh and Russia, but no caravan had come through from China for three years because of the 'incessant and continuall warres' and trade on all routes was much diminished.[9] Jenkinson mentions the wars of the sedentary powers against the nomad Kazakhs and Kirghiz and there were also the campaigns of the khans of Moghulistan against the Uighurs in Hami and western Kansu. But the most potent cause of violence along the central land route was the Safavid reformation which turned Persia into a Shiite stronghold, split orthodox Islam in two and led to repeated wars in the west with the Ottomans, in the east with the Uzbeks, in which the cities and trade of Azerbaijan and Khorasan suffered. 'Little utterance and small profit' was Jenkinson's verdict on the area's potential.[10]

With the universal depression of the seventeenth century the position worsened. Between 1600 and 1643 the embassies recorded by the Chinese were Hami three, Turfan three, Samarkand, Arabia and Rum one each. Bento de Goes who went from India to China via Central Asia between 1602 and 1605 saw only second-class trade. Yet the glory did not entirely depart. Alexandre de Rhodes who visited Tabriz in the late 1640s could still write (and he had spent twelve years in China), 'in all my travels I never saw a city larger, more populous or more mercantile than that one or where anything was cheaper'.[11] The prosperity of Europe injected itself into Asia to some extent.

The southern sea route

The effect of the great discoveries and the establishment of the new Cape and Pacific routes was much greater on the southern sea route. The origin of its decline, however, lay further back. For if the history of the central land route between 1350 and 1650 was dominated by Tamerlane, the history of the southern sea route was dominated by Cheng Ho, the Chinese Moslem eunuch admiral who commanded the six Chinese naval expeditions to the Indian Ocean between 1405 and 1433. Indeed the two histories were linked.

What were the reasons for Cheng Ho's voyages? A primary motive was to keep the southern sea route open and amenable to Chinese influence during the difficult negotiations with Shah Rukh. The Yung-lo emperor was interested in security rather than trade. Until the 1420s he could not be sure that the Timurids might not prove to be new Chinggisids who would compel him to withdraw behind the Yangtze like the southern Sung. That possibility also provided another motive for the voyages. Yung-lo was a usurper. He came to the throne in 1402 after waging from Peking a bitter three-year civil war against the legitimate heir, Hung-wu's grandson, in Nanking. This civil war, an episode in the long Ming conflict between state and society, had left society defeated but unreconciled. Yung-lo knew he was detested by the ruling class of the lower Yangtze. It was important therefore, if the Timurids were going to force a retreat to Nanking – and as former commander in the north Yung-lo was well placed to weigh the possibilities – to root out any legitimism in the overseas Chinese communities built up in the Sung-Yüan period. The ostensible purpose of finding Hung-wu's grandson who had disappeared in the final assault on Nanking concealed the real one of overaweing those communities. Finally, the early Ming state disliked private enterprise and the overseas Chinese communities and their shipping systems had been built up by it outside official channels. A subsidiary purpose of the voyages was thus to reactivate the tribute system, recombine trade and diplomacy and end the anomaly of foreign countries having relations with China through Chinese merchants. Relations with China, too, must as far as possible be *immediatized*, and before the fleets were despatched, missions were sent to all known countries inviting them to enter China's world order by sending tribute.

Cheng Ho's policy, though criticized for its expense by regular officials such as Hsia Yüan-chi, the minister of finance, produced results. A Ming presence was established from Srivijaya to Zanzibar, over thirty new countries were brought into the tribute system, opponents such as the head of an overseas Chinese community and an unfriendly king of Ceylon were extradited, protégés in Malacca and Cochin were confirmed. It was a notable exercise of seapower. Yet with the cessation of the voyages after 1433, as a result of economy, bureaucratic jealousy and a shortage of masts, the number of tribute missions fell to below the pre-1405 level. Ceylon only sent two more missions, in 1445 and 1459; Bengal only one, in 1438. Malacca and Java each sent ten embassies between 1430 and 1481. In the Wan-li *hui-tien*, Malacca having then fallen to the Portuguese, Java was accorded first a three-year, then an indefinite cycle which probably concealed a revival of private Chinese shipping.

By 1500 China's brief Indian Ocean empire was no more. The Venetian Nicolo de Conti who was in India in the 1430s saw Chinese ships and was impressed with their size. Tomé Pires in his *Suma Oriental* of c. 1510 knew of Chinese ships, and of no particular size either, only east of Malacca and they only constituted 10 per cent of the shipping in the port. It is hard to resist the conclusion that the long-term effect of Cheng Ho's voyages was to reduce the Chinese presence along the southern sea route by killing, or at least forcing into smaller dimension, the private enterprise on which it was based. In the late Sung, Chinese shipping was based on joint stock companies *lien-ts'ai ho-pen* and sailed to Malabar; in the late Ming, it was based on simple partnerships and sailed only to Malaya. True, absence of Chinese ships need not mean absence of Chinese goods which were certainly purchasable by Indian merchants at Malacca as well as, though more rarely, direct from China. But with silk now produced in Bengal and Persia, the China trade at Malacca definitely held second place to the spice trade.

The concentration of Chinese trade at Malacca meant that when the Portuguese captured the city in 1511 and diverted its trade to their new Cape route, the southern sea route abruptly ceased being a major avenue of contact between China and the outside world. The capture of Malacca, it is true, did not stop Indian merchants going to China, or prevent them from buying Chinese goods at ports such as Achin and Johore which the Chinese tried to substitute as entrepôts for Malacca, but the scale of operations was reduced. Even areas not directly controlled by the Portuguese suffered their influence. Not long after the Portuguese took Malacca, the king of Pasé in Sumatra offered them his entire silk re-export which had up till then been bought by Gujeratis from Cambay in exchange for cottons. At first the Portuguese encouraged the Chinese to continue coming to Malacca. They wanted Chinese goods for the home trade and also for the country trade in the archipelago in which they soon became involved. With the establishment of Macao in 1557, however, the Portuguese obtained their goods direct. They began to suspect the Chinese of selling to their competitors en route and the junks were discouraged. Malacca therefore ceased to be a major entrepôt for Chinese goods.

In the case of spices, despite their occupation of Ormuz and occasional presence off Socotra, the Portuguese, lacking control of Aden, were unable to destroy the southern sea route which fought back and eventually won, as Braudel showed. In the case of Chinese goods they were more successful, though in the long run the Pacific benefited more than the Cape. The relative prosperity of the central land route was a tribute to their success. Whatever the hazards by land, a load of porcelain might be more likely to reach the West by Samarkand and Tabriz than by Malacca, Ormuz or Aden. Furthermore, rhubarb, the newcomer to the trade, did not travel well by sea and never established itself on the southern sea route. The southern sea route survived but, as regards China, was reduced to second-class traffic in the hands of humbler merchants – Parsees, Armenians and Jews.

The northern land route

If Tamerlane dominated the history of the central land route, and Cheng Ho that of the southern sea route, the history of the northern land route was dominated by Sokollu Mehmet Pasha who made a determined though unavailing attempt to restore its activity.[12]

The northern land route was the greatest sufferer from Tamerlane's systematic, externalized vandalism. He regarded the Golden Horde as his greatest enemy, rightly since not only did it control a route which actively competed with his own but also it represented Chinggisid legitimism and was in a position to destroy him. Tamerlane's campaigns against the Golden Horde are his most interesting militarily as they display the first victories of the revived Iranian heavy cavalry over the light steppe horse of the *ordo* state.[13] The Golden Horde never recovered from Tamerlane. Though the puppet khan Edigü he had installed after the overthrow of Toktamish made himself independent, defeated the Lithuanians and recovered Urgench, the revival was ephemeral.

In the fifteenth century, the Horde fragmented. In the west there were city states: from 1430, the Crimea, originally under Polish protection and, after 1478, a valuable military satellite of the Ottoman empire; from 1440, Kazan, disputed between Crim Tartary and Muscovy; and from 1466, Astrakhan which, to survive Crimean pressure, turned increasingly to Muscovy. In the east there were nomad states: from the late thirteenth century, the Noghais, in the steppe north of the Caucasus, the old lands of the Alans; from 1456, the Kazakhs, often divided into three sub-hordes, Little, Middle and Great from west to east; and from 1470, to the north of them in the Ob-Irtysh valley, the khans of Sibir, cousins of the Shibanids of Uzbekistan. Fragmentation with concomitant war did not make for communication. The Genoese maintained their treaty port of Caffa in the Crimea until 1475 but its trade was purely local. Trebizond at the southern outlet remained a Christian enclave open to Western trade till 1461 but its contacts were now no more than Caucasian. The Ottomans developed the Black Sea via Greek shipowners as a source of grain and slaves for Constantinople and as an avenue for fur imports from Russia, but until the late sixteenth century their vision did not extend beyond the Don. The advance of the Russians down the Volga made things worse and Jenkinson found little trade at Astrakhan and Urgench, the natural stepping stones of the route.

Ottoman lack of interest in the northern land route was not accidental. It was related to the primitive dervish concept of the Ottoman state as a community of *akhis* and *gazis* directed against the infidel in the west rather than against fellow believers in the east. War in Asia was seen as distraction from war in Europe. With the increasing predominance of the canonists over the dervishes in the second half of the sixteenth century, this ideological perspective changed. Just as the Spanish empire in the latter part of the reign of Philip II turned its back on the Mediterranean to fight heretics in a new battle of the Atlantic, so the Ottoman empire in the latter part of the reign of Selim II turned its back on the Mediterranean to fight heretics in a new battle of the continental routes. It was a battle not so much for the sources of wealth, as Braudel thought, as for satellites, legitimacy and the prestige of orthodoxy, though economic interests were not absent in an Islam where the *haj* was a means of profit as well as merit. With this new mood of the empire, which was encouraged by appeals from the Uzbeks, Sokollu Mehmet Pasha, though himself a Bosnian convert, a navalist, a westerner, and a patron of Timurid culture and dervish syncretism, produced his grand design for Suez and Don canals: continental ends by maritime means, a scheme worthy of Mackinder and Mahan.

In this scheme, the northern pincer from Azov via the Don and Astrakhan to the Caspian and the Oxus, which until 1573 still entered the Caspian, had priority. This was the route of the *haj* pilgrimages, organized by the Naqshbandiyya and the Yassawiyya, of the orthodox of Turkestan who could no longer use the central land route because of the Safavid blockade. From the Crimea, the pilgrims went to Sinope and thence via Ankara, Aleppo and Damascus to the Holy Places or to Trebizond and thence via Erzerum, Mosul, Baghdad and Basra.

In 1569–70 the Ottomans made a major effort to recover Astrakhan from the Russians: there was a massive build-up at Azov, Rumanian peasants were conscripted for earth works, one third of the Don–Volga canal was built; and in 1588 a second offensive was seriously considered. On both occasions the initiative came as much from the east as from the Porte: in 1569 from Haji Muhammed I, khan of Khiva, and in 1588 from Abdullah II of Bokhara and Urus Bey the leading prince of the Noghais. On both occasions the cause of failure was not so much the strength of the Russians as disunity among the participants. In 1569 the Crims preferred their alternative plan of a looting raid on Moscow and Bokhara refused to cooperate with Khiva. In 1588, though Bokhara was keen on an expedition, Khiva was allied with the Safavids, the Crims feared to strengthen their Ottoman overlords, and the Ottomans themselves were worried lest the reconquest of Astrakhan might dangerously expand the growing power of Abdullah II who might turn into a new Tamerlane. In the end, with unreliable allies in the north and the naval defeat of Mombasa in 1589 in the south, Sokullu Mehmet's pincers were abandoned for frontal attack along the central land route in Azerbaijan, a strategy more consistent with the new climate of opinion in the empire which preferred to achieve continental ends with continental means. For the victory of the canonists over the dervishes was also the victory of the generals over the admirals. As a result of Sokollu's failure, the northern land route remained blocked and lifeless.[14]

The far southern sea route

By the age of the Renaissance the raftmen had long ceased to ride the equatorial currents. The Indonesian colony of the Zanj coast, forced to retreat by the Bantu to the highlands of Madagascar, was forgetting and forgot by its now increasingly Moslem mother country. However a new version of this route to China was developed by the Dutch, which, going even further south, used, not the equatorial currents, but the prevailing westerlies of the roaring forties. In 1611 Commander Brouwer first took this route from the Cape to Batavia and made the journey in half the usual time for crossing the Indian Ocean. In 1616 the Dutch East India company prescribed it for their captains, though even in the eighteenth century when navigation and geography had improved, it was never used as frequently as the diagonal route across the Indian Ocean, for fear of ending on the reefs of western Australia which were discovered by Dirck Hartog, Frederick de Houtman and others between 1616 and 1622. Tasman's journey in 1642, from Batavia to the south of Australia, New Zealand and back to Batavia, showed in principle how this problem might be solved and a direct route to Canton be established. Dutch shipping coming from Europe, however, was nearly always headed for Batavia, where the company, like the Spaniards in Manila, made contact with China through the junk trade.

The Cape route

More immediately significant, though in the long run less revolutionary because it found no new continent for European colonization, only a peninsula of Africa, was the Cape route, first of the Portuguese, then of the Dutch. The Macao system of the Portuguese provided direct, territorial contact through the medium of bullion. The Batavia system of the

Dutch provided indirect offshore contact through the medium of goods.

Unlike Christopher Columbus, Vasco da Gama did not aim to reach China. It was not until the Portuguese took Malacca in 1511 that they became involved in contact with China and their motive for taking it was to make their spice monopoly more effective, not to extend it to silks and porcelain. Once in Malacca, Portuguese like Tomé Pires, the apothecary turned geographer and business promoter, saw the possibilities of the China trade and hoped they could step into the shoes of the sultan as the recognized managers of the staple. Here they reckoned without the Ming government which valued its Malaccan satellite as the gateway to the West, gave vassals aid, or at least sympathy, against rebels and regarded the Portuguese as predators. The first Portuguese embassy to Peking, in 1520 under Tomé Pires, was not a success. The Ming government demanded the evacuation of Malacca and on Pires' refusal to discuss the question, imprisoned him in Canton until his death in 1524. Attempts to trade at Canton and Ningpo were repulsed. However in the long run, the local authorities proved more flexible than the central government. It was by informal agreement with them that in 1557 the Portuguese, as reward for services against pirates, were allowed to occupy the Macao peninsula. The date was significant. At the mid-century, East Asia, like Europe, experienced a pause in the economic expansion of the sixteenth century, which turned bad debts, unemployment and idle ships into piracy, a protest of the litoral against the interior. The officials at Canton therefore needed the aid of the further shore against the nearer, and the Portuguese were established at Macao.

The Macao system, the Portuguese network through which Chinese goods were acquired for the European market, rested on four pillars. First, there was the 'city of the Name of God' itself, essentially a privileged hole in the Ming system of coastal evacuation, maritime prohibition and commercial embargo directed against native shipping suspected of piracy. Second, there were the carracks, the supertankers whose immunity from pirate attack allowed the Portuguese to exploit their adventitious monopoly of the navigation of the China seas by shipping goods on behalf of Chinese merchants as well as on their own. Third, there was Nagasaki and the Portuguese contacts in Japan through the Jesuit mission, whence, by selling Chinese silk and sugar, Macao acquired the silver to buy goods at Canton for Europe. For at Canton, unlike other parts of their thalassocracy, the Portuguese could not raid, or obtain goods as security payments, but must trade, and trade in silver since they had no other marketable commodity. Japan, the 'little Mexico of the Far East' was the nearest source of silver.[15] Finally, there was Malacca which secured the return route to Goa and the Cape.

The Macao system was the first instance of using what was later called the country trade, intra-Asiatic traffic, to finance extra-Asiatic traffic. Because the intra-Asiatic traffic in question was limited to that between China and Japan it was a vulnerable system. The weakest pillar, and the most vital was Nagasaki, because the essential silver came by grace only and early in the seventeenth century the Tokugawa withdrew their grace, expelled the Jesuits under suspicion of being forerunners of an Iberian invasion, and forbad the carracks to come from Macao. The Tokugawa could do this partly because other holes were appearing in the Ming anti-piracy system, via Canton and Ayudhya, for example, and a direct junk trade from Foochow to Nagasaki was developing. Finally in 1641 the Dutch captured Malacca and cut the route to the west. Long before this, however, Macao was forced into the first of its many humiliating but effective expedients for survival. She entered into a junior partnership with the rising star of the long-distance China trade: Manila. Of all the Portuguese colonies, Macao was the most reluctant to join the national revolution against Spain.

The Batavia system, the Dutch network through which Chinese goods were acquired for the European market, was structured on different lines. Unlike Macao, Batavia was not a mere hole in an Asian continental system, but the active centre of what aspired to be a European world spice monopoly. Unlike Portuguese seapower which by the seventeenth century was defensive and restrictive, Dutch seapower was aggressive and expansionary. The Portuguese avoided pirates, the Dutch attacked them. Unlike the Portuguese base at Nagasaki which propagated religion and mobilized silver, the Dutch artificial island of Deshima tapped supplies of

Chinese goods and mobilized copper. The Dutch commercial empire, unlike the Iberian, was not bullionist. Both at home and abroad it operated through a fiduciary system of clearing houses and credit mechanisms which minimized the use of silver which was increasingly in short supply as the seventeenth century depression intensified. Japanese copper did not play the earlier role of Japanese silver and if any commodity held primacy in Sino–Dutch contact it was pepper. Unlike Malacca which held the windpipe of Macao, the straits of Sunda were securely held by Batavia, and with Mauritius occupied from 1598 and a colony at the Cape from 1652, the Dutch enjoyed better communications home than the Portuguese.

The Batavia system was more rational than the Macao system. Just as the Dutch went to the root of the spice trade where the Portuguese only went to its outlets, so Batavia sought the country trade of all Asia as the base of its home export not just Macao's Sino–Japanese segment. Organizationally too the *Vereenigde Oost-Indische Compagnie*, the herald of private enterprise, was superior to the Portuguese state trading institutions. Yet despite these advantages, Batavia was curiously ineffective in developing Sino–foreign contact. Jan Pieterszoon Coen complained that he did not have the capital resources of the Iberians. Dutch seapower failed to take Manila in 1617, Macao in 1622, and failed to protect Taiwan from the pirates in 1662. Dutch diplomacy failed to secure the opening of either Amoy or Canton to their trade. This was because, for Batavia, China was only a secondary investment in a well spread portfolio designed to exploit a fundamentally bearish situation. In the last resort, Amsterdam, for all its sophistication, reflected Seville.[16]

The Pacific route

The most important link between China and the outside world in the age of the Renaissance was, paradoxically, along the longest, newest and most precarious of the routes, in a direction which had hitherto seen the least contact. The paradox, however, is resolved in that behind the Pacific lay the Atlantic, the most dynamic economic area then existing and the prime mover of the first world economy. The Manila system, the Spanish network through which Chinese goods were acquired for the American or European market, was Pacific in terms of space, but Atlantic in terms of time.[17]

Christopher Columbus, unlike Vasco de Gama, aimed to reach China. This objective remained with the conquistadors so that, even when revealed as part of a continent, Mexico continued to be an isthmus on the way to Cathay. The voyage of Magellan, however, which led to the discovery of the Philippines in 1521, was motivated by the desire of the Spanish government to secure its share of the spice islands under the papal demarcation as modified by the treaty of Tordesillas rather than as a move towards China. The second Spanish Pacific expedition, that of Garcia de Loaisa in 1525, likewise was directed to the spice islands, while the third, that of Alvaro de Saavedra in 1527, sent from Mexico by Cortes, was simply reinforcement.

In 1529, however, on his marriage to a Portuguese infanta, Charles V renounced Spanish claims to the spice islands, a decision confirmed by the union of the crowns in 1580. The fourth expedition, therefore, that of Ruy Lopez de Villalobos in 1542, was of purely Mexican origin and went to the Philippines which were given their name in 1543 in honour of the heir apparent. The Villalobos expedition was the precursor of the expedition of Miguel Lopez de Legazpi in 1564 which, although started as a pepper venture, turned north to conquer the Philippines and found Manila in 1572. For the route, as important as the foundation of the city, was due to the discovery, comparable to that of the roaring forties by Brouwer, of the prevailing westerlies of the north Pacific and the Kurosiwo drift by Andres de Urdaneta, Legazpi's chaplain and scientific adviser, on his return to Mexico in 1565. The Augustinian Urdaneta, who had been on the Loaisa expedition, was thus the real founder of the Manila system. His discovery made possible the circuit of the Manila galleon: out from Mexico along the north-east trades and north equatorial current to Manila; back along the prevailing westerlies and the Kurosiwo to a landfall in California. This circuit became the economic basis of Manila for the next two centuries.

Manila enjoyed advantages over Macao and Batavia. Essentially a colony of Mexico, it had behind it an abundant and reliable source of silver, so that the Mexican dollar eventually became the currency of China. Not only had Mexico more silver than Japan, but it exploited it by the more intensive amalgam method. Manila was not dependent on a straits of Malacca; the galleons required no way stations across the Pacific. No other ports competed with Acapulco and Manila and, except for the occasional Protestant privateer, there were no pirates. Unlike Macao, Manila was not troubled by Chinese officialdom since it traded offshore served by Chinese private enterprise. Unlike Batavia, Manila operated a simple, barter-like trading mechanism and did not have to juxtapose a number of balances. Back home, Manila the colony of a colony, found a growing market. The conquistadors had not gone to Mexico to lower their standards of living. A new elite, they wanted the silk Grenada had provided in Spain. While at first they sought it locally by production in Mixteca and manufacture in Mexico city, they preferred the Chinese product and were prepared to sacrifice the native industry.

The merchants of Mexico, however, did more than import. They re-exported, to Peru and to Spain itself, and by thus paying for imports increased the proportion of its own silver that the colony could retain for its own purposes. Seville blamed Acapulco for the decline of its silver imports – wrongly, Pierre Chaunu has shown, since in fact the quantities of bullion crossing the Atlantic and the Pacific correlated directly not inversely. Despite the critics, the king stood by Manila and paid its considerable overheads for non-economic reasons. As the Jesuit Francesco Colin put it in 1663: 'Our lord the late king Philip II used to say that for the sake of a single friary in the Philippines which kept the Holy Name of God, he was ready to spend all the revenue of his kingdoms.'[18] With these imperial advantages Manila throve for two centuries, where Macao dwindled as an isolated city state, and the *Vereenigde Oost-Indische Compagnie,* for all its modernity, stumbled into bankruptcy under the weight of its territorial imperatives.

Manila was part of the Atlantic of Seville. Of all the routes between China and the outside world in the age of the Renaissance, its system carried the most significant volume of goods in both directions. By the same token, the Manila system was highly sensitive to the contraction of the Spanish Atlantic which underlay the general crisis of the seventeenth century.

Between 1636 and 1640 the *almojarifazgo*, or tax on silver exported from Acapulco to Manila, which had been steady since 1606 at around 8000 pesos a year, fell to 3000, and except in the quinquennium 1656–60, it never regained its former figure. The number of junks from Kwangtung and Fukien entering the port of Manila fell from 123 between 1636 and 1640, to 83 between 1641 and 1645, 58 between 1646 and 1650, 25 between 1656 and 1660. To survive, Manila, like Macao, had to regionalize and seek contacts in the Indonesian archipelago, Indo-China and India.

All the routes in fact were affected by the decline of the Spanish Atlantic and the rarefaction of silver which was the symptom of the temporary halt to the seizure of American space, its profound cause. An age of copper succeeded an age of silver and only the Dutch, masters of world copper supplies in Sweden and Japan and of the arts of fiduciary currency, were able to ride out the storm, and that not without losses. By 1650 contacts between China and the outside world, which had multiplied ever since Shah Rukh and the Yung-lo emperor negotiated their agreement, were again in retreat, and Europe regrouped her forces and shifted to a new basis for a further advance in the Enlightenment.

INTERCHANGES, 1350 TO 1650

China's relative position in the world had deteriorated since the middle ages. Latin Christendom in the Renaissance had built on its medieval foundations, adding achievement to earlier promise. China in the Ming restoration had narrowed her foundations, curtailing previous achievement. At the same time the avenues of contact between China and the outside world had been renovated and extended. The result for the pattern of interchange was twofold.

On the one hand, interchanges multiplied. Chaunu, thinking of just material goods, supposes that the volume of exchange between Europe and the Far East by the Levantine and Cape routes alone increased maybe tenfold in the sixteenth century, not to speak of the Pacific route and invisible goods in the categories of people, flora and fauna, and ideas.[19] On the other hand, the terms of interchange altered. Europe's imports and exports shifted from the simple to the complex; China's from the complex to the simple. Europe, breaking out of its medieval confines, was eager to lend its higher culture and was willing to borrow the advanced achievements of what she recognized to be in some respects still a superior civilization. China, imprisoned by the Ming restoration within the conditions of her earlier successes, preferred to import things rather than institutions or people and could only export techniques and images rather than ideas. Europe was moving from nature to culture, China from culture to nature, although only an elite, the more critical missionaries and the more reflective converts, were aware of what was happening.

People

From China came the unwelcomed, plebeian emigration of the China-towns. Overseas China was the product of private enterprise, much of it small scale, non-establishment, criminal even. There was a Chinese pirate community at Tumasik on the Malay Peninsula in the middle of the fourteenth century; Grise, the Javanese port which dominated the trade to the spice islands, was founded by Chinese between 1350 and 1400; and Surabaya had a Chinese community at the beginning of the fifteenth century.

The attack on Overseas China by the Ming in Cheng Ho's expeditions drove it further in the direction of tongs, capitan-Chinas and piracy. On his first voyage Cheng Ho came into conflict with the China-town boss, Ch'en Tsu-i, at Palembang and with the possibly Chinese pretender, Su Kan-lo, in north-western Sumatra, both of whom were taken to Nanking and executed as rebels. The cessation of the expeditions gave the Overseas Chinese respite if not legality and they continued to spread. In the early sixteenth century there was a community at Brunei and the king was reputed to be of Chinese descent. There were Chinese at Achin, the Asian rival to Portuguese Malacca, and the Dutch found the Chinese their principal rivals for the pepper monopoly. There was a substantial Chinese colony at Bantam with its own quarter, fine stone houses and representatives on the king's council. At Japara and Jambi, Chinese held the office of *shahbandar* or consular doyen. At Macassar, which replaced Grise as the connection between central Indonesia and the spice islands, there was a Chinese community in the eighteenth, probably in the seventeenth century. The Chinese preceded Legazpi at Manila; their community grew with the Spanish colony and was a source of both wealth and danger to it. From Manila, Chinese crossed the Pacific by the galleon to Mexico city where in 1635 the Spanish barbers complained of unfair competition. Later, the Chinese, like the Blacks, acted as middlemen between the Spaniards and the Indians, and like them were regarded as potential organizers of revolt. Though creators of wealth, the Overseas Chinese were unwelcome both as emigrants and immigrants.

To China, admired at its place of departure but at its destination welcome only to an elite, came the patrician immigration of the Catholic missionaries: the Jesuits with their new *pietas literata, par excellence*, but also the friars who, trained in the old scholasticism of the universities, did not deserve the description of *fraile idiota* given them by Rodriguez. The missionary activity of the counter-reformation was rooted in Franciscan millenarism, to which the Jesuits were heir. The convent of La Rabida had been the intermediary between Columbus and the crown of Castile, and Franciscan marialism, the immaculate conception and the feast of candlemas, allied to the Hieronymite cult of Our Lady of Guadalupe, was an important element in the spirituality of Iberian America. In China, although St Francis Xavier was the first missionary of the post-medieval wave, from 1552 to 1582 the Jesuits were confined to Macao and the friars seemed to be making the running. The first two sixteenth-century books devoted solely to China, the Dominican Gaspar da Cruz's *Tractado* and the Augustinian Juan Gonzalez de Mendoza's *Gran Reyno de la China*, reflect their friars' backgrounds.

Nevertheless, although justice has not always been done to the initiative of the friars, from the arrival of Matteo Ricci and the adoption of Valignano's accommodation policy, the Jesuits dominated the China mission, as they came to dominate Catholic reform as a whole.[20] If the friars were educated men – de Rada, Cocchi and Caballero, the founders of the Augustinian, Dominican and Franciscan missions, had all been to Salamanca – the Jesuits were an intellectual elite, a generation of giants, as George H. Dunne calls them. Ricci himself was a pupil of Clavius the mathematician of the Gregorian calendar; Johann Schreck was a foundation member of the Academia dei Lincei, the prototype of all royal societies; Michael Boym was the son of the royal physician of Poland and himself a notable botanist; Giacomo Rho was a brilliant mathematician; Michele Ruggieri was a doctor of civil law. In the Jesuit immigration, China was receiving the kind of brain-drain a Timurid court had set out to induce. In Europe, St Francis Xavier was one of the most popular of the counter-reformation saints and assignment to China was a prize to be sought. The Chinese, however, except for an elite, did not welcome their distinguished guests, and Ricci was struck by the intensity of Chinese popular xenophobia.

Flora and fauna

Here exchanges were almost entirely in one direction, from the outside world to China, and fell into the two categories of American plants and European germs. Sociological and climatic factors were responsible for this disparity. Europe did not need new food grains such as the Chinese varieties of millet and she was not yet sufficiently affluent to ransack China for flowers for her gardens as she was to do in the eighteenth and nineteenth centuries. At the same time, the climate did not permit her to acclimatize the lichee, pomelo, grapefruit and kumquat described by Gaspar de Cruz, or the tea praised by Semedo. On the other hand, having acquired tropical and sub-tropical colonies in America, Europe could contribute to all parts of a China which was pressing particularly on its own agricultural frontier.

The sixteenth century saw the worldwide diffusion of American plants: maize, sweet potatoes, peanuts, Irish potatoes, manioc; tomatoes, pineapples, avocados, guavas; cocoa, tobacco, allspice, chilli, haricot beans and cactus – the green bullion of Columbus, as valuable as the gold and silver. The ability to absorb this wealth was an index of capacity for growth. Europe absorbed most, Africa least (only manioc), with Islam and India in between, and China next after Europe.

In the Ming period China absorbed maize, sweet potatoes, peanuts and tobacco. Maize was the most important potentially because it was the ideal pioneer's crop. It could be grown without irrigation on previously uncultivated hillsides, required little labour and became edible quickly, and so was perfect for cultivation while rice terraces were being laboriously prepared. According to Ho Ping-ti, 'the 1574 edition of the history of Yunnan province lists maize as a product of as many as six prefectures and two department counties'.[21] Mendoza, no doubt on the basis of de Rada's observations in Fukien in 1576, describes in his book of 1585 the mountain uplands sown with maize. Maize is also mentioned in the *Pen-tsao kang-mu* (A Synopsis of the Pharmacopeia) completed by the famous naturalist Li Shih-chen in 1590. The references to Yunnan and Fukien, plus a similar one in Shantung, together with an early appearance of maize at Mecca, suggest a distribution through the *haj* mechanism along the central land route in one of its variants.

Sweet potatoes were a complement of maize. They grew on shaded hillsides where maize required full sun and had a yield in calories per acre second only to rice. Their chronology and geography in China was similar to maize, so the Moslem route is most likely, but the sweet potato was also brought to the Philippines by the Spaniards via the Pacific and thence was carried to Fukien around 1590. Peanuts were a useful adjunct. They grew well on sandy soils deep in river valleys and assisted another kind of agricultural frontier. Possibly a reintroduction, since evidence of peanuts has been found on prehistoric sites, they are noted in the 1530s in the Lower Yangtze provinces. Ho Ping-ti therefore suggests transference by the Portuguese along the Cape route. Tobacco, which Ho Ping-ti calls 'one of the most profitable crops introduced into China during the late Ming period'[22] probably came across the Pacific via Manila, first to Fukien and thence to Kiangsi, which became a leading producer. Tobacco was at Manila before 1575, Japan around 1590, Macao in 1600, Java in 1601, and India and Ceylon in 1605–10.

The impact of the American food plants on Chinese agriculture was initially limited. None of them are mentioned in Sung Ying-hsing's *T'ien-kung k'ai-wu* (Creations of Nature and Man) of 1637.[23] Both Yunnan and Fukien were in different ways frontier provinces without much agricultural potential and in the beginning maize and sweet potatoes were only secondary crops in areas where food was expensive and in short supply. The mechanism of planting maize and sweet potatoes on newly cleared hillside to support the family while rice terraces were being prepared, a system which was to transform Chinese landscape and demography in the eighteenth century, had not yet been developed. Peanuts, too, at this stage were an exotic luxury rather than a pioneer's staple. The demographic revolution, which had started as a mere rebound from the losses of the Mongol period, slackened in the sixteenth century due to hotter weather and more drought famine. Its later acceleration must therefore have been due to other factors beside the American food plants; they owed their importance to it rather than vice versa.

The impact of tobacco, however, was greater. By the end of the Ming, smoking was said to be universal in southern Fukien and Chekiang, even among children. In Chihli its use was creeping up from soldiers and servants to their masters and mistresses. Edicts were issued against both the use of and the trade in tobacco in 1638 and 1643, just as vainly as similar issue by rulers in Europe. Further, while in Europe tobacco smoking spontaneously declined in the eighteenth century, perhaps as a result of greater nasal sensibility and the feminization of manners, in China it progressed steadily. In 1793 Lord Macartney wrote of the Chinese that, 'They almost all smoke tobacco and consider it as a compliment to offer each other a whiff of their pipes.'[24] Already in the sixteenth century, through whatever mechanism of eroticism, a foundation was being laid for a more sinister kind of addiction.

During the course of the sixteenth century a new layer was added to the microbian common market by the worldwide diffusion of syphilis. The diffusion of syphilis had been described by Calvin Wells as 'one of the most puzzling enigmas in the history of disease'.[25] It is a field in which a layman must tread with caution. Renaissance Europeans were convinced that they were being attacked by a new, virulent epidemic. Some, though not all, believed that it had been introduced from America by Columbus' sailors, that it was, as Oviedo said 'the malady of the Indies'.[26] Similarly Li Shihchen was convinced that the Chinese were being attacked by a new, virulent epidemic:

In ancient times this was unknown; only with the reigns of Hung-chih (1488–1505) and Cheng-te (1506–11) did it become prevalent, the people taking mercury as a cure. The sickness first appeared in Kuangtung, spread north-wards, and then to all parts of the empire.[27]

In spite of this concordance of independent conviction, there are strong objections to the theory of American origin, convenient though it might be in explaining the low natality of pre-Columbian demography. The bone evidence for pre-Columbian syphilis in Europe is almost as strong as it is in America and the lack of public comment may have been due to a confusion of the disease with certain kinds of leprosy puzzlingly endemic in medieval Europe. Further, there are obvious statistical difficulties about the role placed on Columbus' fifty sailors. Calvin Wells concludes, 'the balance of evidence tilts to the view that syphilis is an infection of hoary antiquity on both sides of the Atlantic'.[28] One might add, in China too, to judge by the emphasis on the value of mercury by Chinese medical authors.

However, the convergent evidence for an intensification of the disease around 1500 cannot be entirely discounted. The agent of syphilis, *Treponema pallidum*, is part of a family of treponemes responsible, in addition to syphilis, for yaws, pinta and a non-venereal endemic syphilis, some of whose effects are indistinguishable from one another. It would seem possible that a conjuncture of hitherto separate treponeme systems may have given rise to a new and more virulent mutation. If not American, syphilis may have been born in America, though by the time it reached China, it would have become European.

The effect of syphilis in China during the Ming period, like that of the American food plants, appears to have been limited, though if Freud was correct in ascribing counter-reformation asceticism – or as one might now say Michael Foucault's 'grand renfermement' – to its action, perhaps its influence might be sought in the rigorist stream of Neo-Confucian moralism, which descended from Wang Yang-ming via Ch'ien Te-hung, rejecting the master's more authentic anti-nomianism continued by his other disciple Wang Chi. Where however syphilis did affect China was indirectly via the nomads of Inner Asia. Syphilis, like alcoholism and tuberculosis, became very widely diffused among the Mongols, and while the decline of the nomads as a political and military force was a complex matter, the advance of syphilis may have been one factor.

Commodities

In the course of the sixteenth century the structure of international trade underwent a major mutation. It not only expanded but also diversified. This diversification was rooted in the new consumerism of Renaissance society, a phenomenon distinct in origin from the oceanic revolution which lay behind the expansion. Its principal agents were the Dutch, 'the wagoners of all seas',[29] 'the common carriers of the world',[30] and its shop window was Amsterdam, Descartes' enormous inventory of the possible,[31] which another contemporary described as 'la boutique des curiosités de ce monde et le magazin de l'univers'.[32] In the last resort, Amsterdam too, depended on Seville, on the prosperity of its customers; but in the short and middle term, Dutch supply multiplied European demand. With this diversification, the old trinity of textiles, minerals and spices lost its primacy as sugar, tobacco, slaves, leather goods, dyestuffs, medicines, drinks, salt, grain and timber began to be traded long distance. Though the commodities of the China trade remained relatively conservative, here too medicines and drink made their appearance.

The mainstay of both the Goa carracks and the Manila galleons remained the interchange of minerals and silk: silver, German, Japanese or Mexican, for Chinese silk. Chaunu has estimated that a quarter of the silver produced in America was exported across the Pacific and that, if to this is added the quantities exported by the Levant and the Cape, China's total dividend from Columbus may have amounted to a third of the distribution. In return came silk. Richard Hakluyt in his catalogue of the cargo of the *Madre de Dios*, a typical carrack captured by the English in 1592, lists 'silks, damasks, taffetas, sarcenets, altobassos, that is, counterfeit cloth of gold, unwrought China silks, sleaved silk, white twisted silk, curled cypresse', mostly of Chinese provenance, though some may have come from Persia via Ormuz.[33] Botero remarks that:

> the quantity of silk that is carried out of China is almost not credible. A thousand of quintals of silk are yearly carried thence for the Portuguese Indies, for the Philippines they lade out fifteen ships. There are carried out to Japan an inestimable sum... And they sell their works and their labours (by reason of the infinite store that is made) so cheap and at so easy price as the merchants of Nova Hispania that trade unto the Philippines to make their marts (unto which place the Chinese themselves do traffic) do wonder at it much.[34]

The effect of this interchange was considerable. Though Chinese imports competed with the European silk industry of Lucca, Milan, Lyon, Toledo and Grenada (Botero thought that 'the traffic with the Philippines falls out to be rather hurtful than profitable unto the King of Spain'[35]) they also stimulated it by diffusing the taste for silk in concord with the new consumerism of the Renaissance. From the capture of the *Santa Catharina* off Johore by van Heemskerck in 1603, which opportunely coincided with a failure of the Italian silk harvest, Amsterdam became 'le grand marché européen de la soie' and 'foi et sole', Protestant business and high-grade textiles, long remained in alliance.[36] By diffusing the taste for silk, the imports also encouraged the search for cheaper substitutes for it. Thus the *Madre de Dios* also carried 'book-calicos, calico-launes, broad white calicos, fine starched calicos, course white calicos, brown broad calicos, browne course calicos'.[37] Cotton, most revolutionary of textiles, was the daughter of silk.

Meanwhile, the converse import into China of American silver, combined with the parallel import of Japanese silver via Macao, had an impact on the Chinese economy. A school of communist historians has seen the late Ming period as manifesting 'sprouts of capitalism' *(Tzu-pen chu-i meng-ya)*, even incipient industrialization, and while Western scholars have been sceptical of any qualitative change, business activity certainly rose to high levels. While the influx of silver does not seem to have produced even the mild inflation of the 'great' European price rise (great only to Victorians and with other reasons beside monetary), it may have avoided deflation and kept China's excessive interest rates within bounds, thus raising business levels. The Wan-li period was a silver age of private enterprise. The inflow of silver, by stimulating the market sector of the economy, facilitated Chang Chü-cheng's dismantling of the corporatist state and the switch from taxation in kind to taxation in money in the single whip reform (*i-t'iao pien-fa*). Although China did not experience the Renaissance consumer revolution (thus showing that American silver was not its cause but only the means of satisfying it), the Wan-li period was a lavish one and extravagance had even found praise among Chinese scholars. The emperor himself was buried in a tomb of unparalleled magnificence, built at the cost of 8 million taels at the height of the 'royal cycle of silver', and containing gold, in bowls, cups, vases and ingots, of nearly a quarter of a ton.

Three other minerals or mineral products figured in the China trade of the Renaissance, though in the opposite direction. The most important was porcelain. The quantity exported from China and the area over which it was diffused increased during the sixteenth century. At this time the great courtly collections of Ardebil and Topkapi, showpieces of Timurid culture, were built up probably by trade along the central land route. Ardebil, the shrine of the Sufi founder of the Safavids, was endowed by Shah Abbas in a *waqf* document of 1611. The original collection consisted of 1162 pieces of which 805, covering items dated 1369–1610, survive to the present. The Seraglio collection was much larger: 10 512 pieces survive, covering items from Sung to late Ch'ing. Inventories of 1495, 1501 and 1503 mentioning porcelain take the collection back to Beyazid II, though one would expect that very Timurid ruler Mehmet II to have been a collector. Selim the Grim, aesthete as well as warrior, reputedly took porcelain as booty in his campaign against Shah Ismail, and Sinan built Suleiman the Magnificent a *cinihane* or China house. Turkish non-porcelain ceramics from Isnik were strongly influenced by Chinese styles. Collections were not only courtly. In the late 1960s 800 Ming pieces came to light in the wealthy land agents' village of Douma outside Damascus and stray finds have appeared from Aleppo, Homs and Beirut, suggesting the existence of a private, provincial Timuridism.[38]

From Islam the taste for porcelain spread to Christendom. Odd pieces may have arrived before and been treasured, but regular collection and import now began; the cargo of the *Madre de Dios* included porcelain. Philip II had 3000 pieces according to an inventory of 1611; his cousin the Archduke Ferdinand had 241 pieces in his *Kunstkammer* at Ambras; and Rudolf II at the Hradschin had over 700 pieces. François Premier had a collection of vases and bowls, Cosimo I of Tuscany possessed 873 pieces and his successor Francesco I was one of the first in Europe to try to imitate Chinese wares. Bartholomew of the Martyrs advised Pius IV to replace his plate with porcelain; Henry VIII owned at least one piece; and Cecil more. Porcelain deeply affected European sensibility and manners. As it escaped from the *Wunderkammer* of princes to the tables and sideboards of the gentility, it fostered a new rococo grace and a new refinement of behaviour. Porcelain, as a commodity and as a way of life, was an ingredient in feminization.

The other two minerals in the China trade, tutenag and paktung, both owed their import to the silver shortage of the seventeenth century. Tutenag, or zinc – from the Persian *tutiya* meaning calamine, the ore of zinc – first appeared in Europe as an import from China in 1605. In China itself zinc was regularly used in an alloy with copper to make cash. It was therefore imported by the Dutch as part of their world copper monopoly at a time when governments were increasingly being forced to turn to base metals for their currency. Paktung, or cupro-nickel, then unique to China, was first described by Libavius in 1599. Although it had been used in the coinage of the Graeco–Bactrian kings and had a great monetary future before it as a universal *ersatz* silver, in the seventeenth century, paktung substituted for the commodity aspect of silver in candlesticks and fire grates as a kind of brass. Before 1650 neither tutenag or paktung were traded in any quantity. Their interest is that of a symptom of the conjuncture.

In the age of the Renaissance, the spice trade, in preservatives, condiments and aromatics, so long a mainstay of international commerce, reached its apogee and went into relative decline. The underlying reason for this was consumptivity levels: the move to luxury in Europe, the move against it in

China; but changes in consumer preferences were also involved.

First, the great preservative, pepper. Here Europe and China continued to share the production of Indonesia, but in changing proportions in a market which was not expanding. Marco Polo, no doubt with hyperbole, had claimed that 'for one spice ship that goes to Alexandria or elsewhere to pick up pepper for export to Christendom, Zaiton is visited by a hundred'.[39] At the beginning of the sixteenth century, F.C. Lane has estimated the European import of pepper at between one and a half and two million pounds annually. Giovanni da Empoli who went to the Indies in 1503 as the agent of the Florentine merchant house of Bartolomeo Marchione believed that the production of Sumatra alone was 6 million pounds a year, so that the total production of Indonesia would have been around 10 million pounds. Though there was local trade and some export for Indian consumption, most pepper not exported to Europe went to China, whose consumption must have been around 6 million pounds, as Empoli implies. Both Cruz and Rada, one recalls, regarded the Chinese as a nation of beef-eaters. By 1560 Lane believes Europe was importing over 3 million pounds annually and, by the end of the century, the addition of probable imports through Lisbon, Alexandria and Aleppo points to a figure of 6 million pounds. In 1621 the directors of the Dutch East India company estimated the maximum possible sale of pepper per year at 7 million pounds. Meanwhile Chinese imports had fallen: to just over 3 million pounds at the beginning of the seventeenth century, 1 or 2 million by the middle of it. In the eighteenth century, total Indonesian production of pepper averaged 5 million pounds a year, only occasionally reaching peaks of 10 million pounds. The European share of the pepper market had increased, though less than the tenfold increase in economic activity according to Chaunu, and the market itself had remained stable or contracted.

Two sets of factors lay behind this development. On the one hand, although the Chinese pepper trade was injured by Dutch attempts to canalize it through their staple at Batavia, a more basic cause of its decline were changes in Chinese demography, farming and diet. As family units were multiplied by early marriage, as farmlets proliferated and absorbed marginal pasture, the number of cattle fell, the consumption of beef declined and with it the need for pepper. For the time being the loss of protein was compensated by an increased consumption of chickens, ducks, geese, fish, pigs and even dogs, but the course of Chinese diet was set away from protein. On the other hand, in Europe, while the need for pepper was increased by the rising consumption of meat, it was reduced by the rising production of winter feed for animals (another result of the same rising consumption) which finally eliminated pepper altogether except as a condiment. A country-by-country breakdown in 1579–80 by the Augsburg merchant and would-be pepper monopolitan, Konrad Rott, shows that it was backward Europe east of the Rhine which consumed most pepper. Spain and England, though pastoralists and beef-eaters, consumed relatively little. As has often been observed, the Dutch obtained a world monopoly of pepper just when, for different reasons in Europe and China, it was losing its traditional importance.

Next, condiments. Under the heading spices, Hakluyt names two which may have come from China: cinnamon and ginger. Perhaps the cinnamon came from Ceylon where the Portuguese had been installed since 1517, but late-sixteenth-century Jesuit sources mention it as a product of China and in the eighteenth century it was the practice to adulterate the more expensive and superior Singhalese product with it. Ceylon had taken the lead from China in cinnamon as it was later to do in tea. The best ginger, however, came still from China, hand in hand with porcelain ginger jars. Of activity in the other direction there is little sign: no more turmeric or curry powder from India, though cloves from Ternate and Tidore came via Macassar and Macao. But in general Chinese cuisine had lost its taste for the exotic, except for birds' nests and *beche de mer*.

Finally, in this category, aromatics. This had always been China's special interest in the spice trade, one intensified by Buddhism and maintained by the secular luxury of the Sung. It continued into the early modern period and produced the import by Macao of sandalwood from Timor, which became the lifeline of the Portuguese colony after its links with Manila were cut by the separation of the crowns in 1640. Relatively, however, the aromatics trade had declined in importance since the days of the T'ang and Macao was able to monopolize sandalwood partly because it was worth no one else's while to take the monopoly from her. Frankincense, myrrh and storax no longer appear in the trade. Europeans, conversely, were becoming more interested in aromatics partly as a result of plague which alerted noses to bad air and odours. Musk, rather sketchily described by Marco Polo, was regarded by Cruz as second only to silk as a Portuguese export from Macao, and it figured, along with ambergris, in the cargo of the *Madre de Dios*. The European perfume industry, especially in Cologne, was getting under way in response first to Spanish fashion and then to French. Camphor, probably from Taiwan, was another aromatic noted in the *Madre de Dios*.

What the *Madre de Dios* did not contain – or the sailors got away with them too quickly for Hakluyt – were the two best known medicines from China, which first made a considerable appearance in trade in the Renaissance: China root and rhubarb. China root was the bulb of *Smilax China*, a kind of sarsaparilla. It was used early in the sixteenth century by pharmacists in Lisbon and Seville, possibly described to Ramusio at the mid-century but not known to him personally, and shipped to England to the quantity of 10 000 pounds by Captain John Weddell on his voyage to Canton in 1637. It was regarded as a remedy against syphilis, one of a number of such medicines – *gaiac* from Yucatan was another – whose sudden appearance inclines one to believe in the novelty, or at least increased virulence of the disease in the sixteenth century.

More significant was rhubarb, listed by Dioscorides, mentioned by Marco Polo, but not widely used in the West, until the Renaissance. Commercial rhubarb was not the now familiar stalk of *Rheum rhaponticum*, but the root, once equally familiar in the nursery as a nauseous but effective anti-dysenteric, cathartic at first but constipative over time. Medicinal rhubarb of good quality was the product of a restricted area of north-west Szechwan and south-east Chinghai on either side of the Bayan Kara range, the two chief commercial outlets being Kuanhsien and Sining. Most of the English words referring to it, Rha, from a Greek term for the Volga, Rhabarbarum, Rhapontic, and rhubarb itself, appear in the sixteenth century and suggest an original connection with the northern land route.

The chief witness to its diffusion in Renaissance Europe is Ramusio.[40] He describes a dinner party with his friend San-michele of Verona in Murano around 1550, where he met a Persian merchant from Yazd, Hajji Muhammed, who had just landed a consignment of rhubarb in Venice. Hajji Muhammed had gone to China via the central land route: Tabriz, Kasvin, Herat, Bokhara, Samarkand, Kashgar, Turfan, Hami, to Su-chou in the Kansu panhandle where he bought his rhubarb. Because of the war of religion between the Uzbeks and Per-sians, he was unable to return this way, but went by the north-ern land route, which he implies was largely under Uzbek control, to Caffa and thence via Constantinople to Venice. Ramusio then adds that rhubarb was in universal use in Venice and this comment is almost as interesting as Hajji Muham-med's witness to the state of the land routes. In the pre-mod-ern pharmacopeia, rhubarb was a medicine for children. It was for a long time the only even partly effective weapon against summer dysentery, what the Victorians called infantile cholera, which was the major cause of the high infantile and juvenile mortalities of traditional societies. Its widespread use in Venice is thus early evidence of that new sensibility to the 'massacre of the innocents' which, as part of a general femini-zation of values, was to have so profound an effect on Euro-pean demography, education and psychology. In China chil-dren were valued as future farm labourers and mothers of farm labourers. In Europe they were beginning to be valued as present human persons.

Finally in the diversifying category of commodities, the quasi medicine and exotic drink: tea; in the Renaissance no more than a gleam on the horizon, but worth noting because of its revolutionary future. Hajji Muhammed reported the Chinese as saying that if the Europeans knew about tea they would give up rhubarb, but Ramusio apparently had not tried it. For Gaspar da Cruz in 1569 tea was still an exotic, 'a drink of warm water which they call cha... somewhat red and very medicinal'.[41] Botero too in 1589 wrote of 'the herb out of which they press a delicate juice which serves them for drink instead of wine. It also preserves their health and frees them from all these evils that the immoderate use of wine doth breed unto us'.[42]

The first commercial tea in Europe appeared in Holland in 1610. Although expensive it quickly became fashionable among the merchant aristocracy, some said on account of the bad water in Amsterdam, the overuse of tobacco and the constant smell of turbot and herrings! In 1637 the directors of the East India Company ordered the governor of Batavia to send home some cases with every ship. Dutch doctors – Leyden was a famous medical centre, though one, it was said, was paid to say so by the East India Company – recommended tea against indigestion and against the new feminine (and possibly contraceptive) disease of migraine. From Holland, capital of European consumption, tea spread to France and England. Cardinal Mazarin, a natural valetudinarian and a collector of porcelain, took it for rheumatism and in 1657 Thomas Garraway, a café proprietor, opened the first teashop in London. Athanasius Kircher, the Jesuit magus, in his *China Illustrata* of 1667 summed up the European experience of tea:

It is of a diuretic faculty, much fortifies the stomach, exhilarates the spirits, and wonderfully openeth all the Nephritick passages or Reins; it freeth the head by suppressing of fuliginous vapours so that it is a most excellent drink for studious and sedentary persons, to quicken them in their operations.[43]

Techniques

In the Renaissance China's material life remained generally at a higher level than Europe's, despite the progress of Latin Christendom since the middle ages and its hopeful institutional and intellectual foundations. The flow of technology therefore continued to be from East to West. Where Europe's progress showed was in the quality of her imports. Two of her major borrowings, printing and the written examination, were imported to reinforce her growing intellectual power, while the third, alcohol distillation, was part of her general trend to luxury. To this westward flow the only exceptions were the crankshaft and certain hydraulic devices introduced to China by the Jesuits, which were only decoration, not acceleration, of major currents of Chinese history.

The East Asian origin of European printing by movable metal type was demonstrated by T.F. Carter in 1931 though it had been guessed at as early as the middle of the sixteenth century itself by the humanist bishop Paolo Giovio.[44] Carter traced the use of inscribed seals in China, probably copied from the West, in the time of Ch'in Shih Huang-ti; the beginning of lithography, rubbings from inscriptions of the Confucian classics, under the eastern Han; the use of seals in relief around 500; the development of xylography, wooden block printing, for Buddhist scriptures and Taoist charms under the T'ang; the adoption of xylography by Confucianism with the printing of the classics by the Five Dynasties prime minister Feng Tao in 932; the proliferation under the Sung of wood block printing not only for books but also for money, religious prints, playing cards and textiles; the spread of printing to Tun-huang, Seoul, Turfan and, under the Il-khans, Tabriz; the simultaneous invention of movable type in earthenware, wood and metal for Chinese phrases, Uighur words and Korean syllables; all these leading to Gutenberg's new synthesis at Mainz in 1440 of movable type for letters set in a machine modelled on a Moselle wine press, a piece of technology hardly improved upon until the nineteenth century.

Ever since Bacon in the *Novum Organon* claimed that printing, gunpowder and the magnet had 'changed the whole face and state of things throughout the world'[45] and made the difference between antiquity and modernity, the importance of Gutenberg's invention has been generally recognized. Indeed the danger has been to exaggerate it: to see it as a cause of the Renaissance and the reformations, even modern mass literacy, where it was only a technical precondition; to fail to see that despite it, literacy rates in China fell in the early modern period. Printing was the consequence as much as the cause of a drive to literacy in both China and Europe, a drive which in China was not sustained. In Europe its adoption must be associated with changes in the family, the valorization of the child, greater willingness to invest in education, and the new subjectivist lay piety of prayer books and paraliturgies. It was adopted in a world which was not yet Renaissance or reformation but still a waning of the middle ages: the Burgundian epoch of d'Ailly, Gerson, Reginal Pecocke, Thomas à Kempis and Jan Van Eyck, a generation of recovery.

In China, written examinations went back tentatively to the Han and the usurper emperor Wang Mang, definitely to Sui

Wen-ti and the T'ang. Under the T'ang, written examinations were used to recruit a substantial, at times a dominant part of the civil service in the Chinese sense of the political elite. Under the Sung and the Ming, through lower degrees which gave status but not access to the bureaucracy, recruitment by written examination was extended to the social elite as well. At all levels Ming society offered the career open to talent by intellectual competition. In medieval Europe too, there had been examinations, but, except in the doubtful case of the Salerno medical school, oral not written, usually in the form of the *disputatio*.

Early European visitors were struck by the non-aristocratic, meritocratic character of Chinese society which they compared to Plato's republic. Galeote Pereira, Rada and Mendoza all noted the examinations but were not clear that they were written. The first definite statement of this was in the synopsis of Jesuit reports made by Giovanni Maffei in 1588, his source being the relation of Valignano, the famous visitor of the East who devised the accommodation policy which Ricci put into practice. Valignano was the trusted colleague of the Jesuit general, Claudio Aquaviva, the second founder of the order. The first prescription of written examination in European educational literature was in the *Ratio Studiorum* of 1599 for Jesuit schools compiled under his direction. The *Ratio* contains a section *(Scribendi ad examen leges)* on school examinations and in Jesuit colleges promotion from one form to another was by examination. In addition there was provision for competition for individual prize essays. Written examinations were slow to spread beyond the Jesuit colleges and *viva voce* died hard. Cambridge did not have them till they were introduced by Bentley to Trinity in 1702 and Oxford not till the time of Cyril Jackson, Dean of Christ Church 1783–1809. The Jesuits indeed were criticized for excessive *aemulatio*. In China written examinations led to formalism and preoccupation with style and encouraged the retreat from philosophy to myth. In Europe, where the intellectual milieu was more dynamic, written examinations led to less rhetoric and tighter argument and encouraged the advance from philosophy to science. Descartes, one remembers, was a pupil of the Jesuits, part of the new meritocracy they trained.

It was in the prosperous but socially divided sixteenth century that distilled liquor – brandy, liqueur (Benedictine is said to have been invented in 1510 by Dom Bernado Vincelli of Fécamp, while Chartreuse is attributed to a formula given by Maréchal d'Estrées to the Carthusians in 1607), gin, whisky and vodka – first assumed a significant role in European diet. In general, spirits were a luxury of the poor, a replacement for the meat they could no longer afford as prices rose and real wages fell. Liqueurs and cognac, however, were luxuries of the rich, additions to the meal rather than substitutes for it. In both cases, distilled liquor expressed that drive to affluence of Europe which underlay all her borrowings. Amsterdam, at the confluence of the wine-based liquors of the south, the grain-based alcohols of the north, the molasses-based rum of the West Indies, was the home of Dutch courage, a natural entrepôt of spirits as it was of other expressions of affluence.

In Europe distillation was older than distillation for alcohol. Aristotle knew that pure water could be made from brine. In later times the invention of the retort was ascribed to the second-century Alexandrian alchemists Pseudo Cleopatra and Maria Prophetissa who used it in the investigation of sulphur, arsenic and mercury. Stills were used in Persia under the Sassanians for making perfume from roses, and al-Kindi in the ninth century described the distillation of camphor. Distillation for spirits was borrowed from China in the fourteenth century, probably as part of the alchemical package. Its invention was ascribed to the famous alchemist Arnold of Villanova (Arnauld de Villeneuve) who, in a work with the Taoist-sounding title *La Conservation de la Jeunesse*, described the medical properties of brandy. *Aquaviva*, used for both brandy and whisky, was one of the alchemists' synonyms for their mysterious *materia prima*, as was *vinum ardens*. It was not, however, until the sixteenth century that distilling became an industry.

In China possible references to distillation can be found in the writings of Liu An, the author of the *Huai-nan tzu*, c.150–120 BC, in the earliest extant book on alchemy, the *Ts'an-t'ung chi* of Wei Po-yang in the second century AD, and in the *Pao-p'u tzu* of Ko Hung, c.300 AD. All three references are to the distillation of mercury from cinnabar. A clearer reference is the account by Wu Shu, c. 975, of the woman alchemist Keng in the reign of the T'ang emperor, the second Hsüan-tsung 847–860, who distilled camphor from camphor wood about the same time as al-Kindi.

For the distillation of alcohol, however, a key statement is that of Li Shih-chen in the *Pen-ts'ao kang-mu* that the distillation of spirits from grain in China only went back as far as the Yüan dynasty. Certainly the provisions of the late T'ang liquor monopoly seem only to envisage breweries not distilleries, though it is possible that the rise in the yield of the monopoly under the northern Sung represents the introduction of spirits. Marco Polo clearly describes spirits:

> You must know that most of the inhabitants of the province of Cathay drink a wine such as I will describe to you. They make a drink of rice and an assortment of excellent spices, prepared in such a way that it is better to drink than any other wine. It is beautifully clear and it intoxicates more speedily than any other wine, because it is very heating.[46]

Cathay here means north China. As Polo's account of the wineshops of south China do not suggest the presence of spirits, it may be that large-scale distilling developed first in the north in response to the needs of the nomad conquerors. If so, it became a deadly weapon. Alcoholism became endemic in Mongol society and, like syphilis, a factor in the decline of the nomads. In later times large fortified distilleries were a feature of Chinese colonial society in Manchuria.

In Europe the gift was less deadly, despite the gin craze in Georgian London and near vodka addiction in Ruthenia, the Bukovina and other parts of eastern Europe including much of central Russia. The imagination was stimulated as well as the blood. Thus for Athanasius Kircher in his *Mundus subterraneus* of 1665, nature itself was a huge distillery operating on a manifold of materials to produce a variety of precipitates. A new cosmological paradigm had been born.

Compared to this, compared to printing and written examinations, the few mechanical devices the Jesuits introduced to China in the late Ming made little impact. They were most significant in the field of hydraulics, but even here Chinese technology, as represented by the Ming hydraulic engineer P'an Chi-hsun, had reached such a degree of pre-modern maturity that a work such as the *T'ai-hsi shui-fa* of Sabatino de Ursis and Hsü Kuang-ch'i, concerned mainly with fountains and cascades, had little to teach it in essentials. Hsü Kuang-ch'i, as well as being a high official and the most famous of the Christian converts, was a noted agriculturalist, a leader among the Kiang-nan gentry who were gradually taking over control of the Lower Yangtze irrigation system from the state. The fact that he included the *T'ai-hsi shui-fa* in his greatest work, the *Nung-cheng ch'üan-shu* (Complete Treatise on Agriculture) indicates that he saw Western hydraulics as relevant to the renovation of Chinese agriculture, but this is the most which can be said.

Ideas

Intellectual currents moved in both directions in the age of the Renaissance, but in contrasting fashions and with opposite results. In Europe, Chinese influence, essentially alchemy and China itself as presented by the missionaries, was indirect, considerable and absorbed. In China, European influence, essentially Aristotelianism and humanism as presented by the Jesuits, was direct, inconsiderable and, except by an elite, rejected. Whereas in China the Jesuits could only found a sect not a school, in Europe, alchemy and an idealized China combined in what may be called the anti-classical tradition of European thought: the appeal from Greece and Rome to Egypt (the supposed home of alchemy), China and nature. Of this tradition, Athanasius Kircher, alchemist and Sinophile, was the leading exponent in Catholic Europe in the Baroque age.

In the sixteenth century the assimilation of Chinese alchemy, which had been proceeding by periodic quanta since antiquity, reached its conclusion in the work of Paracelsus, c. 1490–1541.[47] By whatever channels it was derived, Paracelsus' thought was highly Chinese. He articulated clearly that the aim of alchemy was not metallic but medical; in Needham's language neither aurifiction nor aurifaction, but the elixir and the *enchymoma*; especially if this last be understood psychologically as well as chemically, the product of archetypes as much as endocrinology. His fundamental entities, salt, sulphur and mercury, were not elements as in the Greek cosmological tradition but processes, like the *hsing* of Tsou Yen and Tung Chung-shu, which operated on the elements. Indeed Paracelsus made a frontal assault on the classical medicine of Galen and Avicenna. Appealing to nature, he presented an alternative picture of the human body as an interlocking set of laboratory processes, a remarkable anticipation of the biochemical approach to medicine. A pioneer, Paracelsus' expression was obscure. In Taoist fashion he drew no clear distinction between physics and psychology. Nevertheless, in the century after his death, his ideas were highly influential in medical circles and beyond.

This influence culminated in the Rhineland school of alchemy whose publishing centres were Mainz, Frankfurt and Basle, whose patron was Rudolf II, and whose leading members were his doctor Michael Maier, Gerhard Dorn and the Pole, Michael Sendivogius. From the Rhineland, Paracelsism passed to Athanasius Kircher, who received part of his education at Mainz when it was a refuge for ex-members of Rudolf's court. Kircher was critical of Paracelsus and of particular alchemical theories, but his *Mundus subterraneus*, a farrago of apparent nonsense and anticipations of the future development of science, was the last major expression of the image of the world as a laboratory (specifically a distillery) before the increasingly dominant image of the world as a clock. Yet without the laboratory to discredit Aristotelian deductivism and to appeal to nature, the clock might not have won so easily.

While Chinese alchemy made its final penetration and won its last triumphs, Europe was acquiring new information about China from the Catholic missionaries. This information was first systematically used by Giovanni Botero in his *Greatness of Cities* of 1588. The *Greatness of Cities* is a kind of universal urban sociology in which Asian as well as European examples are used to criticize Machiavelli's notion of the city as a political community based on free, arms-bearing farmers. As secretary to St Carlo Borromeo, Botero disliked the secularism, indeed paganism, implicit in Machiavelli's sociology, but he was also concerned to show its irrelevance to much of European and almost all Asian urban experience.

Anticipating Montesquieu, the Machiavellian counterblast to himself, Botero was interested in the geography of urbanism. China, as described by the missionaries, provided him with an extreme example. The East, he supposed, was more ecologically favoured than the West, and China, the Far East, most of all, in such matters as soil fertility and availability of water for irrigation and communication:

> The country is for the most part very plain and of nature very apt to produce not only things necessary for the use and sustenance of the life of man, but also all sorts of dainty things for man's delight and pleasure... More than this, the rivers and waters of all sorts run gallantly through all those countries with an unspeakable profit and commodity for navigation and tillage.[48]

Consequently there was no ecological ceiling to Chinese population:

> By these things I have declared, it appeareth plain that China hath the means, partly by the benefit of nature and partly by the industry and art of man, to sustain an infinite sight of people.[49]

Urbanization, too, *pace* Machiavelli, must be unlimited: 'it is of necessity that the number of people do become inestimable, and of consequence the cities exceeding great, the towns infinite, and that China itself should rather, in a manner, be but one body and but one city'.[50] Panopolis was possible.

Botero's ideas were taken up by Athanasius Kircher in the next generation. In his *China Illustrata* of 1667, Kircher provided not only a summary of the latest missionary information about China from Trigault, Semedo, Martini, Boym and Grueber who had written since Botero, but also a universal cultural history in which to fit it. Kircher was, with qualifications, an alchemist and a Paracelsian. He was also an Egyptomane, devoting much of his life to an effort to decipher the hieroglyphs which he believed contained an arcane wisdom, the principle of all the sciences. To reconcile Egyptomania and Sinophilia, Kircher advanced a theory of radical diffusionism similar to that of Sir Grafton Elliot Smith at the beginning of the twentieth century. All culture was derived from Ancient Egypt and the Chinese were originally an Egyptian colony – a view not definitely abandoned until the controversies of its lay exponents Mairan de Dortous and Joseph de Guignes with the eighteenth-century Jesuit Sinologists Parrenin, Gaubil and Cibot. In Kircher, therefore, alchemy and Sinophile utopianism fused in a mixture which, however bizarre, was temporarily compelling and helped to overthrow a narrow classicism by appealing to an older and a wider world. China became the keystone of the anti-classical tradition.

Meanwhile Kircher's fellow Jesuits brought the West to China. In the first half of the seventeenth century a section of the Confucian meritocracy was in a mood to accept ideas from abroad. 'I am of the opinion', wrote Ricci, 'that the Chinese possess the ingenuous trait of preferring that which comes from without to that which they possess themselves once they realize the superior quality of the foreign product.'[51] Yang T'ing-yün, censor and convert, one of the 'three pillars of the beginning of the Catholic church', wrote in 1623:

> Some seven thousand titles of Western books have come to this country from overseas, all of which ought to be translated... If I had ten years to collaborate with a score or more persons of like ambitions we together could complete the task.[52]

This renewed xenophilia, almost comparable to the days of the T'ang in certain literati circles in Kiang-nan and Shensi, was due to a combination of circumstances. The conflict between state and society which underlay Ming history was intensifying. Chang Chü-cheng's successors, lacking his skill, lost control of the government to the eunuchs, and the government, to meet the cost of war against Japan and to respond to the first premonitory tremors of the seventeenth-century general crisis, raised taxes. There was, among the ruling class, increasing alienation from the government, even the dynasty, an incipient *fronde* of Nanking, Soochow and Sian against Peking, and rising dissatisfaction with the ruling philosophy of Wang Yang-ming whose self-contained existentialism now appeared as an avoidance of both deeper issues and practical problems. These discontents expressed themselves in the active political reformism of the Tung-lin academy, in the anti-existentialist school of Han learning which called for a return to exact philology in studying the classics, and in a group interested in science and technology whose most notable work was the *T'ien-kung K'ai-wu* of Sung Ying-hsing.

To these currents of thought the Jesuits had much to offer. Court and country conflict was no stranger to an order which had just operated the League to save Catholicism in France. The school of Han learning had something in common with the higher criticism of the Bollandists. Ricci came from a world which had just reformed its calendar on the basis of improved mathematics. Beyond these details, the monist philosophy of Scotus to which many Jesuits, following Suarez, inclined in preference to Thomism, was congruent with the Chinese rejection of dualism since the time of Wang Yang-ming. Convergence was aided by the opportune discovery in 1625 of the Nestorian monument at Sian which made Christianity both ancient and Chinese. To a select group of literati – Hsü Kuang-ch'i, Yang T'ing-yün, Li Chih-tsao, Wang Cheng – Catholicism as presented by the Jesuits offered a new transcendentalism 'to complete Confucianism and avoid Buddhism', superior predictive technology with which to dominate the board of astronomy and so capture the ideologically crucial board of rites of which it was part; and a freemasonry to unite families and cover political and social activism.

Intellectually, except for Johann Schreck, who had less than ten years in China, the early Jesuits belonged to the pre-Galilean era before the full articulation of scientific method. What they transmitted therefore was, on the one hand, Aristotelian deductivist theory as represented by Ricci and Hsü Kuang-ch'i's translation of Euclid's *Elements* and, on the other, Aristotelian systematic practice as represented by Luigi Buglio's translation of the *Summa Theologica*. In China, however, axiomatization and systematization were novelties which, if they had been absorbed by more than an elite, would have spared China its retreat into myth and provided a basis for the Galilean revolution once it became available. For although the Jesuits, after Galileo's condemnation, were not free to teach heliocentrism, they were free to teach the scientific method on which it was based and the mathematical techniques with which it was constructed. The church rejected, temporarily, the *eureka*, but never the *heuresis*, and it was this that the Chinese were not to absorb until the nineteenth century. Spherical trigonometry and logarithms, introduced by Giacomo Rho and Jan Nikolaj Smogulecki, served only to stimulate a mild revival of interest in the Sung algebra of Mei Wen-ting.

WORLD INSTITUTIONS, 1350 TO 1650

In the Renaissance world institutions acquired greater strength and began to impinge on the behaviour of states, societies and civilizations.

On the one hand, the two existing institutional layers thickened. In the microbian common market, *Treponema pallidum* was added to *Yersinia pestis* as a universal presence, smallpox, measles and influenza spread from Europe to the New World, yellow fever from Africa to Latin America and South-east Asia, while urbanization made tuberculosis everywhere a graver problem. Modernity began in worsening biological conditions, in America with a holocaust comparable to the Black Death. In the deterioration, East Asia's role was that of the prime donor of plague and the prime recipient of syphilis, the epicentre in both cases being eastern Mongolia. In the information circuit, Europe now possessed scientific descriptions of America such as that of José de Acosta, and scientific descriptions of China such as those of Mendoza, Semedo and Kircher. Similarly, China now possessed Ricci's world atlas with the explanatory notes *expanded by Yang T'ing-yün to form a description of all the countries of the world. Ch'en Ch'eng had extended Chinese knowledge of Central Asia, Cheng Ho of the south seas and Indian ocean. In Hsü Hsia-k'o, the intrepid traveller in the fastnesses of the south-west, China had an explorer of her own. Li Chih-tsao translated the De Coelo et Mundo into wen-yen*, Ricci translated the *Four Books* into Latin, Manuel Dias described Saturn's rings and Jupiter's moons to the Chinese, Kircher described Chinese iron-chain suspension bridges to Europeans, Philip II had Chinese books in the Escorial, the Wan-li emperor had European books in the Forbidden City. Not by Magellan only was the world encompassed.

On the other hand, two new institutional layers were added to the world network: a world economy and a set of religious internationals. In one of these internationals, conscious planetization began to turn a network into a system. In both, China held a notable place.

It is over twenty years since Pierre Chaunu in *Seville et L'Atlantique* put forward the theory that between 1500 and 1650 the *Carrera de las Indias* established 'la première esquisse combien grossière d'une économie-monde' and set 'un rythme du monde'.[53] Thanks to the records of the *Casa de Contratacion*, Chaunu was able to establish, with an exactness unique in the pre-statistical era, the conjuncture of the Spanish Atlantic. It consisted of five movements: moderate boom 1500–40, moderate recession 1540–60, strong boom 1560–1600, plateau 1600–20, strong recession 1620–50. Chaunu claimed to find a similar conjuncture in the trade of the Manila galleon which he himself examined; in the Brazilian sugar trade analysed by Frederic Mauro; in the Baltic trade of Amsterdam and Lubeck studied by Posthumus, Bang, Christensen and Jeannin; in the economic fluctuations of the Beauvaisis investigated by Pierre Goubert; in the history of papal finance as revealed by Jean Delumeau; and in many other particular or local studies. Chaunu concluded that, 'La conjuncture de l'Atlantique hispano-americain commande l'ensemble de la conjuncture européenne'.[54] Louis Dermigny made the pattern universal by finding it in East Asia: in Chinese ships going to Manila and Nagasaki; in bullion entering China from Manila, Japan, Macao and Central Asia. The only modification which Chaunu's theory seemed to require in its early days was that the onset of the strong recession had been later in north-west Europe than in the Mediterranean: 1640 rather than 1620. Recession in the south had intensified boom in the north before extinguishing it. The Harrods of Seville was hit before the Marks and Spencers of Amsterdam.

The Chaunu theory has stood up to subsequent testing well. It was essentially a statistical theory about a supposed frequency and as such did not demand complete absence of counter-examples but only that the departures from the system were themselves non-systematic. The only suggestion so far of a systematic departure is Richard Gascon's study of Lyon – by implication, of northern France, for 'C'est par Lyon que la France est entrée plus profondement dans l'Europe de la lettre de change, dans l'Europe des affaires, ce qui est tout un'.[55] Lyon had a different conjuncture from Seville: strong boom 1520–50, moderate recession 1550–60, strong recession 1560–80, moderate recovery on a new basis 1580–1620, moderate recession 1620–50. The difference is only partly explained by the wars of religion and Gascon argues for an autonomous conjuncture of France, perhaps of Franco–Burgundian consumption generally. However, the existence of secondary conjunctures does not necessarily deny the existence of a primary one, provided they stand to it in a genuine relationship of counterpoint, autonomous but subordinate, as would seem to be the case here. Gascon himself writes: 'Certes, la conjuncture atlantique est un élément majeur de la ou des conjunctures européennes, mais elle ne suffis pas, à elle seule, à la ou les definir. L'essentiel est precisement de déterminer dans quelle mesure la première definit la ou les secondes.'[56] A dominant conjuncture must dominate something without defining it, and it may be expected that further secondary conjunctures will be discovered, particularly in continental East Asia, without overthrowing the Chaunu theory.

A more general criticism of the theory – begun by Réné Baehrel's study of Provence, reinforced by the work of Emmanuel Le Roy Ladurie first on Languedoc and then on French agricultural production, and supported by Braudel – is that it exaggerates the significance of trade. In a traditional economy goods traded were a low percentage of goods produced and consumed. Chaunu assumes that the unified but small mobile sector determined the large but disunited immobile sector. Surely, it is argued, this is unlikely and certainly should not be assumed. To this it may be replied that while the facts of the relationship between major, minor and mini conjunctures can only be established by further evidence, such an assumption is not improbable. It appears to be in accord with current monetary theory and with the views of the Cambridge school on the role of the balance of trade in determining the level of activity in a modern economy. Can one be sure that a traditional economy was different? The seventeenth-century mercantilists believed in export-led boom as much as their twentieth-century counterparts. The Chaunu theory, while it may be refuted by further evidence, should not be dismissed *a priori* on neo-physiocratic principles. Until refuted, it should be accepted as having established the existence in the sixteenth century of a real, if limited, world economy. Of this economy, China, through the Manila system principally, formed a not inconsiderable part.

The first of the new religious internationals was the Naqshbandiyya, the Naqshbandi dervish order, which by the mid-

dle of the seventeenth century was dominant in the two Turkestans, influential in both the Ottoman and Moghul empires,
and acquiring pre-eminence in the intellectual capitals of
Islam in Cairo, Medina and the Yemen. Like most Sufi orders
the Naqshbandiyya emerged out of legend as a grassroots
resistance movement to the de-Islamization threatened by the
Mongolian explosion. It traced its origins to the Iraqi Sufi
Abu Yusuf Hamdani who at the beginning of the twelfth
century moved to Central Asia where his disciples founded
two parallel *tariqats* or orders: among the sedentary, Iranian
population, the Khwajagan which was introvert, mystical and
stressed *dhikr-i khafi*, mental prayer; among the nomadic, Turkish population, the Yasawiyya, which was extravert, evangelical and stressed *dhikr-i jahri*, vocal prayer. In the middle of
the fourteenth century, when conditions were at their worst
in Central Asia with the breakdown of the Chaghatai khanate,
the Khwajagan branch was refounded and given its name by
Baha al-Din Naqshband, a somewhat apolitical protégé of
Tamerlane's, who confirmed the original emphasis on *dhikr-i
khafi*. In the next century, however, under its next notable
leader, Khoja Ahrar, the Naqshbandiyya became a fully political movement, the heart and soul of the opposition of the
puritan small craftsmen to the secularist Timurid courts.
Khoja Ahrar extended the Naqshbandiyya from the sedentarists to the nomads and in the process reimbibed *dhikr-i
jahri*, so that in the next generation there were both mystical
and evangelical wings of the order, the *Khafiyya*, the silent or
secret sect, and the *Jahriyya*, the noisy or open sect.

Khoja Ahrar died in 1490, having done more than anyone
to destroy Timurid Central Asia, but his sons – for the leadership of the order was now hereditary – failed to make the
transition from the Timurids to the Shibanids. However, the
Shibanids, only momentarily anti-clerical, were soon forced
to conciliate an equally formidable dervish leader, the
Makhdum-i Azam, or grand master, Ahmad Kwajagi Kasani
who reconstituted Khoja Ahrar's organization and extended
its influence more widely. Before establishing his headquarters at Bokhara in 1512, the Makhdum-i Azam had been to
Iraq, the Ottoman empire, Egypt, Mecca, and after in 1531
he went to India where he ran foul of Emperor Humayun.

Following his death in 1542 the order became yet more
powerful and international. At home, his lieutenant Khoja

Islam acquired immense *waqf* properties, for his organization, the Juybari shaikhs, dominated the Bokharan trade to Moscow and was the kingmaker behind Abdullah I. Abroad, his second son Ishaq Wali and his grandson Muhammed Amin founded rival branches of the order in eastern Turkestan, his great-grandson Muhammed Yusuf proselytized in China and married into the Karakhanid royal house, and his great-great-grandson Khoja Afaq was the friend of the Dalai Lama, the ally and the viceroy of the Zunghar khan and the husband of a Chinggisid princess. Meanwhile the order also spread west, to the Ottoman empire and India. It was through the Ottoman connection, which was encouraged by the law doctors to counteract the more liberal orders of the west, the Mevleviyya and the Bektashiyya, that the Naqshbandiyya established itself as an intellectual force in the Azhar in Cairo and in the religious schools of Medina and the Yemen. Here, strategically placed on the doorstep of the *haj*, the order, and particularly its aggressive, extravert *Jahriyya* branch, became the champion of a militant neo-orthodoxy which went beyond that of the Ottoman *ulema* and in the following generations became the breeding place of a family of revivalisms in all parts of the Moslem world: Wahhabism, the Sanusi, the *Jihads* of Senegal and Nigeria, neo-orthodoxy in India, movements in Kurdistan and Caucasia, and in China the *hsin-chiao* or new sect of Ma Ming-hsin, was really a reintroduction of the *Jahriyya*. The Naqshbandiyya had become a world power except in America, a federation of cells, schools, shrines and hostels whose very looseness allowed it to survive or proliferate in a variety of circumstances.

The second of the new religious internationals was the Gelugspa, the 'virtuous sect' of Tibetan lamaism, founded by Tsong-kha-pa in 1392, which, after a period as a local reform movement, turned missionary and by the middle of the seventeenth century was a significant force from the Volga to Peking. Tsong-kha-pa was born in 1357 in the Amdo country south of the Kokonor: the Navarre of traditional Tibet, its frontier with Mongolia, Islam, China and a wider world, where Central Asian Nestorianism and Manichaeism were still alive. On coming to study in Central Tibet, Tsong-kha-pa's frontier intransigence led him to reject the lax, laicized, half-magical practice of the older Red Hat orders and to found his own Yellow Hat order which stood for a return to the rule, monastic celibacy, literal adherence to scholastic logic. Using Nagarjuna rather as Calvin used St Augustine, Tsong-kha-pa, a great spiritual director, was a disciplinarian and an ascetic rather than either a mystic or an evangelical. He and his successors, the first two Dalai Lamas (though the title only dates from 1578), founded a more unified organization than the Naqshbandiyya, a monastic confederation in its centralization on the houses of Galdan and Drepung reminiscent of Cluny. Because of its rigorist clericalism it met increasing and successful opposition from the lay aristocracy of central Tibet.

From the 1560s the third Dalai Lama, Sodnam Gyatso, turned back to the periphery, to Amdo where the monastery of Kumbum was founded in 1578 as a refuge and outreach, and beyond, to the patronage of the rulers of Mongolia and China. In 1577 Sodnam Gyatso went to meet the Altan Khan, the paramount ruler of the eastern Mongols, and his conversion marked the beginning of the Gelugspa as an international. In the course of the same journey Sodnam Gyatso established diplomatic contact with Chang Chü-cheng and strengthened his influence among the monasteries and princes of Kham, i.e. eastern Tibet. A second visit to Inner Mongolia in 1586 consolidated the alliance and the fourth Dalai Lama was a Mongol, the great-grandson of the Altan Khan, though he was taken to Lhasa to be educated. During his pontificate, a Gelugspa missionary, Zaya Pandita, brought the rising power of the Oirats, the western Mongols, into the order's net.

Around 1625 a split within the Oirats and the subsequent migration of their west wing, the Torghuts, later known to the Russians as the Kalmuks, carried the Gelugspa across Moslem Kazakhstan to the Volga and north Caucasian steppe. At about the same time, the Mongols of the Koko nor, the Qosot, another Oirat splinter group, once a danger to Tibetan predominance, became loyal adherents of the order. The monastery of Kumbum was expanded under Chinese protection. In 1642 the fifth Dalai Lama used the periphery to establish his power at home. The Qosot ruler Gushi Khan headed a grand coalition of all the external Gelugspa supporters, a Yellow Hat crusade, which overthrew the Dalai Lama's lay enemies in central Tibet and installed him as temporal as well as spiritual chief in the gilded Potala, the Escorial of Lhasa, paid for by contributions from all over central Eurasia. In 1643 the Dalai Lama exchanged embassies with the ruler of the Manchus and in 1652 he visited Peking where the Manchu chief was now Chinese emperor. In the south, Ladakh, Sikkim and Bhutan had become satellites of Lhasa. From Astrakhan to Peking, from Lake Baikail to the foothills of the Himalayas, the Gelugspa was an international power.

Its secret was organization and literacy in an area which was short of both. In a world of shifting nomad encampments and ephemeral caravanserais, the Gelugspa monastery was a fixed point for trade, administration or pastoral management, with the educated men with more than local horizons that these activities increasingly required. The seventeenth century depression brought changes to Inner Asia as elsewhere: fresh patterns of trade, north–south rather than east–west; ranch rather than nomadic pastoralism; the tribe as territory rather than kinship; aristocracy rather than monarchy. Of these changes and the new identity they brought to Inner Asia the Gelugspa was the agent and the expression. Anyone, whether in Inner Asia or its neighbours, who sought to manipulate the changes or take advantage of the identity, had to reckon with the Gelugspa international.

The third of the new religious internationals was that of the Jesuits. By the middle of the seventeenth century, 15 000 of them were operating over 500 institutions – parishes, schools, seminaries and mission stations – in nearly every country of the world. Where the Gelugspa operated in only two of the four primary civilizations and the Naqshbandiyya in three, the Jesuits were active in all four: in Paraguay no less than France, in Angola as well as China.

The Jesuits combined Gelugspa centralization with Naqshbandi flexibility. At the centre, their generalate, perfected by their second founder Claudio Aquaviva, based on the fortress-like Collegium Romanum, was almost an independent power, the black papacy. At the circumference, their provincials had sufficient independence to practice accommodation in China, persecution in Bohemia, toleration in Poland, triumphalism in Flanders, a low profile in England. In Vienna the Jesuits were friends of Spain, in Lisbon her enemies; in Peking they were Erastians, in Asuncion, hierocrats. Yet diversity of means, being all things to all men, served a single end: the presentation of an unwatered-down Catholicism at the highest possible level of human culture. Like the Gelugspa and the Naqshbandiyya the Jesuits were fundamentalists: 'To arrive at the truth in all things we ought always to be ready to believe that what seems to us white is black if the hierarchical Church so defines it'.[57] Unlike them, however, the Jesuits were also developmentalists: 'between Christ our Lord the Bridegroom and the Church His Bride there is one and the same Spirit' who would lead into all truth.[58] Their revelation was closed in one direction, open in another. Like the Gelugspa the Jesuits were disciplinarians. Like the Naqshbandiyya they had evangelical and mystical wings, though their evolution was the opposite: from the evangelicalism of St Ignatius and St Francis Xavier to the mysticism of Lallemant, Surin and Caussade. Like both, the Jesuits were suspect to the secular monarchies under whose patronage they lived.

Behind Jesuit organization lay method – the systematic meditations of the *Spiritual Exercises*, the systematic curriculum of the *Ratio Studiorum*, the systematic missiology of the *De procuranda Indorum salute*, the systematic polemic of Bellarmine's *De Controversiis* – a method which pointed in the direction of Descartes' *Discours*. Ahead of it was a much more consciously global picture of the future than those possessed by the Gelugspa or the Naqshbandiyya. Joseph de Acosta saw 'this new Christendom which these last ages have planted in the farthest bounds of the earth' as a counterbalance to heresy: 'Christianity, without doubt, augments and increaseth and brings forth daily more fruit among the Indian slaves: and contrariwise ruin is threatened in other partes where have been more happy beginnings'.[59]

Antonio Vieira, missiologue, philosemite and millenarist who saw the Portuguese revolution of 1640 as the commencement of the fifth monarchy, envisaged the new order in yet wider terms. In a sermon on the eve of Pentecost about St Ignatius he said:

Two new worlds had been discovered in his time, one oriental in Asia, another occidental in America. New men and new nations had appeared, as different in language as in colour. The fame of the new heathendoms – unknown and unnamed in the days of the Apostles – had reached men's ears. What could the fire that blazed in that great heart do to embrace and consume them all? What St Ignatius in fact did was to found and raise a third tower, also furnished and equipped with all tongues, so that his sons could use them to teach and convert the nations. The first tower was that of Babel in which the tongues were confounded. The second tower was that of the Holy Spirit in which they were infused. The third was that of St Ignatius in which they were neither confounded nor infused... but were acquired at the cost of great study and labour.[60]

The Jesuits were the first planetary men, the first in whom the world network became, to some degree, a world system.

In this vision of the Jesuits, the China mission had a special role. It was the most prestigious of the mission fields, the most demanding intellectually, the least likely from which to return, the most adapted to the Jesuits' mysticism of action, their ascesis of mind rather than body. Similarly in the world economy of Seville, the China trade had a peculiar role. It had the longest turnover cycle, required the greatest profit for viability, raised the most doubts because of its outlay in silver, provided the most prestigious prize for Protestant pirates, crossed the greatest ocean. For both religious international and world economy China was the horizon, just as it continued to provide the largest single ingredients to the microbian common market and the world information circuit.

5 World Within a World: China in the Enlighten- ment, 1650 to 1833

In the Enlightenment – for China the early and middle Ch'ing – China reached a peak of influence in world history. On the one hand, China became more than before part of the Europe-centred world order. The European conquest of America, intensified during the Enlightenment and extended by the annexation of Australasia, had altered the shape of the globe. The Chinese economy beat to the rhythms of Europe relayed through Manila, Canton and Kiakhta, her regional conjunctures being no more than counterpoint to the dominant theme. China now figured in universal histories, universal geographies. Her philosophy, flowers and physiocracy were closely observed and her evidence felt to be essential. As Father Amiot said, China was 'the Peru and Potosi of the republic of letters'.[1]

On the other hand, China retained its autonomy, both political and cultural. Europe, having conquered the primary civilization of America, did not go on to conquer those of Africa and East Asia. On the contrary traditional Chinese civilization enjoyed a final floruit under the three great Ch'ing emperors – K'ang-hsi, Yung-cheng and Ch'ien-lung – who rationalized the state, expanded the frontiers, yet left society to follow its bent. Despite a slackening of intellectual drive and a demographic option for quantity rather than quality, traditional China had not lost all creativity or yielded up all her riches. China in the Enlightenment was a world within a world and this situation provided optimal conditions for influence. At no other time in history was the China trade so relatively significant, so much intellectual interest focused on China, or the image of China so influential in forming the picture of the world, as in the Enlightenment. In no other period could a minister of France have told his sovereign on taking office that he intended to inject France with the spirit of

China. Yet to this influence, China, cocooned by defensive diplomacy, popular xenophobia and cultural solipsism, remained largely indifferent–indeed ignorant.

CHINA'S PLACE IN THE WORLD, 1650–1833

Two soundings may be taken to gauge China's standing in the world of the Enlightenment. First, the Chinese empire in the latter part of the reign of Ch'ien-lung will be compared *structurally* with its nearest analogue in the West, the British empire in the latter part of the reign of George III. This sounding will establish the immense gulf which already before the industrial revolution yawned between China and the most advanced Western countries, a gulf reflected in Lord Macartney's irony, so different from Kircher's admiration or Marco Polo's astonishment. Second, to explain this gulf, China and Europe in the Enlightenment will be compared *conjuncturally*: what had happened in Europe, what had not happened in China, and vice versa. This sounding will establish that while both China and Europe matured in the Enlightenment and perfected a traditional equipment – physical, social and intellectual – the maturities were different. Imperial China was not in decline in 1800, nor did it face some plurisecular general crisis which only forces from outside could resolve. It was simply that traditional China had matured at a lower level than traditional Europe, though at a higher level than Black Africa which perhaps also reached maturity in the eighteenth century. China's maturity remained within traditional limits, Europe's went beyond them. It is not only China's relative stagnation which is in need of explanation but Europe's absolute dynamism.

The empires of Ch'ien-lung and George III

Contrasts may be drawn with respect to the state, society, and intellect.

The state
With regard to the state, there were contrasts of organization and scale. Both empires mixed bureaucracy, aristocracy and plutocracy, but in different orders. In England aristocracy

was primary. At the centre of power was the House of Commons with its front-bench politicians, its cross-bench placemen, its back-bench country gentlemen, its ear open to opinion out of doors. It was supported by the House of Lords, the higher aristocracy essentially, political and apolitical, but laced with dependent Scottish peers and Anglican bishops, and it supported a king who was more than a figurehead but less than a chief executive. Next, came plutocracy: the city of London, its patricians essential for customs and loans, its plebeians forming half of what was meant by public opinion. Finally, hardly perceived as such, even repudiated, came bureaucracy: in the navy always, in Ireland sometimes, in India eventually. In this machine, politics was in command, as in the younger Pitt, his great-grandfather a nabob, his father a friend of the city, but himself, despite his administrative brilliance, primarily a professional politician, the successor of North, the Pelhams and Walpole.

In China, on the other hand, bureaucracy was primary. At the centre of power was the imperial study where the emperor handled up to 100 state papers a day; aided by the grand council, a cabinet office of personal assistants chosen from the top echelon of the regular bureaucracy, the grand secretariat; and advised by the six specialist metropolitan boards. Next, came plutocracy: the salt merchants of Yangchow and Tientsin, the Shansi bankers, the Canton co-hong, through whom the empire operated its most readily expandable revenues and from whom it raised emergency benevolences. Finally, hardly perceived as such, even repudiated, came the informal organizations of the local elite – the *shu-yüan* or liberal arts colleges, the committees for building town walls, the conservancy boards, the militia associations – without whom China could not *de facto* be governed. In this machine, red tape was in command, not Ch'ien-lung the ageing superman with work overload; not Ho-shen, his Martin Bormann whom Macartney admired and the mandarins detested; not the grand council collectively; but its secretariat who knew the regulations, did the drafts, and pre-empted the decisions – men like Chia I who while still a supernumerary ran the conquest of Turkestan.

In scale, the Chinese state was larger but lighter, the English state was smaller but heavier. The Ch'ing empire embraced 5 million square miles and 300 million people. The British empire, even allowing generous estimates for North America and India only embraced 2 million square miles and 70 million people. However, from these dominions, the Ch'ing state raised a revenue of 100 million taels, the English state a revenue of 75 million taels. Chinese taxation therefore was at the rate of one third of a tael per capita, English taxation at the rate of a full tael per capita. If India, America and Ireland are left out of account, the discrepancy is still more striking. The 10 million inhabitants of Great Britain paid 45 million taels taxation a year, four and a half taels per head. Turning to the relationship between taxation and gross national product, if 300 million Chinese had an average income of 7 taels per capita, taxation of 100 million taels would represent 5 per cent of GNP. If 10 million British had an average income of 45 taels per capita, taxation of 45 million taels would represent 10 per cent of GNP. Even if 10 million overseas British and 50 million Indians with an average· income of 5 taels per capita are added to make a GNP of 1150 million taels, total British taxation of 75 million taels would represent 7 per cent of GNP. In addition, the British state had a greater capacity than the Chinese to borrow. China had no bank, national debt or bill market. Again, Chinese revenue was less consolidated than British. Only the first third was sent to Peking; the second was legally retained in the provinces, while the last was not even reported to the capital.

The same contrast is found in the armed forces. Though the Ch'ing military establishment was nominally 800 000, its real strength was nearer half a million and it is doubtful if more than 100 000 men were ever put into the field at once. Shipbuilding was reduced to discourage piracy and there was no longer a high seas fleet. In the British empire, though the peacetime army at home was small, there were 100 000 men under arms in India, Wellington had 78 000 men at Vitoria and 200 000 in the Waterloo campaign. Similarly, though the peacetime naval establishment was only 15–20 thousand, a hundred battleships were in cold storage, there was considerable expenditure on dockyards, and in wartime, personnel could be rapidly increased to 100 000 and more.

The English forces were superior in horsepower and firepower. Though the Ch'ing doubled their military horse establishment from 100 000 to 200 000 through the establishment of *ma-ch'ang* or studs along the Inner Asian frontier, the quotas were not always met and the animals were only Mongolian ponies. The British cavalry was only 50 000 horses in peacetime, but all were thoroughbreds and it had behind it the resources of a horse-breeding society not just a few studs. The Chinese forces were also inferior in artillery. The typical war junk, displacing 250 to 350 tons, carried only thirteen guns, compared to the standard ship of the line, of 1500 tons, which carried seventy-four. The largest Chinese wooden battleship, built in the mid-nineteenth century, only had thirty-six guns, most of them 9–12 pounders, compared to HMS *Victory's* hundred: thirty 12-pounders, twenty-eight 24-pounders, thirty 32-pounders and two 64-pounder carronades. Wellington and Nelson would have had little difficulty in disposing of any Ch'ing general or admiral. Furthermore, the Chinese state did not have the pocket or the popularity to sustain a long war in which numbers and space might have told.

Society

With regard to society there were contrasts of articulation and use of energy. In both England and China society was stronger than the state in that it commanded more men, money and material, and possessed considerable autonomy. English society was highly articulated. It was rooted in the revolution of 1688 which was the victory of social institutions – the church, the universities, corporations, counties, companies – over state institutions. The revolution was the result of the power of society and became a further cause of it. Following the revolution, society developed new articulations in many directions: in business with the stock exchange, Lloyds, fire and life insurance companies, country banks; in the professions with the Smeatonian, the Surveyors' Club, the Institution of Civil Engineers, the Royal Academy of Music, the British Association for the Advancement of Science, the British Institute of Architects; in medicine with the new hospitals, Guy's, Westminster, St George's, Middlesex; in the arts with new theatres like Covent Garden, publishing houses like Longman, local literary and philosophical societies, subscription libraries; and in social life at large with the spas – Bath, Cheltenham, Scarborough and Buxton – the hunts – the Badminton, the Pytchley, the Quorn – the cricket clubs, and the newspapers such as *The Times* and *Morning Post*.

In China, on the other hand, though change was in the same direction, it was slower. In China, too, society had in a sense defeated the state. Early Ming etatism was no more and the Ch'ing did not revive it. Instead they contracted the frontiers of state action yet further, concentrating on rationalizing the functions they retained. In 1712 the land tax was frozen and the poll tax abolished. In the salt administration the tendency was to less official intervention and, in the reforms of T'ao Chu in Huai-pei in the 1830s, an approximation to the notion of *laissez-faire* was reached. Officials showed a new awareness of market forces. In town planning, irrigation and flood prevention, Confucian propaganda, and the maintenance of law and order, magistrates were encouraged to work with the informal leaders of society. Beyond this sphere of state/society partnership those leaders were developing literary societies, colleges, partnerships, local improvement boards, banking networks, not without analogy to the developments in England. Yet the result was different. In England the institutions of society coalesced into a country of public opinion to which the court was ultimately responsible. In China, there was a court but no country, interests but no public opinion. Greater articulation contrasted with lesser.

It was the same with the use of energy. Braudel has estimated total and per capita energy consumption in Europe around 1800.[2] There were in Europe around 14 million horses and 24 million cows. About 120 million tons of wood a year were used as fuel; 50 million workers laboured with their hands and muscles; there were half a million watermills, some tens of thousands of windmills, 3½ million tons of sailing ships. Converting these different kinds of energy into a uniform horsepower equivalence, Braudel arrives at a figure of 25 million energy units for a population of 200 million, or roughly one unit for every ten people.

Similar estimates can be made for China. There were in China around 5 million horses and 23 million oxen and water buffaloes. About 10 million tons of wood a year were used as fuel; 75 million workers laboured with their hands and muscles; there were half a million watermills, some tens of thousands of windmills, 2½ million tons of sailing ships. Converting these different kinds of energy into a uniform horsepower equivalence, one arrives at a figure of 13 million energy units for a population of 300 million, or roughly one unit for every twenty people. Even allowing considerable latitude for error, these figures are striking. They mean that even before the industrial revolution, Europe's consumption of energy, total and per capita, was double that of China. When and how was this lead achieved? As it is most marked in the amount of wood and the number of horses, it may be ascribed, first, to the opening of the Baltic timber supply in the sixteenth century and, second, to the multiplication of horses, the hippocultural revolution starting in eastern Europe, in the eighteenth century.

If Europe as a whole consumed double the energy of China in 1800, the gap between England and China was even wider. Prescinding from the latest increases in coal consumption with the beginning of the industrial revolution, say 6 million tons, English energy consumption may be computed as follows. There were 1½ million horses and 3 million cows. Five million tons of wood and 3 million tons of coal were used as fuel; 2½ million workers laboured with their hands and muscles; there were 50 000 watermills, 5000 windmills, and a million tons of sailing ships. Converting these different kinds of energy into a uniform horsepower equivalent, one arrives at a figure of 2½ million energy units for a population of 10 million, or roughly one unit for every four people, five times the corresponding figure for China. England's lead, like Europe's, was most marked in fuel and animal power. It was due, even before the industrial revolution, to her precocious use of coal, particularly London's domestic reliance on Newcastle, and to her adoption to a unique degree of the hippocultural revolution. Coal fires and Corinthians made England the biggest per capita energy consumer in the world. The industrial revolution simply took this lead further.

Intellect
With regard to intellect, the contrast was between the presence and absence of scientific method, for the birth of science affected all thought by providing a new standard of rationality. In their actual achievements, European and Chinese science

might not yet be so different. It was in method that the two parted company. European scientists, though not always European theoreticians of science, had understood since Newton, that what distinguishes a scientific from a non-scientific hypothesis is its falsifiability, its greater negative information content, i.e. what it forbids, and consequent greater testability. They further understood that this enrichment of hypothesis was achieved by abstraction and mathematicization.

Chinese scientists, on the other hand, stressed the positive information content of a hypothesis, i.e. what it asserts. They tried to make hypotheses compatible not only with present but future facts. They were haunted by the irrefutable *I-ching* proposition that everything is either positive or negative. Chinese science did not understand the crucial role of testability nor the place of abstraction and mathematicization in achieving it. It was empirical but not experimental. It was not experimental because in the Renaissance it had not advanced from philosophy but had retreated towards myth. In Europe, the ambiguities of traditional metaphysics had been resolved by Newton's *Principia* and Kant's *Critique* into natural science on the one hand and cognitional theory on the other. In China, the ambiguities of traditional metaphysics had been compounded by the abandonment of critical philosophy by early Neo-Confucianism, by the emphasis on self-evidence by both Wang Yang-ming and his opponents, and by the elevation of practice to be the only test by most schools of later Neo-Confucianism.

English science under George III was preparing for the great leap foward which was to culminate in the work of Clerk Maxwell. The first triumphs of modern science had been in physics, specifically astronomy. The second phase began in France with Lavoisier's breakthrough in chemistry. It was continued in England by Dalton, Davy and Faraday, chemists who returned to physics via Boscovich's law and electromagnetism. Discovery returned from the heavens to earth.

Chinese science under Ch'ien-lung was abandoning the relatively scientific philology of the school of Han learning, which had culminated in the work of Ch'ien Ta-hsin, in favour of the esoteric oracularism of the New Text School or the purely practical institutional studies of the *Ching-shih* school. Truth was now sought in revelation or action. Between the two, human knowledge disappeared except in the thought of the lone thinker Chang Hsüeh-ch'eng who, like Vico and Hegel, sought in philosophical history a knowledge more meaningful than philology, more factual than metaphysics. Unfortunately, Chang entangled himself in the question of who could write such a history. He arrived at a Confucian ultra-montanism in which only an infallible sage ruler, such as Ch'ien-lung claimed to be, could produce, with his bureaucracy, truth in public collections and official histories. Chang thereby became the apologist, if he were not the inspiration, for the *Ssu-k'u Ch'üan-shu*, the huge officially edited library of classics in which Ch'ien-lung sought all too successfully to freeze the achievements of the Chinese mind. Chang Hsüeh-ch'eng gave way to mystical institutionalism: in England a breakthrough, in China a breakdown.[3]

European and Chinese conjunctures

Behind these contrasts of structure between the British empire under George III and the Ch'ing empire under Ch'ien-lung lay contrasts of conjuncture, or long-term trends, between European and Chinese history over the preceding century and a half. These conjunctures may be described as institutional, climatic, demographic, urban, educational and topographic.

Institutions

The first conjuncture was institutional. In both Europe and China the civilization of the Enlightenment emerged out of the general crisis of the seventeenth century. In both areas the cause was the same: the contraction of the Sevillean world economy when its initial spatial conquests had yielded their windfalls, when the stock of Indian labour had been run down by European diseases and when white America became sufficiently established to retain its bullion locally. So too were the symptoms: an exacerbation of political and social tensions which, according to original fault lines, produced protest, rebellions, secessions and revolutions, all of which may be analysed in terms of a conflict between court and country, state and society. The outcome of the crisis, however, differed markedly in West and East: in part of Europe at least a profound institutional transformation; in China only superficial institutional adjustments.

At bottom the seventeenth century general crisis consisted in an imbalance between the cost of the state and what society was able or willing to pay. The courts, tolerable in the boom, became intolerable in the slump. Statesmen sought to rectify this imbalance in three ways: reduction of the cost of the court, enrichment of the country, and less frictionful mobilization of society's resources by the state. In north-west Europe this search led to fruitful institutional innovations. Economy produced cheaper, less corrupt, more professional civil services, best epitomized by Samuel Pepys and the Admiralty. Mercantilist enrichment produced joint stock companies, navigation acts and supported passage for skilled artisans. The search for less painful ways of raising funds produced national banks and more extensive gilt-edged markets, which not only increased the state's financial resources, but also promoted mutual confidence between it and its subjects. Indeed all three kinds of institutions – administrative, mercantilist and public credit – created a new relationship between state and society which made the state more powerful yet left society stronger and less alienated. It was a breakthrough to a new symbiosis, a new integration, in the body politic.

In China, on the other hand, there was no such breakthrough, only a restarting of the mechanisms under better management. The same situation faced China, the same general objectives were sought. K'ang-hsi resembled Louis XIV in trying to create a style of monarchy at once cheaper and more businesslike.[4] Pepys would have admired Yung-cheng who paid officials a second salary, *yang-lien yin* ('nourish honesty money') to reduce dependence on fees and commissions. Chinese officials such as Ts'ao Yin, the Liang-huai salt censor, ceased to be contemptuous of trade and tried, like Colbert, to understand and foster it. K'ang-hsi and Ch'ien-lung went on progress to meet the people and cultivate better public relations. But these things were matters of personality and policy only. They did not involve any basic recasting of the system, nor did they produce new institutions. The three major achievements of the European restoration – incorrupt administration, mercantilism and companies, banks and gilt-edged markets – found no parallel in China. Chinese officials continued to be paid by their clients, customers and victims; their efforts at economic promotion were intermittent and often unauthorized, and the closest the Chinese came to loans from the public were benevolences and the sale of degrees and office. The Ch'ing rationalized the machinery of Chinese government with their palace memorials, their grand council, their imperial dictatorship. They did not raise the level of integration between state and society or make the relationship between the two other than that of splendid parasite to indifferent host.[5]

Climate
The second conjuncture was climatic. In the period 1650 to 1833, the evidence of Alpine glaciers and moraines, tree rings in the Urals, Alaska and Arizona, wine harvest dates in France, cherry blossom times in Kyoto, thaws at Riga, freezing at Lake Suwa, and Greenland ice caves, suggests that both Europe and China experienced a period of colder and wetter weather, the little ice age of the seventeenth century. But, as in late antiquity, they experienced it differently. For Europe, the little ice age was a period of difficulty. The European wheat economy, particularly outside the Mediterranean, was constantly threatened by too much water. Increased humidity was good for fleas and produced a recrudescence of plague, especially in the north-west. It was the more remarkable then that, under the leadership of the north-west, famine was eliminated by better barns and transportation, and plague was banished by international quarantine and better hygiene, both domestic and personal. Despite optimal conditions, death was thrown back and life advanced by the elimination of the amenorrhoea of famine. Europe survived a minor ecological crisis and emerged adaptable and used to hard conditions.

For China, on the other hand, the little ice age was a period of ease. The Chinese wheat economy, particularly north of the Yangtze, was constantly threatened by too little water. Flea-carried disease was not a major problem in China, particularly after the Ch'ing isolated the plague reservoirs of Northern Manchuria by the willow pallisade. Consequently the early and middle Ch'ing saw an expansion of the agricultural frontier and an increase of population in north China, particularly the north-west, the old metropolitan province of Shensi. A system of mini-farms was established on a precarious ecological basis which was to prove highly vulnerable to the drought famines of the nineteenth and twentieth centuries. Until then China enjoyed an ecological bonanza, became inadaptable and used to easy conditions. As the general crisis produced no institutional breakthrough, so the little ice age stimulated no technological vitality.

Demography

The third conjuncture was demographic. In both Europe and China the Enlightenment saw a population increase of roughly 100 per cent: in Europe from 100 million in 1600 to 200 million in 1800; in China from 150 million in 1600 to 300 million in 1800. The causes and the pattern of population produced, however, were different. In Europe, the increase of population was due to a fall in the death rate not a rise in the birth rate. Indeed, paradoxically, a *fall* in the birth rate increased the size of the population, because the biggest component in the decline of the death rate was not the elimination of plague and famine, nor the micro-improvements to hygiene through stone houses and more water, but the reduction of infantile and juvenile mortality which *followed* the decline in the birth rate rather than preceded it. Fewer children meant better cared-for children: improved midwifery, fewer accidental suffocations, less premature weaning, fewer rustications to the 'tristes villages' of commercial wetnursing,[6] a reduction in infantile dysentery, fewer whooping cough deaths among toddler girls, and better care of the diseases of childhood generally. This higher regard for individual children was an expression of that more general feminization of values which grew out of the uniquely European pattern of late, equal-age, companionate marriage with the encouragement, in different ways, of the Protestant and Catholic reformations. However, it was not only the size but the pattern of population which changed. Fewer children meant proportionately more adults, more workers, more literates, higher productivity, increased inventiveness. European demography was set towards progress.[7]

In China, on the other hand, the increase in population was due to a rise in the birth rate not a fall in the death rate.

Possibly there was marginal improvement in the death rate as a result of better hygiene, with the greater use of tea (and hence boiling of water) and easily washed cotton cloth, more efficient administration by the Ch'ing of reserve granaries, and a greater number of orphanages. Primarily, however, the birth rate was responsible and here the chief factor was earlier and more universal marriage. The foundation of new households was made possible by the doubling between 1650 and 1800 of China's cultivated acreage (yield increases came later) by the opening up of new hillside fields, first for maize and sweet potatoes, then after terracing for rice. This set up an accelerating cycle of land – population – land, people supplying not only labour for terracing but refuse for manuring, either directly in nightsoil or, more importantly, indirectly via the pigs who lived off human leavings. Unlike Europe, where an intellectual factor, the revaluation of the child and the feminization of values was fundamental for demography, it was this material factor, the American food plants, which was the primary factor behind the invasion of China by the Chinese. The European population boom was a phenomenon of culture; the Chinese, in the main, one of nature. Nevertheless there was in China a shift in collective psychology and values towards children, though in the opposite direction from Europe: from quality to quantity – at least, quantity of sons because, as Jesuit sources make clear, female infanticide was still prevalent, possibly increasing. However, it was not only the size but the pattern of population which changed. More children meant proportionately fewer adults, fewer workers, fewer literates, lower productivity, diminished inventiveness. Chinese demography was set towards decline.

Urbanization
The fourth conjuncture was urban. As the population increased in both Europe and China, so did the number of towns and the size of the urban population; but the distribution was different. In Europe the increase was macro-urban and it involved a fall in the percentage of the population which was rural. The significant urban expansion was not in the foundation of new towns – that had been more characteristic of the Renaissance when the Iberians had peppered their new worlds with *neapoleis* – but the enlargement of existing

centres, particularly capitals. Thus London had 152 000 inhabitants at the end of the sixteenth century, 317 000 in the mid-seventeenth century, 700 000 at the beginning of the eighteenth century, 860 000 at the end of it, 1 274 000 in 1820, and over 2 million in 1841. Paris had 180 000 inhabitants at the end of the sixteenth century, 360 000 under Richelieu, 400 000 in 1700, 550 000 in 1800, and over 1 million in 1851. Vienna had 60,000 inhabitants in 1637, 100 000 in 1700, 175 000 in 1754, 232 000 in 1800, and 680 000 in 1875. Naples had 300 000 inhabitants in 1600, and half a million in 1800. St Petersburg had 74 000 inhabitants in 1750, 192 000 in 1784, and 218 000 in 1789.

In this megalopolitan revolution the chief factors were not commerce or industry, although London perhaps owed its supereminence to the fact that it alone among European metropolises was an ocean emporium as well as a capital, but government and consumption. The European super-cities, like those of China before them, were the creation of the state, but unlike those of China, they did not remain its property. The capitals first imposed their character on the state: Protestant and mercantile in England, Catholic and administrative in France, Biedermeier in Austria, *lazzarone* in the Two Sicilies, despotic in Russia; and then recreated the country in their own image. This double urban domination was particularly evident in the case of London. London rejected clericalist royal despotism in 1641, London restored church and monarchy in 1660, London was worth a communion service in 1688. In the eighteenth century, London had 10 per cent of the population, absorbed half its natural increase, and disposed of between a quarter and a third of its spending power. One person in six in England passed through London during their life cycle, absorbing not only its high consumptivity but also its high literacy: by 1840, 88 per cent for men, 76 per cent for women. Thus London became the school of England, an economic luxury no doubt, but one which the country made sure it could afford.

In China, on the other hand, the increase was micro-urban and it involved a rise in the percentage of the population which was rural.[8] The significant expansion was not at the apex of the urban pyramid but at the base. During the Ch'ing many new towns were founded in frontier provinces like

Szechwan, Kweichow, Yunnan, Taiwan and Sinkiang.[9] For example, in Chin-t'ang district in Szechwan on the edge of the Chengtu plain the number of small market towns increased from four in 1662, to thirteen in 1875 to thirty-two in 1921. Existing lesser centres swelled. The number of medium-sized market towns in China increased from 2500 in 1700, to 6000 in 1800. For example, the population of Lu-chou district in Szechwan, which contained the typical lesser river port of that name, rose from 40 000 in 1758 to 140 000 in 1817 and over half a million in 1882. The largest cities, however, appear to have been declining. Peking, the 'incomparable imperial city',[10] reliably reported to have had 2–3 million inhabitants in the eighteenth century, had only 700 000 by the beginning of the twentieth. Nanking, 'the perfection of the whole realm. . . it seemeth to me to be the best and greatest city of the whole kingdome',[11] bigger than Peking in the estimates of Mendoza, Semedo and Le Compte, was credited with 7 million inhabitants in the seventeenth century, but had less than one million by the beginning of the nineteenth. Yangchow, capital of the Liang-huai salt trade, had 2 million inhabitants in the eighteenth century, one million or less in the nineteenth. The triple city of Wuhan, 'the best peopled and of the greatest report in China'[12] according to de Halde, with one million in Wuchang, 500 000 in Hanyang, and more in Hankow according to Father Loppin who lived there three years, had only 1 200 000 inhabitants at the beginning of the twentieth century.

The cause of this anti-megalopolitan revolution, this flattening of the urban pyramid, was economic rather than political. Unlike Europe where the state created the capital and the capital recreated the country, in China it was the country, the hinterland, which determined the pattern of urbanization. It was the expanding internal agricultural frontier of maize/ sweet potatoes and rice which drained the lifeblood of the big cities into the petty market towns. Thanks to the progressive withdrawal of the state, China's was a market economy, but a market economy in which the dominant figure was not the entrepreneur who sought to maximize the economic threads in his hands, but the broker who sought to minimize his risks while maximizing his contacts. The seats of the brokers were the river ports, the points of trans-shipment, the relay towns, the up-country distribution centres, the forwarding offices, the depots, the yards, the godowns; and it was these which gave rise to the market towns. But while the urban population of such places was expanding it is doubtful if it was keeping pace with the rural population which they served. In China it was the village and even more the farm which made the running. The Chinese market towns did not have the resonance of the European megalopolis. They were not schools of literacy and high consumption, 'electrical transformers' of culture in Braudel's phrase.[13] They were not luxuries, reckless gambles on the possibility of increasing production. Seats of closed guilds, *mafias* and gombeenism, they were the reluctant necessity of a rural society in the grip of demographic repetition compulsion.

Education

The fifth conjuncture was educational. In Europe, especially the north-west, the eighteenth century saw a literacy breakthrough from town to country, from elite to masses. In Normandy literacy rates rose from 10 per cent for men and 7.5 per cent for women in 1700, to 80 per cent for men and 65 per cent for women in 1800. England was already ahead of France in 1600 and Lowland Scotland overtook both by 1700 to become, with New England and Sweden, one of the areas of highest literacy in the world. It was not only literacy *rates* that were improving. Since population was increasing at the same time, the total increase in the number of literates was even more striking: between six and tenfold. Furthermore the quality was improving as well as the quantity. Elementary literacy, reading rather than writing, was the product of religious competition: the parish school, the Protestant attack, the Catholic counter-attack. Advanced literacy, writing as well as reading, was the product of economic circulation: the urban environment of a culture mediated by addresses, contracts, bills, letters, endorsements and signatures. The two literacies had different geographies: Sweden, one of the highest in elementary literacy in 1700 was one of the lowest in advanced by 1800, while north-east France came from behind into the highest bracket. If literacy was not reading, education was not literacy. In addition there was technical education: an improved ability to handle the traditional tools which in the eighteenth century reached a high point of maturity and technical perfection. Again, there was musical education which combined elements of both technique and literacy, as well as providing, as the modern mythology, new categories of sensibility and imagination. Led first by Protestant middle Germany, then by Catholic Vienna, musicality was the predecessor of literacy in the Enlightenment, as it has been, in our own day, its survivor. Karl Popper has drawn attention to the connection between the rise of polyphony and origins of the critical outlook.[14] Bach was as unique to the West as Newton.

In China, on the other hand, the eighteenth century saw a literacy breakdown, a retreat from country to town, from masses to elite. In the middle ages, China, thanks to paper, printing, Neo-Confucianism and the growth of megalopolises like Hangchow, Soochow and Zayton, enjoyed exceptional literacy rates both elementary and advanced. Mendoza believed that literacy was almost universal in China especially in the urbanized south. By the nineteenth century, however, literacy rates were down to 50 per cent in the towns, 25 per cent in the countryside, which, given an optimistic urban/rural ratio of 1:4, would produce an overall literacy rate of 30 per cent. If male literacy were double female, this would give 40 per cent for males, 20 per cent for females, rates well below the national English average in 1800 of 67 per cent and 51 per cent, though still high for a pre-modern country.

The decline of literacy in the early and middle Ch'ing was due fundamentally to the demographic and urban patterns outlined above. Literacy in a pre-modern society was a function of urbanization, particularly macro-urbanization. There may have been more teachers in China, as the increasing number of candidates for the imperial examinations turned, when unsuccessful, to education for a career, but they were in the wrong place: in declining large and medium-sized *kulturstadt*s rather than in the mushrooming market towns on the maize/sweet potato frontier. Chinese zeal for education was no less. Indeed, Wang Yang-ming's existentialism encouraged education by its belief that every man could become a sage. But with more children, with population less concentrated, with the mass separating itself from the elite in space, educational facilities were not what they had been. A symptom of the cultural gap that was developing was the rise of heterodox, non-Confucian folk religions, such as the White Lotus, with their own simplified scriptures, which reflected the end of mass literacy, just as the European folk religions, such as Methodism, represented its beginnings.[15] Neither in technical skills nor in music was there the same advance as in Europe. China now imported Swiss watches to be repaired by Jesuit horologists and while the Ming prince Chu Tsai-yü knew as much about equal temperament as Bach, there were no organs on which he might have played and no polyphony to play.

Topography

The sixth conjuncture was topographical. In Europe, a new area, the north-west, and a new ideology, Protestantism, took the lead in the civilization of the Enlightenment, with a corresponding increase in dynamism. In China there were no such innovations, no such increase.

Duality was characteristic of Europe. In Caesar's day there had been a Mediterranean and an extra-Mediterranean. Under the classical Roman empire, the Mediterranean was the centre. In late antiquity the balance swung to the extra-Mediterranean, to the imperial capitals of the *limes*: Trier, Milan, Sirmium. In the Gothic middle ages the centre of Christendom remained in the north, among the heavy populations of northern France, Midland England and Old Castile. With the Black Death, however, the balance again swung south, to be confirmed by the oceanic empires of Lisbon and Seville, the industrial empires of Tolfa, Lucca and Bologna. Not the least of the renaissances of the sixteenth century was the renaissance of the Mediterranean itself, against which Erasmism, the Protestant reformation and the revolt of the Netherlands protested in the name of deeper piety, greater literacy and older culture. As Braudel saw, the re-elevation of the Mediterranean on the back of the ocean was unnatural in terms of geohistory and the seventeenth century saw a revival of the north, particularly the north-west, which was able to take over the Atlantic economy from the flagging strength of Spain and reconstruct it on a firmer basis. The north-west already enjoyed advantages: a more productive agriculture, reserves of timber and coal, earlier and more complete adoption of the early modern family, longer life expectancy, better education, fewer imperial burdens, less threat from Islam. These advantages, coupled with a less grave form of the great depression and more political skill in confronting it, gave the north-west the leadership of the European community by the end of the seventeenth century.

Within the north-west England and Holland were pre-eminent. France might supply the quantity for the Enlightenment, 20 million people; but England and Holland, with only a third of that, supplied the quality: Newton, Locke, de Witt, Spinoza, William III, Marlborough. England and Holland were Protestant and one may ask what part did the new religion play in their leadership of modernity. The advantage of Protestantism was cultural rather than intellectual. In themselves, Protestant doctrines, the triple *sola* of scripture, grace and faith, Protestant method, biblicism whether critical or fundamentalist, were less rational than the Catholic doctrines of imparted grace and faith formed by hope and charity, the Catholic method of scripture, tradition, argument and authority. Protestantism was simplistic in both doctrine and method; Catholicism allowed for complexity in both, and so stood closer to the rationality of science. Yet this did not matter at the time. What mattered was that Protestants were people of superior culture who invested in superior culture. Protestantism was a religion of literacy, of late marriage, of the conjugal family, of fewer children, of more education, of longer life expectancy, and it promoted these things. Civilization is the combined product of intellect, culture and institutions. The intellectual roots of the Enlightenment were Catholic: Galileo, Palestrina, Descartes, St François de Sales. What Protestantism generally contributed was the appropriate culture for their growth and what English Protestantism specifically contributed was institutions: constitutionalism and a non-theocratic, pluralistic church which formed part of society rather than the state. In Catholic countries, neither culture nor institutions were as propitious, the one too raw, the other too rotted by absorption into the state. The shift in topography, in itself liberating, from the Mediterranean to the lands where Protestantism was the heir of Burgundian civilization, therefore, meant a power accretion of dynamism via higher culture and improved institutions.

In China, on the other hand, there was nothing to compare to this shift or its consequences. The heart of Chinese civilization continued where it had been since the Sung, in the lower Yangtze, especially the Kiangnan triangle Chinkiang–Hangchow–Shanghai. Since the Sung, China had had its own dualism: the political and military capital in the north; the economic and cultural capitals in the south. This, however, was a division of function rather than an ambivalence of centre and it was accentuated by the advent of the Ch'ing state.

As barbarians whose power within the Wall rested on their power byond it, the Ch'ing were even more tied to Peking than the Ming. By the same token they made more effort to conciliate and compensate the south by their patronage, ideological stance and Confucian whistle-stop tours. The social change, the expansion of agriculture up the hillside armed with the American food plants, likewise did not alter Chinese topography. It simply lengthened the Yangtze and gave the economic and cultural centres in Kiang-nan a longer radius. Szechwan, the boom province of the eighteenth century, remained dependent on the lower Yangtze for high-grade textiles and on the middle Yangtze for raw cotton. It was an internal colony rather than a new metropolis, though, like Mexico in the Spanish empire, it tried to exercise this role *vis-à-vis* Kweichow and Sikang. Within Kiang-nan there was only a slight shift from sea to canal: Hangchow to Soochow. Essentially, from Ming to Ch'ing, Kiang-nan remained dominated by the urban quadrilateral of Nanking the *kulturstadt*, Yangchow the salt emporium, Sung-kiang the cotton factory and Hui-chou the tea centre, with Soochow in the middle, 'the most fashionable city of the Celestial Empire', 'the great emporium of the central provinces of China', combining cultuire and commerce.[16] Its high-productivity agriculture, its superb network of waterways, its pyramid of large cities and small markets, its unique concentration of Confucian scholarship, left Kiang-nan without rival in China: a super-Holland presiding over a greater Rhine. Yet the fact that Kiang-nan had, in 1800, held this primacy for eight centuries left it without much potential for the future. It could not give China the kind of dynamism, mental or material, provided by the Protestant north-west in Europe.

Lord Macartney, George III's ambassador to Ch'ien-lung in 1793, is the best witness to China's relative standing towards the end of the Enlightenment. Macartney found much to admire in China. The Grand Canal, he conceded, was 'a most stupendous work'.[17] Of Kiang-nan he wrote, 'All the advantages of climate, soil and production have been lavished here by nature with an unsparing hand' and 'The country seems to be one continued village on both sides as far as we can see, wonderfully beautiful and rich'.[18] Hangchow, he noted:

> is a very populous, extensive and flourishing city. . . The environs of the town are very beautiful, embellished by an extensive lake, a noble canal with several inferior ones, and gentle hills cultivated to the summit, interspersed with plantations of mulberries and dwarf fruit-trees, sheltered by oaks, planes, sycamores and camphors.[19]

China and England were still comparable:

> The city of Tientsin is one of the largest in the empire. I think its extent along the river cannot be less than from Milbank to Limehouse. Along the quays on each side are many conspicuous buildings, chiefly temples, warehouses, magazines and public edifices.[20]

> Pekin stands on at least a third less ground than London, including Westminster and Southwark, but still it is one of the largest cities in the world, and justly to be admired for its walls and gates, the distribution of its quarters, the width and allineation of its streets, the grandeur of its triumphal arches and the number and magnificence of its palaces.[21]

Yet Macartney had no doubt of the superiority of England, and China for him was no utopia, even a dystopia. He wrote that England 'from the weight of her riches and the genius and spirit of her people, is become the first political, marine and commercial power on the globe'.[22] China, on the other hand, 'is an old, crazy, first rate man-of-war, which a fortunate succession of able and vigilant officers has continued to keep afloat for these one hundred and fifty years past, and to overawe their neighbours merely by her bulk and appearance'.[23] Locally China was impressive, globally she was not.

AVENUES OF CONTACT, 1650 TO 1833

There were two major innovations in the avenues of contact between China and the outside world in the Enlightenment. First, thanks to the European East India companies and the English tea market, the Cape route became predominant, taking the place of the Pacific route in the Renaissance. Where Macao had been marginal and subordinate, Canton was central and dominant. Second, thanks to the Muscovite state and the Russian tea market, a new route, the far northern land route, was initiated which rapidly came to hold second place among the avenues of contact. In addition there were significant developments in three out of the four other avenues, so that China was more closely linked to the outside world than ever before.

The central land route

As the scale of traffic along the central land route in the days of its prosperity has been exaggerated, so it has been underestimated in the days of its decline. Certainly it did not enjoy in the Enlightenment the affluence it had had under the Timurids, but equally it did not fall into the broken back condition sometimes portrayed. Admittedly the period 1650 to 1760 saw the route at a low ebb. Both the Safavid and Astrakhanid states were falling into anarchy. There was war between the Ottomans and the Persians in the first third of the eighteenth century and between the Ch'ing and the west Mongols, the Zunghars, in the second. In the K'ang-hsi and Yung-cheng editions of the imperial statutes, Turfan was the only regular Central Asian tributary mentioned. It was allocated a quinquennial cycle, but embassies were only noted in 1673 and 1686. Gaubil, writing in November 1726, stated that Moslem commerce from Persia had been interrupted since K'ang-hsi's time. In Transoxania the chief cities were in decline in the late Astrakhanid period. Samarkand, which should have been the pivot of any intercontinental traffic, is described as being completely deserted at the beginning of the eighteenth century. Yet even then a trickle passed through. J. Savary des Brulons in his *Dictionnaire Universel de Commerce*, first published in Paris in 1723–30 and then in an enlarged Copenhagen edition of 1759–65, having described the source of rhubarb, continued: 'De là les Caravanes Persanes et Turques la portent à Alep et à Smirne, c'est la Rhubarbe de la France'.[24] There was enough trade for Nadir Shah, the Turkoman soldier of fortune who tried to reconstruct the Iranian empire between 1736 and 1747, to wish to make Meshed his capital in order to control it, though it cannot have been substantial.

From around 1760, however, the situation improved. Between 1755 and 1759 the Ch'ing overthrew the Zunghar empire and imposed their rule on eastern Turkestan. For the first time since the thirteenth century there was a single government from Sian to Ili. In Transoxania three tidy city-states emerged out of the anarchy of the later Astrakhanids: Kokand from 1753, Bokhara from 1785 and Khiva from 1805. In eastern Iran a new area of order was produced by the creation of the Afghan state by Ahmad Shah Durrani 1747–73. In 1760 Ahmad Shah organized a coalition of Moslem states for a *jihad* against any further Ch'ing advance west. In 1762/63, Ch'ien-lung having decided against advance beyond the T'ien-shan, he sent an embassy to Peking with four superb large horses, a threat and a promise, duly recorded with statistics by Castiglione. In Persia the confusion left by Nadir Shah was ended by the rise of the Qajar dynasty, while in the Ottoman empire the palace complex of the marcher lord Ishak Pasha at Dogubeyezit, completed in 1784, suggests a considerable degree of both order and prosperity on the Persian frontier. Herat, which came under the Durrani ruler, was said to have a population of 100 000 at the beginning of the nineteenth century. Generally, Moslem Central Asia was reviving at the beginning of the nineteenth century.

The lead in the revival of trade was taken by Kokand. Between 1759 and 1809, under Erdeni Beg, the first ruler, and his two successors, Kokand sent twenty-three missions to Peking, and under Omar Khan, 1809–22, twenty-five. The scale of the trade covered by these missions may be gauged from the fact that one of them on its return was accompanied by eighty-eight wagons carrying tea, pepper, silks and ceramics. In spite of these exports, China ran an adverse balance of trade. As early as 1760 a Ch'ing official urged an increase in silk exports to stem an outflow of silver. From Kokand, China imported large Ferghana horses, Persian and Indian opium, Russian furs, and European woollens and

metal goods, probably from Russia, though in view of
Dogubeyezit, the Levant is a possibility. The Ch'ing did not
like the Kokand trade, but they tolerated it for political
reasons. Kokand, a military as well as commercial state, was
host to the exiled descendants of Khoja Afak, the Afaqi
Makhdumzadas, hereditary chiefs of the Naqshbandiyya in
eastern Turkestan, whose periodic returns with Kokandi support if trade was interrupted caused rebellion. In 1835 the
Ch'ing granted the ruler of Kokand a semi-monopoly of Sino–
Central Asian trade – Bokhara had been trying to cut in –
and allowed his consul, the *aqsaqal*, to exercise jurisdiction
over Kokandi subjects on Chinese soil. This treaty system
later became the prototype for that with the Europeans on
the China coast after 1842.

The comparative prosperity of the central land route in
the early nineteenth century is clear from the report of Sir
Alexander Burnes who was in Central Asia on behalf of the
government of India between 1831 and 1833. At Kabul, 'a
most bustling and populous city',[25] he found an active commercial international, the Hindu Shikarpooree merchants
from Upper Sind who were able to give bills on Nijni Nov-
gorod, Astrakhan and Bokhara, as well as having an outpost
on the island of Kishem in the Persian Gulf. At Kunduz he
met tea merchants from Yarkand about to go home. Bokhara,
a city of 150 000, was cosmopolitan. Natives of Persia, Turkey,
Russia and China were to be seen and European cutlery,
Chinese tea, Indian sugar and Manila spices were on sale in
the bazaar. The vizier got quinine from Constantinople, an
old merchant had been both there and Canton, there were
twenty caravanserais, and in general, the 'country is flourishing, trade prospers and property is protected'.[26] The tea trade
was particularly large: 950 horse loads, according to Burnes,
some of it re-exported to Russia via Astrakhan. Relations with
Persia were less good because of Sunni/Shia conflict, but
opium was imported and re-exported to Yarkand. The picture
is of a modest but real affluence.

The southern sea route

As an avenue of contact between China and the far West, the
southern sea route did not fully recover from Cheng Ho,

Albuquerque and Urdaneta till the opening of the Suez canal in 1869. In the latter part of the eighteenth century, however, its importance as an avenue of contact between China and India increased through the rise of the so-called country trade. This rise was at first the by-product of the initially greater expansion of the Cape route, but by 1833 the Cape was falling tributary to the Indian Ocean.

Until the rise of the country trade after 1750, the southern sea route was significant only for the *haj*, Chinese Moslems from Yunnan especially, and for minor currents of trade, in particular coffee and indigo, conducted by *Gemeinschaft* merchants, Armenians, Parsees and Jews in roughly that order of importance.

A fresh diffusion of Armenian trade began in 1602–4 when Shah Abbas, in the course of counter-attack against the Ottomans, overran Armenia and captured the emporium of Julfa. He transported the commercial community to a suburb, renamed New Julfa, of Isfahan and made them the privileged merchants of his empire. Careful to distinguish themselves from the eastern orthodox Greeks, the Armenians, with both Uniat and non-Uniat sections, were well placed to circumvent ideological barriers. In the seventeenth century, they were silk merchants at Aleppo, coffee importers, bankers and caravan operators at Constantinople and, according to Tavernier, were active in Tongking, Java and the Philippines. In the 1690s there was an Armenian route to China from Surat via Agra and Lhasa to Sining which handled indigo, coffee, musk, tea, tobacco and porcelain and was sufficiently sophisticated to use letters of credit to settle its accounts. In Lhasa the Armenians were on good terms with the Gelugspa international, while in Shansi in 1703 they gave 100 gold pieces to found a Catholic church. At the beginning of the eighteenth century New Julfa merchants moved via Shiraz and Bushire to Madras and via Astrakhan to Moscow. In 1722 an Armenian ship arrived from Bengal at Canton.

Meanwhile there was expansion west as well. In 1717 there was an Armenian colony at Leghorn, and in 1786 the Madras Armenian, Agavelli Satur, was being considered for enoblement at Trieste. By this time New Julfa was so prosperous that it possessed thirty churches.[27] A striking instance of the wandering Armenian was Francisco Namtella: born in Diarbekir, traded in Aleppo, learnt Spanish in Manila, visited Canton twice, had agents in Saint-Malo and died in Marseille worth half a million.

Behind the Armenians came the Parsees and the Jews. The Parsees had long been established as merchants at Surat and Bombay. They retained links with the Zoroastrian community at Yezd and as early as the sixteenth century traded in Bengal and at Malacca. The advent of the *raj* gave them further opportunities for expansion and in 1845 there were eighteen Parsee firms in Canton. A Parsee, Sir Jamsetjee Jejeebhoy, was the first Indian baronet, and at Canton the community was sufficiently prosperous to found the Canton Zoroastrian Anjuman charity fund. The Jewish community, particularly active in indigo as the Armenians were in coffee, was further flung. The heart of it, so far as the southern sea route was concerned, was the Portuguese, or at least Portuguese-named, community of Kerala which was in touch with smaller communities in Bombay, Surat and Madras, with Macao and the subterranean Jewries of China, and with the Jews of Leghorn, half-Sephardic, half-Levantine who dominated the trade of North Africa. Leghorn Jews specialized in coral, Kerala Jews in diamonds, Constantinople Jews in pearls. Jewish carpet merchants in Constantinople imported indigo from India via their co-religionists at Kabul, Ghazni and Teheran.

The major development along the southern sea route was the rise of the country trade. Until the second half of the eighteenth century, Indian commerce had operated largely within the subcontinent, the essential articulation being the exchange of Bengal silk, cottons and sugar for Bombay raw cotton, silver and horses. From the mid-century, this was replaced by a one-direction trade link between Bombay and Canton, with Bengal, close to Burmese sources of teak, contibuting the shipping. Although conditions in Bengal and the advent of Java sugar played a part in this change, its most powerful cause lay in China.

At Canton the English East India company was short of saleable commodities with which to finance its growing purchases of tea. English goods did not sell, so the company licensed the so-called country traders to bring, first, raw cotton and, later, opium to Canton. There the proceeds of the sale were transferred to the company in return for a draft on India, or increasingly London. For although Armenians, Parsees and Jews helped organize the partnerships which initially conducted the country trade, most of the capital belonged to the company's English servants. It was in fact their profit on the government of India and they sought to repatriate it. It was difficult to do so directly in the form of Indian goods since the market for these was limited and the company itself until 1813 enjoyed a monopoly of the home trade. Repatriation, however, could be done easily, and with the company's encouragement, in the form of Canton drafts on London. In London the drafts plus appropriate interest were met by the company out of the proceeds of the sale of the tea. The company got its capital at Canton, its servants got theirs repatriated, the English public got increasing quantities of cheap tea which put the foreign smugglers out of business. Even India was not the loser, since the real source of the company's servants' profit was not it, but the subsidies which the Treasury in London paid the company. It was this ingenious bullionless system which swelled the shipping between India and China from 33 in the decade 1764–73 to 291 in the decade 1804–13. By 1833 the Bombay connection was essential to the Canton trade, and the local agency houses, such as Jardine Matheson, which now conducted it in place of the Indian partnerships, were the dominating figures on the China coast.

The northern land route

If the southern sea route was in temporary eclipse until the rise of the Anglo–Indian trade to China, the northern land route was more permanently eclipsed. Little traffic travelled across the steppe from the Black Sea to China or vice versa. Golden Sarai had been destroyed, rhubarb merchants no longer returned this way from Su-chou to Constantinople, and since the failure of Sokollu Mehmet's grand design, not many *hajjis* took this route. All that remained was the intermittent commercial activity of Khiva on the one hand and of the Zunghar empire on the other.

Khiva, though not devoid of civilization, as the writings of its most famous ruler Abul Ghazi Bahadur Khan 1643–63 show, was a military rather than a commercial state. Such trade as it had was north and south rather than east and west and Alexander Burnes described the Khivans as banditti living in an entrepôt since slavery was much of their business. Nevertheless there was some improvement in the early nineteenth century and some Chinese tea took this route to Russia. Lake Yamysh, on the edge of the Zunghar empire, whose annual salt fair attracted traders from all over Inner Asia, had a brief period of importance between 1640 and 1695. Russian and Tartar traders from Tobolsk, Kazan and Moscow accompanied the salt caravans to the lake where they exchanged Russian leather and fur for the Chinese silks, rhubarb, cottons, tea and porcelain which Bukhariot and Zunghar traders brought with the salt caravans from the opposite direction. The trade was not large, thousands rather than tens of thousands of roubles, but it helped to give Russia a taste for Chinese goods which the far northern land route then exploited. There was another burst of activity when the Zunghar empire was at its height under Galdan Tseren, 1727–45, indicated by six embassies to Peking between 1735 and 1746, but after this, night descended just as it was lifting on the central land and southern sea routes. Thereafter the only notable travellers were the Torghuts, the western Mongols returning from the Volga to their homeland in Zungharia in 1770–1 to escape increasing Russian control.

The far southern sea route

In its modern form the far southern sea route had begun as simply a quicker passage to either Batavia or Canton, depending on whether Australia was passed on the west or the east. For example in 1794, Captain Thomas Butler of the *Walpole* arrived at the Cape from England late in September just as the north-east monsoon was starting in the Indian Ocean. He therefore headed south, ran before the roaring forties, swung through the Tasman with the south-east trades, and finally used the north-east trades to bring him to Macao in January, a journey of nearly 10 000 miles in 102 days. He commented on arrival that he was 'sure we could not so soon have got here by any other way at this season'.[28] The *Walpole*, however, did not find many imitators because although fast, it was a bumpy ride in which the rig might be damaged; but closer inspection, starting with Cook, had already revealed two other ways in which Australasia might be linked to China.

First, its sub-Antarctic waters and offshore islands were seal-bearing and this was discovered just as the sea otter of Oregon and British Columbia, with which a lucrative trade had been developed at Canton, was becoming exhausted. Second, New Zealand at least had excellent mast timber in the *kauri*, 'a pine which rises sixty and sometimes eighty feet before the first branch',[29] conveniently available in the Auckland district just where shipping needed it after passage through the roaring forties. The earliest phase of New Zealand history, that of the sealers and whalers (whale oil was needed for cheaper and better candles for literate England) and *kauri*, was therefore intimately bound up with the Canton trade. The penal settlement at Port Jackson in 1788 which became Sydney was designed to protect what was in effect an offshore island, a greater Taiwan with better than camphor for the China trade. Both seals and *kauri* were soon exhausted, but native flax for rope was not. In 1838, 130 vessels, British, American and French, called at the Bay of Islands, north of Auckland.

The Cape route

The rise of the Cape route to become the leading channel for Sino–foreign contact was the result of two factors both related to the progress of consumerism in Europe.

The first was the seventeenth-century shift from bullion to commodities in world trade pioneered by the Dutch and the Amsterdam commodity markets. In the Renaissance, the age of Seville, Europe wanted the *means* of consumption: initially gold, whose value had risen thanks to the production of silver in central Germany, and latterly silver, when Mexico and Peru were revealed. When bullion was the *primum mobile*, China was a secondary element in the European world economy and the preferred avenue of approach was the Pacific with the best access to supplies of silver. In the plateau of the seventeenth century, the age of Amsterdam, and still more in the Enlightenment, the age of London, Europe wanted the *ends* of consumption: sugar, tobacco, cocoa, coffee and tea. With commodities the *primum mobile*, China could be a primary element in the European world economy and the preferred avenue of approach would be the Cape with the lowest, because most maritime, transportation costs.

The second factor, which actualized these possibilities, was the transformation of tea from a medicine to a commodity. Although the English East India Company was ultimately to be the prime beneficiary of this transformation, it was effected initially by its continental rivals, in particular the Ostend Company and its successors which began the large-scale importation of tea to Europe in the early eighteenth century.

The importance of the Ostend Company has been underlined by Louis Dermigny. Although its charter was issued in Vienna in 1722 by Charles VI and may be seen as part of a policy to develop his new dominions in the Low Countries after the war of the Spanish succession, the Ostend Company was essentially a flag of convenience. Behind it was an international consortium: Antwerp merchants long excluded from the ocean by the closing of the Scheldt, English Jacobites, Huguenots, Dutch republicans, people with capital who could operate on both sides of the Channel. For although most of the shareholders came from Antwerp (in name at least; some may have been nominees), most of the ships were English, suitably rechristened with Habsburg names, so were the captains and supercargoes, as were the envisaged customers. Thomas Ray, an Irish Catholic married to a Belgian, who had organized the expedition to India in 1715 of the *Saint Matthew* commanded by Xavier Sarsfield, was one of the seven directors, along with five Antwerp merchants and Jacques Maelcamp of Ghent, whose firm of Craywinckel and Maelcamp had useful links at Cadiz with the bullion trade. Between 1724 and 1732 the company sent eleven ships to China and ten to Bengal. Between 1724 and 1727, the profit of nine vessels exceeded the company's entire capital, primarily through the sale of tea smuggled into England from the continent to undercut the smaller and heavily taxed imports of the English East India Company.

The success of Ostend thoroughly alarmed London and forced the English East India Company to increase its imports. The author of a history of the Ostend Company which appeared in the 1764 edition of Harris's *Voyages*, expressed these fears vividly: 'The Trade of the Indies was the great Wheel which moved the whole commercial System in Europe . . . . *Flanders* was, for several Ages, the Centre of the Commerce of Europe; among such a people therefore Trade might easily be revived ... the great success this Company had, during the short time it continued, was a very strong and prevailing argument to persuade the setting up a Company in any other place.'[30] Had not the English government put pressure on the emperor to dissolve the company, he concluded, 'the whole *East India* trade, in less than a century, would have been confined to the *Austrian* Netherlands, and perhaps, the greatest Part of the Trade in Europe must have followed it.'[31]

Under the combined pressure of England, France and Holland, the emperor, whose priority in foreign policy was the recognition of the Pragmatic Sanction by the powers, was forced, first, in 1727 to suspend the company for seven years and, then, in 1731 to put it into definite liquidation. The interests behind the company, however, sought other flags of convenience. The Swedish East India Company, which received a charter from Frederick I in 1731, was founded at the instance of Colin Campbell, a former shareholder and ex-supercargo of the Ostend Company who had made friends with the pro-Jacobite Swedish ambassador to London, Karl Gyllenborg. Many Jacobites were among the shareholders, as was a group from Ghent including Jacques Maelcamp the former Ostend director. Charles Pike who had commanded a ship for Ostend became a director and one of its ships, the *Apollo*, had formerly been to Canton as the *Archduchess*. Until the late 1740s when genuine Swedes began to take over, captains and ships' officers were British, mostly Scots and generally semi-Jacobites. China was the centre of the company's activities: between 1732 and 1805 it sent 126 ships to Canton. The Danish East India Company, given a charter by Christian VI in 1732, also had Ostend affiliations. Among the directors were Frederick de Coninck from Antwerp, a relative of one of the Ostend directors, Pieter van Hurck a former supercargo, and John Brown, son of a Jacobite killed at Culloden, with, presumably Catholic, relatives in France. Flemish capital was also invested in the Asiatic Company of Emden which operated briefly from 1750 to 1756 under the auspices of Frederick the Great. One of the two ships it sent to Canton in 1752 was commanded by Peter Dens of Ostend who had been in the service of both the Ostend and Swedish companies and made in all eleven voyages to the East.

Finally, the same interests were also behind the Asiatic Company of Trieste, which received a charter from Maria Teresa in 1775, and lasted with a reorganization in 1781 until 1785. It too was a flag of convenience organization which exploited Austria's neutrality during the War of American Independence. Its links with Trieste were tenuous. The Proli family of Antwerp, one of whose members had been a director of the Ostend Company, was a principal shareholder; a Scots captain commanded the *Kaunitz* which went to Canton in 1790; and Ostend was the main centre of its activities. It was the competition of the Trieste company which led the Earl of Pembroke to exclaim in 1781, 'Will Washington take America or the smugglers England first?'[32] and which led the British government and the East India Company to abandon their restrictionist policy of small purchases and high taxation in favour of large purchases and low taxation. Even after its defeat by the new English policy, Anglo–Belgian business was not quite dead. In Asia John Reid, the Trieste company's business manager at Canton, formed the agency house of Cox, Beale and Reid, which eventually, after several changes of partner, became Jardine and Matheson. In Europe, after a period of eclipse Anglo–Belgian business turned inwards and in the persons of Lieven Bauwens and the two Cockerills, William and John, laid the Walloon foundation for the continental industrial revolution.[33] The virus of capitalism at Antwerp was not easily suppressed.

The Pacific route

Although dethroned by Macao's successor, the Canton of the East India companies, the Pacific route continued to exist and developed a second articulation. Until Mexico revolted from Spain, the galleons continued to ply between Acapulco and Manila. However, despite the recovery of the Mexican mines in the eighteenth century, as the white population built up to replace the lost Indians, the number of Chinese ships coming down from Kwangtung and Fukien to Manila never consistently reached the best pre-depression levels. Manila, like Macao after 1640, had to diversify its trade and become more South-east Asian. Consequently the galleon trade came under increasing criticism in the Philippines, as well as in

Spain where the mercantilist politicians behind the Royal Philippine Company of 1733 (in which Antwerp interests were involved) wanted to use its silver while taking its silk direct to Spain. The galleon interest, however, 'the city and commerce of Manila', really the religious houses, some charities and a few established families, fought back, and in 1769 established their own *consulado* or chamber of commerce, to protect their position, which they succeeded in doing until the Spanish empire itself disintegrated in the wars of independence.[34]

The new articulation was the sea otter route from Oregon and British Colombia operated by the Americans and British and attempted by the Russians. American trade to Canton, via the Atlantic and the Cape, began in 1784 with the arrival of the *Empress of China* under the direction of Major Samuel Shaw. It was the work of New England interests, which needed a new field of action after their exclusion from the triangular trade with West Africa and the British West Indies. With small, lightly manned, low-cost ships, the Americans were well placed to find themselves a role on the China coast. The continental companies had been driven off the seas by English competition in peace and English blockade in war. Most of their trade had been, via the smugglers, with England and that was captured by the English East India Company. But into that part which was genuinely with the continent, the Americans, as neutrals, inserted themselves. However, not having the country trade system of the English or at this date ready access to Mexican silver, they needed a commodity with which to trade at Canton. Having experimented with North American ginseng, they fixed on fur.

The sea otter of the north Pacific was already being traded by the Russians at Kiakhta. The possibility of selling it at Canton was revealed by the ships of Cook's last voyage which called there in 1779 under King and Clerke. Between 1779 and 1787 a kind of fur rush to Oregon occurred among the country and private traders at Canton, John Reid ex-Trieste Company manager being one. In 1787 the Bostonian John Kendrick took the *Columbia* to Canton via the Horn, Juan Fernandez and the Oregon coast, while the New Yorker Simon Metcalf brought the *Eleonora* to the same destination with seal skins from the Falklands before himself sailing to Oregon for more. In 1789 Spain asserted her claims over the area in the Nootka sound crisis but, unsupported by France, was forced to give way to England backed up by Vancouver's expedition of 1791–2. The Americans, although neutral in the crisis, were its real beneficiaries. During the wars American shipping at Canton grew phenomenally, from an average of six ships in 1792–4, to forty-one in 1805, and became predominant on the sea otter coast. From Oregon the Americans sailed via Hawaii, where they could pick up useful sandalwood, to Canton and thence home to New England via the Cape. The Russians too, who had had outposts in Alaska from the 1790s, wanted to use the north Pacific route to Canton instead of the tedious porterages to Kiakhta, and they ran a way station in Hawaii between 1806 and 1820, but were refused permission to trade by the Chinese authorities since they already had facilities in the north. They therefore sold their fur to the Americans who thus received a further boost. Meanwhile, the fur trade stimulated J.J. Astor with the American Fur Company and a Montreal consortium, the North West Company, to develop land links between the eastern United States and Canada, and the Pacific coast. By 1825, however, the sea otter was becoming rare. The brief efflorescence of its route had nonetheless deeply influenced European patterns of discovery and settlement in the north Pacific. It was also the beginning of the opening of Japan. Vancouver to Yokohama had joined Acapulco to Manila and the Pacific now had two strings to its bow.

The far northern land route

The opening of the Siberian route to China, first to Peking and later, after 1727, to Kiakhta on the Russo–Mongolian frontier, may be seen as part of Europe's flight forward in response to the seventeenth-century general crisis. Russia, blockaded by Sweden, Poland and the Ottomans, experienced the crisis in a particularly prolonged and acute form, a true time of troubles which started in the late sixteenth century and did not end till Peter the Great opened his window to the west in 1703. Unlike Poland, Russian agriculture, despite serfdom – or because of serfdom – did not then yield an export surplus. Russia's timber reserves were too distant as yet to be mobilized, the slave trade was no longer respectable, honey was being replaced by sugar, beeswax by whale oil. Russia's sole marketable asset was fur: sable, ermine, marten, fox and squirrel. With fur Russia paid her subsidy to the ecumenical patriarchate and financed her purchases from the West and the Ottoman empire, in particular the incense needed by the orthodox church. The western fur market, however, while boosted by Renaissance luxury, was reduced by seventeenth-century austerity, and always liable to political interference. It was an obvious move then, one first suggested to the tsar by the English Muscovy company merchant and diplomatic agent Sir John Meyrick at the beginning of the seventeenth century, to turn east rather than west, particularly as the retreating fur frontier, as animals were hunted out, was already moving in that direction. With fur, silk might be purchased from China, and re-exported to the West for foreign exchange.

Russian approaches to China took two forms. First, there was the Cossack approach. The Cossacks employed by the fur monopolitans, having crossed Siberia to the Pacific by 1638 in search of fur, turned south to the Amur in search of land sufficiently temperate to grow grain to support the chain of *ostrogs* – strongpoints for collecting fur levied as tribute from native trade – which had been precariously established in eastern Siberia. In the Amur valley, in their attempt to assert paramountcy over the local tribes, the Cossacks came into contact, and increasingly into conflict, with the authority of the 'bogdoiskii tsar' of the 'Nikanskii land'.[35] Although the Cossacks did not realise it, this was the Manchu ruler who was in the process of becoming emperor of China by invited conquest.

Second, there was the diplomatic approach. This proceeded from Tobolsk and Kazan as well as Moscow and resulted in the missions of Ivashko Petlin, 1618, Feodor Isakovich Baykov, 1653–6, and Nikolai Gavrilovich Milescu, 1675–8, which went to Peking via the Ob, Irtish and Mongolia. The missions aimed to make contact with the emperor of China, but not until the time of Milescu was it realized that since 1644 the ruler in Peking was the same 'bogdoiskii tsar' on whose territories the Cossacks had been trespassing in the Amur, whose vassal Gantimur they had enticed away and from whom they had

had the temerity to demand submission in the Milovanov embassy of 1670. Nor was it appreciated that the 'Nikanskii land' was simply the Manchu for China.

The Ch'ing government, too, had difficulty in identifying the Russian (*O-lo-ssu*) envoys with the Russian (*Lo-ch'a*) marauders in the Amur. By the time of the Milescu mission, however, it had made the identification and was determined not to grant regular tributary status and the right to trade until satisfaction had been received over Gantimur and the frontier. The position was complicated by the fact that in 1675–8, the K'ang-hsi emperor was engaged in the real conquest of China by the Manchus, the suppression of the *san-fan* rebellion in south China. The Ch'ing were further worried by the possibility of an alliance of the Russians with their enemies in Inner Asia, the Zunghars: the nightmare of a new Chinggis Khan reinforced with European artillary. Milescu therefore was treated with considerable reserve of which he was only half aware.

In 1682 having defeated the *san-fan* and in expectation of a decisive war with the Zunghars, K'ang-hsi began a careful military build up in Manchuria. In 1685 he commenced operations against the Cossacks in the Amur valley with the object of bringing the Russians to the conference table. The stratagem was highly successful. After the fall of the Russian fort at Albazin, a conference assembled at Nerchinsk further west and, through the mediation of the Jesuits Pereira and Gerbillon, an agreement was reached in August 1689. The treaty was based on the principle of equality: a Ch'ing concession and evidence of K'ang-hsi's desire for a settlement since this was contrary to Chinese protocol. The Russians agreed explicitly to withdraw from the Amur (though Gantimur stayed with them) and implicitly not to ally with the Zunghars. In return they received the right to send caravans to Peking to sell fur and buy silk. The Jesuits, as the honest brokers, got an edict of toleration from K'ang-hsi and a half-promise from the Russians of the right to use the Siberian route to Europe. It was a good bargain for all concerned: the Ch'ing benefited politically, the Russians economically and the Jesuits religiously.

In essentials the system established at Nerchinsk lasted 150 years, but in important details it was modified by the Kiakhta settlement of 1728, which followed commercial difficulties at Peking, Russian flirtations with the Zunghars, and fresh negotiations through the Jesuits Parrenin and Gaubil. The demarcation of the frontier was extended from the Amur to Mongolia which effectively excluded any Russian interference in Inner Asia. The place of trade was transferred from Peking to Kiakhta, which on the one hand gave the Russians access to a wider market, and on the other took undesirable foreigners away from the imperial capital. In compensation the Russians were allowed to establish an ecclesiastical mission in Peking, nominally to minister to the Albazinians, the Cossack captives of 1685 who had stayed on in China, but in reality to act as a minimum embassy and cut out the Jesuits. As modified by Kiakhta the Nerchinsk system functioned well. The Russians obtained a stable basis of trade; the Ch'ing obtained elbow room to conquer the Zunghars. The Jesuits, however, having served their turn, were discarded by both parties.[36]

INTERCHANGES, 1650 TO 1833

In the Enlightenment Europe and the European world progressed: not so much in breadth, as in the Renaissance, or quantity, for some sixteenth-century indices were not exceeded by the eighteenth, as in depth; settlement rather than conquest; and quality, education and health, rather than numbers. Yet it would be hard to say that China declined except relatively. The Ch'ing was an era of creativity. Ch'ien-lung ruled over more territory than T'ang Hsüan-tsung or Mao Tse-tung. China was paramount from the Caspian to the Sea of Japan, from the Stanovoi mountains to the Bay of Bengal. Without, the Ch'ing had solved the Inner Asian problem which had baffled the Han, the T'ang, the Sung and the Ming. Within, they provided some of the best government China ever saw and also the peace which allowed Chinese society to indulge in an unparalleled increase in population. It was two booming worlds then which were increasingly involved with each other through Canton and Kiakhta, through the Jesuits in Peking, and through the Ch'ing conquests in Central Asia. But the two worlds, Chinese and European, inscribed and circumscribed, ran on different time-scales. They were desynchronized, China conscious of the past, Europe conscious of the future; China living from hand to mouth, Europe building for the long term. The pattern of exchanges in the Enlightenment was shaped by these differences of temporal orientation.

People

As in the Renaissance, the pattern was quantity from China, quality from Europe. What was new in the Enlightenment was that the channels of population movement were now continental as well as maritime. To the overseas Chinese were added the overland Chinese. To the Jesuits were added the Albazinians and the Russian ecclesiastical mission.

The expansion of the overseas Chinese continued under the Ch'ing. When Koxinga captured the Dutch forts of Zelandia and Provintia in 1662, Taiwan was still largely aboriginal. Both the regent Oboi and the K'ang-hsi emperor contemplated returning it to Dutch rule if the authorities at Batavia would assist them in the overthrow of the pirates. Shih Lang's occupation in 1683, however, was followed by considerable immigration. Tainan received walls in 1723, Hsin-chu was founded in 1733 and walled in 1827–9, I-lan was founded in 1813. By 1833, though the aboriginal headhunters were still a problem, Taiwan was definitely Chinese territory, no longer part of South-east Asia. In Vietnam, a number of Chinese families arrived as refugees after the fall of the Ming. They remained, in places such as Quang Nam and Bien Hoa, a distinct community, the Minh-huong, who were admitted to the local bureaucracy and were significant purveyors of northern culture to the southern court. Distinct and later in origin was the Chinese mercantile community at Hanoi which dominated the trade of its hosts while retaining links with its land of origin, especially via Hainan. In Phnom-Penh, there were 3000 Chinese as early as 1606, but they were reinforced in the seventeenth century by Ming refugees under the adventurer Mao Cuu, who established a semi-independent state on the Cambodia–Vietnam border, which flourished on the basis of trade in pepper until the nineteenth century. In Thailand the Chinese merchant community was even more important than in Vietnam or Cambodia. In particular, emigrants from Ch'ao-chou (Teochiu) became the partner of the Rama dynasty in the national revival after the fall of Ayuthia in 1767, organizing the building of Bangkok, managing the sugar monopoly for the king, supplying wives for his harem, farming taxes on gambling and distilleries, and conducting the trade to Canton in timber and rice. During the reign of Rama II, the Chinese community received an average of 7000 immigrants a year. Finally, there was Singapore, founded by Raffles in 1819, but made by Chinese immigrants into his dream of 'the emporium and the pride of the East'.[37] Continental south-east Asia was now as bespattered with China-towns as maritime south-east Asia.

At the same time, with more official consent, Chinese emigration began to follow in the wake of the Ch'ing conquest of Inner Asia. The primary political expansion beyond the Wall was Manchu rather than Chinese and the Ch'ing kept official positions a Banner preserve. However, like most Inner Asian empires, the Ch'ing needed assistant conquerors: clerks, merchants, carters, artisans and factotums, to operate the lower levels of their system; and here there was a place for the Chinese.

Emigration was of two kinds. On the one hand, there was a mainly administrative emigration of Chinese-speaking Moslems, Tungans, from Shensi and Kansu to the political headquarters of Sinkiang, Ili and Urumchi. Here they acted as a buffer between the non-Moslem Ch'ing authorities and their Moslem, Turki subjects. In the short run, the Tungans in Sinkiang were a convenience to the Ch'ing and a source of strength because they made possible a light and inconspicuous regime in the new dominions. In the long run they were an inconvenience and a source of weakness because they imbibed Jahriyya radicalism from their co-religionists and transmitted it back to the Tungan communities in Shensi and Kansu, with serious consequences in the nineteenth century. On the other hand, there was a mainly mercantile emigration of Chinese from Shansi to the monastic settlements of Mongolia, Urga, Uliassutai and Kobdo. In Mongolia the Chinese merchants became the agents of profound changes in steppe society: sedentarization, rising consumption for the few, pauperization for the many. In the short run, these changes facilitated

Ch'ing rule by making Mongolia harmless because divided. In the long run, they made it impossible, as lesser nobles and commoners combined against both magnates and Chinese creditors in the programme of social radicalism and national assertion. The overland Chinese were a two-edged weapon for their homeland. The same could also be said of the overseas Chinese.

As Chinese plebeian emigration to South-east Asia continued under the Ch'ing, so did Jesuit patrician emigration to China. In the late Ming the Jesuits had acclimatized themselves as intellectual advisers to a country party in the lower Yangtze opposed to the eunuch-dominated court. The Manchu conquest by invitation, and still more the defeat of the *san-fan* rebellion of 1676, ended the hopes of the country parties. Thanks to the commanding personality and astronomical skill of Adam Schall and the personal finesse and diplomatic expertise, especially at the time of the Milescu mission, of Ferdinand Verbiest, the Jesuits made the difficult transition from Ming country intellectuals to Ch'ing court technicians. They became experts in diplomacy, cartography, astronomy, medicine, artillery and art to a reformist but generalist government which lacked technical services. In 1688, on the appeal of Verbiest, the Portuguese Jesuit mission – in the seventeenth century often Belgians and in the eighteenth century often Germans – was reinforced by the French mission patronized by Louis XIV and initially composed primarily of mathematicians. Less numerous and less well-supplied with funds, the French Jesuits added the new cultural distinction of the Christian Enlightenment to the Catholic presence in Peking just as it was winning its greatest success.

For two decades after the treaty of Nerchinsk, it looked as if the Jesuits and their now predominantly Manchu converts might become an established echelon of the Ch'ing state. Catholicism was now a legal religion, the Jesuits controlled a number of institutions such as the board of astronomy, they were useful allies and could command influential friends. Suddenly, however, conditions changed: not so much the famous rites controversy to which too much has been attributed, but through the changing configuration of Ch'ing politics. At K'ang-hsi's court there were two factions: the 'Manchu' faction of Banner aristocrats, imperial in-laws and old cronies, and the 'Chinese' faction of Yangtze meritocrats, some Manchu military gentry and the Jesuits as a group of civilian experts. K'ang-hsi kept a balance. He intended that the Manchus should rule in his life time, the Chinese after his death. In pursuance of this policy, in the early eighteenth century, K'ang-hsi temporarily restricted the Chinese faction (and the Jesuits) in favour of the Manchu grandees. When the Chinese faction covertly returned to favour in K'ang-hsi's last years and openly took power under his successor Yung-cheng, it was under new leadership unsympathetic to the Jesuits and prepared to jettison them from the party to placate rival native experts and signify a policy of sinofication. The Jesuits were the fall guys of Chinese politics as they were of Sino–Russian relations. The Kiakhta negotiations and the flurry of diplomacy which followed it gave the Jesuits the illusion of a second chance, but thereafter they were of no political significance, mere *virtuosi* in a court whose only genuine interest in things foreign was aesthetic: Castiglione's paintings and the rococo old summer palace.

As a result of the Kiakhta settlement, the Jesuits were joined, much to the alarm of Father Parrenin, their effective head and chief diplomat, by a Russian eastern orthodox mission. In 1712 the Ch'ing government accepted the petition of a Russian caravan leader that orthodox priests be allowed to come and minister to the Albazinians, the Cossack prisoners of 1685 and their descendants, now in Ch'ing service as soldiers and language experts, whose Christianity was at a low ebb. In 1715 the archimandrite Hilarion, plus seven clerics, arrived and were given *de facto* right of residence. In 1728 the orthodox ecclesiastical mission was given *de jure* status as one of the official institutions of the Nerchinsk-Kiakhta system.

After 1730 there were two orthodox churches in Peking: in the *O-lo-ssu pei-kuan*, the Russian north hostel, was the Albazinian church dedicated first to St Nicholas the Miracle Worker, then to St Sophia and finally to the Assumption, founded in the 1690s and supplied with priests from Tobolsk; and in the *O-lo-ssu nan-kuan*, the Russian south hostel, to which the Peking caravans came, was the church of the Purification (Presentation, Candlemas) founded in 1728. Both churches were built and paid for by the Ch'ing authorities, who saw themselves as possible patrons of eastern orthodoxy in eastern Siberia as they were of lamaism in Inner Asia. The Russian government, on the other hand, had the right to send a number of purely secular students to study Chinese and Manchu at a school, the *O-lo-ssu hsüeh*, in the grounds of the *O-lo-ssu nan-kuan*. The early orthodox missionaries were not edifying: alcoholism, insanity and scandals marked their history, while the Albazinians, only a pretext anyway, went completely native. The secular students, however, were much better and on their return laid the foundations of Russian Sinology at the university of Kazan. Diplomatically, the orthodox ecclesiastical mission was never the counterweight to the Jesuits that Peter the Great hoped, and Father Parrenin feared, it might be. Similarly, the Ch'ing protectorate of orthodoxy never developed.[38]

Flora and fauna

The same pattern, plebeian/patrician, also governed exchanges of flora in the Enlightenment, but with the roles reversed. With one exception there were no significant exchanges of fauna in the Enlightenment.

Chinese imports of flora were plebeian. The early and middle Ch'ing saw the spectrum of the American food plants enlarged by Irish potatoes and reach its maximum effect on Chinese agriculture. Irish potatoes, really from Peru, were slow to spread outside the New World. Their diffusion in both Europe and China was an eighteenth, even a nineteenth-century phenomenon. In China they appeared first in northern Fukien shortly before 1700. As this area was in contact with Manila, and the Cape route had not yet established its pre-eminence, the Pacific seems the most likely course for it to have followed. Where maize grew on sunny hillsides, sweet potatoes on shady, and peanuts on sandy bottomland, Irish potatoes could be grown high up above the mist level. This was one reason for their late adoption: they only came into their own when the best land had been used. Thus in the mountainous Hupei-Szechwan divide, an important area of agricultural expansion, the potato was only cultivated after 1800. The 1866 edition of the gazetteer of Fang-hsien, an agricultural frontier town here, stated unenthusiastically that, 'in the lofty mountains where maize cannot be successfully grown the only source of food is the Irish potato'.[39] Another reason was that potatoes in China were a northern crop which did best in Shansi, Kansu and Feng-t'ien where population pressures came later than in the south.

The American food plants made their greatest impact in China in the middle Ch'ing. A stream of well-organized migrants moved from the rich province of Kiangsi, north-west to the hills of Hupei, south-west to the hills of Hunan, to meet in the interior basin of Szechwan which became the *chef d'oeuvre* of the new colonization and the most affluent pro- in China. Before the middle of the eighteenth century Szechwan was only thickly settled and intensively cultivated in the Chengtu plain, that magnificent artificial delta created by Chinese hydraulic skill. The census of 1776 showed a population of 8 million only. By 1819, however, the provincial gazetteer showed 25 million, by the 1870s it was 35 million and by the beginning of the twentieth century 45 million. The American food plants, however, had less happy long-term results. They were used, as far as possible, as transitional crops, to support the family during the preparation of rice terraces. They became therefore instruments of inertia, allowing the rice economy to repeat itself endlessly without regard to circumstances or cost. The American food plants were applied with ecological recklessness. As Dermigny neatly says, the flood of Chinese farmers going up the hill was matched by a flood of earth coming down.[40] Soil erosion through deforestation produced dustbowls above and raised river beds below. Furthermore, the hillsides had been sources of timber and pasture, both in short supply in traditional Chinese agriculture. Energy levels were going to fall as a result. Many of these evils lay in the future in 1833, but like the urge to marriage and the natalist fury of the Chinese farmer, they exemplify his short-term perspectives.

European imports of flora were patrician. It was in the Enlightenment that Europe began that massive importation of plants from China that was to transform European horticulture by making possible Chinese landscapes in Western parks and gardens. The origin of this movement was Father Attiret's description in 1743 of the gardens of the summer palace, later published in the *Lettres Edifiantes*. Its theoretician was Sir William Chambers, son of a Scots, probably Jacobite, merchant at Göteborg, himself a supercargo in the Swedish East India Company, voyager to Canton on three occasions and, on retirement, *virtuoso* and architect of the Kew Gardens pagoda (1761–2) and of Somerset House (1776–86). His *Dissertation on Oriental Gardening* of 1772, although including fanciful elements and over-schematized, contained the essential Taoist notion that a garden should be natural rather than artificial and encouraged gardeners to think that there was something to be learnt from China.

The first conscious practitioner of the movement, however, was Sir Joseph Banks, president of the Royal Society from 1778 to 1820, Cook's colleague on the first voyage, and a universal man. Through his contacts with the East India Company, he introduced to his garden at Spring Grove near Isleworth, the tree paeony in 1787 and the tea rose and the chrysanthemum in 1789, the latter having been imported earlier by the Dutch in the wake of the tulip craze but subsequently dying out. Banks also introduced hydrangeas, magnolias and the tiger lily. The Royal Horticultural Society, which was founded in 1804, soon made contact with China. Its correspondent was John Reeves, an inspector of tea in the service of the East India Company, who was at Canton 1812–31. Reeves was responsible for the introduction of wistaria, from the garden of the co-hong merchant Consequa, to Chiswick in 1818. He was also instrumental in the decision of the Royal Horticultural Society to send Robert Fortune to China in 1843. Fortune's journeys resulted in the introduction of a wide range of Chinese plants, forsythia for example, but in particular rhododendrons. The first rhododendrons had come to England from the Indian Himalayas around 1810, but their real wealth, over 150 species, lay in Szechwan under the eaves of the mountains which had preserved them from the last ice age. It was this wealth which Fortune began to tap through the gardens of eastern China. As Chinese agriculture destroyed the upland flora of Szechwan with maize walks and rice paddies, European horticulture preserved it with vistas and shrubberies. Meanwhile Father Joao de Loureiro had made the first systematic survey of Chinese plants in his *Flora*

Cochinchinensis of 1790 which listed 254 species peculiar to the Canton area. By the mid-nineteenth century China had provided some of the most splended ingredients of the Victorian garden, giving it a Baroque luxuriance of mass, colour and fragrance it would otherwise have lacked.[41]

The exception to the absence of significant interchange of fauna was Koch's *vibrio*, the agent of cholera. In 1817 it broke out of its ancient home in Bengal and attacked the Near East, eastern Russia, and Europe in one direction, China in the other. Although China was protected to some extent by the habit of boiling water for tea and the practice of collecting nightsoil for manure, there were further attacks in 1822, 1826 and 1837, and in 1838 a Chinese scholar published a treatise on the disease. Cholera is relatively simple. Its bacillus, the *vibrio*, is pecular to man and the disease spreads by contamination, either directly through contact with the excrement of people with the disease, or indirectly through the intermediary of flies and water. The surprise therefore is not that cholera expanded, but that it never did so before the early nineteenth century.

Cholera at first travelled by land: to Europe via Persia, Bokhara and Russia, to China via Central Asia; and its routes show a considerable overlap with those of the *haj*. It may be that the nineteenth-century pandemics of cholera are to be associated with an increase of *haj* traffic due partly to improved communications, but more to the movement of Islamic neo-orthodoxy cradled by the Naqshbandi international. India was an area of expansion for the order in the eighteenth century, particularly Bengal, placed under infidel rule and subject to economic depression. Once the *vibrio* was in the *haj* circuit, it would easily be picked up by non-Indian *hajjis* in the insanitary conditions which often prevailed on the pilgrimage and thence taken to their various countries. But cholera also travelled by sea, particularly in its later attacks, and here it must be regarded as a product of the rise of the country trade. In the ports of the China coast, death rates from cholera were lower than in the early industrial towns of Europe, probably because of the sanitary practices mentioned above. It was, nevertheless, a very unwelcome import from the West, more deadly than opium.

Commodities

The development of the commodities trade may be summed up in the formula: expansion, absolute diversification, relative specialization. If the volume of exchanges between Europe and China increased tenfold in the Renaissance, it increased more than tenfold in the Enlightenment, with the huge increase of traffic round the Cape, the rise of the country trade, the new route through Siberia, the second line across the Pacific. Concomitantly, in line with the shift of the world economic system from bullion to commodities, the range of objects traded widened. Within the old trinity of textiles, minerals and spices, still important in the conservative China trade because of the on-going significance of silk (in 1867 still one third of Chinese exports by value), textiles expanded to include furs, woollens, nankeens and Indian raw cotton; minerals expanded to include English lead, Banka tin, Cantonese mercury, Taiwanese gold and Prussian blue; and spices expanded to include Chinese sugar and Indian indigo. Within the new category of medicines introduced by the Renaissance, rhubarb and *Smilax China* were joined by Canadian ginseng (discovered by Father Lafitau), Malwa, Persian and Turkish opium, Peruvian quinine, Kwangsi aniseed and Tibetan borax. Within the new category of drinks, tea was joined, very marginally by coffee through the Armenians at Sining, but not it seems by that other conqueror, cocoa, no doubt because China was weak in its two partners, milk and sugar, the reflections of pastoralism and modest luxury. However, despite this diversification the greatest change in commodities in the Enlightenment was the symbiotic rise of tea and opium. In 1867 tea amounted to 59 per cent of China's exports in value, opium amounted to 46 per cent of China's imports in value. In 1833 the percentages were probably higher.

The tea trade was not a uniform whole. There was the brick tea trade from Tachienlu and Sung-p'an to Tibet and Koko-nor which handled about 100 000 piculs a year. There was the trade in green tea from T'un-ch'i (the English Twankay) via Yarkand and Badakhshan to Bokhara of a few thousand piculs a year. There was the small trade in a very sweet mint tea which the English introduced to Morocco in the eighteenth century. There was the brick tea trade from Hankow via Kiakhta to Siberia and Russia of about 50 000 piculs a year. There was the leaf tea trade, both green and black, from Canton to Europe of, by the middle of the nineteenth century, 350 000 piculs a year. In all, around 500 000 piculs or 25 000 tons was exported. All these trades had their own schedules of demand. Tea was a foodstuff in Tibet, a soup, the basis of *tsamba* the national dish, as it was in parts of Siberia. In Islamic Central Asia, tea was a cheaper provincial substitute for Turkish coffee: in prosperous Morocco it was an exotic European luxury. The essential, however, was the European, really the English demand, for although on the eve of the Commutation Act of 1784 only one third of the tea leaving Canton left it in English ships, almost all, except for modest quantities sold in Holland, ended in England. It arrived there, in the case of tea not transported in English ships, via the well-organized smuggling system which encircled England from the Isle of Man via the Shetlands and Orkneys through to Göteborg, Amsterdam, the East Anglian and Kentish coasts and thence via the Channel to Brittany and Cornwall and round via the Irish seas to Man again. It was the English demand for tea which ruled the Canton system, indeed the whole pattern of the relationship between China and the outside world in the Enlightenment.

Between 1650 and 1833 English demand for tea passed through three stages. Before 1720 when the annual import was 10 000 piculs or less, tea was a medicine, a tonic and a stimulant: for men, an alternative to coffee for the *cognoscenti*, for women a palliative for the new feminine psychosomatisms of migraine, vapours and *crise de foie*. It was primarily a Dutch import and its chief exponent was the medical faculty of Leyden.

Between 1720 and 1800 when the annual import rose from 10 000 piculs to 200 000, tea became a social accomplishment: feminine essentially, round which was constructed a new feminization of time, space and inter-familial relations. Tea demanded its own room, time and clothes; it imposed its own pattern of behaviour; it required its own set of social skills. As this kind of commodity, tea was primarily the import of the Ostend Company and its continental successors, though the English East India Company, if crippled by heavy import duties, was not behind in taking up its possibilities. Its chief exponent was Bath, the diffusion point for the fashions of the capital to the provinces.

Between 1800 and 1833, when the annual import rose from 200 000 piculs to 350 000, tea became, as in Tibet and Siberia, a foodstuff: family high tea, rich in milk and sugar, the crude but effective alimentary infrastructure for the longer hours and higher natality of the early industrial revolution. As an object of mass consumption, tea was primarily the import of the English East India Company, its heavy duties removed by the Commutation Act in 1784, its capital at Canton swollen by nabobs' piles in search of repatriation, and its continental competitors put out of business by the end of smuggling, the new scale of operations and, after 1793, by the navy. Its chief exponent was the north of England, where cold and winter darkness had always argued in favour of an early evening meal and where nascent industry sought the waterpower which rather than steam was its initial prime mover. Yorkshire probably set the style, rather than Lancashire, because it was larger, more thickly populated and older in terms of intensive settlement, and sociologically advanced where Lancashire was technologically advanced.

Of these three stages, the second was the most important for Europe. Civilization will always have its placebos; high tea was simply part of the temporary regression in living standards which industrialization involved; but afternoon tea was a change in values, in consumer patterns and in the ancient cycle of meals which went back to prehistory.

Afternoon tea was the most artificial and superfluous of meals. Not a square meal, it postulated leisure and did not seek to satisfy hunger after work. It inverted the normal dichotomy of hot food and cold drink: tea and coffee had not yet invaded the breakfast table. Except for milk, cream and butter, in limited quantities, it excluded animal products, but perhaps not fish, since salmon, sardines and gentleman's relish made concessions to the occasional male trespasser. Its appeal was to the eye rather than to the nose: all dishes were on the table simultaneously. On Lévi-Strauss' culinary triangle it rejected both roast meat and rotten cheese, but while it had no strict succession of courses, it generally followed a movement from the lightly elaborated, such as cucumber sandwiches, to the heavily elaborated, such as chocolate cake. Afternoon tea was an affirmation of high culture masquerading as a return to nature. The alfresco setting, the honeycomb, the watercress, spoke of nature; the carefully prepared tea leaves, the highly fired porcelain encircling them, the silver teapot, spoke of culture. Only a civilization which was in no danger of going hungry could present a succession of increasingly rich carbohydrates as social entertainment. In China on the other hand, it was the third stage of the demand for tea which was the most important, because it was then that tea became conjoined with another kind of ashes: opium.

Like tea, the opium trade was not a uniform whole. Besides the opium brought by the country traders to Canton which came variously from India (the Rajputana mainly), Persia and the Ottoman empire, there was also an import of Indian and Persian opium through Central Asia organized by Kokand. In addition opium was grown in the western provinces of China at least as early as the first quarter of the nineteenth century. It had probably been introduced along the central land route by the Moslem communities because botanically Chinese opium was closer to the Persian than the Indian form.[42] By the middle of the nineteenth century, there was more native opium consumed in China than imported. However, though opium came from different sources and Indian was stronger than Chinese, unlike tea, it was for the consumer a single commodity.

It is surprising that the reasons for opium addiction in China, the only example of a drug-permissive society on a large scale in modern times, have not been more seriously studied. Too often it has been assumed that the supply, especially the foreign supply, created the demand and that the demand itself requires no further explanation, though the fact that no such demand was created in the countries which supplied China militates against this view. China consumed a few hundred piculs of opium in 1700, 1000 in 1767, several thousand in 1800, several tens of thousands in 1833, 100,000 in 1850, and over 400,000 piculs in 1900. One must look at who consumed opium and why.

The Royal Commission on Opium 1894/95 showed that the use of opium in China fell into three categories which strangely parody the stages of tea in England.[43] First, opium was a medicine or a prophylactic, particularly in relation to malaria, but also to tuberculosis and dysentery. This was the initial use of opium when it was still a rare Arab drug hardly known outside the pharmacopeias. This was still its prime purpose for most of the 8 000 000 people who smoked it when its use was at maximum in 1900. Second, opium was a social accomplishment. Its use, begun in sickness, was continued in health by certain semi-affluent urban groups: government clerks, soldiers, Manchu women, ne'er-do-well sons of officials and gentry; as a symbol of leisure, conviviality and the ability not to work. Third, opium was a food, or rather a food substitute. As a stimulant, it reduced appetite and was therefore used by workers with irregular mealtimes: coolies, boatmen, and round-the-clock operatives such as those at the salt works at Tzu-liu-ching in Szechwan. As Dermigny points out, this kind of proletarian opiomania was akin to the gin craze in early eighteenth-century London or vodka alcoholism in late nineteenth-century Russia: a phenomenon of proto-industrial growth.

These three kinds of opium consumption were of unequal size and different location. The first, medical opium, was the largest and was concentrated in the inland provinces of the south-west, Szechwan and Yunnan in particular, which were also the largest producers. The second, social opium, was the next largest, but was diffused wherever appropriate social circumstances existed, which was predominantly in the declining cities of eastern China, especially the lower Yangtze area. The third, food-substitute opium, was the smallest and was also diffused, more typically in the market towns of central China, in accordance with the location of trails, water routes and factories.

Explanations can now be advanced. First, the origin of opiomania in China was Islamic, a fruit of the anti-alcoholic but drug-tolerant culture of hashish and the hubble pipe, part of the Islamic invasion of China which followed the Ch'ing conquest of Moslem Central Asia. Yunnan, probably the first province to grow opium, was a Moslem stronghold until the great Panthay rebellion of the mid-nineteenth century. Second, the development of opium *smoking*, in its Chinese form unknown in Islam, was facilitated by the absence of good competing alcohols and the presence of wide-spread use of tobacco. Opium smoking grew as an intensifier to tobacco. Third, the medicinal use of opium is associated with migration from non-malarious to malarious regions, the moving frontier of Chinese agriculture. Szechwan and Yun-nan were frontier provinces with populations of newcomers. In addition Szechwan was urbanized and humid, prime conditions for tuberculosis. Fourth, the social use of opium may be associated with the Chinese pattern of urbanization in the Enlightenment, the decline or stagnation of official and gentry cities, the growth of market towns, in both of which the relatively affluent had little to do and much frustration. Fifth, the industrial use of opium may be associated with the growing spatial extension of China, the lengthening distances between towns to be travelled by coolies and boatmen, possibly with lower wages as population mounted.

Unlike tea consumption in England, opium consumption was never a mass phenomenon. The opium of the masses was not opium. It was the recourse of a minority of a minority: mobile China of the agricultural frontier with its necessary superstructure of markets and routes; a gesture of culture in defiance of the general return to nature. No more than tea, was the demand for it the creation of the smugglers. Tea and opium expressed the directions European and Chinese society were taking.

Techniques

Despite the increased level of contact, there was little technological exchange between China and the outside world in the Enlightenment. This is not surprising. The civilizations of China and Europe, though at different levels of culture, were both at a high degree of maturity. Their traditional technologies had nearly reached perfection and were not susceptible of improvement, only radical transformation. Consequently such borrowing as there was tended to be decorative rather than structural. Thus China half-heartedly borrowed the European technique of perspective, while Europe acquired the Chinese technique of porcelain. In addition, Europe acquired from China a new appreciation of the importance of the division of labour for technology. Finally

China's contribution to the prehistory of the steam engine must be noted.

Painting was one of the greatest achievements of Chinese civilization. If the peak was reached under the Sung a high level continued under the Ming and Ch'ing. Painting was an extension of calligraphy, so every literate person took an interest in it, and practised it as an amateur. It was natural that Matteo Ricci should use this common interest of Chinese and Europeans, and although not a painter himself, should expound the mathematical principles of Renaissance perspective.

This policy was continued when the centre of Jesuit activity became the court rather than the opposition scholars. In 1667 Luigi Buglio presented K'ang-hsi with three landscapes in the European manner: one by Johann Grueber and two by himself and two Chinese assistants whom he had trained. K'ang-hsi himself studied with the Modenese painter Giovanni Gherardini, whom the French Jesuits brought to China in 1698 and, according to Matteo Ripa, 'the emperor in the first place esteems perspective'.[44] Ministers followed suit. In 1729, Nien Hsi-yao, minister of the household and brother of the viceroy Nien Keng-yao who helped to bring the Yung-cheng emperor to the throne, published in collaboration with Castiglione the *Shih-hsüeh*, a free translation with illustrations of Andrea Pozzo's *Perspectiva Pictorum et Architectorum*. A second enlarged edition was brought out in 1735. In the next generation, under Ch'ien-lung, Attiret painted 200 portraits for the court and decorated the ceilings of the summer palace. Castiglione, 'whom the emperor very much esteemed and beloved much more than a prince ordinarily does',[45] was the favourite, but other foreign artists were the Jesuits Panzi, Sichelbarth and de Poirot and the Augustinian Serafino di San Giovanni Battista. Yet the effect was small: the Chinese tradition was too well established, too mature easily to admit new conventions. In 1733 the art historian Chang Keng chronicled Ricci's ideas and noted a Chinese imitator: 'Chiao acquired this art, and modified his style accordingly, but the result was not refined and convincing. Lovers of antiquity would do well not to adopt this method.'[46] In such a climate of taste it is not surprising that the more radical innovations of European polyphony hardly received a hearing.

If China received but hardly used the European technique of perspective, Europe received and fully used the Chinese technique of porcelain. Porcelain first entered Europe in the middle ages, the earliest collections were built up in the Renaissance, and importation continued in the Enlightenment as tea increased the demand. Imitation was almost as old. The Hispano–Moresque pottery which inspired *maiolica* was based on earlier Islamic imitations, and majolica itself, with its semi-vitrified glaze was an *ersatz* for the now more widely available Chinese product. Of these early high-grade ceramics it was Delft, blue and white like contemporary Ming wares, which most consciously imitated porcelain.

None of them, however, was porcelain. It was not until the eighteenth century, when further information from the Jesuits about Chinese technology became available, that true porcelain was made in Europe: first by the alchemist Friedrich Böttger at Meissen in 1708, then by Jean Hellot at Sevres around 1743, and finally by William Cookworthy at Plymouth in 1768. Although the Jesuits supplied information from the late seventeenth century, the most significant transmissions were made in the two letters of Father Dentrecolles of 1712 and 1722, which described the processes used at Ching-te-chen, the porcelain city in Kiangsi. It was these which allowed the English industry to take off under the leadership of Josiah Wedgwood. Most of Wedgwood's wares were not true porcelain, but his Queen ware, named in 1765 from Queen Charlotte's patronage, was a close approximation, and it became the first mass brand-name product. Wedgwood's successor, Josiah Spode, finally developed the process for the large-scale production of bone china, the industrial form of porcelain. Wedgwood, however, had gone beyond Chinese technology. In 1782 he ordered his first steam engine for grinding and clay mixing and the demand for Cornish clay encouraged the introduction of Watt's machines there. The Potteries indeed were the first branch of industry to move completely to the new source of energy, since both Lancashire and Yorkshire still used more water than steam. The forward linkages of porcelain in Europe were considerable.

Father Dentrecolles' descriptions of Ching-te-chen were also important in another direction. In his letter of 25 January 1722, he emphasised the division of labour in the process of manufacture: 'Une pièce de porcelaine, avant que d'en sortir pour être portée au fourneau, passe par les mains de plus de vingt personnes, et cela sans confusion. On a sans doute éprouvé que l'ouvrage se fait ainsi beaucoup plus vite . . .Le travail de la peinture est partagé dans un même laboratoire entre un grand nombre d'ouvriers'.[47] China's high labour productivity was one of the things Europeans most admired about it and Dentrecolles' letter was intended as an explanation as well as a description of Ching-te-chen. It seems that this and similar passages influenced Adam Smith in his famous account of the division of labour in the early chapters of the *Wealth of Nations*. Adam Smith is sometimes regarded as a prophet of modern industry, but a closer reading suggests that he had no concept of limitless industrial growth based on new sources of energy, but envisaged only limited growth based on more rational methods of organization of which the division of labour was the principle. Dentrecolles gave an explanation for China's economic maturity based on what he saw at Ching-te-chen. Adam Smith drew from that explanation a formula by which to achieve Europe's economic maturity.

Neither Dentrecolles nor Adam Smith envisaged the revolutionary role of steam power as developed by Josiah Wedgwood and his successors. Here too China played a part. In the 1670s Father Claudio Grimaldi demonstrated to the K'ang-hsi emperor a small vehicle operated by a steam turbine. The Ch'ing officials who watched it with the emperor probably saw it as no more than an ingenious mechanical toy – like the nightingale in the fairy story – but what they were looking at was the first locomotive and the first operating steam engine. True, the steam engine which introduced the industrial revolution to Europe was not the turbine but the reciprocator or piston engine. Nevertheless, the Jesuit machine, which was well publicized in du Halde's handbook, was good news for all steam power and will have encouraged experimenters working on other lines. Grimaldi's machine was not a direct ancestor of those of Papin, Savery, Newcomen and Watt, but it was a successful cousin. Too advanced in principle for the technology of its day, it was the ancestor of the turbine engines of the late nineteenth century which, with the aid of improved steel technology, largely replaced the steam reciprocators.

Ideas

Where the exchanges in technology in the Enlightenment were similar in kind but different in effect, the exchanges in ideas were different in both kind and effect. China imported at the level of low culture where her society and intellectual life were most active, the effects being negative. Europe imported at the level of high culture where her society and intellectual life were most active, the effects being positive.

One of the strongest currents of Chinese intellectual life in the eighteenth century was the rise of non-Confucian popular folk religion, chapel sects which may be associated with the various alienations of the agricultural frontier, the rise of market towns and the increasing illiteracy. In this current, a major component was the growth among Chinese-speaking Moslems in Shensi, Kansu and probably Yunnan of the movement known to Ch'ing officials as the *hsin-chiao* or new religion. Joseph Fletcher has identified the *hsin-chiao*, whose origins and character long puzzled scholars, as the *Jahriyya* branch of the Naqshbandi dervish order and shown that it was an eighteenth-century import to China from the neo-orthodox Moslem schools of the Middle East, that of Zabid in the Yemen in particular.

The Naqshbandiyya had been active in north-west China since the end of the sixteenth century. First came the Isaqiya, the line of Ishaq Wali, the Makhdum-i Azam's second son, the Black Mountain khojas who inclined in devotion to the non-mystical *Jahriyya*. Later came the Ishaniya, the line of Ishan Kalan, the Makhdum-i Azam's first son, the White Mountain khojas, who inclined to the mystical *Khafiyya*. One or other of these lines may have been involved in the Kansu Moslem revolt of 1648–49, although no direct evidence of Naqshbandi participation has yet been found. However, perhaps as a result of the defeat of non-mystical militancy, the *Khafiyya* became the predominant spirituality among Chinese speaking Moslems, so that those reacting against it, or seeing others do so, called it the old religion. By this time the Naqshbandi order was a worldwide movement and in the eighteenth century the *Jahriyya* experienced a revival in the pilgrimage centres of the Middle East.

This revival was introduced to China as the new religion by Ma Ming-hsin, a Chinese Moslem who studied at Zabid with the Naqshbandi Shaikhs of the Mizjaji family before returning to China in 1781. The *Jahriyya* was extravert, evangelical and stressed vocal prayer. In addition, from the eighteenth century at least, it preached political activism, the *jihad*, to combat the increasingly manifest decline of Islam, of whose worldwide dimensions pilgrims learnt during the *haj* and of which the Ch'ing conquest of half Moslem Central Asia was a conspicuous part. The *hsin-chiao* therefore was explicitly anti-Ch'ing. It raised minor rebellions in 1781 and 1784, collaborated with the Kokand–Khoja invasions of Sinkiang in 1820 and 1830 and raised a major rebellion in northwest China in 1862–73. Moslem neo-orthodoxy, intrajected by the Ch'ing conquest of Inner Asia, was a major element in the Western challenge to traditional China in the nineteenth century. Though ultimately defeated and rejected, it was a political poison, no less dangerous than the, also Islamic, opium, and its suppression necessitated a perhaps crucial diversion of effort from the coast to the interior.

While China imported, perhaps only could import, at the level of the little tradition, the sects, Europe imported at the level of the great tradition, the mainstream. The Enlightenment saw the high tide of the Sinophilia which had been launched by Botero, Kircher and the anti-classical stream of the Renaissance. Three kinds of Sinophilia made a significant contribution to the evolution of European thought in the Enlightenment.

First, China, by figuring as a Utopia in space rather than time, a living Egypt rather than a dead one, contributed to the victory of the moderns over the ancients. She made Europeans realize that their vocation was not merely to restore the glories of antiquity, but to surpass them. China thus helped to replace a degenerative view of history with a progressive one. Again, the realization during the eighteenth century that China was not in fact a colony of Egypt opened the way to a less unilinear view of the past and to a more rational approach to the history of Egypt and the ancient Near East. The Great Pyramid was no longer the beginning of wisdom.

Second, China, which Kircher had invoked, along with Egypt, India and Mexico, against Machiavellian classical paganism, on closer inspection served de-Christianization better. She served it intellectually through the apostate Jesuit van Ende with whom Spinoza studied and whose presentation of non-theistic Chinese philosophy may have been a source of Spinoza's *Deus sive Natura* pantheism, one of the fountainheads of modern agnosticism. She served it in morals via Jesuit praise of China which, once it was accepted that China was not in receipt of a primordial revelation, led to the conclusion that true religion was not necessary to good ethical practice. She served it socially through the portrayal of China as a land of essentially secular government and society, a country without priests, a model for European anti-clericalism. De-Christianization was Europe Sinofied.

Third, China, the lightness and legality of whose government was defended by the Jesuits, particularly Cibot, against Montesquieu's accusations of oriental despotism (really a misidentification of China and India) became, in the writings of the physiocrats, Poivre, Quesnay and La Mercier de la Riviere, the exemplar of minimum government, *laissez-faire* and the night-watchman theory of the state. Chinese government might not in fact be as liberal as these authors supposed – though light it was pervasive – but until the late eighteenth century the example of China was part of the anti-monopolistic polemic of people like the Abbé Morellet and the enemies of the East India companies. In Quesnay, in particular, scholasticism and Sinophilia converged to champion market economy in opposition to mercantilism. Progress, unbelief and free trade, the three nostrums of the Enlightenment, thus all had Chinese elements in their origin.

WORLD INSTITUTIONS, 1650 TO 1833

In the Enlightenment as in the Renaissance, the institutions of the world order both thickened and multiplied. Microbian common market, information circuit, world economy and religious internationals all thickened, and a naval *pax Britan-*

nica and a republic of letters was added to them. As a result, global consciousness increased and terms like cosmopolitanism and *Weltburgertum* acquired new currency and meaning. In these institutions China's part was not inconsiderable.

In the microbian common market, as a result of the incorporation of Bengal into the world economy and of the particular directions of the *haj* routes, Koch's *vibrio* had been added to *Yersinia pestis, Treponema pallidum*, tuberculosis and yellow fever. Nevertheless, world health was better in 1800 than in 1600. The anti-microbian common market, the antidote to the universalization of disease initiated by the Black Death, was slowly coming into existence.

Medicines were universalized. Mercury was everywhere used as a remedy against syphilis. The Jesuits introduced quinine to China, ginseng to the West. Quarantine was extended. Before 1500 it had been municipal. In the sixteenth century it became regional. After 1600 in response to a new pulsation of plague supercharged by the recovery of trade and the humidity of the little ice age, quarantine began to be applied nationally, first by the Spanish government, then by Colbert in the north-western outbreak of 1664 to 1670. Against the Marseille outbreak of 1720 there was, for the first time, a measure of international cooperation, particularly between France and Spain. In 1779 Johann Peter Frank, who served as public health adviser to governments all over Europe, brought out his *System einer Vollständigen Medizinischen Polizei*, the first modern treatise on preventive medicine. By the beginning of the nineteenth century, quarantine procedures were being extended to Egypt and the Ottoman empire, key points for the control of plague and cholera. Regional health organizations were established in Alexandria in 1831 and Constantinople in 1839. In 1834 the first suggestion for an international sanitary conference was made by Segur du Peyron, head of the French sanitary service. As yet China was not included in this system. Yet the Ch'ing institution of the willow pallisade, which aimed to keep north Manchuria as a strategic reserve and to exclude Chinese immigration, also acted as a *cordon sanitaire* against the plague reservoir of the Lake Baikal region. Whether it realized it or not the Ch'ing government interrupted the further advance of plague.

In the Enlightenment the basic information circuit became ever more complete. By 1833 there was more known in geography than unknown and it had become a question of filling in gaps. In this process the Peking Jesuits played a significant role both in supplying Europe with fresh information and transmitting to China what Europe already knew. Father Gaubil corrected the maps which Guillaume Delisle produced in Europe, particularly with regard to Central Asia where there was a Jesuit surveying party, and established the proper location of places such as Chia-yü-kuan, Hami, Turfan and Kashgar. In 1727 he gave Prince I, the Yung-cheng emperor's brother and prime minister, an extended tutorial in geography: 'Le Regulo nous interrogea sur plusieurs royaumes d'Asie, et quelques réponses que je lui fis luy ayant donné envie de parler au long sur cette matière, il nous ordonna d'aller á son hôtel, et un mandarin eut ordre de nous suivre et d'aporter des atlas et des cartes d'Europe, d'Afrique, d'Asie et d'Amérique'.[48] A year later, history and politics were included: 'Le P. Parennin et moy avons eu bien souvent à répondre aux questions du Regulo sur la révolution de Perse, sur les intéréts des Turcq avec les Russiens, sur les guerres des Suédois, sur le grand nombre d'Européans qui sont en Russie dans les troupes, et sur ceux qui y sont allés pour les sciences et les arts, mais surtout sur les raports des Moscovites avec les autres Européans'.[49] Gaubil also collated much information about Korea, Hokkaido, Sakhalin, Kamchatka and the Bering strait, using both Russian and Chinese sources, which was new to both his European and Ch'ing correspondents. Gaubil's correspondence shows him to have been familiar with the basic geography, history and politics of most parts of the world. The basic information circuit was there for those who wanted to use it.

Pierre Chaunu has not yet given us his promised volumes on the second Atlantic, the Enlightenment world economy, but its main features are clear from his other writings. London, the new centre, as Seville had been the old, was a more sophisticated emporium. Seville's monopoly had not been artificial. It rested on its position, its port, and its command over its rich hinterland's corn, oil and wine. But Seville was not a major centre of manufacture, banking, shipping or marine insurance. London, on the other hand, besides being a port and commanding the resources of lowland England and access to the Continent, was an industrial city and the home of the world's biggest gilt-edged market, its only discount market, the Baltic exchange and Lloyds. Nevertheless, despite these advantages, London's position was a less dominant one than Seville's because the system was a more complex one. It was grounded on a series of commodity markets rather than a single exchange of foodstuffs and bullion. Amsterdam, Riga, Rouen, Bordeaux, Lisbon, Cadiz, Leghorn, Smyrna, Boston, Porto Bello, Rio de Janeiro, Bombay and Canton were junior partners of London rather than satellites.

The Atlantic of London was not, except in particulars, larger than the Atlantic of Seville. Canton was little further from the Thames than Macao from the Tagus. East Indiamen were not much larger than carracks. The greater scale of the world economy was due to implosion rather than explosion, in particular the in-depth penetration of the West Indies, north-east Brazil, the eastern seaboard of North America and the Canton hinterland of the tea routes. The new system moved faster than the old, perhaps 100 per cent faster and, in the aggregate, more safely. Thanks to better knowledge of wind regimes, copper bottoming, cleaner lines and chronometers, the East Indiamen made better passages than the carracks. Where the economy of Seville was dominated by the four-year cycle of Peru, the economy of London was dominated by the two-year cycle of Canton. Profit per turn-over could fall and still remain above the floor of the ruling rate of interest, so the volume of business increased. The extreme profitability of the first Atlantic had made long turn-overs possible: the second Atlantic by increasing speed made such profitability no longer necessary. On land, Guy Arbellot has shown that more and stronger horses, rationalized time-tables, improved roads ('hippoways') cut public coach times in France by half between 1750 and 1780.[50] For inland goods there was the massive canal-building in England, France and the Low Countries which cut times as well as costs.

Another difference between the two Atlantics was in the means of consumption. Where Seville had operated a silver standard, London moved onto a gold standard, a move from a commoner, cheaper, less stable reserve to one rarer, less cheap and more stable. Initially the China trade was directly involved in this change, as China, or rather Taiwan, Tibet and Siberia were significant sources of gold before the revolutionary discoveries of Minas Gerais. Later China was indirectly benefited by it as it made European governments less unwilling to see silver exported to Canton to buy tea. The tea trade indeed became a means whereby continental countries could tap England's monopoly of gold. The change from silver to gold tied China more closely to the world economy. Externally the world economy of London with its tall ships, its horsedrawn carriages, its letters of credit, its underwriters, looked not so different from that of Seville. Internally it was of a different degree of complexity and Canton was a significant element in that complexity.

The three religious internationals had fluctuations of fortune in the Enlightenment, but despite the rise of secularism, indeed, in reaction to the rise of secularism, they emerged from it on balance strengthened.

The Naqshbandiyya increased its influence through association with the growing movement of neo-orthodoxy in Islam. The Enlightenment was a bad period for Islam. Half the Balkans was lost to the Habsburgs; the Moghul empire dissolved, parts of Moslem India came under Hindu or English rule; Moslem Indonesia fell to the Dutch; the Ch'ing conquered eastern Turkestan; the Russians occupied the Crimea, overran the Kazakh steppe and penetrated the Caucasus; Napoleon invaded Egypt. Faced with this decline, whose generality and gravity was most clearly perceived at the crossroads of the *haj* routes in Egypt, the Hijaz and the Yemen, Moslems turned for revitalization to the integralist neo-orthodoxy preached by the schools of those places which could not be held politically responsible for the situation. Neo-orthodoxy was wider than dervishism, but the Naqshbandi shaikhs of Zabid and Medina were close to its heart. Muhammed ibn Abd al-Wahhab, the founder of the Wahhabi movement which conquered eastern Arabia in the later part of the eighteenth century, had studied with the Naqshbandi shaikh Muhammed Hayya al-Sindi of Medina. Ma Ming-hsin, the founder of the *hsin-chiao*, had studied with the Naqshbandi shaikhs of the Mizjaji family of Zabid. Muhammed ben Ali ben as-Sanusi, the founder of the Senussi order which came to dominate Libya, the eastern Sudan and Somalia, came under similar influences during his stay in Arabia. The most prominent Indian Naqshbandi of the eighteenth century Shah Wali Allah studied in Medina at the same time as Muhammed ibn Abd al-Wahhab. The Naqshbandiyya was the expanding infrastructure of neo-orthodoxy. Not the least of its expansions in the Enlightenment was that of the *Jahriyya* into China.

The Gelugspa had a more chequered career, but by 1833 it was recovering ground as the spearhead of Tibetan and Mongolian nationalism. Between 1642 and 1705, the Gelugspa, first headed by the fifth Dalai Lama and then by the regent for his successor, maintained itself as an independent theocracy by balancing between the rival patronages of the Zunghars and the Ch'ing. In 1705 Tibet became an indirect Ch'ing protectorate under first the Qosot khan Lajang and then under the anti-Gelugspa Tibetan nobleman P'o-lha-nas. In 1750 the Ch'ing protectorate became direct. Ambans or high commissioners were appointed to the court of the Dalai Lama and during the Gurkha wars at the end of the century, Ch'ing control was extended further. Yet there were compensations for this increase in the power of the *danapati* or lay protector. Once the Ch'ing emperor felt he had the Lhasa hierarchy in his pocket, he was prepared to be advised by leading ecclesiastics, to recognize only Tibetan incarnations to the Jebtsun-damba Hutuktu of Urga and the Chang-chia Hutuktu of Inner Mongolia, and to allow Lhasa more than its fair share of power in Kham where the non-Gelugspa orders remained strong. It only needed imperial control to be relaxed for Gelugspa theocracy to re-emerge in both Tibet and Mongolia with increased ambitions. A first instance occurred in the Dogra invasion of 1841–42. The Ch'ing government, preoccupied with the opium war against England, left the Tibetan authorities to deal with the situation not unsuccessfully on their own. The ambans increasingly lost control of the government and a new note of independence and aggressiveness crept into Tibetan policies.

Like the Gelugspa, the Jesuits had a chequered career in the Enlightenment, but by 1833 were recovering ground as the spearhead of the Catholic restoration. In the Christian Enlightenment before Voltaire, the Jesuits, particularly the French Jesuits, were leaders. Their journal, the *Memoirs de Trevoux*, supported scientific method and its application to the social sciences. The Bollandists, the Jesuit editors of the *Acta Sanctorum*, helped to lay the foundations of critical history. Denis Petau introduced the historical approach to theology and anticipated Newman's doctrine of development, while Boscovich advanced the first unified field theory. The Jesuits were the schoolmasters of the middle class in half of Europe. It is to this first phase of the Enlightenment that the *Lettres Edifiantes, les Memoires concernant la Chine* and Gaubil's correspondence belong.

In the next phase, the anti-Christian Enlightenment, the Jesuits, partly as a result of their failure in China and the doctrinal modernism and moral probabilism with which it had been associated, steadily lost ground until their dissolution in 1773 by the bull *Dominus ac Redemptor*, extracted from Clement XIV by the enlightened obscurantism of the Bourbons. The order, however, survived under the protection of Catherine the Great, who refused to allow the bull to be promulgated in her dominions and a novitiate was reopened in 1780. In 1801 Pius VII approved the restoration of the order in White Russia, Gabriel Gruber who hoped to work in China becoming local general in 1802. In 1814 Pius VII restored the order generally by the bull *Sollicitudo Omnium Ecclesiarum*, the Pole Thaddeus Brzozowsky becoming general. The order made a quick recovery by championing the ideas of de Maistre, by regaining control of seminaries, by becoming publicists for ultra-montanism, and by reviving missions. In 1832 a group of Chinese Christians petitioned for the restoration of the China mission. Propaganda authorized the Jesuits to go back, and not long after the opium war, they returned to their observatory at Siccawei.

In addition to the four existing world institutions – microbian common market, information circuit, world economy and religious internationals – two new ones came into existence during the Enlightenment. These were the global seapower of the *pax Britannica* and the universal science of the republic of letters.

During the Enlightenment, there was an evolution from local seapower to global seapower and then to British global seapower, the *pax Britannica*. In the Renaissance there was a world economy, but no world seapower. The empire of Seville was only partly protected by fleets and these fleets did not form a single navy. Before Drake, the Pacific was virtually undefended and the Mediterranean squadron of galleys did not cohere with the Indian guard of galleons. The Dutch seaborne empire was likewise only intermittently and imperfectly covered by naval squadrons, though one of them, Balthasar Bort's fleet, active on the China coast in 1662–64, was the first effective exercise of European seapower in Chinese waters. The change from local to global seapower came in the eighteenth century with the standardization of warships, the establishment of permanent overseas naval bases like Mauritius, and the multiplication of theatres of operation which made the Seven Years War and the War of American Independence the first two world wars. Mahan's maxim of one sea, one fleet came to be acted on: the whole now became more than the parts.

It was during the second of these wars, with her resources overstrained and the consequences of its loss manifest at Yorktown, that England first grasped the significance of overall seapower, and in its latter stages, sought and achieved it. Rodney's victory at the Saints' passage, incomplete though it was, both in strategy and tactics anticipated Nelson's at Trafalgar: the aim of annihilation, the method of line breaking. It was however the revolutionary and Napoleonic wars with its destruction of the fleets of France, Spain, Holland and Denmark which established England as the monopolitan of world seapower. Lord Fisher argued that '5 strategic keys lock up the world'.[51] By 1833, four of them – Dover, Gibraltar, the Cape and Singapore – were in English hands; and the fifth, Alexandria, had been and would be again.

English seapower first came into the China seas with the capture of Manila in 1762. Macartney was aware of its potential when he asked rhetorically of the Chinese authorities: 'Can they be ignorant that a couple of English frigates would be an overmatch for the whole naval force of their empire, that in half a summer they could totally destroy all the navigation of their coasts and reduce the inhabitants of the maritime provinces, who subsist chiefly on fish, to absolute famine?'[52] China, however, with her elaborate system of in-depth defence of inland waters by forts, booms, fireships and shallows, was a less negligible naval force than Macartney imagined, and British seapower had to be established by an accumulation of skills, information and techniques.[53] A Chinese embargo checked Britain's attempt to occupy Macao in 1808; the coastal defences of the Canton estuary thwarted Napier's diplomatic pressure in 1834 and Elliot's military moves in 1841. It was not until Pottinger and Parker's successful penetration of the Yangtze in 1842 that Britain overcame China's peculiar kind of naval force, and the Tientsin estuary, protected by distance and weather, gave trouble in 1859 and again in 1900. Command of another country's defended inland waters is perhaps the highest form of seapower. By the mid-nineteenth century Britain had achieved it in China. Her navy was the temporary embodiment of a world power which in the suppression of piracy, the inhibition of the slave trade, the development of maritime law, the regulation of the conventions of rescue and salvage, and the enforcement of freedom of the seas, made a significant contribution to the emerging world system, not least in China.

The second new world institution was that loose assemblage of learned societies, astronomical observatories, botanical gardens, scholarly publications, corresponding members and a small public of amateurs which contemporaries called the republic of letters. The term first gained currency in the early seventeenth century, the age of Bacon, Rubens and Grotius, but it was not until the second half of the century that it began to refer to a recognizable institutional entity, spread thin no doubt, but real.

In this entity China participated through the secular science and scholarship of the Jesuits. Thus Gaubil referred to the *respublica litteraria* in a letter to Cromwell Mortimer, secretary of the Royal Society in November 1749, and again to his successor Thomas Birch in November 1753. Amiot, confronted with yet another proof that Chinese was the clue to the hieroglyphs, exclaimed sceptically 'quelle conquête pour la république des lettres si elle a jamais lieu!'[54] In addition to his associations with the Academie Royal des Sciences and the Académie Royal des Inscriptions et Belles-Lettres, Gaubil was a member of the Imperial Academy of St Petersburg and a foreign associate of the Royal Society. Besides the *Memoires de Trevoux*, he read regularly the *Acta Eruditorum* from Leipzig, the *Miscellanéa Berolinensia*, and the *Philosophical Transactions*. Among the savants with whom he was in touch were César-

François Cassini of the Observatory of Paris; the physicist Dortous de Mairan of the Académie de Sciences; Lorenz Lange, the former Russian diplomat in Peking; Joseph Nicolas Deliste, a French astronomer who lived at St Petersburg from 1726 to 1747; his brother, Guillaume, royal geographer in France; James Bradley, professor of astronomy at Oxford; Joseph de Guignes, professor of oriental languages in Paris; Nicolas Freret, perpetual secretary of the Académie des Inscriptions et Belles-Lettres; Louis Bertrand Castel the Cartesian critic of Newton; and Anquetil du Perron, the founder of Zoroastrian studies. On his death in July 1759, his friend Gabriel Boussel wrote to Berthier, the editor of the *Memoires de Trevoux*, 'L'Europe savante regrettera la perte d'un savant du premier ordre . . . il étoit à notre Chine ce que vous étes à la France.'[55]

Cosmopolitanism increased during the Enlightenment. One finds it near the beginning in Montesquieu:

> If I knew of something beneficial to me but harmful to my family, I would eject it from my mind. If I knew of something beneficial to my family but not to my country, I would try to forget it. If I knew of something beneficial to my country but harmful to Europe – or beneficial to Europe but harmful to the human race, I would regard it as a crime.[56]

One finds it near the end in Metternich's remark to Wellington in 1824: 'C'est que depuis longtemps l'Europe a pris pour moi la valeur d'une patrie'.[57] One finds it in the middle in Amiot's letter to Macartney in which the interests of China, the church, France and Britain are all seen as ultimately convergent. Even the Ch'ing government was forced to think globally: Prince I poring over the maps with Parennin and Gaubil and being briefed on the basic geography, history and politics of Europe. The Ch'ing government sent embassies to Batavia, the Lower Volga, Moscow and St Petersburg and considered sending them to Persia and Europe. Its rejection of Macartney's request for a seacoast Nerchinsk in favour of England, was based not on *a priori* diplomatic rigidity, but on its appreciation of the current situation on the Himalayas, in India and in revolutionary Europe. However impressive Macartney's embassy and however skilful the ambassador, it was best not to move house in the hurricane season. China might still be a world on its own and wish to remain so, but its ministers, less blinkered than they seemed, realized dimly that China was now a world within a world.

6 Between Two Worlds: China in the Modern Age, 1833 to 1976

In the modern age, which in Chinese history may be defined as the late Ch'ing, the early republic and the people's republic to the death of Mao Tse-tung, China lay between two worlds, in several senses.

First, China lay between its own world, in the early nineteenth century still autonomous, vital and dynamic, and the world order of the Europeans which possessed these qualities to even higher degrees. The European world order, which in the Renaissance and the Enlightenment had encompassed China and shaped her history indirectly, now began direct penetration. Second, that penetration came from two directions, the sea and the land. Besides the Western Europeans, the Americans and the Europeanized Japanese on the China coast, there were the Islamic revolt and the Russian advance on the Inner Asian frontier, so that China had to deal with two Wests not one. Third, the course which China charted under this double challenge from the West and her own internal imperatives, was a diagonal which, up to the death of Chairman Mao, rejected both tradition and modernity. Fourth, because Mao's version of this rejection was psychistic and existential where Lenin's was materialist and technocratic, China found herself in the last third of the twentieth century with her own brand of communism, between the European world order now centred on the United States of America and the totalitarian revolt against it centred on the Soviet Union.

In these dualities China was more often passive than active. Although more deeply involved with the outside world than at any time since the T'ang, China contributed less and received more than in any of the preceding periods. The event most comparable to the reception of Marxism in the modern age was the reception of Buddhism in late antiquity, but to date the *réclame* of Chinese Marxism has been less than that of Chinese Buddhism. Both K'ang Yu-wei, the last Confucian sage, and Mao, the first Marxist sage, dreamed of a future when China would once again be the centre of the world, as under the T'ang, but it was clear in 1976 that their dreams were very far from realization. The osmosis of China and the world remained incomplete and, as far as we can see, the long dialogue between the two must continue to be a theme of history.

CHINA'S PLACE IN THE WORLD, 1833 TO 1976

At first sight it would seem that the trajectory of China's place in the world between 1833 and 1976 was one of decline under the late Ch'ing and early republic followed by recovery under the people's republic. Thus Jacques Gernet entitled the last two books of his history 'Du Declin à L' Aliénation' and 'La Chine Crucifiée' and Mao Tse-tung proclaimed in 1949 that the Chinese people had at last stood up: 'Our nation will never again be an insulted nation... our revolution has gained the sympathy and acclamation of the broad masses throughout the world ... we will emerge in the world as a nation with a high culture.'[1] While this overview may be correct so long as the horizon is confined to politics, if it is enlarged to include other kinds of history, a different pattern emerges: a fishhook course of advance until around 1916, followed by loss of impetus and reversal of direction.

This may be seen from an analysis of state and society in China between 1833 and 1976, taking as the object of comparison, not the two superpowers, the Soviet Union and the USA, but another medio-power, the European community. For if the people's republic was the residuary legatee of the successive Chinas we have traced, Europe of the Nine was the heir of the successive Europes. Though the differences between the new China and the new Europe were immense, there are enough similarities for comparison. Both faced problems of adjustment to an increasingly demanding world order no longer under their leadership either in government or opposition. Neither enjoyed the local predominance which had once been theirs. Chairman Mao, the typical Chinese, and President de Gaulle, the typical European, had much in common. Both were post-imperial figures, heirs to superannuated revolutionary traditions, nationalists by temperament though internationalists by circumstances, heads of lesser consortia dwarfed by greater. Both knew that their successors would have to rule in a different fashion from themselves and both fought against this knowledge. Both, in different ways, stood between two worlds.

The Chinese state 1833 to 1976

Here, there are two processes to be considered: changes in absolute power and changes in relative power. First, changes in absolute power.

In the days of the Ch'ien-lung emperor, the Chinese state raised 100 million taels in taxes, about 5 per cent of the GNP of the society over which it ruled; it commanded some 500 000 soldiers, one person in every 600 of its subjects; and it operated through a ruling class, the *shih* or scholar gentry, who numbered just over one million individuals. In the latter days of Chairman Mao, the Chinese state raised the equivalent of 13 000 million taels, about 35 per cent of the GNP of the society over which it ruled; it commanded some 3 million soldiers, one person in every 200 of its subjects; and it operated through a ruling class, the Communist Party who numbered just over 30 million individuals. The people's republic exercised more power over its society than any preceding regime in Chinese history, and it was appropriate that Chairman Mao should be widely compared to Ch'in Shih Huang-ti.[2]

State-building was also a feature of modern European history. In the days of Napoleon, the European states raised £60 million in taxes, the equivalent of 180 million taels, about 6 per cent of the GNP of the societies over which they ruled; they commanded some 2 million soldiers and sailors, one person in every 100 of their subjects; and they operated through a composite ruling class of nobles, bureaucrats, gentry, army officers, lawyers and greater merchants of about 400 000. In the latter days of President de Gaulle, the European states raised the equivalent, allowing for inflation, of £20 000 million, or 60 000 million taels, about 33 per cent of the GNP of the societies over which they ruled; they commanded 2 million soldiers, sailors and airmen, one person in every 125 of their subjects and they operated through a ruling class of 10 million civil servants plus about the same number of key personnel in the law, business, the professions and the armed services. The European welfare states absorbed more of their societies' resources than any previous regime in the continent's history.

Yet, despite not incomparable figures, the changes in China were much greater than in Europe. In Europe, although between Napoleon and de Gaulle, European countries had experienced two if not three industrial revolutions, the acquisition and loss of colonial empires, two world wars and the rise of modern welfare, the state had not fundamentally altered its character. It had grown parallel with society, expanded its functions, but it still recognized a distinction between itself and society and the non-identity of church and state. In China, on the other hand, the state had been transformed from the limited physiocracy described by the Jesuits under the Ming and Ch'ing which, for all its pervasiveness, left much *de facto* independence to non-political life and thought, into a modern totalitarianism which controlled both society and ideology to a degree unparalleled in the past. In China, what has been called a political conquest of society had occurred;[3] in Europe it had not.

The expansion of the Chinese state: 130-fold in money, 6-fold in military manpower, 30-fold in political personnel; was not of course uniform and continuous between 1833 and 1976. But neither was it concentrated solely into the period of the communists. It came rather in four successive and discontinuous waves.

First, the state expanded in the Victorian era in response to the mid-century rebellions and the second European war, 1856 to 1860.

The mid-century rebellions – the Taipings, the Nien, the Moslems in Kansu, Yunnan and Sinkiang – have generally been regarded as the expression of overpopulation and growing misery in the countryside. More truly they were the outcome of that growth at the base of society, the lack of concurrent extension of the state, and the consequent tendency to secession by the margins, which had become characteristic of China since the introduction of the American food plants.

The secessions, formerly incomplete and static, as in the White Lotus rebellion from 1795 to 1805 on the internal agricultural frontier between Hupei and Szechwan, now became total and mobile, as in the long march of the Taipings from the back-blocks of Kwangsi to the heartland of Kiangnan, or in the mounted looting expeditions of the Nien from their nest area in Huaipei. No-go areas turned into migratory juggernauts not because of misery, but according to the logic of organiza-tion and ideology. To survive, government had to expand. Taxation was doubled by surcharges to the land tax, increases in the price of salt, and the imposition of *likin* or transit taxes.

The level of militarization was raised, in quality as much as quantity, by the creation in partnership with regional gentry of *yung-ying* task forces, which could deal with the new forms of rebellion because they were larger and more professional than the units of the *Lu-ying* or local constabulary, and closer to the ground and less alien than those of the *Ch'i-ping* or imperial army. The number of the ruling class was enlarged 50 per cent by the sale of degrees and the inclusion of new talent, military, mercantile and modern.

The Arrow War (1856–60), more national and less local than the Opium War (1838–42) worked in the same direction. The foreigners' weapons at least were convincing. In 1862 the Lay-Osborne flotilla was ordered, in 1865 the Kiangnan arsenal was founded outside Shanghai by Li Hung-chang, and in 1866 the Foochow shipyard, planned by Tso Tsung-t'ang, was opened. At Peking, a special committee of the privy council (*i-cheng wang ta-ch'en*) known as the *tsungli yamen* or general affairs office, was set up in 1861 as a foreign ministry and coordination centre for modernization; in 1862 the *O-lo-ssu wen-kuan*, the Russian language school founded after the treaty of Nerchinsk, was transformed into the *T'ung-wen kuan*, a modern interpreters' college with branches in Shanghai and Canton; and in 1863 Robert Hart became head of the imperial maritime customs which he turned into a national revenue institution. In this first phase of state-building, the dominant figures were the greater regional governors-general and, thanks to the rise of the treaty ports and of certain inland cities like Sian or Tzu-liu-ching, the growth of the state was paralleled and supported by the growth of society.

A second wave of expansion took place between the Sino-

Japanese war of 1894–95 and the death of Yüan Shih-k'ai, the first president of the Chinese republic, in 1916. Between 1895 and 1912 when the monarchy fell, rising expenditure on foreign indemnities for two lost wars, naval and military development, railway building, a new school system and reassertion of imperial authority in Manchuria and Tibet, raised revenue from 200 to 300 million taels. Yüan Shih-k'ai's army reforms in the decade preceding the revolution increased the number of effective soldiers and the scale of military hardware, and the revolution itself increased the number of all kinds of soldier from 500 000 to nearly a million. As for the ruling class, it expanded from roughly 1½ million to 2 million, not only through this militarization, but also through the growth of business and the professions, and by the replacement in 1906 of the imperial examinations by a decentralized system of school accrediting which gave elite status to previously excluded strata of the provincial gentry.

As president of the republic, Yüan Shih-k'ai endeavoured to rationalize the state-building of the last years of the empire. He strengthened the power of the Peking ministries, particularly those of foreign affairs, finance and communications, giving them executive and not merely advisory authority and recruiting talent for them among returned students through specialist examinations. With the aid of foreign advisers he created a new salt administration which not only, through the new banks set up in the late empire, centralized the receipts, but also, more significantly, increased the quantity of salt subject to taxation by nearly 50 per cent. He also established a land tax administration to make this source of revenue, like the salt and the maritime customs, national and comprehensive. In politics, Yüan attempted to push the clearing house between the bureaucracy and the non-bureaucratic elite down from the *sheng* or province, to the next unit, the *tao* or circuit, and to appeal over the heads of the elite to the people. It was these state-building activities quite as much as the accidental monarchic form in which he embodied them, that generated the revolt against Yüan Shih-k'ai in 1916.[4]

A third wave of expansion took place in the days of the Kuomintang, though not only under its auspices, since for much of Chiang Kai-shek's reign, there were in effect four expanding states on Chinese soil: in addition to his own, those

of the warlords, the communists and the Japanese satellites
– Manchukuo, Meng-chiang, Hua-pei-kuo and Wang Ching-
wei's Kuomintang at Nanking. Although different currencies
and inflation make estimates conjectural, it would seem that
by 1945 the revenue raised by these states reached a total
equivalent to 1000 million taels, and that all the communists
did initially was to centralize receipts already being collected.
From 1930 the Kuomintang increased the rate of the salt tax;
in 1932 it established an internal revenue administration to
manage excises on tobacco and liquor; and in 1936 an income
tax department was initiated. During the war there were compulsory purchases of grain to feed the army and the inflation
which was used to finance them was in effect a capital levy,
informal expropriation by the Kuomintang preceding formal
expropriation by the communists. The level of militarization,
already raised by the early warlord era 1916–26 and the revolution of 1926–27 to over 2 million under arms, rose again
between 1927 and 1937 as the Kuomintang, the communists,
the warlords and the satellites built up their armies to perhaps
3 million by the eve of the second Sino–Japanese war.

The war itself of course established even higher levels: 4
million at least for the Kuomintang, 1 million each for the
communists, warlords and satellites, a total militarization of
7 million. The subsequent communist stabilization of the
armed forces at around 3 million therefore represented a
return to pre-war levels of militarization. As regards ruling
class, the official membership of the Kuomintang at its height
was given as 8½ million, but as soldiers were automatically
deemed members, Ch'ien Tuan-sheng considers that the
effective membership was between 2 and 4 million.[5] If to
these, say, 3 million, are added the cadres of the Communist
Party (which had a membership of over a million in 1945)
and the personnel of the warlords and satellites (Hua-pei-kuo
had half a million members in its mass organization the *Hsin-
min-hui*) one will reach a total ruling class not far short of the
5 million members with which the communists began to govern China in 1949.

Finally the state expanded again under Mao Tse-tung. The
revenue rose from 7500 million yüan in 1950/51, about 10
per cent of GNP, to 100 000 million yüan in the 1970s, over

35 per cent of GNP. The party expanded its membership from 5 million in 1949 to 17 million in 1960, and 30 million in 1975. The increase in the scale of the state, however, was greater than these figures would suggest, because it also underwent institutional magnification. During the Great Leap Forward of 1957 to 1961, Mao's moment of instant industrialization, the state practically swallowed society. The party cadres were made responsible for the day-to-day running of the 25 000 communes, urban and rural, through which China's whole life was channelled. The resultant institutional indigestion led to a partial regurgitation during the retreat from the Great Leap from 1961 to 1965, but the party never shed all the functions it had acquired, and with the increasing complexity of its task, its apparatus continued to expand from the 1960s to the 1970s despite the attempt of the cultural revolution to de-bureaucratize it. Whatever his intentions, Mao must go down in Chinese history as the creator of a huge, privileged, hierarchic and red-tape ridden bureaucratic machine, radically different from the traditional state to which it succeeded but hardly modern in character.

Second, changes in relative power. Just as in both Europe and China the state grew in absolute power and, to differing degrees, in control over society, so in both it contracted in relative predominance in relation to other states in its vicinity: on the one hand to the USA and Russia, and on the other to Japan.

The emergence of Japan as a Great Power, an independent pole both traditional and modern where communist China was neither, an alternative centre for the world of East Asia, was the most significant factor in determining China's relative predominances in the modern world, one whose full implications have not yet worked themselves out. For most of Chinese history, Japan had been an intermittent, inactive satellite, wrapped in the mists of the sea, of less significance in the Confucian firmament than Korea or Vietnam. It was good only for ideological propaganda, Buddhist or Confucian: bad only for piracy; a source of gold, silver, copper and armour; an outlet for silks. In 1800 Japan had only a tenth of the population of China and was doubtfully richer in per capita terms. By the 1970s, however, Japan had a sixth of the population of China, a gross national product 50 per cent larger than China's, and was ten times richer than China in per capita terms.

The rise of Japan was less sudden than it seemed, being masked by the isolationism of the Tokugawa. In 1400 the population of Japan had been about 5 million, less than that of Korea or Vietnam, and only one sixteenth of China's. Between 1400 and 1600, unrestricted by Mongol invasion or Black Death, buoyed up by a rise of commoner classes and, despite or because of political disunion and civil war, the population increased to 20 million, one seventh that of late Ming China. The dynamism of Renaissance Japan expressed itself in its vigorous response, first positive and then negative, to the Jesuits. Even after the proscription of Christianity, the shogunate continued to patronize the scholars of the Rangaku or Dutch learning, who studied the culture of the West, especially medicine, through the keyhole of the Netherlands trading post at Nagasaki. In the seventeenth century, thanks to Tokugawa peace and isolationism, Japan avoided the world depression and its population rose to around 30 million by 1700, a fifth of China's under K'ang-hsi. Japan's eighteenth century was even more original: a Malthusianism which stabilized the population at the 30 million mark; rising rates of literacy which put her at the head of the world league for reading and writing; and an urban pyramid the opposite of China's showing growth in the apex, the major centres of Edo, Osaka and Kyoto rather than at the base; a highly European profile which foreshadowed the modernization of the Meiji era. Japan's modernization after 1868 was an earthquake which altered the contours of East Asian political space. China was no longer the unquestionable centre of the East; no longer its richest, most powerful, most successful, most civilized political community. From 1894 to 1945, by way of action and reaction, Chinese history was largely made in Tokyo. After 1945, the Japanese economic miracle mocked Chinese communist planners and the possibility of Soviet–Japanese encirclement haunted Chinese communist diplomats.

Yet the displacement of China by Japan was less significant than the dwarfing of Europe by the USA and Russia. It could be regarded as reversible: a mere conjunctural accident which left the structural foundations unchanged and which another conjuncture could change. China retained its lead over Japan

in size, numbers and resources and, given rational government, could hope to recover it in other fields. Whether this
prove so or not, China need not feel she had lost her relative
predominance for ever. Some Japanese agreed, preferring
to become China's satellite once more rather than the Soviet
Union's. China therefore lost ground externally less than
Europe between 1833 and 1976. In terms of the state then,
China improved its standing relative to Europe in the modern
age and its history showed considerable consistency of direction.

Chinese society 1833 to 1976

Chinese social history, on the other hand, was much less consistent. In the first half of the nineteenth century it was still
dominated by its internal frontier and the tendency of its
rural base to atomize itself into ever more micro-units of the
same kind. A powerful undertow increased population, the
rural percentage of population, illiteracy and cultural alienation, and reduced the average size of cities by subtraction
from major centres and multiplication of country towns and
local markets. Around the middle of the nineteenth century,
however, a contra tendency emerged. A powerful upsurge
increased Malthusianism, the urban percentage of the population, the average size of cities, literacy and cultural participation. The early years of the people's republic, *per contra*,
saw a partial reversal of this countercurrent: an attempt to
limit the growth of cities and their natural diversification; a
return to a pattern of organization which stressed micro-units,
larger but more autarchic; and a consequent provincialism
which threatened a return to demographic explosion and at
best promised a Malthusianism of hopelessness. As a result
of these oscillations, the gap between European and Chinese
society widened between 1800 and 1970. In 1800, the gross
national product of Europe was only 50 per cent more than
China's, and the per capita income only a little more than
double. By 1970, the gross national product of Europe was
over four times that of China, and the per capita income
more than ten times. While China hesitated, Europe advanced
consistently along the lines laid down by the Renaissance and
the Enlightenment, reinforced by the industrial revolution

and Victorianism, her pace accelerating noticeably after the Second World War with the Marshall Plan and the Common Market.

For most of the nineteenth century the internal frontier of China continued to expand: in Fengtien, in Inner Mongolia, Ninghsia, Ili, Shensi-Kansu, Chinghai, Szechwan, Yunnan, Kweichow, Kwangsi, Hainan, Taiwan and the Chusan archipelago – a vast three-quarters of a circle round the rim of the Chinese heartland of the lower Huang-ho and Yangtze. In Szechwan, the broadest sector, the population increased from 20 million in 1800, to 25 million in 1819, 35 million in 1851, 40 million in 1890, advancing from the lowland valleys of the Chia-ling, T'o and Min into the highlands of the Ta-pa-shan, the Yun-kwei plateau and the Himalayan foothills. In south-west China, at least, outwards meant upwards. The conquest of China by the Chinese continued to be mainly by arable agriculture, but not exclusively so. In Kansu, Chinghai and parts of Sinkiang, there were pastoral frontiers; in Kirin, Kwangsi and Taiwan, there were mining frontiers; in Sinkiang and Sikang, there were military frontiers, the soldier–settler replacing the settler pure and simple; in Kweichow, there were mixed frontiers, arable, mineral and forest.

Behind this frontier, and serving it, there developed local markets, particularly in Szechwan where beyond the indi-vidual farms, as Colborne Baber observed, there were 'few villages in agricultural Ssu-ch'uan, but a great many market places'.[6] Above these were country towns: in Szechwan, Yu-ting-p'u on the Chungking-to-Chengtu road whose 'chief industry is the manufacture of agricultural implements',[7] Chung-pa a local entrepôt on the upper Fu-chiang, Ya-chou the brick tea centre, a 'busy little town'[8], or Sung-p'an, the garrison town and Moslem emporium founded in 1775; in Taiwan, I-lan, founded in 1813 and Hsin-chu, given walls for the first time in 1827–29; in Manchuria, mining camps like Chia-p'i-kou or Mo-ho. All, for the most part, were unofficial, non-mandarin towns created by society rather than the state. By contrast the great cities at the apex of the urban pyramid were, with the exception of Canton, the monopolitan of West-ern European trade, stagnant or declining. Robert Fortune visited the cities of Kiangnan in the 1840s and found them prosperous enough, but he felt it necessary to observe about

Soochow that it 'is evidently the seal of luxury and wealth, and has none of those signs of delapidation and decay which one sees in such towns as Ning-po', as if the case of Ning-po was more typical.[9] The base ruled in Chinese society not the apex, and the mid-century rebellions are best understood as an inversion of the frontier, attempts by the backcountry to conquer the heartlands.

In the last quarter of the nineteenth century, however, the progress of population and the frontier slackened, except in Manchuria, and a new current set in commanded by the great cities. Part of China at any rate returned to the megalopolitan traditions of the Sung. On the one hand, the growth, first of steamer, then rail, and finally of road transport, removed inhibitions to the mobilization of grain for people, cotton for machines and coal for furnaces. On the other hand, a variety of positive factors, endogenous as well as exogenous, traditional alongside modern, gave an impetus to the growth once more of large cities. The inversion of the frontier in itself released a flood of refugees in the direction of the main centres.

Shanghai, the most conspicuous of the new generation of giants, was the product mainly of modern, exogenous factors and foreign trade; the Sino-foreign community; virtual independence as an international city-state; new services like shipping, banking and insurance; new industries like Chinese machine textiles; though it also became the capital of the river and the home of 50 000 junks. Chungking on the other hand, 'the Liverpool of West China', was more traditional and endogenous; the outlet for Szechwan salt and opium; the ingress for Hupei cotton, boom commodities in the nineteenth century: the trans-shipment point between the Chia-ling and the Yangtze; the refuge for Chiang Kai-shek's government during the Second World War: a point in time as well as space, Wuhan stood midway sociologically as well as geographically: served both by the traditional economies of the Tung-t'ing and Po-yang lakes and by the Peking to Hankow railway; the capital of the Hu-kuang vice-royalty but a notable treaty port with British, Russian, French, German and Japanese concessions; the greatest junk port on the Yangtze and also the seat of the Han-yeh-p'ing steel complex.

The most significant growth, however, was not along the

Yangtze but in the north-east below the Wall, at selected points in the interior, and above all in Manchuria. Thus Tientsin grew as the port of Peking, Li Hung-chang's headquarters, the capital of the Ch'ang-lu salt division, the terminus of the railway to Nanking and the head-office for coal mines along the Chihli coast. Tsingtao was a railway terminus and a naval base, always seen by its German developers as the Hong Kong of the north, but also a centre of the refined salt industry and a rising junk port. In the interior, Sian recovered some of the glory of Ch'ang-an as the expression of China's new ascendancy in Central Asia following Tso Tsung-t'ang's expedition, and as the western terminus of the Belgian-built Lunghai railway; Tzu-liu-ching, the booming capital of the Szechwan salt industry, surprised foreigners with its natural gas wells, its million population and air of industrial bustle. In Manchuria, Dairen developed as a civilian seaport with a rate of growth at times faster than Shanghai's; Mukden as the company town for the coal mines of Fu-shun and the steel works of An-shan; Ch'ang-ch'un as the headquarters of the soya bean industry; and Harbin as the capital of the Chinese eastern railway zone and a White Russian refuge from Bolshevism.

A number of lesser centres also came to the fore: Taiyuan, headquarters of the progressive warlord Yen Hsi-shan and site of a major communist industrial project; Cheng-chou, railway junction and textile workshop; Ho-fei, Li Hung-chang's home town and communist provincial capital; Kunming, railway terminus and head-office for the tin industry; Taipei, colonial capital and refuge for the Kuomintang; Pao-t'ou, Inner Mongolian product of first five-year plan industrialization.

The most important single factor in this re-urbanization of China was the railways. Indeed the whole period 1833 to 1976 might be called the railway age in China. China's initial opposition to railways was indicative of her centrifugal orientation. In 1863 even so enlightened an official as Li Hung-chang, then governor of Kiangsu, turned down a proposal by the foreign community at Shanghai to build a line to Soochow. In April 1867, *The North China Herald* expressed the differences between Chinese and foreigners on this point: 'To us, railways mean free intercourse, enlightenment, commerce and wealth; to the mandarins they suggest rowdyism, the overthrow of time-honoured custom and tradition, distur- bance and ruin'.[10] In October 1867, the Tsungli Yamen, a new and by no means immobilist body, in a letter seeking the comments of high officials on the barbarian problem, expres- sed its opposition to the building of railways in China on the grounds of stategic risk, popular religious hostility and the danger of unemployment. All seventeen of its correspon- dents, including Li Hung-chang, now Hukuang viceroy, Tso Tsung-t'ang Shen-Kan viceroy and patron of the Foochow shipyard, and Ting Pao-chen, perhaps the best administrator in China, then governor of Shantung, agreed with this oppos- ition. In 1877, a short line built by the foreign community from Shanghai to Woosung without Chinese authorization was hurriedly purchased by Liang-kiang governor-general Shen Pao-chen, a relatively progressive figure, and destroyed. In 1880 a proposal from one of Li Hung-chang's subordinates, Liu Ming-ch'uan for a railway from Peking to Huai-yin half- way down the Grand Canal met with no official support. China preferred her isolation.

Progress began in the 1880s. In 1881, C.W. Kinder, the engineer of the Kaiping coal mining company, part of Li Hung-chang's empire, converted the company's seven-mile mule-drawn tramway from T'ang-shan to the Pei-t'ang river to locomotion, thus establishing the first permanent railway in China. In 1886 the line was extended to Lu-t'ai, and in 1887 imperial consent was given for extensions to Tientsin, Peking and Shanhaikuan, the whole complex coming under the control of a vice-regal agency, the Imperial Railways of North China. In 1887 another state railway from Taipei to Kelung was begun by Liu Ming-ch'uan, now governor of Taiwan.

The real breakthrough came in 1889. A proposal by the navy yamen to build a railway from Tientsin, Li Hung-chang's headquarters, to T'ung-chou just outside Peking was debated among the high officials. It drew a vigorous memorial from Liu Ming-ch'uan who made a frontal assault on the arguments based on strategic risk, popular hostility and the danger of unemployment still being championed by the censorate, and called for a general programme of railway building by a national development corporation. This was followed by a

counter-proposal from Liang-kuang governor-general Chang
Chih-tung for a much longer line from Peking to Hankow
which would be less exposed to foreign attack than the navy
yamen's scheme, could virtually replace the Grand Canal, and
could be extended north to Manchuria, west to Kansu, south
to Canton, as resources allowed. Chang's memorial, skilfully
blending conservative arguments for radical measures, won
the day and on 27 August a commission was set up to build
the first Chinese trunk line. Work was delayed by the Sino–
Japanese war and the inability of the commission to raise
sufficient Chinese capital, so that the first trunk line actually
commenced was the T-shaped Chinese eastern and South
Manchuria system begun by the Russians under the Li Hung-
chang/Cassini agreement of 22 May 1896. In 1898, however,
the Peking–Hankow project was resumed with Belgian capital
and a Belgian chief engineer, Jean Jadot, and was successfully
brought to completion in 1905.[11]

The first decade of the twentieth century saw a railway
boom in China unequalled even by that of the early days of
the communists. Between 1901 and 1912, 5000 miles were
completed. These included the Manchurian T, the A-shaped
trunk lines of north China, Peking–Hankow, Tientsin–Pukow,
Kaifeng–Loyang; two sets of metropolitan branch lines round
Peking and Shanghai, the former including the purely
Chinese-built Peking to Kalgan line of the engineer Chan
T'ien-yü; and a number of significant provincial lines, for
example Tsingtao to Tsinan and Kunming to Hanoi. In addition, at least the same mileage was projected as every level
of state and society – the court, the governors-general, the
provincial gentry, merchants and foreigners – sought to graft
itself on to a development which seemed certain to be profitable, politically advantageous and prestigious. Contracts were
signed, in 1911 with a consortium of British, French, German
and American bankers for the Hu-kuang railways, Hankow
to Canton, Hankow to Chengtu; in 1912 with a Belgian company for the Lunghai line extending the Kaifeng–Loyang to
Lanchow in Kansu and Haichow on the Kiangsu coast; in
1913 with a Franco–Belgian group for the T'ung-ch'eng line
from Ta-t'ung on the Wall to Chengtu in Szechwan; and in
1914 with a French company for the U-shaped Ching-Yu line
from Yamchow (Ch'in-chou) on the south-west Kwangtung
coast via Kunming and Sui-fu to Chungking.

Lack of capital, mismanagement of what there was, revolution, world war and civil wars interrupted these projects. The early republic extended the Lunghai line eastward to Hsuchou in 1921 and to Haichow before 1928, while the Kuomintang extended it westward to Sian by 1934 and to Pao-chi in the upper Wei valley by 1937. The Kuomintang's most notable railway achievement, however, was the completion in 1936 of the Hankow to Canton line. The early republic and Kuomintang between them added some 2500 miles of line to the railway network, and about 2000 miles was added by the warlord and puppet regimes in Manchuria, making a total for China in 1949 of nearly 10 000 miles.

The communists resumed the building programme of the late empire and the presidency of Yüan Shih-k'ai. Under the first five-year plan the chief projects were the extension of the Lunghai line across Kansu and Sinkiang to meet the Turksib just east of Lake Balkash; a line from Pao-chi to Chengtu, a version of the Belgian T'ung-ch'eng line of 1913 for which more preliminary work was done in 1936; a westward extension of the Inner Mongolian line to Lanchow and a northward projection to Ulan Bator and Kiakhta; and a line from Chengtu to Chungking, a section of the Hu-kuang railways of 1911 again under active reconsideration in 1936. All these projects were completed by the mid-1960s. By the time Chairman Mao died, total railway mileage in China was over 20 000, small compared to the 100 000 miles of Europe of the Nine, but equal to Britain's in 1900, Brazil's in 1950. The geotechtonics of China provided better water communication east/west than north/south, an imbalance not rectified by the artificial Nile of the Grand Canal. But the natural interchange of commodities was north/south since latitude, through climate, diversifies products more than longitude. The railways redressed this asymmetry of communications and commodities and reorientated China from the line of the Yangtze, which had been dominant since the Sung period, to a new line of great cities from Harbin through Mukden, Peking and Wuhan to Canton.

This re-urbanization deeply affected Chinese society: the upper classes, the *shih*, directly; the other, less urban classes, indirectly. The effect on the upper classes was a double movement of diversification and polarization; the effect on the other classes was a more hesitant movement of demography.

First, diversification, that is the rise alongside the officials and community leaders of the traditional *shih* of groups with a different basis of legitimation. On the one hand, there was the development of private business, particularly in Shanghai and the Tientsin area. Modern industry in China began under official patronage, within the cocoon, half protective, half inhibitory, of the *kuan-tu shang-pan* system of official/merchant chant partnership. Following the Sino–Japanese war and particularly during the First World War which gave it a temporary monopoly of its own market, it broke out of this protection and created not only partnerships, companies, chambers of commerce and stock markets, but also the ancillary welfare institutions of an urban society – schools, hospitals, libraries.

Thus in the north, Chou Hsüeh-hsi, son of a viceroy, friend of Yüan Shih-k'ai, not only established an industrial empire centred on the Chee Hsin cement company at T'ang-shan outside Tientsin which supplied much of the cement for the railways, but was also the founder of Peking Central Hospital.[12] Thus Chang Chien, *optimus* in the *chin-shih* examination of 1894, protégé of Chang Chih-tung, president of the Kiangsu provincial assembly, not only established an industrial empire centred on the Dah Sun cotton mill at Nan-t'ung outside Shanghai which supplied machine-made yarn to the hand looms of the Kiangnan hinterland, but was also the founder of teachers' training colleges, primary schools, a museum, a subscription library and a primitive university at his company town.[13] Other notable business pioneers were Meng Lo-Ch'uan, a traditional merchant from Tsinan who organized a chain of drapery stores in Peking, Tientsin and Shanghai; the Jung brothers, minor officials and local bankers who founded the Mou-hsin flour mill which supplied the new-found tastes of Shanghai and later became the cotton kings of the city; the Kuo brothers, Cantonese remigrants who set up the Wing On department store in Shanghai on the model of David Jones in Sydney; Ching Pen-po, theoretician of salt reform who founded the Chiu Ta salt refining company at Tientsin and was partner of Fan Hsü-tung in the Pacific Alkali company; Mu Ou-ch'u, returned student from Texas and Shanghai.[14] All these businessmen built on the consumerism of the growing cities.

On the other hand there was the development of the professions. Under the old regime, the nearest equivalent to a professional class were the *mu-yu* (lit. 'tent friends'), the specialist advisers whom all levels of the Ch'ing bureaucracy found it increasingly prudent to employ on an individual basis. The *mu-yu* were members of the *shih* who had either withdrawn from the official *cursus* or paused on the examination ladder, to concentrate on some branch of the administration – law, taxation, salt, hydraulics or border problems – in which the regular officials did not possess sufficient expertise, The *mu-yu* were specialists but, lacking formal training or institutional qualification, they were hardly professionals.

Professional classes only began to emerge in the twentieth century with re-urbanization, the railways and the rise of business. They included engineers such as Chan T'ien-yu, the technologist of the first entirely Chinese-built railway, the Peking to Kalgan, and the first president of the Chinese Institute of Engineers; doctors such as the Malay-born and Cambridge-educated Wu Lien-teh, founder of the Manchurian plague prevention service in 1912, the national quarantine service in 1930 and of fourteen hospitals: scientists such as Ting Wen-chiang, the creator of the geological survey of China, also indefatigable traveller, managing director of a coal mine, mayor of Shanghai and friend, despite his positivism, of Teilhard de Chardin; lawyers such as Wang Ch'ung-hui, DCL from Yale, member of the Middle Temple, chairman of the judicial *yuan* and judge of the international court at the Hague; journalists such as Ying Hua (Ying Lien-chih), Manchu bannerman, founder of the Tientsin newspaper *Ta Kung Pao*, also, as a convert to Catholicism, of Fu-jen university at Peking; publishers such as Chang Yüan-chi, *chin-shih* from Chekiang 1892, manager of the Commercial Press at Shanghai, also bibliophile and editor of the magazine *Tung-fang tsa-chih* (Eastern Miscellany); educationalists such as the feminist Chang Mo-chün, first principal of the Shen-chou girls' school at Shanghai.[15] All these pioneers, whether in private practice or employed by public or private institutions, received their impetus from the new urban context.

Second, polarization. The new blossoming of the *shih* in the cities was accompanied by growing estrangement between its urban and rural moieties. Despite the English connotations of their name, the scholar gentry had always been predominantly an urban class. Most of the *shih* derived most of their income from essentially urban activities: government, management, arbitration, brokerage, trade or teaching. However, in all provinces there were *shih* landlords, rural scholars, and in some, like Hunan and Anhwei, a true squirearchy, even a landed aristocracy. The abolition of the imperial examinations, the replacement of tutors by schools, the growth of large cities and access to them by rail polarized the urban and rural components. Facilities – educational, professional, commercial and bureaucratic – were now more than ever urban and those unable to use them necessarily became more rustic. The counterpart of the rise of business and the professions was the rise of a rural counter-elite: landlords, market town *mafia* bosses, leaders of folk religions, the officers of warlord armies, the cadres of rural Soviets; not a single group but united in opposition to the urban elite.

Such polarization is characteristic of modernizing countries. Lawrence Durrell describes it in fictional form for Egypt under the *raj* in the two Hosnani brothers: Nessim, the smooth urban financier and manipulator, Narouz, the rough backcountry farmer, the man of the people and, if necessary, of violence. In China, the rural counter-elite included people as varied as the leaders of the Szechwan railway protection league in 1911, such as Lo Lun, a *chü-jen* but not an official, vice-president of the provincial assembly, his father a prominent *Ko-lao-hui* member; the organizers of the Red Spears of Honan in 1926 whom Mde. Vishnyakova-Akimova described as a mixture of 'monks, landlords and *shenshih*';[16] their opponent, Hu Ching-i, commander of the ragtag second national army, ex-lieutenant of the bandit White Wolf, ally of the self-consciously homespun warlord Feng Yü-hsiang; the 'country boys' of the Kwangsi military clique – Li Tsung-jen, the two Huangs and Pai Chung-hsi – military sons of civilian failures in the old examination system, radical but Spartan;[17] their counterpart inside the Kuomintang, the *tsa-pai* clique of Ch'en Ch'eng; communist marshals such as the converted warlord Chu Te or Ho Lung, the elder brother who outgrew the *Ko-lao-hui*; cadres such as the provincial schoolmaster Liu Shao-ch'i or Liu Chih-tan, from a gentry family in Shansi, another ex *Ko-lao-hui* man. All these people, in different ways, reacted against an urban world which by expanding had cast them off.

Beyond the *shih*, re-urbanization had its effects on the urban lower classes and in the countryside mainly in demography. First, the cities changed their character. As Braudel observed, pre-modern Chinese cities were expressions of rural over-population rather than economic organization.[18] Because they were essentially temporary places of work for the rustic immigrant, they contained more males than females (in Peking 63.5 per thousand to 36.5 per thousand), had low birth rates (in Peking 12 per thousand) and, because of the youth of the population, low death rates at least for males (in Peking 21.6 per thousand for males against 33.2 per thousand for females). With re-urbanization Chinese large cities became places of permanent residence. The male/female ratio approached unity; the huge prostitute population of Shanghai, the world of Suzie Wong, was one aspect of this. The birth rate rose in Shanghai to 45 per thousand in 1957. So did the death rate, particularly the female tuberculosis death rate, as housing failed to keep pace with population increase and living space per capita in Shanghai fell from 3.7 square metres in 1949 to 2.1 square metres in 1957. The average death rate for males and females together rose to perhaps 30 per cent until checked by modern medicine; in Shanghai the death rate was down to 20 per cent by 1957. In these circumstances, the family (both marriage and *de facto* relation-ships important in big cities) became more conjugal and less filial, as wives less frequently lived with their parents-in-law in the village while their husbands worked in the town, and the basic unit became the co-resident husband and wife. The fact that immigrants now came from farther away – in the case of Shanghai, Kiang-pei rather than Kiang-nan – retain-ing fewer links with their villages of origin, worked in the same direction. Conjugality pointed towards later marriage and fewer, better educated children.

Next, urban values reached out to the countryside. Between 1920 and 1937 some 50 000 miles of road were constructed, mostly surfaced with sand, clay and gravel it is true, but effec-tive enough for the 50 000 odd buses, lorries, cars and motor-cycles which used them. These roads were arterial rather than local, for example the Silan highway of 480 miles from Sian to Lanchow built by O.J. Todd between 1930 and 1934, or the road from Chungking to Yunnan completed just before the outbreak of hostilities in 1937; and the villages resented the loss of land, the exclusion of their carts and the imposition of corvée. However, since the traditional Chinese village was seldom autarchic but formed part of a system of interlocking markets which handled half its production and consumption, it benefited by the fall in transport costs and by the wider diffusion of technology: in particular the *san-chuan*, or 'three things that go round', that girls insisted that suitors should guarantee them before agreeing to marriage – the watch, the bicycle and the sewing machine.[19] Already in 1935, O.J. Todd noted in Shansi that: 'Bicycles are cheap and therefore are within the reach of thousands. Many a merchant's clerk or a family cook owns his bicycle and uses it constantly, or rents it out by the day. Students travel long journeys to and from school or on short trips into the country in this way'.[20] As in Europe, the bicycle affected marriage patterns and the structure of marriage by enabling young people to choose partners outside their village and beyond family supervision. With the closing of the rural frontier as new land became scarce, and the opening of the urban frontier through re-urbanization and improved communications, demographic configurations even in the countryside changed. It seems likely that the stabilization of the population between 1850 and 1950 owed more to these factors than to the political disorder to which it is often attibuted. Down to 1949 concentration at the top rather than proliferation at the bottom was the dominant theme of Chinese society at all levels.

The victory of Chinese communism in 1949 represented in social terms the success of one section of what we have called the rural counter-elite. It was from the country town of Yenan, the Geneva of Chinese communism, that Mao, the provincial teachers' training college principal, masterminded the growth of Soviet areas during the war with Japan which, by 1945, had put the party half-way to supreme power in China. It was from the backwoods of Manchuria that Mao's marshals, gathering in the forces of the former warlord Chang Hsüeh-liang, sprung the trap on Chiang Kai-shek's overextended city garrisons which completed the ascent.

The victory of the party, however, was made possible by

the series of disasters which the Chinese middle classes, the successors of the *shih*, suffered between 1937 and 1949. First, their base, the cities of the eastern seaboard, were successively bombed, looted and occupied by the Japanese between 1937 and 1941. Next, after heroic efforts to save themselves – the long march of factories, offices, laboratories and libraries to shanty towns, converted temples and caves in Szechwan and Yunnan – their capital was confiscated, their service refused and their status depressed by the inflation, nationalization and hostility of the Chungking government. Finally, the predatory return of the Kuomintang to the coast in 1945, its reluctance to return property to its rightful owners, its demonetization of the satellite currencies, its vindictive attitude towards anyone who had remained in the east, its continued and aggravated mismanagement of the currency, extended these evils to the nucleus of the middle class which had survived under Japanese and satellite protection.

These disasters produced in urban China a kind of flight from society: capitalists despaired of capitalism, professional people of independence, democrats of democracy. The middle classes saw their future not in a restoration of pre-war society, but in a rejuvenated and extended bureaucratic state. This attitude did not lead automatically to active support, except in the case of students, for the communists. In most cases it led only to withdrawal of support from the Kuomintang or passive sympathy with its anti-mainstream faction. But it created a climate of opinion favourable to Mao, so that when the Red Army began to win in the field, the Kuomintang had no reserves of civilian strength, while the communists could expand their membership rapidly to govern as well as conquer. Mao was carried to power, not, as he may have imagined, on the swell of peasant discontent, but like Hitler, on the sudden crest of a temporarily despairing middle class.[21] His crucial margin of support came not from the countryside but from the big cities: from enlightened technocrats like Wong Wen-hao, businessmen like the Nan-yang brother Chien Yu-chien, professional people like Chang Yüan-chi the publisher or Hou Te-pang the chemical engineer, all of whom remained on the mainland after 1949.

Of itself the advent of communism need not have checked re-urbanization, though clearly it was going to absorb business and the professions into the bureaucracy. Indeed, the early adoption by Mao of the Soviet model of development, i.e. priority for heavy industry under the leadership of a managerial technostructure, encouraged the growth of urban population, the improvement of communications and the diversification of elites. Despite hostility to Shanghai as the capital of imperialism and attacks on business and some parts of the intelligentsia, the early years of Mao were an Indian summer for Chinese cities.

From 1957, however, specific policies of the party counteracted the dominant tendency of society. First, the Great Leap Forward, Mao's own formula for development – an adaptation of the Yenan model for revolution to the problems of socialist construction, with its emphasis on 'red rather than expert', ideological fervour in the cadres rather than managerial or professional skill – checked the diversification of elites. Simplicity of mind was preferred to complexity. Similarly, its adoption of the autarchic people's commune as the dominant institution in the countryside and ideally in the towns as well, stressed self-sufficiency rather than intercommunication. The intention was to reduce the number of cells in Chinese society to facilitate communist leadership: 25 000 communes, later increased by subdivision to 75 000, replaced 100 million family farms and workshops as the basic units of organization; but the effect was to reassert the dominance of lowest level institutions in Chinese society and to re-emphasize its cellular rather than organic character. Second, the retreat from the Great Leap, the party's readjustment of institutions, reversed the encouragement of urban population growth by its formalization of the practice of *hsia-fang* (lit. 'downward transfer'), the compulsory rustication of urban youth, into a conscious programme of de-urbanization. *Hsia-fang* produced 'a decline in the urban component of the total population from 18.5 per cent in 1960 to 14 per cent in 1969',[22] and an absolute reduction of 18 million of urban population in the twenty years from 1959 to 1979. Bitterly opposed by urban youth and a major ingredient in the cultural revolution, 1966 to 1969, it was resumed thereafter and was still in force as policy at Mao's death. The tendency to megapolis was, temporarily at any rate, abated.

The evolution of the family under communism also fell into this pattern of early advance, later retreat. On the one hand, the party inherited and continued the feminism of 4 May movement, the intellectual awakening at Peking university between 1916 and 1922. It attacked the early, universal, family-arranged, filial and fertile marriages of teenagers characteristic of the peasant frontier, and advocated the later, less-than-universal, individual-arranged, conjugal and Malthusian marriages of adults characteristic of the big city. Under the marriage law of 1950, which outlawed polygamy and the sale of wives and daughters and redefined divorce and abortion, the legal age of marriage was fixed at 20 for men and 18 for women, but the party recommended 22/23 and 20/21 as the optimum, and later raised this recommendation to 25 and 23 in the countryside, 28 and 26 in the towns. The party could be construed as the modernizer of the family.

On the other hand, the institutions of the regime worked against its professed ideals. *Hsia-fang*, while it reduced birth rates to low levels in the towns (in Shanghai in the 1970s to 10 thousand or less), raised them in the countryside where they were still high, families with five or six children being not uncommon. The autarchic and labour-intensive commune put a premium on hands. In 1965 Edgar Snow asked Ch'en Yung-kuei, then head of the Ta-chai brigade of a model commune in Shansi and later a politbureau member, about birth control. He replied 'No we don't need that. We need able-bodied workers'.[23] In 1956, 90 per cent of the marriages in rural Shansi were still arranged by the parents, many of them early marriages. Even in the towns old attitudes died hard. In 1971 Ross Terrill talked to six silk-spinners in Wushih, four women, two men, with an average age of 35. Five were married and four had employed go-betweens to arrange their marriages.[24] During the cultural revolution when external constraints temporarily broke down, there were many early marriages and the birth rate in the towns revived. Though the party willed the form of the modern urban family, it did not will the content nor provide the appropriate institutional context. The family was not encouraged to be a centre of initiative either socially or psychologically. As Yao Wen-yüan. Mao's son-in-law, put it in 1963: 'The warriors of the revolution should put revolutionary pursuits in the centre of their lives and subject their personal loves to the needs of the revolution'.[25]

In these circumstances, the family, perhaps the ultimate

secret of the West's dynamism, became in China, at best, the lowest cell of the party's organization, at worst, a secret society against it: brothers with the party, brothers against it. Consequently at the death of Chairman Mao, China had a family system neither filial nor conjugal, neither traditional nor modern, but fraternal, a reflection of the ambivalence of totalitarian society as a whole.

It would therefore be an oversimplification to see the trajectory of China's place in the world in the modern age as decline in the nineteenth century and recovery in the twentieth, unless the curve is defined in exclusively political terms. Indeed, if the history of society is given proper consideration, the opposite would seem nearer the truth: a healthy increase of complexity in the nineteenth century, an unhealthy resimplification into officials and peasants in the twentieth century. If Mao's China compared better to de Gaulle's Europe than Ch'ien-lung's to Napoleon's, it was little thanks to Mao. Between 1949 and 1976 both China and Europe experienced renaissances, but the two renaissances were more different than similar. That of China was primarily in the fields of force and diplomacy. That of Europe was in every field except those of force and diplomacy. Post-war Europe, like post-war Japan, had sophistication without power. China, like the Soviet Union had power without sophistication. Only the USA had power and sophistication. Hence the world order became a *pax Americana* and only those naive enough to believe that all power grows out of the barrel of a gun, would think that China had improved her position within it under Chairman Mao.

AVENUES OF CONTACT, 1833 TO 1976

Just as the internal development of China in the nineteenth and twentieth centuries was dominated by the revolution in transport, so too the principal factor affecting the avenues of contact between China and the outside world in the modern age was the coming of steamers, railways, automobiles and aeroplanes. Although no new routes were opened except by the aeroplane, the revolution in transport altered the hierarchy of existing routes and made all of them wider and smoother except where interrupted by political factors. The interruptions, however, were considerable, so that while contacts between China and the outside world multiplied, they did not do so to the extent that the technology alone would have warranted.

The central land route

Here, the transport possibilities were largely checked by polit ical factors. The modest revival which the route was experiencing at the beginning of the nineteenth century, thanks to Kokandi and Tungan mercantile enterprise and the impetus given to *haj* traffic by the *Jahriyya*, was not maintained and extended by railways and roads. Although much of the traditional terrain was in fact eventually traversed by railways – the Turkish Anatolian lines from 1888, the Russian Trans-Caspian from Krasnovodsk via Samarkand to Tashkent 1885–98, the Sino–Soviet Lanchow to Balkash line 1955–65 – the parts did not make a whole, and there was the Persian gap where Reza Shah's north/south Trans-Iranian line set an orientation on a different alignment. Roads might generally improve between Constantinople and Peking, but here again politics took away what technology gave, as enterprises such as the *Croisiere Jaune*, the Haardt–Citroen expedition of 1930–32, proved. From China's point of view only Mao's military highway from Kashgar to Gilgit was of much significance. The result of this failure to exploit the possibilities of the new transportation was that the central land route lost importance relatively in the modern age.

The two principal forms of political interference were the disorders caused by dervishism and the mutually hostile partition of Central Asia by Britain, Russia and China, in particular the Sinification policies of Tso Tsung-t'ang.

As may be seen from the writings of the Hungarian traveller Arminius Vambery, who travelled extensively in Central Asia in the mid-nineteenth century disguised as a dervish, the Sufi *tariqats*, in particular the Naqshbandiyya, provided – in their hostels, *haj* caravans and contacts between sedentarists with goods and nomads with animals – a permanent infrastructure for circulation all the way from Constantinople to Peking. At the same time, the political ambitions of different sections of the order, its Islamic fundamentalism, and its systematic rejection of the European world order, were formidable obstacles to the development of such circulation.

In western Turkestan clerically-dominated Bokhara launched attacks on the more commercially-oriented Kokand in 1839, 1863 and 1865 which undermined its prosperity and cohesion, so that it became easier prey for the Russians. After the Russian conquest, there were dervish disturbances in Ferghana in 1885, 1891 and 1898; in 1916, the Tsar's attempt to impose conscription produced a major revolt in Kazakhstan; and the Bolsheviks found the Moslem Basmachi movement in Uzbekistan from 1918 to 1934 one of their most determined opponents. In eastern Turkestan, the Afaqi Makhdumzada khojas, the leaders of the Naqshbandiyya exiled to Kokand by the Ch'ing conquest, organized unsuccessful but destructive rebellions in 1827, 1847, and 1857, as well as minor outbreaks in 1814, 1852, 1856 and 1861. In 1862 the Tungans, the Chinese-speaking Moslems of Kansu, revolted under the leadership of Ma Hua-lung, a chief of the militant *Jahriyya* sub-group of the Naqshbandiyya which had been introduced to China in the late eighteenth century. Over the next three years the rebellion spread to the Moslems of Sinkiang both Chinese and Turkish-speaking. In 1865 the exiled khoja returned from Kokand and Ch'ing authority collapsed completely, but power was taken by the Kokandi general Yakub beg who sent the khoja to Mecca and established a coherent Moslem state in Sinkiang, which lasted nearly ten years until it was overpowered by Tso Tsung-t'ang in 1878. Yakub's regime was pan-Turkish rather than Pan-Islamic, but the *sharia* was enforced and, according to Sir Douglas Forsyth who visited Yarkland in 1873, it was generally disliked by the commercial classes.

Tso Tsung-t'ang's defeat of both the Kansu and the Sinkiang rebellions brought only temporary peace. There were serious Tungan disturbances in 1895–96 in Kansu in areas which had been active in 1862–73; between 1930 and 1937 there was the major revolt of both Kansu Tungens and Sinkiang Turks led by the Moslem warlord Ma Chung-ying; and in 1944 there was an uprising of Kazakhs, some of whom were still in arms in 1951 and eventually found refuge in Turkey. Westward from Central Asia, the Naqshbandiyya was active in resisting

Russia in the Caucasus and in resisting Turkey, Iraq and Persia in Kurdistan. Tso Tsung-t'ang's remarkable and, to contemporaries, surprising reconquest of Sinkiang was closely bound up with transportation factors. His problem was to feed his armies in a province without a food surplus and, in particular, to build up a reserve in his beach-head in the north, Uighuristan, sufficient to support an offensive against the south, Altishahr, where lay the heartland of the rebellion. The traditional solution, advocated by his commissary Yüan Pao-heng, was to use donkey carts to move grain from central China (the Yüans came from Honan and may have been suppliers themselves) up the silk road from Sian via Lanchow, Su-chow, An-hsi and Hami to Barkol and Ku-ch'eng, and some supplies did take this route. Tso, however, calculated that the animals and drivers would consume too high a proportion of the grain they carried, suspected the efficiency of Yüan's office, and insisted on the use of two additional routes which between them carried more than the traditional one and made the crucial difference to the success of the campaign.

First, he used the desert road to Turkestan from Kuei-hua via Pao-t'ou and the wastes of Alashan and the Etzin Gol direct to Barkol and Ku-ch'eng: a purely pack camel route whose utilization thus signalized the last victory of the Islamic Bactrian camel, whose ascent we noted in the middle ages, over the Chinese cart. As Tso argued:

> In a word, the best means of transportation in the northwest are camels, because they eat less and carry more, and are able to cross the difficult mountain passes and deserts... Once they get out of the Great Wall, the camels can depend almost entirely on natural feed and need grain only in rare cases when they are really tired.[26]

Second, he used the Irtish route via Lake Zaisan and northern Zungharia, a variant of the far northern land route, to bring Siberian grain by riverboat and *tarantass* (a four-wheeled Russian *troika*) to Ku-ch'eng: a much more forward move foreshadowing the age of the steamer, railway and truck. By adding these two new routes, one implicitly traditional, the other implicitly modern, to the one already in use, Tso secured supplies sufficient for a rapid, mobile and victorious campaign.

The reconquest of Sinkiang was followed externally by a confrontation with Russia and internally by the erection of the area into a regular Chinese province. Both events restricted the use of the central land route. During the rebellion, Russia had occupied Ili ostensibly to protect her commercial rights under the treaty of Kuldja of 1851, but in reality with a view to annexation, a move which would have made Sinkiang virtually a Russian dependency. China was sufficiently strong, and sufficiently self-confident after Tso's campaign, to obtain the retrocession of Ili at the treaty of St Petersburg in 1881, but the episode left her with a disinclination for closer contact on this frontier than she was already committed to by the establishment of a Russian consulate-general at Kashgar in 1866. So long as the empire lasted, China was successful in preventing contact rising beyond what she considered a safe level. Internally, the conversion in 1884 of the Manchu military dependency governed by a dyarchy of banner officers and local notables into a regular Chinese province, and the limited encouragement of Chinese immigration – sufficient to lay a basis for future Sinicization but insufficient to cause a native rebellion – were moves with the same ends in view. Between 1912 and 1949 these checks weakened and collapsed; Russian influence, Chinese immigration, native rebellion all increased. But, despite all, a semblance of Chinese control, and a considerable degree of isolation was maintained, particularly by the pro-Soviet warlord Sheng Shih-ts'ai who was in charge of the province from 1933 to 1944.[27] When Mao came to power in 1949, he favoured cooperation with the Soviet Union on this as on other frontiers, but while the Sino–Soviet dispute was not the result of border disputes, it had the result of once more closing the route from Kashgar to Kokand. Mao in effect returned to an intensified form of the policies of Tso Tsung-t'ang: isolation and Sinification. In these circumstances the silk road could not flourish.

The southern sea route

On the central land route, technology and politics in the modern age were discordant. On the southern sea route they were concordant. In the Renaissance and early Enlightenment, the southern sea route, traditionally the most important link between China and the West, had been eclipsed first by the Pacific, then by the Cape. In the latter part of the eighteenth century it had been partially revived by the country trade in raw cotton and opium from India to China. In the modern age this revival was completed by, on the one hand, the opening of the Suez canal in 1869 and the progressive substitution thereafter of steam for sail and, on the other, the emergence, particularly during the ministries of Salisbury, of the line Suez, Bombay, Colombo, Singapore and Shanghai as the jugular vein of the British empire. Together these two factors produced the brief age of the ocean liners with their six weeks' journeys mixing tedium, snobbery, romance and seasickness. Thereafter politics and technology moved together to dethrone the southern sea route. Singapore fell, India became independent, China went communist, Suez was evacuated, while BOAC replaced P&O and supertankers replaced colliers. By the time the Suez canal was closed in 1967 by the six-day war, the southern sea route had lost its recovered primacy, and when it reopened in 1975 following the Yom Kippur war, politics and technology had, temporarily at any rate, bypassed it. Further east, supertankers sailed from the Gulf, but to East Asia's modern rim, Japan, not to the primitivist China of Chairman Mao.

The revival of the southern sea route which expanded the volume of shipping entering and leaving Chinese ports from 7 million tons in 1864 to 72 million in 1905, and by the 1930s made Shanghai nearly as big a port as London, involved a much wider range of institutions than simply the canal and the steamship.

In China it required not only the agency houses and compradors already in place in 1833, but also the suppression of piracy by the Royal Navy; the compilation of charts of the China coast by Kellet and Collinson; the construction of lighthouses, lightships, buoys and beacons by the marine department of the maritime customs; the establishment of the Siccawei observatory and its typhoon warning system by the Shanghai Jesuits; the initiation of a Sino–foreign pilotage service the appointment of harbour masters and quarantine officers; the creation of the Hai-ho and Whangpoo conservancies which maintained the approaches to Tientsin and Shanghai. In Europe, it required not only shipyards, graving docks, wet docks and warehouses, but also the shipping companies

such as P&O, North German Lloyd and Messageries
Maritimes; the syndicate system at Lloyds; the sometimes
tortuous finance and diplomacy of the Suez canal company;
the development of banking networks. In between, it required
not only the existence of ports of call, but also the provision
of coal and other facilities at them; the establishment of local
sub-systems of trade; and, not least, the suitable adjustment
of freight rates. For example, the advantageous freight rates
offered by British colliers allowed salt manufacturers in the
Red Sea to build up a lucrative trade to India, which Chinese
producers around 1913 feared might be extended to China,
and which in the 1960s did in fact supply part of Japan's large
import. Such cabotage formed part of the infrastructure of
the liners. Indeed, the careful fulfilment of all these require-
ments lay behind, say, the repeated commutings of Teilhard
de Chardin between Paris and Peking, his stopovers and side-
trips in Ethiopia, India, Ceylon, Burma and Java, in the last
years of the P&O era. A general condition, of course, was
the security provided by the British navy.

The northern land route

Here too, as with the central land route, the transport revolution was largely aborted by political factors. Railways were
only built in the twentieth century: the Orenburg–Tashkent,
during 1900–06, from the Urals across the Kazakh steppe to
the capital of Russian Central Asia; the Turksib (Turkestan–
Siberian), during 1912–31 with work effectively interrupted
from 1913 to 1927, from Novosibirsk on the Trans-Siberian
to Tashkent; the Sino–Soviet Lanchow to Balkash, begun in
1955 with the Russian section, Aktogai to Ching-ho being
complete by 1958, the Chinese section, Pao-chi to Ching-ho,
not till 1965. Even when built, not much use was made of
them thanks to Russian fears of Chinese immigration,
Chinese fears of Russian subversion in Sinkiang and the Sino–
Soviet schism under Khrushchev and Mao. The northern
land route never recovered the pre-eminence it had had in
the days of Pegolotti and the Golden Horde, nor achieved
what Mackinder's theory of the heartland might have led one
to expect of it.

Nevertheless Ili and Chuguchak were more significant

points of contact between China and the outside world in the modern age than Kashgar and Yarkand.

In the late eighteenth and early nineteenth centuries the Ch'ing authorities in Ili had pursued a closed border policy with respect to the Kazakh 'hordes' or confederations to their west. Though they accepted occasional tribute missions and permitted tributary trade on what might be considered the frontier, they did not want more subjects who were both Moslems, under the influence of a Sufi *tariqat*, the Yassawiyya which, like the radical wing of the Naqshbandiyya, practised *dhikr-i jahri*, and nomads. Between 1822 and 1848, however, the Russians turned a nominal suzerainty over the Kazakh hordes (shared, did they but know it, with the Ch'ing) into a real one by forcing the Khans to come and live in Russian border fortresses and by establishing strategic garrisons and settlements of Cossacks to maintain a Russian presence. At the same time, Russian trade, sometimes disguising itself in the form of the Kazakh–Ch'ing tributary relationship, began to spill over from the Siberia–Kiakhta system to Semipalatinsk on the Irtish and thence to Chuguchak and Ili. Russian diplomacy pressed the Ch'ing government to legalize this trade and in 1851, having already given ground to the British in the treaty of Nanking, and with the Taiping rebellion already under way, it agreed. The treaty of Kuldja, signed between I-shan the tartar-general of Ili and the Russian plenipotentiary Kovalevsky, opened Chuguchak and Ili to Russian trade, on terms less restrictive than those of the Kiakhta system but less generous than those in operation on the coast. The trade only amounted to a trickle, and except for a certain amount of espionage in Sinkiang by agents like Valikhanov, Russia temporarily lost interest in this frontier. In 1871 von Kaufmann, the conqueror of the Central Asian khanates, took advantage of Yakub beg's rebellion to occupy Ili, and for nearly ten years this richest region of Sinkiang was under Russian rule. Forced to disgorge, at least in part, by Tso Tsungt'ang's reconquest and the subsequent diplomatic confrontation, Russia was left with a heightened awareness of the military significance of the Zungharian gate. Tso's ability to threaten central Siberia was not forgotten and part of the indemnity which Russia received in the treaty of St Petersburg in 1881 was put into the Trans-Siberian railway.

Between 1912 and 1949 Russia again had an opportunity of furthering her interests in Zungharia which were heightened by the geological discovery of rich deposits of oil, tin and wolfram in the north of the Ili basin and by the political discovery that the gate was a means of access to China as well as to Russia, whether this means was used to manipulate the Chinese communists in their hour of weakness after the long marches, to counteract Japanese pan-Islamic intrigue, or to reinforce Chiang Kai-shek after the Marco Polo bridge incident. In 1924 a Soviet consulate-general was opened at Urumchi which, particularly during the tenure of G.A. Apresov, 1933–37, became the headquarters for activities in these directions. If their most lasting result was the initiation of the Chinese petroleum industry at Wu-su in Zungharia, their most immediately significant was the military supply line to China in the early days of the second Sino–Japanese war. It should not be forgotten that for a moment in the late 1930s it looked as if Chinese communism might develop under more direct Soviet auspices on a Moslem basis. The radical Moslem leader Ma Chung-ying was brought to Moscow and Mao's brother, Mao Tse-min, became minister of finance in Sheng Shih-ts'ai's government in Urumchi. Apresov, Ma and the younger Mao were all later purged, but the possibilities they represented did not disappear entirely from the minds of the Soviet and Chinese parties, at any rate as long as Chairman Mao lived. Once opened the Zungharian gate was not easily closed, in either direction.

The far southern sea route

The mid-nineteenth century was the last great age of sail. One might have expected an increased, if temporary, use of the roaring forties route to China before its inevitable eclipse with the rise of steam. In fact this did not happen. First, Australia and New Zealand, although developing in other ways, were ceasing to provide either seal fur or *kauri* wood and soon forgot that their existence had anything to do with the China coast. Second, the tea clippers, which dominated the China run before the opening of the Suez canal, were built for speed rather than seaworthiness. Relatively small (700 tons), narrow in the beam, and carrying an excessive spread of canvas, they were liable to submerge their sterns in a high sea with strong tail winds. The *Ariel*, one of the fastest of the clippers with a beam of only 33 ft 9 ins, was lost like this in the roaring forties en route for Sydney in 1872. Other clippers were less extreme in design and more seaworthy, but the route declined in popularity and except for the whaling fleets and the occasional scientific expedition bound for Antarctica, the great southern ocean became as empty as in the days before Captain Cook.

Australasia itself, however, and China, were not without mutual influence in the modern age. Chinese emigrants went to the gold fields of Victoria, Otago and Westland and the White Australia policy was formulated in reaction to this inflow. In 1888 when the Privy Council upheld the legality of Victoria's legislation in this respect, we find Hart writing to Campbell: 'Tibet and Australia will be heard more about. In the first the Peking Govt. *is interested*: as to the second, it is to the interest of somebody else to make it a burning question and then win credit for extinguishing the flames.'[28] Australia took the yellow peril more seriously than anyone else: school cadet corps in the early 1900s expected to have to fight Japan and, when they sailed in 1914 to fight Germany, were amazed to find themselves convoyed by Japanese warships. In return for the unwelcomed immigrants to the goldfields, the southern continent sent a number of notable figures to the China coast. Australia sent George Ernest Morrison, *Times* correspondent in Peking from 1897 to 1912, and William Henry Donald another journalist who became press agent to Chiang Kai-shek. New Zealand sent George William Shepherd, the Plymouth Brother turned American Congregationalist, who became adviser on rural reconstruction to the Kuomintang's New Life Movement, and Rewi Alley, the founder of Indusco *(kung-ho)*, the guerrilla light industrial movement during the Pacific War which was one of the sources for Mao's Great Leap Forward. Canton sent rhododendrons from Szechwan direct to the gardens of Christchurch; Canterbury sent sheep to improve the blood stock of Kansu; Australia made available its eucalyptus for Chinese drought control and, in the first years of the twentieth century, sent coal to support early Chinese industrialization. In the prosperous years following the Pacific War, Australia took China's place in supplying Japan with iron ore, salt and rare minerals. Gough Whitlam made part of his reputation by his pro-Chinese foreign policy. The Sino–Australasian relationship in the modern age was tangential to both partners but it existed.

The Cape route

The return of the southern sea route to pre-eminence at the end of the nineteenth century has obscured the continued importance of the Cape route in the period of thirty-six years of intensified Sino–foreign contact which followed the abolition of the English East India Company's monopoly in 1833 and preceded the opening of the Suez canal in 1869. In these years, the treaty system was created, the imperial maritime customs with its ancillaries was established, the foundations of a new wave of Christian missionary endeavour were laid, two Sino–foreign wars were fought, all on the basis of the Cape route and, predominantly, sail rather than steam. The last age of the Cape saw a decisive mutation in the relations between China and the outside world. In 1833 the tonnage of foreign ships entering and leaving Chinese ports was 200 000; by 1864 it was 7 million. In 1833 only one Chinese port, Canton, was open to European trade by sea. By 1864, fifteen more had been added: Shanghai, Ningpo, Foochow and Amoy by the treaty of Nanking in 1842; Newchwang, Chefoo, Chinkiang, Swatow, Kiungchow, Nanking, Tientsin, Hankow, Kiukiang, Tamsui and Taichung by the treaty of Tientsin in 1858. In 1833, 300 000 piculs of tea were exported annually from China to Europe; by 1864, 1 200 000 piculs. In 1833 the Ch'ing empire was a fully sovereign state with unimpaired territorial integrity. By 1864, it had had to accept a number of limitations to its sovereignty both on the coast and in the interior, it found it prudent to employ foreigners in its own administration, and it had ceded Hong Kong to England and substantial territories in north-east Manchuria to Russia, as well as permitting the growth of what was virtually a free city in the international settlement at Shanghai. In 1833 Christianity in China was an illegal persecuted sect, and foreign missionary activity was tolerated, if at all, only in the European factories at Canton. By 1864 it had been granted toleration by an imperial edict, and foreign missionaries were permitted, under the Sino–French convention of Peking of 1860, to acquire land anywhere in the empire for the purpose of establishing mission stations.

These were remarkable changes to have been effected on so slender, so traditional, a basis: a warning against ascribing the ascendency of Europe over China too exclusively to industrialization. Further, the Suez canal did not rapidly oust the Cape. As late as the 1880s, less than half of India's foreign trade passed through the canal, and, thanks to the tea clippers which continued to frequent the Cape, the same was probably true of China. Iron sailing ships continued to dominate the wool trade to Australia until the 1890s. Eventually, however, as steamers multiplied, as freight rates were adjusted, as speed increased in importance, the Cape lost its primacy. As a result, Britain lost interest in South Africa for a generation. The Boer republics were allowed to drift away, Germany to install itself in Namibia, France in Madagascar and Britain shifted the centre of her interest on the dark continent to East Africa, now of new strategic significance on the flank of the line from Suez to Shanghai. Yet, despite the modernity of its transport, the new route proved less dynamic than the old in terms of its impact upon China. The extensions made to the treaty system by the Chefoo convention of 1876 – the immediate opening of Ichang, Wuhu, Wenchow and Pakhoi; the subsequent opening of Lungchow, Mengtsz and Chungking – were decorative rather than substantial. China's territorial losses between 1869 and 1895 were confined to her tributaries – Liu-ch'iu in 1874, Vietnam in 1885, Burma in 1886, Sikkim (a tributary of a tributary) in 1890 – or her extremities – parts of north-west Sinkiang in 1881, Macao in 1887. Trade expanded, the European presence thickened, but the real changes came overland or across another ocean.

The Pacific route

Although the Acapulco galleon had been relatively predominant in 1600 and the sea otter relatively important in 1800, in absolute terms the volume of traffic on the Pacific route to China was small until the modern age. Acapulco and Vancouver were only portholes in the otherwise blind seawall of the American continent. In the mid-nineteenth century, a set of four changes, not unrelated but without logical sequence, gradually brought the Pacific to life, so that when Chairman Mao died, four years after President Nixon's visit in 1972, it had become again the most significant avenue of contact between China and the outside world.

First, there was the appearance of the United States of America in force on the Pacific during Polk's presidency, as a result of the partition of Oregon in 1846 and the annexation of what were to become California, Nevada, Utah, Arizona and New Mexico at the end of the war with Mexico in 1848. Chaunu has described Polk as the greatest president of the USA – certainly he was the one who acquired most territory – but his importance has been obscured by American reluctance to see their destiny as other than manifest and by European identification of the United States with Yankeedom. In fact, the USA did not grow, it had to be built; and the construction was done initially by the south rather than the north, though the edifice later confronted the builder with the bleak alternatives of political subordination or contested secession. Contrary to myth, both American and European, the construction largely preceded the railway and was effected through the same pre-modern forces of spatial expansion which had built the transcontinental empire of Spain in the sixteenth century.

Second, there was the opening of Japan by the expeditions of Commodore Perry in 1853 and 1854 and the treaties with the USA, Britain and Russia which followed them. Perry sailed to Edo via the Cape. Neither the Massachusetts whalers which frequented the north Pacific, nor the fur clippers crossing it to and from Oregon, castaways from both of which underlined the need for diplomatic contact with Japan, hailed from the west coast. Nevertheless Perry was a product of the age of Polk, whose satiated expansionism was transposed into an oceanic mode before being introjected into the struggle for slavery and secession. Without the new acquisitions on the Pacific, Perry might never have sailed. No doubt the seclusion of Japan would have been broken eventually without Perry, probably by Russia or Britain, already Pacific powers. But the timing and manner of Japan's opening, at once peremptory but non-imperialist, were crucial to her later development.

Third, there was the Alaska purchase by the victorious Yankees in 1867, which by confirming the Pacific role of the United States and removing the American presence of Russia, promoted the use of the ocean. Russia's casual decision to abandon her American ambitions was motivated primarily by her desire to escape from her post-Crimean War diplomatic isolation by cultivating good relations with the USA, but it was not unrelated to her recent acquisition of north-east Manchuria and to Muraviev's vision of the Pacific as the Mediterranean of the future, a means of modernizing Russia through friendly contact with the Americans. Conversely, Secretary of State Seward thought that the USA would eventually embrace Canada and Mexico as well as Alaska and become the founder of a commercial empire of the Pacific which should dominate Asia, 'the chief theater of events in the world's great hereafter'.[29] Two technocratic Utopias thus met in Alaska.

Fourth, there was the Meiji restoration in 1868 and the policies which ensured that the newly-opened Japan should not become a second Korea or a greater Siam, but a leaven of modernization, crucial for all East Asia, indeed for the whole modern world. The establishment of a modernized Japan within China's own traditional sphere of culture was the most important non-Chinese factor in modern Chinese history. The Meiji miracle was not the inevitable outcome of Perry's missions. A lesser degree of modernization might have been undertaken more successfully by the Bakufu, or the sterile xenophobia with which the Bakumatsu started might have become chronic. Time and context were crucial. By the 1870s the Meiji leadership had had time to outgrow their xenophobia yet were still sufficiently young to pursue radicalism of another kind. By the 1870s Victorian civilization was at its most impressive: the alternatives, whether Bohemian or proletarian, had hardly raised their heads; and even China, ahead of Japan, had begun cautiously to modernize. In particular for Meiji Japan, the Pacific was never a dead ocean. In 1860 the Bakufu had dispatched an embassy to the USA in the entirely Japanese-manned *Kanrin-maru*. A Japanese line, the Toyo Kisen Kaisha, founded by the Zaibatsu promoter Asano Soichiro, quickly became the principal company operating the run from San Francisco to Yokohama via Honolulu, while Mitsubishi's Nippon Yusen Kaisha and the

Osaka Shusen Kaisha ran from Tacoma and Seattle to Yokohama and Kobe. Japan's modernization is only intelligible in its Pacific situation.

Unlike the Pacific of the Iberians which appeared almost overnight following the voyages of Legazpi and Urdaneta, the Pacific of the Americans took time to develop. The USA at first left the China coast to British management. Between 1864, the height of the clipper age, and 1905, the tonnage of American shipping entering and clearing Chinese ports actually fell by 50 per cent from 2 600 000 tons to 1 300 000, though the total volume of foreign shipping increased tenfold. Nevertheless, among the various groups of foreigners on the China coast, the American component grew steadily. American influence, boosted by the acquisition of the Philippines in 1898, first showed itself in the missionary interest, especially the Protestant missionary interest. In 1900, of the 3500 Protestant missionaries in China, 1000 were Americans. By the 1930s the 3000 Americans constituted about half the Protestant establishment, which was increasingly shaped by American social concern. Harvard's Yenching was the most prestigious of the foreign-sponsored universities in China; Tsinghua, financed by the remitted American share of the Boxer indemnity was, after Peita, the best of the Chinese universities. Peking Union Medical College backed by the Rockefeller Foundation was the best-equipped medical centre in the capital, while Hsiang-ya, Yale in China, at Changsha, was the most noted medical missionary establishment in the provinces. American business became increasingly active in the 1920s and 1930s, notably Standard Oil, Singer Sewing Machines and the British and American Tobacco Company. The two last heads of the foreign salt gabelle, Frederick A. Cleveland and Oliver C. Lockhart, were Americans. The leading figure in China's hydraulic and road construction activities between the wars was the American engineer Oliver J. Todd, and American journalists like Carl Crow were prominent at Shanghai, while Edgar Snow scooped Mao's autobiography at Pao-an.

As the threat to China from Japan developed in the 1930s, American diplomatic influence at Nanking grew. During the Pacific War, the American ambassador, senior military staff and economic advisers became the most powerful foreigners in China, men like Patrick J. Hurley, Joseph W. Stilwell and

Arthur N. Young being veritable proconsuls, though perhaps both they and their Chinese critics over-estimated their power. In 1949 Chairman Mao excluded American influence from China supposedly for ever, but the Korean and Vietnamese wars underlined, albeit in a confrontational way, the significance of the Pacific as a link between China and the outside world, and by the time of his death Mao had had to call the New World back into existence in East Asia to redress a balance in the Old, which he himself in the Sino–Soviet dispute, had disturbed.

The far northern land route

Like the Pacific route, the far northern land route was transformed by the continental expansion of a new great power and the introduction of modern communications: the Trans-Siberian railway commenced in 1891, its satellites the Chinese Eastern and South Manchuria railways of 1896 and 1898, and the Trans-Mongolian railway from Kiakhta to Kueihua completed by the Chinese communists in 1956. There were, however, profound differences in the nature of the continental expansions. In the fulfilment of American manifest destiny, society led and the state followed. Polk was only the agent not the author of expansion. In Russia the state led and society followed. Men like Baranov, Muraviev, Baryatinsky, von Kaufmann, Ignatiev, Witte were genuine authors of expansion not mere executants. Further, whereas American expansion followed a single direction from east to west, as simple transition from the Atlantic to the Pacific, not seriously deflected by the temptations of Canada and the Caribbean, Russian expansion from its central point of origin in Muscovy had a choice of direction: the Arctic, the Balkans, the Baltic, the Caucasus, Central Asia and the Far East. Again, whereas the American society which led was characterized by a modern demography – late marriage, conjugal orientation, falling birth rate, rising per capita income and a fundamentally urban drive to affluence – the Russian society which followed was characterized by a traditional demography – early marriage, filial orientation, high birth rate, stable per capita income and a fundamentally rural acquiescence in sufficiency. Multiple choice plus lack of societal support meant that Russian expansion oscillated both in direction and intensity.

The far northern land route illustrates this pattern. Between the treaty of Kiakhta in 1727 and Muraviev's appointment as governor-general of eastern Siberia in 1847, Russia made no territorial advance in East Asia beyond probings in Sakhalin and Hokkaido. When Muraviev was appointed, Russia had just suffered setbacks in her endeavours to exploit the rivalry of the Sultan and the Khedive. Furthermore Russian America after a hopeful start under Baranov had ground to a halt for lack of settlers, sea otter and ships. Muraviev thereafter, in his plans for a return to Albazin, a revision of the Nerchinsk–Kiakhta settlement and a re-penetration of the Amur, received a degree of support from the Tsar, if not from the foreign ministry. The Taiping northern expedition of 1854, which according to Russian observers in Peking came close to success, and the Anglo–French attack on Petrapavlovsk in 1855 during the Crimean war, underlined the need for a stronger Russian presence in the area.

In 1856 European peace and Sino–foreign war gave Russian diplomacy the opportunity for which Muraviev's colonization and Nevelskoy's exploration had prepared. Muraviev at Aigun and Putiatin at Tientsin having signed advantageous but contradictory treaties with China in 1860, Ignatiev, specially dispatched from St Petersburg, resolved the situation by the even more advantageous convention of Peking of 1860 which gave the Tsar the large slice of north-east Manchuria on which Vladivostok could be founded. Once born, however, the new Amuria, unlike the new California, failed to grow, despite the presence of gold. For twenty-five years after the foundation of Vladivostok, eastern Siberia stagnated, hardly able to feed itself better with the Amur than without it. Where San Francisco became a metropolis, Vladivostok remained a naval base. Even in Muraviev's time, the Far East had to compete with Baryatinsky's Transcausasia for St Petersburg's support and between 1865 and 1885 the focus of Russian expansionism fluctuated between Central Asia and the Balkans. Colonization faltered. Sir Alexander Hosie, British consul at Newchwang, who returned home in 1900 by the far northern land route while the Trans-Siberian was under construction, was told by a 'Russian gentleman' on the Amur boat that 'he would sooner throw his money into the Shilka than invest a rouble in Siberia'.[30]

It was not until Russia had been checked in the Balkans by

the Congress of Berlin, in Central Asia by the Pendjeh inci-, dent, and her weakness in the Far East revealed by both Tso Tsung-t'ang and the temporary British occupation of Port Hamilton in Korea, that it was decided in 1886 to revitalize eastern Siberia by the construction of a transcontinental rail- way. Work was commenced at both ends in 1891. When Witte became minister of finance in 1893, the project assumed the character of a five-year plan. The trans-Siberian was not only to resume Muraviev's advance to the Pacific, but also to trans- form Russia by its stimulus to heavy industry and the engineer- ing profession, and to unite Russia and China in a Eurasian co-prosperity sphere. In 1896 the Tsar's government used the political credit of its part in the triple intervention against Japan in 1895 to obtain from China a concession to build the Chinese Eastern railway to shorten the route to Vladivostok. In 1898 China leased Port Arthur and Dairen to Russia for twenty-five years and the Chinese Eastern railway was given the right to build the branch line from Harbin to Dairen which became known as the South Manchuria railway. In 1900 the Boxer Rebellion brought the whole of Manchuria under Russian military occupation and, from then until the Russo– Japanese war, the area was almost a Russian province.

Yet the results were disappointing. Russia sowed but Japan harvested. The line was too primitive, Tsarist administration was too clumsy, the support given it by Russian society was too inadequate. A guide book published in 1914 for American tourists gave a gloomy picture of Trans-Siberia:

> Barring magnificent Moscow, which is in every way worthy of the traveler's attention, none of the wayside cities posses- ses vitality, sprightliness, or color, and their cheerless aspect depresses rather than attracts one. The inhospitable towns, with their log cabins and mud streets, are pictures of desol- ation, and are almost as saddening as the blowsy bewhis- kered, sodden, slatternly people, who somehow remind one of emigrants from a land yet in the Stone Age.[31]

If the reconstructed Siberian corridor failed to fulfil the dreams of Muraviev and Witte, and even less the militaristic version of them produced by Admiral Alexeiev, it nevertheless had a considerable impact on China. It created in the Manchu- rian railway zones a new and potent form of foreign penetra- **tion.** It stimulated Chinese nationalism elsewhere, for example in the resistance to German railway expansionism in Shantung, and in the wider railway rights recovery movement. The railways of Manchuria brought Russians into China, particularly after 1917 as refugees, and they were soon the largest group of Europeans. They took Chinese into Russia to participate in the revolution and to return as carriers of Marxism. Along the Manchurian railways, too, travelled the more palpable infection of *Yersinia pestis* which provoked the formation of Wu Lien-teh's North Manchurian plague prevention service, the parent of the national quarantine service and of preventive medicine generally in China. Manchuria, where Chinese authority had to be strengthened to counter Russian and Japanese encroachment, became the pilot for China's constitutional experiments in the last years of the empire. Under the early republic, Manchurian railways were the basis for the satrapy of Chang Tso-lin, greatest of warlords and exponent of armoured trains.[32] Between 1928 and 1949 Manchuria was the prize for which the Kuomintang, the Soviets, the Japanese militarists and the Chinese communists fought, and it was Manchuria that gave the communists victory. After liberation, the need for Sino–Soviet cooperation in Manchurian heavy industry was an important consideration in the adoption by chairman Mao of the Soviet model of economic organization. When that model was dropped and Kao Kang and Jao Shu-shih selected as appropriate purgees, the accusation against them was of attempting to found an independent pro-Soviet Manchuria. Shanghai, the American-style metropolis of the Whangpoo might, thanks to the Yangtze, have reached its pre-eminence without the steamships of the southern sea and Pacific routes. Harbin, the Russian-style metropolis of the Sungari, certainly would not have reached its pre-eminence without the Trans-Siberian, Chinese Eastern and South Manchuria railways. Harbin, like Vladivostok, was a major diffusion point for Bolshevism in China. In political terms, the far northern land route was the most important link between China and the outside world in the modern age.

Air routes

When Mackinder gave his famous lecture to the Geographical Society in 1904, the Wright brothers had only just flown, and

air freight, intercontinental ballistic missiles and earth satellites – which were to undermine his theory of the heartland,
re-emphasise the depths of the ocean as the ultimate launch-
ing pad, and make the very notion of an avenue of contact
between one part of the world and another obsolete – were
still in the realm of science fiction. Airpower, however,
developed rapidly during the First World War – a bomb was
dropped on the Forbidden City during Chang Hsün's restoration of the monarchy in July 1917 – and it established itself
in civilian form during the Nanking decade of the Kuomintang. By 1937 four civilian airlines were in service on Chinese
soil, three of them providing links with the outside world.
The largest, the Sino–American China National Aviation Corporation operated conjointly by the ministry of communications and Pan American Airways, ran services from Shanghai
internally to Peking, Canton and Chengtu and externally to
Hong Kong and Hanoi. The Sino–German Eurasia Aviation
Company flew to Manchuria and the Chinese north-west, and
would have liked to provide a service to Berlin across Russia.
The Sino–Japanese Huitung Air Navigation Company, an
agency of the Peking-based Japanese satellite of Hua-pei-kuo,
ran lines between Tientsin, Peking, Manchuria and Japan.
The purely Chinese Southwest Aviation Company, run by the
provincial governments of Kwangtung and Kwangsi, made
local flights in those areas and connected with Air France at
Hanoi. What all the airlines provided was essentially a passen-
ger service.[33]

During the war an air connection of a new kind was
developed. This was the famous Hump freight service from
Calcutta or points in Assam over the eastern Himalayas to
Kunming and back. The Hump flights were the world's first
airlift, the prototype for that of Berlin, and between March
1942 and August 1945, they moved 650 000 tons of material
to China and brought back much lesser quantities to the
Allies. The Hump route was pioneered by the Chinese
National Aviation Corporation pilots only two weeks before
Pearl Harbor. It was their skill in dealing with the problems
of weather, altitude, navigation and enemy interception which
made its use possible. Though they continued flying it
throughout the war, the leading role was taken over by the
American Army Airforce's air transport command under

Brigadier General Caleb V. Haynes.[34] During the peak Hump month of July 1945, air transport command carried 73 691 tons compared to the Chinese National Aviation Corporation's 2649. The Hump was essential to China's war effort. Between the closing of the Burma road in April 1942 and the opening of the Stilwell road in January 1945, it saved the Kuomintang from complete beleaguerment and probable collapse.

Chiang Kai-shek was over-impressed. His confidence in airlifts, reinforced by the ability of air transport command to move his troops over the heads of the communists to reoccupy the Japanese-held cities of the eastern seaboard, was a factor in the adoption of the Manchurian strategy of the last round of the civil war which so fatally over-extended his forces. Mao Tse-tung, on the other hand, was under-impressed. Consequently airpower whether military or civil, played little part in his five-year plans or in his strategic thinking. It was not until 1957 that the first Soviet sputnik gave him, too, temporarily the rather exaggerated estimate of airpower implied in his 'East wind prevails over the West wind' speech in Moscow which so alarmed his Soviet hosts. Though Mao professed the invulnerability of China's huge population to nuclear attack, even in the period of his greatest emphasis on morale rather than technology as the decisive factor in warfare, he pressed ahead with China's own nuclear project which was successfully achieved in October 1964. Airpower, exercised or non-exercised, effective and non-effective, was therefore a significant factor in the history of modern China and its relations with the outside world.

INTERCHANGES, 1833 TO 1976

The pattern of exchange between China and the outside world in the modern age was shaped by three factors. First, there was the growing superiority of the West: detectable already in the middle ages by institutional analysis, precociously conspicuous in the Renaissance by the conquest of America, demonstrable in the Enlightenment in terms of money, material and mentality. In the modern age it became manifest and self-evident thanks to almost permanent industrial, medical and scientific revolutions. Second, there was the protean but consistent ambivalence of China's attitude towards this superiority which willed the end of joining it but not the means, wanted progress but refused association, hoped for equality but demanded independence. Chairman Mao, the ascetic materialist, who preached technological paradise but practised anti-technological purgatory, perfectly embodied this ambivalence which can be found in other forms in the successive regimes of the late imperial viceroys, Yüan Shih-k'ai the Kuomintang, the warlords and the various Japanese satellites. Third, there was the totalitarian revolt against the West from within the West which, spread to the non-West, allowed China to fulfil its secret wish of accepting but rejecting, breaking with tradition but refusing to modernize, noisy discontinuity but silent perseverance. Consequently, although the volume of interchange between China and the outside world increased in the modern age, particularly in the direction non-China to China, it increased less than it would have done with less ambivalence by China and more unity in the outside world. At the death of Chairman Mao, China remained between two worlds: its own, protected by a new great wall, and the other one.

People

With the development of modern communications by land, sea and air, the number of foreigners coming to China and the number of Chinese going to foreign countries increased dramatically. While the prevailing pattern remained that of quality to China, quantity from China, it was modified by diversification in both directions. Many of the White Russians who formed the majority of the European community in China at the mid-century were of humble origin, and more had to take humble, not to say humiliating, places in Chinese society. Conversely China supplied the world not only with coolies, miners, laundrymen, fruiterers and restaurateurs, but also with students, businessmen, doctors and university professors. Diversification produced osmosis between the two kinds of migration, inward and outward.

First, diversification of inward migration to China. In the Enlightenment, the foreign community in China had consisted of two groups: missionaries in Peking, Catholic and Orthodox, and merchants in Canton and Kiakhta, Western European and Russian – though missionaries underground in the provinces like Jean-Martin Moÿe in Szechwan, itinerant Bokharan dervishes in Kansu, Andijan merchants in Sinkiang need to be borne in mind. By the early twentieth century, to these two groups, themselves becoming more varied – in the case of the missionaries notably by the addition of the Protestants – had been added diplomats, synarchs, professional people, and riff-raff.

The diplomats were the product, first, of successive extensions of the treaty system between 1842 and 1922 and, then, of Soviet expansionism and Japanese satellitism, offshoots of the totalitarian revolt. They included not only the ministers at Peking, Nanking or Hsinking, but also the consuls in the treaty ports, the flag officers of China stations, the commanders of troops stationed in China under the Boxer protocol, the heads of Comintern missions, and League of Nations technical advisers.

Advisory missions shaded into synarchy: foreign participation in Chinese state institutions. The major synarchic institutions of the treaty system were the maritime customs, established by Horatio Lay but developed by Sir Robert Hart, the foreign salt gabelle founded by Sir Richard Dane, and the Chinese post office initiated by Hart but first headed as a separate body by Théophile Piry. These were the prototypes of modern administration in China. The gabelle was particularly significant because, unlike the customs and the post office which were hived off either geographically or functionally, it remained attached to the ministry of finance, so that its example had a wider impact, particularly in the early days of the Kuomintang when T.V. Soong was minister. The chief minor synarchic institutions were the rather unsuccessful British admiralty mission of William M. Lang from 1882 to 1890; the German military mission of Bauer, von Seeckt and Falkenhausen between 1928 and 1938; the British treasury mission of Sir Frederick Leith Ross in 1935 which played a major role in China's shift from silver currency to paper; and the three conservancies: the Whangpoo which under its Dutch chief engineer, de Rijke, removed the Woosung sandbar from outside Shanghai, the Hai-ho which struggled with the silt and the sandstorms of north China to keep Tientsin service-able, and the Chihli river commission whose chief engineer, F.C. Rose, provided the permanent answer to that silt. Beyond the synarchic institutions, individual synarchs contributed to particular Chinese bodies: Ward and Gordon to the Chinese army in the days of Li Hung-chang; Halliday Macartney to the Chinese legation in London where he was secretary and councillor for nearly thirty years; Teilhard de Chardin to the Chinese geological survey; Cyril Rogers and Fenimore B. Lynch to central banking; Claire L. Chennault to the Chinese air force; Arthur N. Young to the ministry of finance in the days of H.H. Kung and T.V. Soong. Synarchy not only brought western techniques to China but also revived neglected elements of China's own tradition.

Outside government service, foreigners practised their professions, often new to China. There were lawyers such as A.S.P. White-Cooper who appeared for a group of Chinese plaintiffs in a case heard in 1906 before the American consular court in Hangchow against a Southern Methodist mission. There were dentists such as Dr Winn at Shanghai who treated Hart in 1876. There were doctors like Peter Parker, the pioneer medical missionary who founded the Canton Ophthalmic Hospital in 1835; Douglas Gray the British legation physician who ran a free clinic in the Chinese city of Peking; Reinhard Hoeppli, professor of parasitology at Peking Union Medical College and Backhouse's last patron; and Norman Bethune who gave his talents and life to the Chinese communist armies. There were veterinarians such as Frank C. Hershberger from Missouri who helped the Manchurian plague prevention service in identifying anthrax in Heilungkiang. There were journalists like the rival *Times* correspondents George Ernest Morrison the radical modernizer and J.O.P. Bland the Burkian conservative. There were conservationists such as Walter C. Lowdermilk, professor of forestry at the University of Nanking 1922–27, expert on the vagaries of the Yellow River, again on location in China 1942–43. There were accountants such as Henry Carter Adams who standardized the accounts of the various Chinese railway companies between 1913 and 1917 or John R. Lyman who went from the Fouke Fur company, St Louis to the Chinese industrial cooperatives in the early 1940s. There were engineers such as Jean Jadot of the Peking to Hankow railway and Oliver J. Todd the hydraulic technocrat. There were architects such as H.K. Murphy who designed the Kuomintang city of Nanking and introduced Bauhaus functionalism to China. These people brought with them to China a vast range of new skills, values and social possibilities.

Among refugees and displaced persons, the most significant and numerous were the White Russians – about a quarter of a million in all. Something like 100 000 of them congregated in Harbin where they formed a third of the population in 1920 and established over the next thirty years, under a variety of political conditions, a coherent expatriate community complete with its own churches, schools, university and primitive municipal institutions. The rest passed on to Peking, Tientsin, Shanghai and beyond China altogether. In Peking the Tsarist legation continued to be recognized down to September 1920 and hence to enjoy the revenue of the Boxer indemnity, but thereafter its members were scattered: V.V. Hagelstrom, for example, to a poultry farm in New Zealand. The concessions at Tientsin and Hankow survived a little longer with foreign support but by 1924 they too were gone. More fortunate were the Russian employees of the customs and salt gabelle who kept their jobs, and the ecclesiastical mission at the *O-lo-ssu pei-kuan* functioned until 1949. In Shanghai some White Russians were reasonably prosperous as restaurateurs, policemen and nannies to Western families in the international settlement, but there rapidly developed an unhappy penumbra of gangsters, rickshaw pullers, wharfies and prostitutes, the first European lumpenproletariat in the Far East.

The Russians were not the only refugees. There were displaced persons from Austria–Hungary: for example, Dr Robert Pollitzer, a Vienna-trained pathologist who, having been successively captured by the Russians and Japanese and restrained from suicide by Wu Lien-teh, entered first the Manchurian plague prevention service then, after its takeover by Manchukuo, the national quarantine service, next, after the Japanese took Shanghai, the American Red Cross, ending as a senior epidemiologist with the World Health Organization. Then there were refugees from Central Asia: Kazakhs notably, fugitives from the anti-conscription rebellion of 1916 and from Bolshevism later. Between 1911 and 1949, despite – or because of – its political confusion China was a zone of relative liberty: German Jews for example found refuge in Shanghai. Finally, exploiting this liberty was the flotsam and jetsam: Sit Edmund Backhouse the confidence-man whose hidden life has been so brilliantly exposed by H.R. Trevor-Roper;[35] the American girls from San Francisco who, in the first decade of the twentieth century, captured the high-class prostitute trade of Shanghai; adventurers like Charles H.A.W. Mason, the customs official who got mixed up in a Chinese secret society conspiracy; or Homer Lea 'military adviser' to Sun Yat-sen; the drunken sailors and common criminals who formed the stock-in-trade of the consular courts; the signers of spurious chits, the drug smugglers and the perpetrators of frauds, who often escaped prosecution.[36]

Second, diversification of outward migration from China. In the Enlightenment, the pattern of Chinese emigration had been relatively simple. By land it went to Chinese Inner Asia: Tungans from Kansu to the capitals of Zungharia, Ili and Urumchi, as police officers, tea exporters and restaurateurs; Shansi business families to the emporia of Uighuristan and Qalqa Mongolia, Ku-ch'eng and Urga, as general traders. By sea it went to Chinese south-east Asia: Hoklos from Amoy to Manila, Taiwan, Hainan (and thence to Hanoi and Saigon-Cholon), Batavia and the ports of Malaya, Penang and Singapore; Hakkas from Swatow, the Boston Irish of south China, to Taiwan; and Teochius from Ch'ao-chou to Bangkok; all taking with them the low-profile capitalism with which the emigrants were familiar in China. In the modern age this kind of emigration continued as Hakkas went to the tin mines in the interior of Malaya and Cantonese went to the outer islands of Indonesia, but its spatial horizons notably expanded. If foreign immigration diversified functionally, Chinese emigration diversified geographically.

Six new areas became significant: Latin America, the United States of America, Australasia, Russia, South Africa and Western Europe. These absorbed, in all, perhaps a million emigrants, at least double the European immigration into China. It was, on the whole, a successful diaspora. The remittances from emigrants in both the old and new areas played a crucial role in China's balance of payments. As invisible earnings, they allowed China to maintain a high level of imports, despite their increasing cost in terms of Chinese silver, and to balance her books without a deflationary export of bullion. More adequately handled, these invisible earnings could have provided the capital for modernization in China.

The first new area to be opened to Chinese emigration was labour-hungry Latin America. With the decline of the African trade and the rise of abolitionism, the coolie replaced the slave. In the late 1840s British merchants at Amoy began sending indentured workers to the plantations of Cuba and the guano islands of Peru. The trade, though subject to much criticism inside China and out, continued till the late 1870s. Peru, which received about 100 000 Chinese immigrants, reached the highest percentage of Chinese in its population of any country outside East Asia. Next, the discovery of gold, first in California in 1849 and then in Victoria in 1851 and Otago in 1861, drew another 100 000 emigrants each to the United States of America and Australasia. California was *Chiu-chin-shan* the old gold mountain, Australia the *Hsin-chin-shan*, and miners moved from one to the other. Thus the Cantonese Charles Sew Hoy had been in both San Francisco and Victoria before settling in Dunedin, New Zealand in 1869 where he became the provisioner of the Chinese miners in Otago and a successful gold dredge operator himself.

In the late nineteenth century the Trans-Siberian railway was an even greater importer of Chinese than it was an exporter of Russians. About 300 000 Chinese emigrants took this route. Most remained in eastern Siberia. In Amur province, there were 102 000 Chinese in 1923, one tenth of the population. Others went on to the Urals, Moscow, Petrograd, Murmansk and the Donbas. In September 1918 the Chinese colony in Moscow organized a pan-Soviet trade union for coolies and published the *Chinese Worker* in a mixture of Chinese and pidgin Russian. Its leadership was the first Chinese communist organization, two years before the first cells in China and three years before the official inauguration of the party. Chinese labour battalions supported the Red Army: there were Chinese among the Red Guards in Petrograd and in the Soviet forces in Bessarabia; and a Chinese regiment fought under Chapaiev against Kolchak. By 1919 there were 10 000 Chinese in the Red Army and 20 000 in auxiliary units.

Some returned to China to become part of the infrastructure of Chinese communism. In 1904 the British government arranged to import 50 000 Chinese indentured workers into South Africa to restart the Rand after the Boer War. The cry of 'Chinese slavery' was an ingredient in the landslide Liberal victory in the general election of 1906. King Leopold of the Belgians was interested in coolies for the Congo railways and the Katanga mines, and Kasuvubu – the Congo's first ruler after independence–was reputed to be of part Chinese descent. Finally the First World War saw the migration of 140 000 Chinese workers to France. It was from them, as well as from Chinese students, that Chou En-lai formed a communist group in Paris in 1920. The sphere of Chinese emigration had expanded from China's environs to the world.

Not all Chinese migration was plebeian. A highly significant development in the modern age was the rise of the *liu-hsüeh-sheng*, 'students remaining abroad to study', often translated 'returned students', though in fact not all of them went back to China. Both the Jesuits and the missionaries sent by Propaganda had sent promising pupils to Europe to study for the priesthood: one thinks especially of the Chinese College of the Holy Family founded by the secular priest Matteo Ripa in his native Naples in 1732 which before its dissolution in 1888 produced a hundred Chinese priests. But the first overseas, or overland, student of the modern age was Yung Wing (Jung Hung) who, after attending missionary schools in Macao and HongKong and being sent in 1847 under missionary sponsorship to high school in Massachusetts, entered Yale in 1850 and graduated in 1854.

On his return to China, Yung, after some false starts, joined the entourage of Tseng Kuo-fan and became overseas buyer for the Kiangnan arsenal. In 1870 he persuaded Tseng, and his obvious successor Li Hung-chang, to sponsor a government scheme for sending a series of groups of boys to America to receive the education he had had. Between 1872 and 1881, when it was wound up because of conservative opposition, the educational mission, as it was called, sent four groups to New England, 120 individuals, among whom were a future prime minister (T'ang Shao-i), foreign minister (Liang Tun-yen), admiral and presidential secretary (Ts'ai T'ing-kan), leading diplomat (Jung K'uei) and railway chief engineer

(Chan T'ien-yu). In 1896 the Chinese government began sending students to Japan, the number was increased after the
Boxer Rebellion, and by 1906 there were said to be 13 000
Chinese students, state-sponsored and private, in Japan. The
abolition of the old examination system in that year,
foreshadowed since 1901, stimulated the demand for modern,
foreign-style education, In 1909 the USA made available its
share of the Boxer indemnity for the purposes of Chinese
education and by 1915 there were around 1200 Chinese students in American schools and colleges. A slightly smaller
number attended similar institutions in Britain, France and
Germany. These figures with fluctuations were roughly maintained until the communist seizure of power in China; for
example in 1942 there were 1500 Chinese students in the
USA, though by 1949 various aid schemes had pushed this
number up to 3900, while numbers in Japan had fallen.

As a body, the *liu-hsüeh-sheng* were one of the most important institutions of contact between China and the outside
world in the modern age. They constituted for China a kind
of western coast which was arguably of greater cultural significance in both directions than the China coast of the Westerners, because they were an elite in absolute terms while most
of the Western denizens of the China coast were so only
relative to the mass of the Chinese population. Some indication of what they took from the West to China may be obtained
from what they studied. Between 1905 and 1960, American
universities granted 2789 PhDs to Chinese students, the leaders being Illinois 204, Columbia 203, Harvard 165 and Michigan 150. Of these, physical sciences accounted for 696,
engineering sciences 590 and biological sciences 439, as
opposed to humanities 327 and social sciences 548.[37] This
suggests that what the Chinese were most interested in was
not the values or institutions of the West but its technology,
a continuation of Chang Chih-tung's formula 'Chinese learning for the substance, Western learning for practical use' –
Chung-hsüeh wei t'i, Hsi-hsüeh wei yung, Chinese values, Western
techniques – which had been the official line of flexible Confucianism in the nineteenth century, and possibly a misunderstanding of where the real strength of the West lay.

Not all Chinese returned home. China also contributed to
the higher levels of non-Chinese society. Among literary

figures, there were S.I. Hsiung, author of *Lady Precious Stream* and lecturer in Chinese at both Oxford and Cambridge; Lin Yu-tang interpreter of China to the outside world; and K'ai-ming Ch'u prince of librarians. Among scientists there were the Nobel prize winners of 1957, the physicists Chen-ning Yang of Princeton and Tsung-dao Lee of Columbia. Among historians there were Lien-sheng Yang of unrivalled scholarship; Achilles Fang at home in the classics of the West as much as in those of China; Ho Ping-ti the demographer: Yeh-chien Wang the fiscal expert; Silas Wu the authority on decision making. Among churchmen, there were Dom Pierre Celestin Lu Cheng-hsiang, former foreign minister, monk of the abbey of Saint-André-les-Bruges in Belgium; and the paradoxical Cardinal Sin, archbishop of Manila. The importance of Chinese wives should not be overlooked, partners in who knows how many American PhDs. In England, Professor Michael Lindsay, son of Lord Lindsay, Master of Balliol, married a Chinese, so at least one member of the House of Lords was half-Chinese. In Africa, the Chinese communist engineers of the Tanzania railway will hardly have seemed proletarian figures to the local inhabitants. All over the world there were political exiles from China's numerous changes of government. A grandson of Prince Ch'un, the last regent, was born in London in 1933; Yüan Shih-k'ai's grandchildren settled in the USA; Ma Pu-fang, warlord of Chinghai, ended up in Arabia. China diffused her elite as well as her mass.

Flora and fauna

The exchange of flora and fauna in the modern age was less significant than the exchange of people. Temporarily at any rate, osmosis of this kind reached an equilibrium, or perhaps social and industrial opportunities led to a neglect of its possibilities. Human planetization was passing from the biosphere to the noosphere, from the socialization of expansion to the socialization of compression. Of the six major floral and faunal exchanges of the modern age, one was residual, two were cosmetic, two were of marginal importance, and only the sixth had real significance because it affected the Chinese economy.

The residual exchange was the belated acquisition by China

of scarlet fever, a last step in the formation of the microbian common market. Scarlet fever, a bacterial disease of temperate climates described by Galen, was probably of European origin. It only appeared in North America in 1735 and was unknown in pre-modern East Asia. It was first reported in China in 1873 and in Japan in 1893, its route probably being across Siberia. An unstable disease fluctuating in virulence, by the early twentieth century it was relatively benign in Europe, but in China because of novelty and lack of resistance, it retained its Victorian power, reaching epidemic proportions and mortality rates of up to 25 per cent, whereas in Europe mortality rates had fallen to between 1 per cent and 3 per cent. After its introduction, scarlet fever was compartmentalized. As Wu Lien-teh summarized, it was 'practically absent in South China, fairly severe in Shanghai and the Central Provinces, and very severe in the north'.[38] The arrival of this unwelcome import, probably from Russia, was at least a local factor in the stabilization of Chinese population between 1850 and 1950.

The two cosmetic exchanges were both prolongations of the Chinese garden introduced to Europe by Attiret, Chambers and Banks. In fauna, the introduction of Chinese ornamental pheasants (Reeve's pheasant, Lady Amherst's pheasant, golden pheasant, silver pheasant) and the crossing in England of the Roman-introduced Colchian pheasant with the Chinese ring-necked version, were of little significance except to connoisseurs. In flora, the systematic cataloguing and ransacking of the floral wealth of China had both more scientific value and deeper aesthetic effects. In the days of Robert Fortune, Europe had tapped this wealth only through the gardens of the Chinese seaboard, but now a series of botanists made direct contact with it in the hinterland. Père David (1826–1900) was responsible for the introduction of cotoneaster, clematis and a number of rhododendrons. Augustine Henry (a customs officer stationed at Ichang 1881–96), was a systematic cataloguer and the discoverer of the *augustinii* species of rhododendron introduced to England in 1899. E.H. Wilson (1876–1930), the greatest of them, introduced no less than sixty species of rhododendron to the West, among them the well-known *discolor* and *sutchuenense* varieties, as well as a number of roses. These introductions made possible hybrids which transformed two of the most basic ingredients of the modern Western garden, the rose and the rhododendron. Szechwan was now in the suburbs, and gardening, the most widespread aesthetic activity perhaps apart from choice of clothes, was deeply affected.

The two exchanges of marginal importance were the belated introduction to China during the nineteenth century of tomatoes and chili from America. Adopted particularly in Szechwan and Hunan where they represented a modest affluence comparable to that represented by quality Tzu-liu-ching salt in the same areas, tomatoes and chili were more than flavourings. They also contributed vitamins and it has been argued that they have 'contributed largely to the rise of China's population and wealth over the last 100 years'[39]. More certainly, tomatoes and chili counteracted the tendency to monotony in Chinese diet and, as acting through the restaurants of places like Chungking and Hsiang-t'an, may be seen as part of the urban offensive in modern China.

The exchange of most significance was China's loss of the monopoly of tea with the establishment of plantations in Assam, Georgia in the Caucasus, Ceylon, South Carolina and East Africa. In 1848 Robert Fortune 'was deputed by the Court of Directors of the East India Company to re-visit China for the purpose of obtaining some tea manufacturers' implements, and a large collection of tea-plants and seeds, from those northern or central districts of the empire where the finest descriptions of tea are made for the European and American markets', with a view to establishing the industry in India.[40] In 1851, Fortune brought 12 838 Chinese plants, 'a large assortment of implements' and a group of manufacturers from Shanghai to the Indian government's botanical garden in the Himalayan foothills near Saharanpur in Uttar Pradesh.[41] It was not here, however, that the Indian tea industry developed, but in Assam and on the basis of an indigenous plant independently discovered by Major Robert Bruce in 1823. Plants were only part of the technology though and Fortune's work was essential both in Assam and in Ceylon where tea was introduced following a failure of the coffee crop in the 1870s. Tea from Assam first came on to the English market in the late 1850s, but in 1867 India only exported 40 000 piculs to China's one and a quarter million. Ceylon tea first arrived in England in 1883 and between 1886 and 1905 South Asia defeated East Asia. In 1905 China supplied England with 49 142 piculs, India with 1 128 978 and Ceylon with 670 394.

More than a substitution was involved. Indian tea was cruder than China, and while it might be popular with plebeian consumers of high tea, it prepared the way for the conquests of coffee among the patrician consumers of afternoon tea. The taste for China tea, once lost, was never recovered except among the *cognoscenti*. In Russia, tea cultivation was introduced as early as 1847, but Georgian production could not develop until Baryatinsky's pacification of Caucasia in the late 1850s; and Georgian tea was not a real rival to China until the twentieth century when its production of 620 000 piculs approximated to the best years for brick tea. In the United States of America there was experiment with tea cultivation in South Carolina between 1890 and 1915 under the direction of Dr Charles V. Shephard, but though the experiments were successful technically, they proved uneconomic and were abandoned. In British East Africa, tea cultivation was introduced in 1890 as part of colonial development and by the middle of the twentieth century the export equalled that of Taiwan. By that time, mainland China had really ceased to be a factor in the international tea trade. 'All the tea in China' was no longer a metonym for boundless wealth.

Commodities

In the Enlightenment, commodity exchange between China and the outside world had followed a pattern of expansion, absolute diversification and relative specialization. In the modern age it followed a pattern of initial expansion/subsequent stagnation, absolute diversification and relative despecialization. In other words, taking the elements in reverse order, there was discontinuity, continuity and a mixture of the two.

Despecialization and discontinuity

In 1833 the staples of the China trade at Canton, and to a lesser extent at Kiakhta and Kashgar too, were tea and opium, which were also major components of world trade. By 1976 both commodities had lost their place as staples. Tea might still figure as a luxury item in the legal trade; opium might still be smuggled, though out of China rather than into it; but neither had their earlier primacy in the China trade nor their importance in the world trading system.

Tea exports from China increased from 500 000 piculs in the 1830s to over 2 million in the peak year of 1886, and thereafter fell away, though brick tea held up better than leaf. The decline of China tea was not simply due to the acclimatization of tea elsewhere and the crude taste of the average consumer in England. Indian production was mechanized where Chinese was not; Chinese export was taxed where Indian was not; and in India cultivation was scientific and organization rationalized, while in China both remained traditional. South Asia, anyway closer to the market, therefore won a battle of comparative costs over East Asia. Like tea, opium imports increased from 30 000 piculs a year in the 1830s to 100 000 in the peak year of 1879, and thereafter fell to 50 000 piculs in 1905 and virtually nothing in 1914.

Two factors lay behind this decline of foreign opium. First, there was the rise of Chinese opium production from a few thousand piculs in Yunnan in the 1830s to 375 000 piculs in the peak year of 1905 when Yunnan produced 30 000 piculs, Kweichow 15 000 and Szechwan 250 000. These south-western provinces had communications and balance of payments problems with the rest of China and the export of the valuable but low freight-cost drug was actively promoted by the import houses of Chungking to provide exchange. They in turn were abetted by the tenant farmers whose crop it was, the landlords whose property values were thereby increased, and by the provincial officials who taxed or mulcted the consequent trade. Second, there was the rise of the Chinese anti-opium movement in the last years of the empire and the first years of the republic under the leadership of Yüan Shih-k'ai. The British government agreed to prohibit exports from India *pari passu* with the suppression of opium production in China which surprised contemporaries by its effectiveness. The anti-opium campaign was not popular: in west China indeed it was an important factor in the genesis of the revolution of 1911; but it changed the attitude of the educated classes in the cities of the eastern seaboard and marked the end of an era. After the death of Yüan Shih-k'ai, the revival of opium consumption on a reduced scale produced a recovery of foreign import, but not to the same degree as that of domestic production, and both of course were killed, officially, by the communists.

Continued diversification and continuity
Tea and opium had no successors as staples. Between 1833 and 1976, and particularly after 1886, the list of items traded lengthened without any of them achieving more than ephemeral predominance. The modern age saw the rise of what the old China hands called 'muck and truck'. In 1886 such miscellaneous goods formed only 10 per cent of the value of the total exported, but by 1905, 58 per cent. Goods other than opium, cottons, woollens and metals formed 20 per cent of the value of the total imported, but by 1905, 40 per cent. On the one hand, China began to supply industrial raw materials, such as soya beans, sesame and wood oil for foreign chemical industries: tin, or rare metals such as antimony and tungsten: and light consumer products such as bristles, matting and firecrackers. On the other hand, China began to demand industrial prerequisites like coal, scrap iron and aniline dyes: industrial consumer goods like kerosene and cigarettes; and basic economic necessities no longer supplied adequately by her own economy like timber and grain. As the twentieth century advanced, the diversity of commodities exchanged increased. By 1976, cheap clocks, shrimps, dehydrated potato and canned food had been added to the list of exports; ammonia fertilizer plant, PVC, machine tools, aero engines, helicopters, rubber, deers' horns and the movie 'Wuthering Heights' to the list of imports. None of these items, however, was very central to either the Chinese or the world economy, except perhaps the chemicals – and those as a group rather than as particular commodities. If the treaty system declined it was not only because of Chinese hostility and Western weakness, but also because economic imperatives on neither side any longer demanded it. At the death of Chairman Mao, China and the world, in terms of commodities, had reached a state of mutual irrelevance.

Initial expansion/subsequent stagnation and a mixture of continuity and discontinuity
Between 1863 and 1910 the value of China's trade with the outside world increased both absolutely and as a percentage of gross national product. In 1863 the total value of China's foreign transactions, imports and exports, visible and invisible, was around 100 million taels, approximately 3 per cent of the gross national product. By 1910 it had risen to 1000 million taels, approximately 20 per cent of the gross national product. China had become highly commercialized and Shanghai, its principal emporium, one of the great ports of the world. Behind this initial expansion was the dynamic of the West which demanded tea and industrial raw materials; the rising per capita wealth of China which expanded imports faster than exports, despite worsening terms of trade, and met the deficit on visible account by repatriation from abroad and foreign spending at home; and the liberalism which kept tariffs low and imposed few restrictions on emigration.

Between 1910 and 1976, transactions between China and the world slackened. They increased absolutely to the equivalent of 2000 million taels but fell relatively, as a percentage of gross national product to around 12.5 per cent. Behind this subsequent stagnation lay the reduced dynamic of the West during the great depression; the falling value of silver which turned Chinese demand to domestic rather than foreign supply; and the general communist preferences for autarchy, the special isolationism of Maoism. Under Chairman Mao, Shanghai, China's window on the world, was deliberately allowed to run down, and only in his last years, under the rule of the cultural revolution radicals, was some of its potential encouraged to revive.

Techniques

In the modern age Pierre Chaunu has argued that technological innovation took the place of spatial acquisition as the prime motor of economic development. For the first time, too, a wide gap opened between China and the outside world, not only in the physical technology of which Chaunu was thinking, but also in biological and social technologies as well.

The pace of technological transmission therefore quickened, though it was not all in one direction. China became a pupil, but still had something to teach.

Physical technology

In the Enlightenment, both China and Europe were based on mature economies which brought to perfection the possibilities of traditional and not dissimilar economies. In Europe alone, however, and only in its privileged north-west, the acquired propensity to consume of the Renaissance, the acquired inducement to invest of the great discoveries, plus the expenditure on literacy of the Enlightenment, broke the bottlenecks of tradition, notably in labour and energy, to reach the new technological horizon of the first industrial revolution. Between 1833 and 1976, China, slower and more reluctantly than Japan, but faster and more enthusiastically than Islam or India, received the new technology based initially on French science, British invention and Belgian diffusion, but soon the property of the whole Western world.

China's reception of industrial technology was shaped by its existing situation which in certain respects was more advanced than Europe's. Cort's puddling process was crucial in a technology which made steel by the recarbonization of wrought iron. It was much less significant in a technology which made steel by the partial decarbonization of cast iron and which had known, but not needed to use, Cort's process since the beginning of the seventeenth century. In general the new technology had the same significance in China as in Europe, but because it was an import, the order of reception was different.

In the West, the order of invention was steam textile machinery (Arkwright and Watt), steam locomotion (Stephenson), steamships (Brunel), steel (Bessemer), heavy chemicals (Solvay) and electrical supply (Edison). In China, the order of adoption was steamships, the first being built at the Kiang-nan arsenal in 1868 for Tseng Kuo-fan; steam locomotion; Li Hung-chang's Kaiping mine line in 1881 followed by the decision for an interior trunk line in 1889; steam textile machinery, the Shanghai Cotton Cloth mill began spinning and weaving under Li Hung-chang's protection in 1890; steel, the completion in 1894 of Chang Chih-tung's Han-yeh-ping complex containing both Bessemer and Siemens-Martin furnaces; electrical supply, initiated by the electricity department of the Shanghai municipal council around 1910; and heavy chemicals, the Solvay ammonia-salt process was first used by Fan Hsü-tung's Pacific Alkali Company at Tientsin in 1921 under the direction of the MIT-trained engineer Hou Te-pang.

Transport came first because of its military applications; textiles only second, partly because Chinese hand-made cloth was cheaper and more durable than Lancashire machine-made cloth. Steel, as in the West, came with railways and continentality. Electrical supply followed as the pre-condition and consequence of serious industrialization. Already in 1921 the customs commissioner could write: 'There is no doubt that the actual industrial prosperity of Shanghai is almost entirely due to the enterprise and energy of the Electricity Department of the Shanghai Municipal Council';[42] and in the inter-war period Shanghai prided itself on having the cheapest electricity in the world and on using more of it than any English city except London. Heavy chemicals, although commenced in the 1920s, really had to wait until the late Mao era emphasis on agricultural fertilizer to see the massive installation of plant from the USA, France and Japan.

In the expansion of physical technology, China was not entirely passive. William Kelly, co-inventor of decarbonization steel, may have learnt the principle, which had been known in China since the eleventh century when it was discussed by the Confucian polymath Shen Kua, from the Chinese workmen he was among the first in the USA to employ. Edwin L. Drake, who laid the foundations for a later phase of the industrial revolution by drilling the first commercial oilwell in Pennsylvania in 1859, may have borrowed his technique from accounts of drilling for brine and natural gas at Tzu-liu-ching in Szechwan, which had appeared in Europe in the late 1820s. Just as Ching-te-chen anticipated the Potteries so Tzu-liu-ching anticipated Paris and London in the use of gas for lighting and heating, and derivation cannot be excluded. Bearing in mind that textile machinery had its origin in the *molino bolognese* which was based on Chinese prototypes, and that the steam engine had antecedents both in Grimaldi's turbine toy and in the steam sufflators of Tibet, it is clear that physical industrialization was not a one-way process, though the flow in the modern age was primarily from West to East.

Biological technology

The five primary steps of the Western medical revolution were quarantine, vaccination, anaesthetics, immunology based on bacteriology, and antibiotics. Quarantine was an invention of the Mediterranean city states generalized after 1600 by the territorial monarchies. In China quarantine followed a similar course. It was begun, against cholera primarily, at the treaty ports by the maritime customs and the foreign consulates, commencing from 1873 in Amoy where the future Sir Patrick Manson was medical officer. It was extended by the North Manchurian plague prevention service established by Dr Wu Lien-teh in 1912 under the auspices of the governor-general, Chao Erh-hsün. It was generalized by the inauguration of the national quarantine service in 1930 by the Kuomintang.

Vaccination was discovered in 1798 by Edward Jenner. Not only did it prevent a disease which afflicted 95 per cent of the population and killed one in seven of its victims, but it also anticipated empirically the scientific immunology of Pasteur. Vaccination was an improved version of variolation which, according to Wu Lien-teh was introduced to China from India in the Sung period and was certainly mentioned in the *Pen-tsao kang-mu* of the late Ming naturalist Li Shih-chen. The West regarded variolation as a Turkish technique because Lady Mary Wortley Montagu, its introducer, first heard of it in Constantinople between 1716 and 1718. Father Dentrecolles, however, who knew the *Pen-tsao kang-mu* reference, gave it as his belief in 1726 that variolation originated either in Central Asia, passing to China through the Armenian network, or in China itself. It is possible that when Dr Alexander Pearson, the East India Company physician, introduced vaccination at Canton at 1805, he was importing something with Chinese antecedents. Vaccination spread slowly: first to ports like Amoy and Swatow when compulsory innoculation for Chinese emigrants was introduced; then to inland treaty ports like Chungking through the maritime customs medical officers; and finally to cities generally mainly through the mission stations. In Szechwan vaccination was first performed in 1890, but by 1920, 100 000 doses a year were being distributed in Chengtu alone, enough to cover all children.

In the West, anaesthetics may be dated from Sir James Simpson's discovery of chloroform in 1847. In China it was first introduced in the 1850s by medical missionaries trained by Peter Parker. For immunology the crucial dates in the West were 1876, Koch's isolation of the organism of anthrax, and 1881, Pasteur's development of an appropriate 'vaccination' against it. In China, the first true case was not plague, which was dealt with by quarantine essentially, but cholera. Over a million people were innoculated in Shanghai during the epidemic of 1932. Antibiotics, developed by Fleming and Florey between 1928 and 1938, were first brought to China during the Second World War over the Hump and sulfadiazine was used against plague in south Manchuria in 1946. Already in 1944 a Chinese laboratory was planning to make penicillin. An important figure in the reception of these latest elements of the medical revolution was Dr Robert K.S. Lim, an Edinburgh graduate and former professor of physiology at Peking Union Medical College, who was surgeon-general of the army 1945–48.

Social technology
During the modern age a vast range of purely institutional techniques entered China from the West. They covered the whole spectrum of the body politic from the state to the family and arguably did more to modernize China than the more obvious physical and biological technologies. At the top, China acquired a series of new political systems: constitutional monarchy in 1908, constitutional republic in 1912, presidential and party dictatorships thereafter with appropriate associated institutions – provincial assemblies, parliaments, parties competitive and monopolistic, central civilian ministries, politically indoctrinated armed forces. In the middle, China acquired municipal authorities, previously unknown in an empire which ignored the corporate existence of cities; a legal system administering a comprehensive code; nationwide services like the post office and the banks; both non-political and political police; professional associations, universities, trade unions and a press. At the bottom, China acquired new concepts of the family, new freedoms for women and children,

new articulations and restrictions of property and human rights. All these things had a technological aspect. In many instances China had to be taught how to do them: as for example by Borodin's mission, 1923–27, which introduced to both the Kuomintang and the infant Chinese Communist Party many of the organizational techniques of the Soviet Union.

In one sphere of social technology there was osmosis rather than transmission. This was bureaucracy where in the modern age the West borrowed the Sui-T'ang technique of recruitment by written examination, while China borrowed the European Enlightenment technique of remuneration by salary alone. Europe had known about Chinese written examinations since the late sixteenth century and it had been progressively adopted by schools and universities beginning with those of the Jesuits. As a method of civil service recruitment however, though advocated by Lord Chesterfield, experimented with by Talleyrand, and used to a minor extent in Prussia, examination did not become the main basis of any Western bureaucracy until, first, 1855, when it was adopted by the Indian civil service and, second 1870 when it was extended to the administrative class of the British home civil service. Both advocates and opponents explicitly recognized the principle to be Chinese and one of the strongest advocates, Thomas Taylor Meadows, was a consular officer on the China coast. The principle was accepted by the Trevelyan–Northcote report in 1853, but the recommendation was not implemented until Gladstone's first ministry. The implementation was a major element in the nineteenth-century revolution in government: it consolidated the distinction between politicians and administrators, and made possible an increase in the range of government by making administration more intelligent.

Remuneration by salary alone and the consequent complete elimination of fees, commissions, gratuities and bribes, was first introduced to China by the maritime customs in 1854. The customs, however, was a new service. It consisted in its upper echelons entirely of foreigners and had only distant relations with its Chinese associate, the superintendencies of trade. A greater effect of diffusion was produced by Sir Richard Dane's salt gabelle after 1913. Here there were fewer foreigners, foreign and Chinese inspectors always worked in

tandem, and there was close contact not only with its Chinese
associate, the salt commissionerships but also with all the
departments of the ministry of finance. Remuneration by
salary reduced costs and made possible the typically Gladsto-
nian legerdemain of simultaneously reducing the rate of a
tax but increasing its yield. Dane and his Chinese colleague
Chang Hu took modern remuneration into the heart of the
traditional Chinese bureaucracy, just as the Trevelyan–Northcote report took modern recruitment into the heart of the
traditional British bureaucracy.[43]

Ideas

In the modern age, the whole intellectual wealth of the West
was poured almost unintentionally on to China's shores. In
return, apart from stimulus to individual Westerners and her
art which influenced the Impressionists indirectly through
Japan, China gave only Maoism: a Chinese confection of
largely Western ingredients. Because of the breadth of the
Western tide it must suffice to mention some significant seg-
ments and their agents.

In front were the translators: Lin Tse-hsü, governor-general at Canton who in 1840 used missionary-trained repat-
riates to translate sections of Vattel's *Law of Nations*; W.A.P.
Martin, president of the T'ung-wen kuan, who in the 1860s
produced versions of Newton's *Principia* and the *Code Napoleon*; John Fryer, at the Kiangnan arsenal, who in 1871 translated D.A. Well's *Principles and Applications of Chemistry*, the
first of a total of 112 scientific textbooks; Yen Fu, superintendent of the Peiyang Naval Academy at Tientsin, who translated Thomas Huxley's *Evolution and Ethics*, *The Wealth of
Nations*, Mills' *Liberty* and *Logic*, *L'Esprit des Lois*, Spencer's *A
Study of Sociology*, Jevons' *Logic*; Wang Kuo-wei, outwardly a
traditional scholar, who translated selections from Kant,
Schopenhauer and Nietzsche; Chu Chih-hsin, anti-Christian,
who produced a version of the *Communist Manifesto* in 1906;
Lin Shu, dean of letters at Peking, who, among 163 Western
works, paraphrased *Ivanhoe*, *David Copperfield* and
Uncle Tom's Cabin; Kuo Mo-jo, leftist litterateur, who translated
Werther, *Faust* and *War and Peace*.

Next, came the converts and pupils: Ying Lien-chih, convert to Catholicism and founder of the Tientsin *Ta-kung pao* and Fu-jen university; Ts'ai Yüan-p'ei, convert to the critical philosophy and chancellor of Peita; Yang Ch'ang-chi, convert to British Hegelianism and teacher and father-in-law of Mao Tse- tung; Ch'en Tu-hsiu and Li Ta-chao, converts to different kinds of Marxism and co-founders of the Communist Party; Hu Shih, convert to pragmatism and pupil of Dewey; Carsun Chang, pupil of Bergson and opponent of Scientism; Ting Wen-chiang, convert to Huxleyite positivism and founder of the Chinese geological survey; Ch'ien San-ch'iang, pupil of the Joliot-Curies and co-father of the Chinese nuclear bomb.

Behind were the distinguished visitors: Paul Claudel in the French consular service; Russell, Dewey and I.A. Richards at Peking university; Rabindranath Tagore, visitor to Peking literary circles in 1924; André Malraux, eyewitness of Borodin's China; Teilhard de Chardin, shuttling between Paris and Peking for twenty years; R.H. Tawney, visitor in 1930, whose *Land and Labour in China* was serialized in the Chinese press. Translators, converts and pupils, distinguished visitors, all were purveyors of Western ideas to China, as were the *liu-hsüeh sheng*, the returned students with their various degrees, their books and experience.

Below the crests of these waves came the long swell of the philosophies: the flow of Christianity and Marxism to China, the ebb of Maoism from it.

Many of the new ideas which came to China from the West came via the mission station. In the nineteenth century it was impossible for any of the Christianities not to practice Hilaire Belloc's doctrine that Europe is the faith and the faith is Europe. The Protestant missions in particular conjoined Christianity and modernization in their missionary strategy. By and large the Chinese took the modernization and rejected the Christianity. Yet too much should not be made of the numerical failure of Christianity in China. In 1948 there were more Christians than communists. The Protestant community, which *modo grosso* went for quality, had half a million members, many of them, like the Generalissimo himself and the Soong family, in strategic places in government, business and the professions. The Catholic community, which *per contra* went for quantity, had 3 million members, not so strategically placed socially, but better organized. Since 1922 it had its own apostolic delagacy, the formidable Mgr, later Cardinal, Celso Constantini, being the first incumbent from 1922 to 1933; since 1926 Chinese bishops; and since 1946 its own hierarchy under a Chinese cardinal archbishop of Peking.

The real weakness of Christianity in China was not numerical but intellectual. Christianity could not aspire to rival communism in organization, but it might have aspired to rival it in intellectual appeal. However, evangelical Protestantism, as represented by the interdenominational China Inland Mission founded in 1860 by Hudson Taylor, was too narrow; social Protestantism, as represented by the Chinese YMCA founded in 1885, was too contentless; and inter-Vatican Catholicism, for all its latent wealth, was too unenterprising, to make much headway in this direction. When Mde Chiang Kai-shek asked the New Zealand-born American Congregationalist and village reform expert, George Shepherd, to become adviser to the New Life movement – her husband's pale attempt at a cultural revolution – he brought no specifically Christian ideas to those he had learnt from James Y.C. Yen, the non-missionary founder of the rural reconstruction movement.[44] Intellectual Protestantism, the fundamentalist dialectical theology of Barth, the modernist demythologization of Bultmann, never reached China. Similarly, the heroic Lazarist Vincent Lebbe, founder of Catholic Action in China and exponent of 'China for the Chinese and the Chinese for Christ' could not inject either the social Catholicism of *Rerum Novarum* or the intellectual Catholicism of the liturgical movement and transcendental Thomism. Teilhard de Chardin found his friends in China not among his fellow Jesuits, but in non-missionary circles: men such as the positivist Ting Wen-chiang, the technocrat Weng Wen-hao, the palaeontologists Davidson Black and Amadeus Grabau. Christianity failed to capture an intellectual elite through which to enlist fellow travellers and mobilize a public in a Chinese Christian democratic movement.

Inversely, the real strength of Marxism in China was organizational not intellectual. It is true that the two co-founders of the party, Ch'en Tu-hsiu and Li Ta-chao, were professors at Peita, that Chou En-lai and Chang Kuo-t'ao, the effective leaders of the party in the 1930s, were university men, that

Mao Tse-tung was a normal school principal, that Liu Shao-
ch'i was a teacher; but the party only captured the intellectual
elite near the end of its ascent to power – after the Second
World War, when the universities turned decisively against
the Kuomintang. Chinese Marxism was always Marxism–
Leninism and its lack of any firm grip on dialectical
materialism facilitated the infiltration of the elements from
Nietzsche, Bergson and Sorel which eventually produced
Maoism. What made the party strong was not its intellectual
appeal – already in the rectifcation campaign of 1942–44 its
ideology had reached a state of mindlessness hardly surpassed
in Stalin's Russia – but its organization, given it first by Borodin, developed by the leaders of the rural Soviets, and completed by Mao during his Yenan period 1937 to 1945. It was
this organization of disciplined party, politicized army and
rural but not really peasant bases, which allowed the party
during the war to expand its territories, soldiers and subjects
enormously, and after it to become an alternative government
which capitalized on the disillusion with the Kuomintang and
the flight from society produced by over a decade of war,
refugeeism and hyperinflation. Maoism, if it appealed at all,
appealed as an ascesis rather than an ideology. As an ideology,
re-exported to the West in the 1960s to the sillier students,
the trendier university teachers and to Latin American
revolutionaries sufficiently naive to take its prescriptions literally, its intellectual content was inconsiderable. It was not, as
its devotees claimed, a Sinification of Marxism–Leninism
adapted to Third World circumstances, but rather a potpourri
of earlier European voluntarisms, its romantic militarism
closer to Nazism than true Marxism, though set in a social
historicist rather than geopolitical setting.

Finally, of some significance for the intellectual relations
between China and the outside world in the modern age were
the ideas which did *not* travel. These would include Keynesian
economics, depth psychology (Freud, Adler and Jung), linguistic analysis (neither the earlier nor the later Wittgenstein
reached China before the death of Chairman Mao), Karl
Popper's philosophy of science and democratic politics, Lévi-
Strauss' structuralism and the protean world of existentialism
(Kierkegaard, Sartre, Marcel and Rahner); the very ideas on
which the European Renaissance following the Second World

War drew for inspiration. The Chinese mind was only genuinely open between 1900 and 1920: long enough to abandon tradition, not long enough to absorb modernity.

WORLD INSTITUTIONS, 1833 TO 1976

In the modern age down to 1914, world institutions not only thickened and multiplied as they had done in the Enlightment, but also, as they had not done since the Renaissance, broadened to include Black Africa and the interior of East Asia. China's increasing participation in the institutions of the European world order was a notable part of this process. By the middle of the twentieth century, government offices, apartment blocks, airports, department stores, hotels, universities, factories, sports stadia and hospitals looked much the same the world over. Further, having encompassed the four primary civilizations in a loose network, the world institutions in the early part of the twentieth century showed signs of coalescing into a definite system which, in China, expressed itself in such things as the international expedition against the Boxers in 1900, the consortium banks' reorganization loan loan and establishment of the foreign salt gabelle in 1913, Sun Yat-sen's proposal for an international agency to inject massive quantities of foreign capital into China in 1921, the provisions of the Washington treaty in 1922, Roosevelt's insistence on China's permanent membership of the Security Council at the Teheran conference of 1943. After 1914, however, as state after state entered the fatal cycle of revolution and its complications – militarism, terror, party seizure of power – the prospects of the world institutions and for the emergence of any world system became much more problematic and remained so at the death of Chairman Mao.

No one was more impressed by the incipient coalescence of world institutions than Teilhard de Chardin, the philosopher of the China coast. In the winter of 1939–40, while Europe froze in the phoney war and China saw – or rather did not see – Mao Tse-tsung so expand Soviet power as to make ultimate communist victory highly probable, Teilhard was completing *Le Phénomène Humain* in which the effects of such a coalescence were analysed, lauded and projected into a metaphysical future. He planned the book late in 1937, began the first chapter in July or August 1938, and, following a year's interruption due to a trip to France and the USA, worked steadily on it from his return to Peking on 30 August 1939. On 8 February 1940, he wrote to his friends the Begouëns '*The Phenomenon of Man* progresses at the rate of a page or two a day';[45] on 7 March, he added, 'By Easter, I don't doubt, I shall be not far from three-quarters of the way through';[46] and on 9 May, as the fall of France was about to begin: 'My book has an excellent chance of being finished before July. In fact, since I'm just up to the last half-chapter, I almost feel that I've finished it'.[47] The central idea of the book was convergence: what Teilhard variously called human planetization, the involution of the noosphere, the socialization of compression or totalization. He assumed the growing importance of what this study has called world institutions. Such institutions, he argued, would eventually become, first, a system and then – through the law of complexity-consciousness, the principle that union differentiates and absolute union differentiates absolutely – a person, the metahistorical Omega point. But did the course of events, especially after 1914, particularly in China, really support even the first stage of Teilhard's vision?

The oldest surviving world institution, the microbian common market, progressed not so much by the interchange of diseases as by the development of international cooperation to combat them. The first international sanitary conference was held in Paris in 1851. Though its convention was not ratified because of differences between the 'sanitationists' of northern Europe and the 'quarantinists' of the Mediterranean, nine further conferences were held before the end of the century. The *intendance sanitaire d'Alexandrie* and the *counseil supérieur de Santé* at Constantinople were developed and lesser bodies were established in Tangier and Teheran. From 1909 the Office International d'Hygiène Publique in Paris collected and distributed information about the 'big five' – plague, cholera, smallpox, typhus and yellow fever. In 1921 the health section of the League of Nations came into existence, headed by Dr Ludwig Rajchman of Poland who visited China in 1925–26, 1929, 1931, 1933–34 and largely took over the functions of the Paris office. It was the parent, after the collapse of the League, of UNRRA which in turn was the parent of the World Heath Organization established in 1948. By the time Chairman Mao died, China had rejoined this, as well as other United Nations' agencies, to make them for the first time fully global bodies. In 1965 Chinese scientists made a major contribution to the microbian common market when they chemically synthesised active insulin for the first time.

Similarly, the newest world institution, the world technological bank created in the modern age by successive industrial revolutions, made steady progress. An index of this progress was the series of world fairs beginning with the Great Exhibition of 1851 at the Crystal Palace which had displays from 13 000 exhibitors arranged under the four categories: raw materials, machinery, manufacturers and fine arts. Between 1867 and 1905 China participated in twenty-eight such fairs, including the unusually successful exhibitions at Vienna in 1873 and at Paris in 1878 and 1900, the choice, arrangement and management of her exhibits being one of the multifarious functions of the maritime customs. In the nineteenth century, China's contribution was to the categories of raw materials and fine arts, but by the death of Chairman Mao, she was holding her own trade fairs twice a year at Canton which featured machine tools and pharmaceuticals as well. Despite the growing imperatives of military secrecy in the twentieth century, the world technological bank was a reality in 1976.

As we have seen, many of its roots lay in pre-modern Chinese technology, and to its fine if fading flower, the petrochemical industry, China had contributed through the Szechwanese technique of deep drilling and might contribute again through the resources of her coastal shelf.

The status of the republic of letters, however, was more ambiguous. In the nineteenth century it expanded in all directions: more scientists and scholars, more journals, more congresses, more books and articles, more translations, more interchange at least of abstracts. The totalitarian revolt — Hitler's rejection of Jewish relativity, Stalag vivisection, the expulsion of Freud, Lysenkoism, Gulag psychiatry, Mao's interventions in quantum mechanics, the state control of history in all Marxist countries, the Marxist hostility to serious sociology — limited but did not reverse this expansion. Nevertheless the limitations, particularly in the field of history were striking, and Teilhard de Chardin hardly took them into consideration in his lyrical accounts of the convergence of the noosphere. Chinese scholars complained discreetly to Western visitors of their isolation from their foreign colleagues.

The evolution of the other four world institutions was even less encouraging. The basic information circuit, after a period of expansion in the nineteenth century when, among other advances, Richthofen completed the geography of China, in the twentieth century became subject to the limitations of official secrets acts, withholding of data, closure of archives, misleading statistics and bland official denials. Passports, visas, work permits and immigration quotas resumed their obstruction of the unofficial traveller and curiosity was increasingly equated with espionage. The number of forbidden cities, few in 1900, multiplied steadily. In this new obfuscation, the special contribution of Mao's China was the systematically stultifying conducted-tour of official parties to produce appropriate fellow travellers' tales.

Windowless monads in information were paralleled by economic autarchy in trade. The world market, in the nineteenth century reaching up the Yangtze and down the Amur, in the twentieth was attenuated first moderately by the reappearance of tariffs, the abandonment of the universal gold standard, the end of convertibility and the imposition of exchange controls, then radically by the emergence of the totalitarian planned economies. Monetary disorder was a major factor in this process and the Chinese hyperinflation during the Second World War and after was one of the worst cases.

As regards the religious internationals, the Naqshbandiyya, the Gelugspa and the Jesuits: all made progress in the nineteenth century. In China, the *Jahriyya* completed its conquest of the Chinese-speaking Moslems, the Tungans, and inspired a series of rebellions against Chinese rule, which after 1912 resulted in virtual autonomy for a group of Tungan warlords in Kansu, Ninghsia, Chinghai and Sinkiang. The hierarchs of the Gelugspa, the Living Buddhas, recast the terms of their partnership with the Ch'ing in Tibet and Mongolia, so that after 1912 the Thirteenth Dalai Lama was temporal ruler in Lhasa, the Eighth Jebtsundamba Khutughtu was head of state in Urga, and even a local figure like the

Fourth Jambyang of Labrang was a prince in his own region. The Jesuits, having recovered Siccawei, established Aurora University in Shanghai and were hosts to the first council of the Catholic church in China in 1924, where Mgr Constantini inaugurated his plans for the Sinification of missions and the eventual establishment of a Chinese hierarchy. As the twentieth century advanced, however, Naqshbandiyya, Gelugspa and Society of Jesus all came under totalitarian attack, in China as elsewhere. Soviet intervention defeated pan-Islamic revolt in Sinkiang; Ma Chung-ying, most charismatic of Moslem leaders, perished in Stalin's purges; and the Chinese communists disposed of the other great Ma's of the northwest. The Eighth Jebtsundamba Khutughtu had no reincarnation in the Mongolian People's Republic when he died in 1924, the Fourteenth Dalai Lama fled from Tibet in 1959, the Sixth Jambyang, though still alive in 1956, had lost all authority in Labrang. The Jesuits were once more expelled from China along with Mgr Riberi the apostolic internuncio, though in 1979 following the election of a Polish pope, there was talk of their return to Aurora to open a medical school.[48]

Finally, the naval *pax Britannica*, which reached its apogee on the China coast at the end of the nineteenth century, proved as ephemeral as the *Weltreich* of the T'ang in the middle of the eighth century. As the product of Britain's virtual naval monopoly after 1815, it ended when successively Russia, Japan, Germany and the USA built fleets, and seapower gave way to airpower. In the absence of any other *pax*, with a *pax Americana* rejected by the rest of the West – indeed by American public opinion – in a polycentric world, piracy, terrorism, hijacking and even the slave trade could raise their heads again.

In short, Teilhard de Chardin's vision of convergence, while it finds some support in modern developments in medicine, pure science and industrial technology, finds less in developments in general information, the arts and in the world market and in the non-development of *paces Anglo-Saxonicae*. In particular, it would seem that Teilhard seriously under-estimated the threat to human unity and progress – for in his view the two were identical – by the modern totalitarianism to which China made so notable a contribution in the person of Chairman Mao and the regime he established.

Teilhard de Chardin's analysis of the totalitarianisms was ambivalent. On the one hand, his optimism led him to take their collectivism at face value and to regard them as crude sketches for his own Utopia. He never paused to wonder whether the individualistic societies of the democracies might not be more totalized in his sense than *soi-disant* totalitarian societies, or to consider the fact that during the Second World War it was only the democracies which were capable of full mobilization of manpower and materials. Thus he could write of 'the first forms, brutally herding men together, assumed by political state control'; 'totalitarian political systems, of which time will correct the excesses but will also no doubt, accentuate the underlying tendencies or intuitions'; 'the modern totalitarian regimes, whatever their initial defects, are neither heresies nor biological regressions: they are in line with the essential trend of "cosmic" movement'; and 'these first attempts ... it is not the principle of totalisation that is at fault, but the clumsy and incomplete way in which it has been applied'.[49] He could even in 1936 propose a 'Human front' of democrats, communists and fascists, or ask in 1948, 'Who can tell whether, in the very interest of the Kingdom of God, a good dose of Marxism is not the thing to save us?'[50] On the strength of such utterances R.C. Zaehner saw Teilhard as the prophet of Christian–Marxist dialogue, Teilhardo–Marxism as Chaunu calls it. In this frame of mind, Teilhard would entirely deny the demonic element of totalitarianism identified by Solzhenitsyn when he wrote that the OSO, the special boards of the secret police, were 'subordinate only to the Minister of Internal Affairs, to Stalin and to Satan'.[51]

On the other hand, Teilhard's intuition led him occasionally to see the darker potentialities of the totalitarian revolt. Thus on 11 December 1939, he wrote to his brother Joseph:

> As you already so wisely wrote in October, the great danger lies in the awakening of Russia ... Some new solution will have to be found for the problem of world organization, but that can hardly be envisaged without a common ideal. That is what makes the Russian schism fundamentally so formidable.[52]

On 16 December he wrote to the Abbé Breuil:

In the end, it is Russia that is becoming public enemy no. 1. According to a recent conversation I had with a person well placed to judge, the danger in that quarter would appear to be no longer Marxism and the Third International (which, but for the jargon, is completely dead): it is the formation of a national group, hostile, watertight, completely ignorant of what lies outside itself, and so incapable of being included in the far-reaching combination of mankind we need.[53]

'The Russian schism', 'public enemy no. 1', this was strong language for Teilhard. In the last chapter of *Le Phénomène Humain*, written the following May, he toyed with the possibility of human unification culminating in an act of discord – 'ramification once again, for the last time'.[54] He wrote: 'Enormous powers will be liberated in mankind by the inner play of its cohesion ... Are we to foresee a mechanizing synergy under brute force, or a synergy of sympathy? ... A conflict may supervene'.[55] After the war too, as the cold war got under way, he observed in 1947:

It is interesting to note the extent to which the lie (a relatively minor evil in more restricted groups) is fast becoming an inhibiting major vice in large social organisms, so that one might say that (like hatred – and the taedium vitae) *it* tends to constitute a major obstacle to the formation of a Noosphere.[56]

Further, he had the sense to refuse Joliot-Curie's invitation to sign the Stockholm peace appeal in 1951 and described it as 'oversimplified in its anti-Americanism'.[57]

Teilhard de Chardin was no politician. Nevertheless, it is a pity that he did not develop these intuitions into a deeper understanding of the totalitarian revolt in terms of his own theories. Had he done so, he would have seen that the totalitarian phenomenon, far from being a crude groping towards the kind of progress he thought was happening and wanted, was a refusal of it, aping change the better to oppose it. As a Frenchman brought up to the ideals of 1789, Teilhard was not well placed to see that most revolutions are conservative, even reactionary, and the complications of revolution, among which totalitarian seizure of power is pre-eminent, even more so. Thus the Puritan revolution opposed the swollen London metropolis which was later to found England's greatness upon commercial capitalism; the French revolution opposed the development of France in the direction of English capitalism and the industrial revolution; the Chinese revolution of 1911 opposed the modernization of China by the late Ch'ing dynasty; and the Russian revolution opposed the development of Russia in the direction of European capitalism and the Eurasian technocracy of its own engineers.

What did the totalitarian seizures of power oppose? Essentially they opposed the rise of world institutions, global capitalism in particular, participation in which would have transformed their countries more profoundly than the noisy but superficial and hysterical changes they themselves introduced. The totalitarians, Teilhard failed to see, were *terribles simplificateurs*, offering in place of the complexity of modern society with its worldwide ramifications, a brutalized version of the old duality of bureaucrats and subjects operating within single states. Because they were simplifiers – *Gleichschaltung* posits fewer elements not more – they were lowerers of consciousness; in terms of his own law of complexity-consciousness, ultimately purveyors of mindlessness. The famous Nazi slogan, 'We don't want higher wages, we don't want lower wages, we don't want the same wages – we want national socialist wages', was a piece of dialectic with which the Maoist theory of contradictions was perfectly consonant. In Teilhardian terms, totalitarianism is the refusal of totalization, the refusal of personalization: a revolution of *nihilismus* in Rauschning's description of Nazism; Gregor Strasser's 'Nazism is the opposite to everything that now is'.[58] As such, totalitarianism would constitute a profoundly negative element in Teilhard's system, a major obstacle to even the first stage of convergence, the development of a real system of world institutions.

Mao Tse-tung and Teilhard de Chardin, two revolutionaries both working in or around Peking in the winter of 1939/40, symbolized another pair of worlds between which China stood in the modern age: a world where contradiction was fundamental; a world where convergence was fundamental.

Notes

CHAPTER 1

1. Pierre Teilhard de Chardin, *Man's Place in Nature* (Collins Fontana Books, London 1973) p. 116.
2. Werner Benndorf, *Das Mittelmeerbuch*, quoted in Fernand Braudel, *La Mediterranée et Le Monde mediterranéen à l'époque de Philippe II* (Librairie Armand Colin, Paris 1949) p. 187.
3. For this paragraph, see Fernand Braudel, *Capitalism and Material Life 1400–1800* (Collins, Fontana Books, London 1974).
4. Ferdinand von Richthofen, *Baron Richtehofen's Letters, 1870–1872* (North China Herald Office, Shanghai 1903) p. 125.
5. Karl A. Wittfogel, *Oriental Despotism, A Comparative Study of Total Power* (Yale University Press, New Haven 1957).
6. Ho Ping-ti, 'The Loess and the Origins of Chinese Agriculture', *American Historical Review*, vol. LXXV, no.1 (October 1969) pp. 1–36.
7. K. Baer, 'Land and Water in Ancient Egypt', paper presented to 28th International Congress of Orientalists, Canberra, 1971.
8. C.S. Lewis, *The Pilgrim's Regress* (Geoffrey Bles, London 1947) p. 154.
9. Quoted in Isaiah Berlin, *Vico and Herder, Two Studies in the History of Ideas* (The Hogarth Press, London 1976) pp. 139.
10. Joseph Needham, *Science and Civilisation in China* Vol. I (Cambridge University Press, Cambridge 1954) pp. 30, 36.
11. Ibid., Vol. IV, part three, p. 29.
12. Pierre Teilhard de Chardin, *Letters from a Traveller* (Collins Fontana Books, London 1967) p. 57.
13. For European and Chinese options in housing, see Pierre Chaunu, 'Le Bâtiment dans L'Économie Traditionnelle', in J-P Bardet, P. Chaunu, G. Désert, P. Gouhier and H. Neveux, *Le Bâtiment: Enquete D'Histoire Économique XIVᵉ – XIXᵉ Siècles* (Mouton, Paris and The Hague 1971) pp. 9–32; and Needham, op. cit. Vol. IV, part three, pp. 60–80.
14. F. Alvarez Semedo, *The History of That Great and Renowned Monarchy of China* (John Crook, London 1655) p. 3; Jan Nieuhof, 'An Appendix or special Remarks taken at large out of Athanasius Kircher his *Antiquities of China*', *An Embassy from the East India Company of the United Provinces to the Grand Tartar Cham Emperor of China* (John Ogilby, London 1669) p. 99; John Francis Gemelli Careri, *A Voyage Round the World, A Collection of Voyages and Travels in Six Volumes*, Vol. IV (London 1745) p. 288; Melchisedec Thevenot, 'Desciption Geographique de L'Empire de la Chine par Le Pêre Martin Martinius', *Relations de Divers Voyages Curieux*, Tome second, (Paris 1696) p. 8.
15. For modern interpretations of the fall of the Roman empire, see Peter Brown, *The World of Late Antiquity from Marcus Aurelius to Muhammed* (Thames and Hudson, London 1971); and Richard W. Bulliet,

The Camel and the Wheel (Harvard University Press, Cambridge, Massachusetts 1975).

16. For the fall of the Han, see Yang Lien-sheng, 'Great Families of Eastern Han', in E-tu Zen Sun and John de Francis (eds) *Chinese Social History* (American Council of Learned Societies, Washington 1956) pp. 103–34; and Etienne Balazs, *Chinese Civilization and Bureaucracy* (Yale University Press, New Haven and London 1964) especially chapters 12–14, pp. 173–254.

17. Richthofen, op.cit p. 149

18. Sir Aurel Stein, *On Ancient Central-Asian Tracks* (Pantheon, New York 1964) pp. 19–20.

19. M.J. Finley, *The Ancient Economy* (Chatto and Windus, London 1973) p. 137.

20. For the cultural functions of the Chinese empire, see Leon E. Stover, *The Cultural Ecology of Chinese Civilization* (Mentor, New American Library, New York and Scarborough, Ontario 1974) pp. 189, 235.

21. Burton Watson, *Records of the Grand Historian of China, Translated from the Shih chi of Ssu-ma Chien, Vol. II: The Age of Emperor Wu 140 to circa 100 BC* (Columbia University Press, New York and London 1961) p. 329.

22. Peter Levi, *The Light Garden of the Angel King* (Collins, London 1972) pp. 132, 256.

23. E. Zurcher, *The Buddhist Conquest of China* (E.J. Brill, Leiden 1959) p.62.

24. Liu Mau-tsai, *Kutscha and Seine Beziehungen zu China Vom 2.JH. V. Bis Zum 6.JH. N. CHR* I Band (Otto Harrassowitz, Wiesbaden 1969), p. 22.

25. John Watson McCrindle, *The Commerce and Navigation of the Erythraean Sea* (Reprint in 1973 of Editions Calcutta and London 1879, 1882) pp. 132, 136, 137.

26. Needham, op.cit., Vol. IV, part three, p. 602.

27. Paul Wheatley, *The Golden Khersonese* (University of Malaya Press, Kuala Lumpur 1961) p. 16.

28. H.A. Giles, *The Travels of Fa-Hsien* (Routledge and Kegan Paul, London 1959) pp. 76, 78.

29. Wheatley, op.cit., p. 16.

30. Propertius, *Elegies*, IV, iii, 8.

31. McCrindle, op.cit., p. 147.

32. Seneca, *De Beneficiis*, VII, 9, 5.

33. J. Innes Miller, *The Spice Trade of the Roman Empire 29BC–AD 641* (Clarendon Press, Oxford 1969).

36. Pliny the Elder, *Naturalis Historia*, XII, 87–88; Innes Miller, op.cit., pp. 153–71.

37. Cicero, *De Re Publica*, ii, 4, quoted in Dimitri Obolensky, *The Byzantine Commonwealth* (Weidenfeld and Nicholson, London 1971) p. 10.

38. Needham, op.cit., Vol. IV, part three, p. 550.

39. Pan Ku, *Ch'ien Han-shu*, Chapter 70, p. 96.

40. Needham, op.cit., Vol. I, p. 237.

41. Burton Watson, op.cit., Vol. II, p. 280.

42. For the history of horsepower, see Miklos Jankovich, *They Rode into Europe* (Harrap, London 1971).
43. St John Chrysostom, *Homily XXV*.
44. Seneca, *De Beneficiis*, VII 9, 5.
45. Fan Yeh, *Hou Han-shu*, Chapter 118, p. 96.
46. McCrindle, op.cit., pp. 108, 123.
47. Fan Yeh, quoted in C.P. Fitzgerald, *China A Short Cultural History* (The Cresset Press, London 1954) p. 199.
48. C.G. Jung, *The Practice of Psychotherapy* (Routledge and Kegan Paul, London 1954) pp. 200, 307. For the history of alchemy, see Needham, op.cit., Vol. V, parts two, three and four.
49. For Zervanism, see R.C. Zachner, *Zurvan, A Zoroastrian Dilemma* (Clarendon Press, Oxford 1955).
50. T.R.V. Murti, *The Central Philosophy of Buddhism. A Study of the Madhyamika System* (Allen and Unwin, London 1953), quoted in Max Loehr, *Buddhist Thought and Imagery* (Harvard University Press, Cambridge, Massachusetts 1961) p. 26.
51. Helen Dunstan, 'The Late Ming Epidemics: A Preliminary Survey', *Ch'ing-shih Wen-t'i*, vol. III, no. 3 (November 1975) pp. 24–6.
52. For the significance of the *Mahaprajnaparamitasastra*, see Etienne Lamotte, *Le Traité de la Grande Vertu de Sagesse*, Tome III (Université de Louvain, Institut Orientaliste, Louvain 1970) pp. V–LX; K. Venkata Ramanan, *Nagarjuna's Philosophy as Presented in the Maha-Prajnaparamita-Sastra* (Harvard-Yenching Institute, Tuttle, Rutland, Vermont and Tokyo 1966); and S.A.M. Adshead, 'Buddhist Scholasticism and Transcendental Thomism', *The Downside Review*, vol. 95, no. 321 (October 1977) pp. 297–305.

CHAPTER 2

1. For T'ang China, see particularly Edward H. Schafer, *The Golden Peaches of Samarkand* (University of California Press, Berkeley and Los Angeles 1963); Edwin G. Pulleyblank, *The Background of the Rebellion of An Lu-shan* (Oxford University Press, Oxford 1955); D.C. Twitchett, *Financial Administration under the T'ang Dynasty* (Cambridge University Press, Cambridge 1963); Arthur F. Wright and Denis Twitchett (eds) *Perspectives on the T'ang* (Yale University Press, New Haven and London 1973).
2. For the empire of Justinian see P. Brown, *The World of Late Antiquity from Marcus Aurelius to Muhammed* (Thames and Hudson, London 1971); W.H.C. Frend, *The Rise of the Monophysite Movement* (Cambridge University Press, Cambridge 1972); Evelyne Patlagean, *Pauvreté Économique et Pauvreté Social à Byzance, 4ᵉ–7ᵉ Siecles* (Mouton, Paris, La Haye 1977).
3. C.P. Fitzgerald, *China. A Short Cultural History* (The Cresset Press, London 1954) p. 884.

4. For monastic capitalism in China, see Jacques Gernet, *Les Aspects Économiques du Bouddhisme dans La Société Chinoise due V^e au Xe Siècle*, (École Française D'Extrême-Orient, Saigon 1956).

5. Quoted in Immanuel Wallerstein, *The Modern World-System* (Academic Press, New York 1974).

6. For plague in late antiquity, see Jean-Noel Biraben, *Les Hommes et la Peste en France et dans les pays européens et mediterranéens. Tome I. La Peste dans L'Histoire* (Mouton, Paris, La Haye 1975).

7. For the Romanitas of the early Byzantine empire, see Gilbert Dagron, *Naissance d'une Capitale, Constantinople et ses Institutions de 330 à 451* (Presses Universitaires de France, Paris 1974).

8. For P'ei Cheng and Chinese law in late antiquity, see Étienne Balazs, *Le Traité Juridique du 'Souei-chou'* (E.J. Brill, Leiden 1954) especially pp. 22, 64, 147–9.

9. For the Chinese horse administration in Central Asia, see Henri Maspero (ed.) *Les Documents Chinois de la Troisième Expedition de Sir Aurel Stein en Asie Centrale* (The Trustees of the British Museum, London 1953) pp. 87–92, 113–49.

10. D. Obolensky, *The Byzantine Commonwealth* (Weidenfeld and Nicholson, London 1971) p. 48.

11. For changes in Chinese agriculture in late antiquity, see Michel Cartier, 'L' Exploitation Agricole Chinois de L'Antiquité au XIVe siècle: Evolution d'un Modele', *Annales, Économies, Sociétés, Civilisations*, vol. 33 no. 2, (March–April 1978) pp. 365–88.

12. For capitalism in Western antiquity, see Paul Veyne, *Le Pain et Le Cirque, Sociologie Historique d'un Pluralisme Politique* (Editions du Seuil, Paris 1976) especially pp. 118–40. Much of what M. Veyne says could be applied to China.

13. Ho Ping-ti 'Lo-yang, A.D. 495–534. A Study of Physical and Socio-Economic Planning of a Metropolitan Area', *Harvard Journal of Asiatic Studies*, vol. 26 (1966) pp. 52–101 and 86.

14. I. Umnyakov and Y. Aleskerov, *Samarkand, A Guide Book* (Progress Publishers, Moscow 1972) pp. 15–16.

15. Ibid., p. 16.

16. For the spread of Nestorianism to China, see P.Y. Saeki, *The Nestorian Documents and Relics in China* (SPCK, Tokyo 1951).

17. Schafer, op.cit., pp. 15, 282.

18. Ibid., p. 282.

19. J.W. McCrindle (ed.) *The Christian Topography of Cosmas, An Egyptian Monk* (Hakluyt Society, London 1897) pp. 365–6, 368.

20. Ibid., pp. 365, 119, 366.

21. Joseph Needham, *Science and Civilisation in China* Vol. I (Cambridge University Press, Cambridge 1954) p. 216.

22. Paul Wheatley, *The Golden Khersonese* (University of Malaya Press, Kuala Lumpur 1961) pp. 218, 219.

23. Raymond K. Kent, *Early Kingdoms in Madagascar, 1500–1700* (Holt, Rinehart and Winston, New York 1970).

24. A.L. Basham, *The Wonder That Was India* (Grove Press, New York 1959) pp. 189, 526.

25. Fernand Braudel, *La Mediterranée et le Monde mediterranéen à l'époque de Philippe II* (Librairie Armand Colin, Paris 1949) p. 336.
26. Schafer, op.cit., p. 140.
27. Ibid., p. 150

CHAPTER 3

1. For the population of Hangchow, see Mark Elvin, *The Pattern of the Chinese Past* (Eyre Methuen, London 1973) p. 177.
2. I owe the phrase 'a cut flower civilization' to Dom Hubert Van Zeller, *The Benedictine Idea* (Burns and Oates, London 1959) p. 225, where he refers to 'what Father Keller calls a cut-flower culture'.
3. Wang Gungwu, *The Structure of Power in North China During the Five Dynasties* (University of Malaya Press, Kuala Lumpur 1963).
4. For the *ordo* and its significance, see Karl A. Wittfogel and Feng Chia-sheng, *History of Chinese Society: Liao (907–1125)* (The American Philosophical Society, Philadelphia 1949) especially Wittfogel's general introduction, pp. 1–35, and pp. 505–39.
5. Dun J. Li, *The Ageless Chinese, A History* (Scribners, New York 1965) p. 216.
6. For southern Sung China, see Jacques Gernet, *Daily Life in China on the Eve of the Mongol Invasion 1250–1276* (George Allen and Unwin, London 1962).
7. K.C. Chang (ed.) *Food in Chinese Culture, Anthropological and Historical Perspectives* (Yale University Press, New Haven and London 1977) pp. 143, 168.
8. Sir Henry Yule, *Cathay and the Way Thither*, Vol. III (Hakluyt Society, London 1915) p. 95.
9. Marco Polo, *The Travels of Marco Polo* (Penguin Books, Harmondsworth, Middlesex 1958).
10. Yule, op.cit., Vol. IV, p. 108.
11. Gernet, op.cit., p. 52.
12. For the T'ang aristocracy, see David G. Johnson, *The Medieval Chinese Oligarchy* (Westview Press, Boulder, Colorado 1977); Patricia Buckley Ebrey, *The Aristocratic Families of Early Imperial China, A Case Study of the Po-ling Ts'ui Family* (Cambridge University Press, Cambridge 1978).
13. Marco Polo, op.cit., p. 197. For the sociology of Sung and Yüan China, see E.A. Kracke, Jr, *Civil Service in Early Sung China 960–1067* (Harvard University Press, Cambridge, Massachusetts 1953); Herbert Franz Schurmann, *Economic Structure of the Yüan Dynasty* (Harvard University Press, Cambridge, Massachusetts 1956); Lo Jung-pang, 'Chinese Shipping and East–West Trade from the Tenth to the Fourteenth Century', in Mickel Mollat (ed.) *Sociétés et Compagnies de Commerce en Orient et dans l'Ocean Indien* (Bibliothèque Général de l'École Pratique des Hautes Études, Paris 1970) pp. 167–78.
14. For the Sung intellectual scene, see A.C. Graham, *Two Chinese*

Philosophers (Lund Humphries, London 1958); Ulrich Libbrecht, *Chinese Mathematics in the Thirteenth Century, The Shu-shu chiu-chang of Ch'in Chiu-shao* (MIT Press, Cambridge, Massachusetts and London 1973).

15. Jean Baechler, *The Origins of Capitalism* (Basil Blackwell, Oxford 1975).
16. For the Avignonese papacy, see Bernard Guillemain, *La Cour Pontificale d'Avignon 1309–1376* (Editions E. de Baccard, Paris 1966).
17. Yule, op.cit., Vol. IV, pp. 137, 111; Joseph Needham, *Science and Civilisation in China*, Vol. IV, part three, (Cambridge University Press, Cambridge 1954) p. 470; and Yule, op.cit., Vol. IV, p. 109.
18. Marco Polo, op.cit., pp. 110, 77.
19. Ibid., p. 209.
20. Yule, op.cit., Vol. II, pp. 179–80.
21. Needham, op.cit., Vol. IV, part three, p. 469.
22. Marco Polo, op.cit., p. 206.
23. Ibid., p.215; Needham, op.cit., Vol. IV, part three, p. 469.
24. Needham, op.cit., vol. IV, part three, p. 468.
25. Wittfogel and Feng, op.cit., p. 533; Harold Lamb, *Genghis Khan, Emperor of all Men* (Thornton Butterworth, London 1928) p. 237.
26. I. Umnyakov and Y. Aleskerov, *Samarkand. A Guide Book* (Progress Publishers, Moscow, 1972) p. 18.
27. Marcus Nathan Adler (ed.) *The Itinerary of Benjamin of Tudela* (Philipp Feldheim, New York 1907) pp. 58–9.
28. Marco Polo, op.cit., pp.3, 50.
29. Ibid., p. 50.
30. Yule, op.cit., Vol. II, pp. 103–4.
31. Ata-Malik Juvaini, *The History of the World Conqueror*, John Andrew Boyle (trans.) 2 vols (Harvard University Press, Cambridge, Massachusetts 1958).
32. Ibid., Vol. I, pp. 213–14.
33. Ibid., Vol. II, p. 603.
34. Ibid., Vol. I, p. 108.
35. Adler, op.cit., p. 76.
36. F. Hirth and W.W. Rockhill (trans.) *Chao Ju-Kua; His Work on the Chinese and Arab Trade in the Twelfth and Thirteenth Centuries Entitled 'Chu Fan Chih'* (Imperial Academy of Sciences, St Petersburg 1911).
37. Marco Polo, op.cit., p. 209.
38. Ibid., p. 261.
39. Ibid., p. 263.
40. Ibid., p. 264.
41. Ibid., p. 282.
42. Ibid., p. 35
43. E. Ashtor, 'Essai sur l'alimentation des diverses classes sociales dans l'Orient médiéval', *Annales, Économies, Sociétés Civilisations*, vol. 23; no. 5 (September–October 1968) pp. 1017–53; Eliyahu Ashtor, *Histoire des Prix et des Salaires dans l'Orient médiéval* (S.E.V. P.E.N., Paris 1969).
44. Dmitri Obolensky, *The Byzantine Commonwealth* (Weidenfeld and Nicholson, London, 1971) p. 182.

45. Adler, op.cit., p. 13.
46. Sir Percy Sykes, *A History of Exploration* (Routledge and Kegan Paul, London 1950) p. 88.
47. Needham, op.cit., Vol. I, p. 188.
48. L. Olschki, *Marco Polo's Asia* (University of California Press, Berkeley, California 1962).
49. Lamb, op.cit., p. 261.
50. Donald F. Lach, *Asia in the Making of Europe. Vol. I, The Century of Discovery*, Book One (The University of Chicago Press, Chicago and London 1965) p. 41.
51. Hsiao Ch'i-ch'ing, *The Military Establishment of the Yüan Dynasty* (Coun- on East Asian Studies, Harvard University, Cambridge, Massachusetts 1978).
52. For the Franciscan mission to China, see I. de Rachelwiltz, *Papal Envoys to the Great Khans* (Faber and Faber, London 1971).
53. Juvaini, op.cit., Vol. II, p. 608.
54. For the long and eventually successful pre-modern struggle against plague in Europe, see Jean-Noel Biraben, *Les Hommes et La Peste en France et dans les Pays européens et mediterranéens. Vol. II, Les Hommes face à la Peste* (Mouton, Paris, La Haye 1976).
55. Lien-sheng Yang, *Money and Credit in China, A Short History* (Harvard University Press, Cambridge, Massachusetts 1952) p. 38.
56. For China's contributions to nautics, see Needham, op.cit., Vol. IV, part three; G.R.G. Worcester, *The Junks and Sampans of the Yangtze* (Naval Institute Press, Annapolis, Maryland 1971).
57. Marco Polo, op.cit., p. 11.
58. Needham, op.cit., Vol. IV, part three, p. 467.
59. Ibid., p. 469.
60. Ibid., p. 600.
61. Elvin, op.cit., p. 195.
62. Ibid., p. 195.
63. Needham, op.cit., Vol. IV, part three, p. 296.
64. Carlo Poni, 'Archéologie de la Fabrique: la diffusion des moulins a soie' alla bolognese 'dans les Etats vénitiens, du XVᵉ au XVIIIᵉ siècles', *Annales, Économies, Sociétés, Civilisations*, vol. 27, no. 6 (November–December 1972) pp. 1475–96.
65. *The Cloud of Unknowing*, Clifton Walters (trans.) (Penguin Books, Harmondsworth, Middlesex 1976) p. 54.
66. Pierre Teilhard de Chardin, *The Phenomenon of Man* (Collins Fontana Books, London 1966) p. 46.
67. Helen Dunstan, 'The Late Ming Epidemics: A Preliminary Survey', *Ch'ing-shih Wen-t'i*, vol. III, no. 3 (November 1975) p. 20.
68. Needham, op.cit., Vol. IV, part three, Plate CDXII following p. 656.

CHAPTER 4

1. For the fall of the Yüan and the rise of the Ming, see John W. Dardess, *Conquerors and Confucians. Aspects of Political Change in Late*

Yüan China (Columbia University Press, New York and London 1973); L. Carrington Goodrich and Chaoying Fang, *Dictionary of Ming Biography*, 2 vols (Columbia University Press, New York and London 1976).

2. For the Islamic revival in the West, see Stanford J. Shaw, *History of the Ottomon Empire and Modern Turkey. Vol. I. Empire of the Gazis: The Rise and Decline of the Ottoman Empire, 1280–1808* (Cambridge University Press, Cambridge 1976); Godfrey Goodwin, *A History of Ottoman Architecture* (Thames and Hudson, London 1971); Halil Inalcik, *The Ottoman Empire, The Classic Age 1300–1600* (Weidenfeld and Nicholson, London 1973).

3. Pierre Chaunu, *L'Amérique et Les Amériques* (Librairie Armand Colin, Paris, 1964) p. 57.

4. Fernand Braudel, *La Mediterranée et le monde mediterranéen à L'époque de Philippe II* (Librairie Armand Colin, Paris 1949) p. 624.

5. For late Ming finance, see Ray Huang, *Taxation and Goverment Finance in Sixteenth-Century Ming China* (Cambridge University Press, Cambridge 1974).

6. See S.A.M. Adshead, 'An Energy Crisis in Early Modern China', *Ch'ing-shih Wen-ti*, vol. III, no. 2 (December 1974) pp. 20–8.

7. Bartolomé Bennassar, *Valladolid au Siècle d'Or* (Mouton, Paris, La Haye 1967) pp. 473–92.

8. Harold Lamb, *Tamerlane, the Earth Shaker* (Thornton Butterworth, London 1929) p. 276.

9. E. Delmar Morgan and C.H. Cook (eds) *Early Voyages and Travels to Russia and Persia* (Hakluyt Society, London 1886) p. 108.

10. Ibid., p. 98.

11. Rhodes of Vietnam, *The Travels and Mission of Father Alexandre de Rhodes in China and Other Kingdoms of the Orient*, Solange Hertz (trans.) (Newman Press, Westminster, Maryland 1966) pp. 226–7.

12. W.E.D. Allen, *Problems of Turkish Power in the Sixteenth Century* (Central Asian Research Centre, London 1963); Braudel, op.cit., pp. 1008–18; C. Max Kortepeter, *Ottoman Imperialism During the Reformation: Europe and the Caucasus* (New York University Press, New York 1972).

13. François-Bernard Charmoy, *Expedition de Timour-i-lenk (Tamerlane) contre Toqtamiche en 1391 de JC* (Academic Imperiale des Sciences de St Petersbourg, 1836, reprinted Phila Press, Amsterdam 1975).

14. Hélène Carrère d'Encausse, 'Les routes commerciales de l'Asie Centrale et les tentatives de reconquête d'Astrakhan', *Cahiers du Monde Russe et Soviétique*, vol. XI (July–September 1970) pp. 391–422.

15. Louis Dermigny, *La Chine et l'Occident. Le Commerce à Canton au XVIIIᵉ Siècle 1719–1833*, Tome I (S.E.V.P.E.N., Paris 1964) p. 118.

16. M.A.P. Meilink-Roelofsz, *Asian Trade and European Influence in the Indonesian Archipelago between 1500 and about 1630* (Martinus Nijhoff, The Hague 1962); John E. Wills, Jr, *Pepper, Guns and Parleys. The Dutch East India Company and China, 1662–1681* (Harvard University Press, Cambridge, Massachusetts 1974).

17. Pierre Chaunu, *Les Philippines et Le Pacifique des Ibériques (XVIᵉ, XVIIᵉ, XVIIIᵉ siècles)* (S.E.V.P.E.N., Paris 1960).

18. Ibid., p. 9.

19. Huguette Chaunu and Pierre Chaunu, *Seville et L'Atlantique (1504–1650)*, Vol. VIII, Part two, 1, (S.E.V.P.E.N., Paris 1955–59) p. 386.
20. Jean Delumeau, *Le Catholicisme entre Luther et Voltaire* (P.U.F., Paris 1971) pp. 75–6.
21. Ho Ping-ti, *Studies on the Population of China, 1368–1953* (Harvard University Press, Cambridge, Massachusetts 1959) p. 187.
22. Ibid., p. 203.
23. Sung Ying-hsing, *Tien-kung K'ai-wu, Chinese Technology in the Seventeenth Century*, E-tu Zen Sun and Shiou-Chuan Sun (trans.) (Pennsylvania State University Press, Pennsylvania and London 1966).
24. Lord Macartney, *An Embassy to China*, J.L. Cranmer-Byng (ed.) (Longman, London 1962) p. 225.
25. Calvin Wells, *Bones, Bodies and Disease* (Thames and Hudson, London 1964) p. 100.
26. Ibid., p. 101.
27. Goodrich and Fang, op.cit., p. 862.
28. Wells, op.cit., p. 105.
29. Harold F.B. Wheeler, *The Story of the British Navy* (Harrap, London 1922) p. 121.
30. G.J. Marcus, *A Naval History of England. Vol. I, The Formative Centuries* (Longman, London, 1961) p. 134.
31. Dermigny, op.cit., Tome I, p. 15.
32. Michel Morineau, 'Quelques remarques sur l'abondance monétaire aux Provinces-Unies', *Annales, Économies, Sociétés, Civilisations*, vol. 29, no. 3 (May–June 1974) p. 767.
33. Donald Lach, *Asia in the Making of Europe. Vol. II, A Century of Wonder* (The University of Chicago Press, Chicago and London 1970) p. 34.
34. Giovanni Botero, *The Reason of State and the Greatness of Cities* (Routledge and Kegan Paul, London 1956) p. 258.
35. Ibid., p. 268.
36. Dermigny, op.cit., Tome I, p. 393; Tome II, p. 588.
37. Lach, op.cit., Vol. II, p. 34.
38. John Carswell, 'China and the Near East: the recent discovery of Chinese porcelain in Syria', in William Watson (ed.) *The Westward Influence of the Cinese Arts* (The University of London Press, London 1972) pp. 20–5.
39. Marco Polo, *The Travels of Marco Polo* (Penguin Books, Harmondsworth, Middlesex 1958) p. 209.
40. Sir Henry Yule, *Cathay and the Way Thither*, Vol. I (Hakluyt Society, London 1915) pp. 290, 295.
41. Lach, op.cit., *Vol. I, The Century of Discovery*, Book Two, p. 772.
42. Botero, op.cit., p. 267.
43. Jan Nieuhof, *An Embassy from the East India Company of The United Provinces to the Grand Tartar Cuam Emperor of China* (John Ogilby, London, 1669) appendix p. 86.
44. T.F. Carter, *The Invention of Printing in China and its Spread Westward* (Columbia University Press, New York 1931).
45. Frances Bacon, *Novum Organum*, Book 1 (Routledge, The New Universal Library, London n.d.) aphorism 129, p. 147.
46. Marco Polo, op.cit., p. 127.

47. Walter Pagel, *Paracelsus, An Introduction to Philosophical Medicine in the Era of the Renaissance* (S. Karger, Basel and New York 1958).
48. Botero, op.cit., p. 267.
49. Ibid., p. 269.
50. Ibid., p. 269.
51. Jonathan Spence, *The China Helpers, Western Advisers in China 1620–1960* (The Bodley Head, London 1969) p. 6.
52. Arthur W. Hummel (ed.) *Eminent Chinese of the Ch'ing Period (1644–1912)*, Vol. II (Government Printing Office, Washington 1943) p. 895.
53. Chaunu and Chaunu, op.cit., Vol. VIII, Part one, pp. 28, 8.
54. Ibid., Vol. VIII, Part two, 1, p. 19.
55. Richard Gascon, *Grand commerce et vie urbaine au XVIe siècle, Lyon et ses marchands (environ de 1520–environ de 1580)* Vol. I (Mouton, Paris, La Haye 1971) p. 339.
56. Ibid., Vol. II, p. 593.
57. W.H. Longridge, S.S.J.E. (ed.) *The Spiritual Exercises of Saint Ignatius Loyola* (Mowbray, London 1955) p. 199.
58. Ibid, p. 199.
59. Joseph de Acosta, *The Natural and Moral History of the Indies*, 2 Vols (Hakluyt Society, London 1880) pp. 532–3.
60. José Pereira, 'Ignazio Arcamone (1615–1683): First Italian Orientalist', *East and West*, New Series, Vol. 24, nos. 1–2 (March–June 1974) p.153. For Vieira, see C.R. Boxer, *A Great Luso–Brazilian Figure, Padre Antonio Vieira S.J. 1608–1697* (Hispanic and Luso–Brazilian Councils, London 1963).

CHAPTER 5

1. *Memoires concernant L'Histoire, Les Sciences, Les Arts des Cinois*, Vol. I (Paris 1776) p. 322.
2. Fernand Braudel, *Capitalism and Material Life, 1400–1800* (Collins Fontana Books, London 1974) pp. 274–5.
3. For Chang Hsüeh-ch'eng, see D.S. Nivison, *The Life and Thought of Chang Hsüeh-ch'eng (1738–1801)* (Stanford University Press, Stanford, California 1966); P. Demieville, 'Chang Hsüeh-ch'eng and His Historiography', in W.G. Beasley and E.G. Pulleyblank (eds) *Historians of China and Japan* (Oxford University Press, London 1961) pp. 167–85.
4. Jonathan D. Spence, *Ts'ao Yin and the K'ang-hsi Emperor: Bond-servant and Master* (Yale University Press, New Haven and London 1966).
5. Thomas A. Metzger, *The Internal Organization of Ch'ing Bureaucracy* (Harvard University Press, Cambridge, Massachusetts 1973).
6. J.-L. Flandrin, 'L'Attitude à L'Egard du Petit Enfant et Les Conduites Sexuelles dans la Civilisation Occidentale', *Annales de Démographie Historique. Enfant et Sociétés* (1973) p. 177.

7. Jean-Louis Flandrin, *Familes: parents, maison, sexualité dans l'ancienne société* (Hachette, Paris 1976).

8. Gilbert Rozman, *Urban Networks in Ch'ing China and Tokugawa Japan* (Princeton University Press, Princeton, New Jersey 1973).

9. Claudine Lombard-Salmon, *Un Exemple D'Acculturation Chinois: La Province du Gui Zhou au XVIIIe Siècle* (École Francaise D'Extrême-Orient, Paris 1972).

10. Jan Nieuhof, *An Embassy from the East India Company of the United Provinces to the Grand Tartar Cham Emperor of China* (John Ogilby, London 1669) p. 114.

11. Alvarez Semedo, *The History of that Great and Renowned Monarchy of China* (John Crook, London 1655) p. 14.

12. J.-B.du Halde, *The General History of China*, Vol. I (John Watts, London 1736) p. 205.

13. Braudel, op.cit., p. 373.

14. Karl Popper, *Unended Quest, An Intellectual Autobiography* (Collins Fontana Books, London 1977) pp. 55–60.

15. Susan Naquin, *Millenarian Rebellion in China, The Eight Trigrams Uprising of 1813* (Yale University Press, New Haven and London 1976); Daniel L. Overmyer, *Folk Buddhist Religion. Dissenting Sects in Late Traditional China* (Harvard University Press, Cambridge, Massachusetts 1976).

16. Robert Fortune, *Two Visits to the Tea Countries of China*, Vol. II (John Murray, London 1853) pp. 194, 196.

17. Lord Macartney, *An Embassy to China*, J.L. Cranmer-Byng (ed.) (Longman, London 1962) p. 171.

18. Ibid., p. 175.

19. Ibid., pp. 177, 179.

20. Ibid., p. 80.

21. Ibid., p. 156.

22. Ibid., p. 213.

23. Ibid., p. 212.

24. Louis Dermigny, *La Chine et L'Occident. Le Commerce à Canton au XVIIIe Siècle 1719–1833* (S.E.V.P.E.N., Paris 1964) Vol. I, p. 377 and Vol. III p. 1474.

25. Alexander Burnes, *Travels into Bokhara*, Vol.I (Murray, London 1834) p. 144.

26. Ibid., Vol. I, pp. 309–10.

27. John Carswell, *New Julfa, The Armenian Churches and Other Buildings* (Oxford University Press, Oxford 1968).

28. Dermigny, op.cit., Vol. I, p. 252.

29. Keith Sinclair, *A History of New Zealand* (Pelican Books, Harmondsworth, Middlesex 1959) p. 39.

30. John Harris, *A Complete Collection of Voyages and Travels*, Vol. I (London 1764) p. 975.

31. Ibid., p. 955.

32. Dermigny, op.cit., Vol. II, p. 682.

33. Joel Mokyr, *Industrialization in the Low Countries 1795–1850* (Yale University Press, New Haven and London 1976).

34. W.E. Cheong, 'Canton and Manila in the Eighteenth Century', in Jerome Ch'en and Nicholas Tarling (eds) *Studies in the Social History of China and South-East Asia* (Cambridge University Press, Cambridge 1969) p. 239.

35. Eric Widmer '"Kitai" and the Ch'ing Empire in Seventeenth Century Russian Documents on China', *Ch'ing-shih wen-t'i*, Vol. II, no. 4 (November 1970) pp. 21–39.

36. Marc Mancall, *Russia and China. Their Diplomatic Relations to 1728* (Harvard University Press, Cambridge, Massachusetts 1971).

37. Sir Reginald Coupland, *Raffles of Singapore* (Collins, London 1946) p. 112.

38. Eric Widmer, *The Russian Ecclesiastical Mission in Peking During The Eighteenth Century* (East Asian Research Center, Harvard University, Cambridge, Massachusetts 1976).

39. Ho Ping-ti, *Studies on the Population of China, 1368–1953* (Harvard University Press, Cambridge, Massachusetts 1959) p. 150.

40. Dermigny, op.cit., Vol. III, p. 1332.

41. E.H.M. Cox, *Plant-Hunting in China* (Collins, London 1945).

42. Ernest H. Wilson, *China, Mother of Gardens* (Arnold Aboretum, Harvard University, Boston, 1929) pp. 365–6.

43. British Parliamentary Papers, Reports from Commissioners, Inspectors and Others, Vols 41, 42 (1894, 1895): *Report of the Royal Commission on Opium 1894–95*, 5 vols.

44. George Loehr, 'European Artists at the Chinese Court', in William Watson (ed.) *The Westward Influence of the Chinese Arts* (The University of London Press, London 1972) p. 34.

45. Ibid., p. 39.

46. Ibid., p. 33.

47. M.L. Aimé-Martin (ed.) *Lettres Edifiantes et Curieuses* Vol. III (Société du Pantheon Litteraire, Paris 1853) pp. 212, 214.

48. Antoine Gaubil, *Correspondence de Pékin 1722–1759* Renée Simon (ed.) (Droz, Geneva 1970) p. 172.

49. Ibid., p. 235.

50. Guy Arbellot, 'La Grande Mutation des routes de France au milieu du XVIIIe siècle', *Annales, Economies, Sociétés, Civilisations*, vol. 28, no. no. 3, (May–June 1973) p. 766.

51. Paul M. Kennedy, *The Rise and Fall of British Naval Mastery* (Allen Lane, London 1976) p. 206.

52. Macartney, op.cit., p. 170.

53. Gerald S. Graham, *The China Station, War and Diplomacy 1830–1860* (Clarendon Press, Oxford 1978).

54. *Memoires concernant l'Histoire, Les Sciences, Les Arts des Chinois*, Vol. I (Paris 1776) p. 276.

55. Gaubil, op.cit., p. 864.

56. Quoted in John U. Nof, *War and Human Progress. An Essay on the Rise of Industrial Civilization* (Routledge and Kegan Paul, London 1950) p. 347.

57. Quoted in 'Metternich', *Encyclopaedia Britannica* (London 1957) p. 369.

CHAPTER 6

1. Jacques Gernet, *Le Monde Chinois* (Librairie Armand Colin, Paris 1972) pp. 459, 519: Stuart Schram, *The Political Thought of Mao Tse-tung* (Praeger, New York 1963) p. 110.
2. Ezra F. Vogel, *Canton under Communism. Programs and Politics in a Provincial Capital, 1949–1968* (Harvard University Press, Cambridge, Massachusetts 1969); Simon Leys, *Chinese Shadows*, (Penguin Books, Harmondsworth, Middlesex 1978).
3. Vogel, op.cit., p. 350.
4. Ernest P. Young, *The Presidency of Yuan Shih-k'ai, Liberalism and Dictatorship in Early Modern China* (The University of Michigan Press, Ann Arbor 1977).
5. Ch'ien Tuan-sheng, *The Government and Politics of China* (Harvard University Press, Cambridge, Massachusetts 1961) p. 117.
6. E. Colborne Baber, *Travels and Researches in Western China* (John Murray, London 1882, reprinted Ch'eng Wen Publishing Company, Taipei 1971) p. 10.
7. Ibid., p. 8.
8. Andre Migot, *Tibetan Marches* (Penguin Books, Harmondsworth, Middlesex 1957) p. 58.
9. Robert Fortune, *Two Visits to the Tea Countries of China*, Vol. I (John Murray, London 1853) p. 194.
10. Mary Clabaugh Wright, *The Last Stand of Chinese Conservatism, the T'ung-chih Restoration 1862–1874* (Stanford University Press, Stanford, California 1962) pp. 177, 361.
11. G. Kurgan-Van Hentenryk, *Léopold II et les groupes financiers Belges en Chine. La politique royale et ses prolongements (1895–1914*, (Académie Royale de Belgique, Brussels 1972).
12. Albert Feuerwerker, 'Industrial Enterprise in Twentieth-Century China: The Chee Hsin Cement Co'. in, Albert Feuerwerker, Rhoads Murphey, Mary C. Wright (eds) *Approaches to Modern Chinese History* (University of California Press, Berkeley and Los Angeles 1967) pp. 304–41; Wu Lien-teh, *Plague Fighter, The Autobiography of a Modern Chinese Physician* (W. Heffer, Cambridge 1959).
13. Samuel C. Chu, *Reformer in Modern China, Chang Chien 1853–1926* (Columbia University Press, New York and London 1965).
14. Wellington K.K. Chan, *Merchants, Mandarins and Modern Enterprise in Late Ch'ing China* (East Asian Research Center, Harvard University, Cambridge, Massachusetts 1977).
15. Howard L. Boorman and Richard C. Howard, *Biographical Dictionary of Republican China*, 4 vols (Columbia University Press, New York and London 1967–71).
16. Vera Vladimirovna Vishnyakova-Akimova, *Two Years in Revolutionary China* (East Asian Research Center, Harvard University, Cambridge, Massachusetts 1971) p. 119.
17. Diana Lary, *Region and Nation, the Kwangsi Clique in Chinese Politics 1925–1937* (Cambridge University Press, Cambridge 1974). p. 34.

18. Fernand Braudel, *La Mediterranée et le monde mediterréen à l'époque de Philippe II* (Librairie Armand Colin, Paris 1949) p. 240.
19. Simon Leys, *Chinese Shadows* (Penguin Books, Harmondsworth, Middlesex 1978) p. 45.
20. O.J. Todd, *Two Decades in China* (Ch'eng Wen Publishing Company, Taipei 1971) pp. 355–6.
21. Suzanne Pepper, *Civil War in China: The Political Struggle 1945–1949* (University of California Press, Berkeley 1978).
22. Peter Worsley, *Inside China* (Allen Lane, London 1975) p. 187.
23. Edgar Snow, *The Long Revolution* (Hutchinson, London 1973) p. 45.
24. Ross Terrill, *800,000,000. The Real China* (Heinemann, London, 1972) pp. 97–8.
25. Aline Kan, 'The Marriage Institution in Present-Day China', *The China Mainland Review*, vol. I, no. 3 (December 1965), p. 9.
26. Chu Wen-djang, *The Moslem Rebellion in Northwest China 1862–1878*, (Mouton, The Hague 1966) p. 188.
27. Peter Fleming, *News from Tartary* (Jonathan Cape, London 1936); Allen S. Whiting and Sheng Shih-ts'ai, *Sinkiang: Pawn or Pivot?* (Michigan State University Press, East Lansing, Michigan 1958).
28. John King Fairbank, Katherine Frost Bruner and Elizabeth Macleod Matheson, *The I.G. in Peking, Letters of Robert Hart, Chinese Maritime Customs 1868–1907*, 2 Vols (The Belknap Press of Harvard University Press, Cambridge, Massachusetts 1975) p. 710.
29. David Gillard, *The Struggle for Asia 1828–1914* (Methuen, London 1977) p. 113.
30. Alexander Hosie, *Manchuria, Its People, Resources and Recent History* (Methuen, London 1901) p. 127.
31. T. Philip Terry, *Terry's Japanese Empire* (Houghton Mifflin, Boston 1914) p. 757.
32. Gavan McCormack, *Chang Tso–lin in Northeast China, 1911–1928, China, Japan and the Manchurian Idea* (Dawson, Folkestone 1977); Donald A. Jordan, *The Northern Expedition, China's National Revolution of 1926–28* (University Press of Hawaii, Honolulu 1976).
33. Arthur N. Young, *China's Nation-Building Effort, 1927–1937* (Hoover Institution Press, Stanford University, Stanford, California 1971) pp. 322–5.
34. Arthur N. Young, *China and the Helping Hand 1937–1945* (Harvard University Press, Cambridge, Massachusetts 1963) pp. 248, 251–2, 339–41.
35. Hugh Trevor-Roper, *A Hidden Life. The Enigma of Sir Edmund Backhouse* (Macmillan, London 1976).
36. Carl Crow, *Foreign Devils in the Flowery Kingdom* (Hamish Hamilton, London 1941).
37. Yuan T'ung-li, *A Guide to Doctoral Dissertations by Chinese Students in America* (Sino–American Cultural Society, Washington 1961).
38. Wu, op.cit., p. 446.
39. K.C. Chang (ed.) *Food in Chinese Culture, Anthropological and Historical Perspectives* (Yale University Press, New Haven and London 1977) p. 329.

40. Fortune, op.cit., Vol. I, p. iii.
41. Fortune, op.cit., Vol. II, p. 286.
42. China, Maritime Customs, *Decennial Reports 1912–1921*, Vol. II (The Statistical Department of the Inspectorate General of Customs, Shanghai 1922) p. 27.
43. See S.A.M. Adshead, *The Modernization of the Chinese Salt Administration 1900–1920* (Harvard University Press, Cambridge, Massachusetts 1970).
44. James C. Thomson, Jr, *While China Faced West, American Reformers in Nationalist China 1928–1937* (Harvard University Press, Cambridge, Massachusetts 1969).
45. Pierre Teilhard de Chardin, *Letters from a Traveller* (Collins Fontana Books, London 1967)
46. Ibid., p. 210
47. Ibid., p. 211.
48. *The Observer*, London, 25 March 1979.
49. Pierre Teilhard de Chardin, *Man's Place in Nature*, (Collins Fontana Books, London 1973) p. 100; Pierre Teilhard de Chardin, *The Futue of Man* (Collins, Fontana Books, London, 1970) pp. 41, 48 and 123.
50. Robert Speaight, *Teilhard de Chardin, A Biography* (Collins, London 1967) p. 280
51. Alexander Solzhenitsyn, *The Gulag Archipelago*, Vol. I (Collins, London 1974) p. 285.
52. Teilhard de Chardin, *Letters from a Traveller*, p. 200.
53. Ibid., p. 203.
54. Teilhard de Chardin, *The Phenomenon of Man*, (Collins Fontana Books, London 19656) p. 317.
55. Ibid., pp. 316–17.
56. Teilhard de Chardin, *The Future of Man*, p. 211 n.
57. Speaight, op.cit., p. 298.
58. I owe Gregor Strasser's remark to Dr Edgar Feuchtwanger of the University of Southampton.

Bibliography

Acosta, Joseph de, *The Natural and Moral History of the Indies*, 2 vols (Hakluyt Society, London 1880).

Adler, Marcus Nathan (ed.) *The Itinerary of Benjamin of Tudela* (Philipp Feldheim, New York 1907).

Adshead, S.A.M., 'Buddhist Scholasticism and Transcendental Thomism', *The Downside Review*, vol. 95, no. 321 (October 1977) pp. 297–305.

Adshead, S.A.M., 'An Energy Crisis in Early Modern China', *Ch'ing-shih Wen-t'i*, vol. III, no. 2 (December 1974) pp. 20–8.

Adshead, S.A.M., *The Modernization of the Chinese Salt Administration* (Harvard University Press, Cambridge, Massachusetts 1970).

Aimé-Martin, M.L. (ed.) *Lettres Edifiantes et Curieuses* (Société du Pantheon Litteraire, Paris 1853).

Allen, W.E.D., *Problems of Turkish Power in the Sixteenth Century* (Central Asian Research Centre, London 1963).

Arbellot, Guy, 'La Grande Mutation des routes de France au milieu du XVIIIe siècle', *Annales, Économies, Sociétés, Civilisations*, vol. 28, no. 3 (May–June 1973) pp. 765–91.

Ashtor, Eliyahu, 'Essai sur l'alimentation des diverses classes sociales dans l'Orient médiéval', *Annales, Économies, Sociétés, Civilisations*, vol. 23, no. 5 (September–October 1968) pp. 1017–53.

Ashtor, Eliyahu, *Histoire des Prix et des Salaires dans l'Orient médiéval* (S.E.V.P.E.N., Paris 1969).

Baber, E. Colborne, *Travels and Researches in Western China* (John Murray, London 1882).

Bacon, Francis, *Novum Organum* (Routledge, The New Universal Library, London n.d.).

Baechler, Jean, *The Origins of Capitalism* (Basil Blackwell, Oxford 1975).

Baer, K., 'Land and Water in Ancient Egypt', paper presented to 28th International Congress of Orientalists, Canberra, 1971.

Balazs, Etienne, *Chinese Civilization and Bureaucracy* (Yale University Press, New Haven and London 1964).

Balazs, Etienne, *Le Traité Juridique du 'Souei-chou'*, (E.J. Brill, Leiden 1954).

Bardet, J.-P., P. Chaunu, G. Désert, P. Gouhier and H. Neveaux, *Le Batiment: Enquête D'Histoire Économique XIVe–XIXe siècles* (Mouton, Paris and The Hague 1971).

Basham, A.L., *The Wonder That Was India* (Grove Press, New York 1959).

Beasley, W.G. and E.G. Putleyblank, *Historians of China and Japan* (Oxford University Press, Oxford 1961).

Bennassar, Bartolomé, *Valladolid au Siècle d'Or* (Mouton, Paris, La Haye 1967).

Berlin, Isaiah, *Vico and Herder, Two Studies in the History of Ideas* (The Hogarth Press, London 1976).

Biraben, Jean-Noel, *Les Hommes et la Peste en France et dans les pays européens et mediterranéens*, 2 vols (Mouton, Paris, La Haye 1975–76).

Boorman, Howard L. and Richard C. Howard, *Biographical Dictionary of Republican China*, 4 vols (Columbia University Press, New York and London 1967–71).

Botero, Giovanni, *The Reason of State and the Greatness of Cities* (Routledge and Kegan Paul, London 1956).

Boxer, C.R., *A Great Luso–Brazilian Figure, Padre Antonio Vieira S.J. 1608–1697* (Hispanic and Luso–Brazilian Councils, London 1963).

Braudel, Fernand, *La Mediterranée et le monde mediterranéen à l'époque de Philippe II* (Librairie Armand Colin, Paris 1949).

Braudel, Fernand, *Capitalism and Material Life 1400–1800* (Collins Fontana Books, London 1974).

British Parliamentary Papers, Reports from Commissioners, Inspectors and Others, Vols. 41, 42 (1894, 1895): *Report of the Royal Commission on Opium 1894–95*, 5 vols.

Brown, Peter, *The World of Late Antiquity from Marcus Aurelius to Muhammed* (Thames and Hudson, London 1971).

Bulliet, Richard W., *The Camel and the Wheel* (Harvard University Press, Cambridge, Massachusetts, 1975).

Burnes, Alexander, *Travels into Bokhara*, 3 vols (Murray, London 1834).

Carrère d'Encausse, Hélène, 'Les routes commercials de l'Asie Centrale et les tentatives de reconquête d'Astrakhan', *Cahiers du Monde Russe et Soviétique*, vol. XI (July–September 1970).

Carswell, John, 'China and the Near East: The Recent Discovery of Chinese Porcelain in Syria', in William Watson (ed.) *The Westward Influence of the Chinese Arts* (The University of London Press, London 1972).

Carswell, John, *New Julfa, The Armenian Churches and Other Buildings* (Oxford University Press, Oxford 1968).

Carter, T.F., *The Invention of Printing in China and its Spread Westward* (Columbia University Press, New York 1931).

Cartier, Michel, 'L'Exploitation Agricole Chinois de L 'Antiquité au XIVe siècle: Evolution d'un Modele', *Annales, Économies, Sociétés, Civilisations*, vol. 33, no. 2 (March–April 1978) pp. 365–88.

Chan, Wellington K.K., *Merchants, Mandarins and Modern Enterprise in Late Ch'ing China* (East Asian Research Center, Harvard University, Cambridge, Massachusetts 1977).

Chang, K.C. (ed.) *Food in Chinese Culture, Anthropological and Historical Perspectives* (Yale University Press, New Haven and London 1977).

Charmay, François Bernard, *Expedition de Timour-i-lenk (Tamerlane) contre Toqtamiche en 1391 de JC* (Academie Imperiale des Sciences de St Petersbourg, 1836, reprinted Philo Press, Amsterdam 1975).

Chaunu, Huguette and Pierre Chaunu, *Séville et L'Atlantique (1504–1650)*, 8 vols (S.E.V.P.E.N., Paris 1955–59).

Chaunu, Pierre, 'Le Batiment dans L'Economie Traditionnelle', in J.P. Bardet, P. Chaunu, G. Désert, P. Gouhier, H. Neveux, *Le Batiment: Enquête D'Histoire Économique XIVe–XIXe siècles* (Mouton, Paris and The Hague 1973) pp. 9–32.

Chaunu, Pierre, *L'Amérique et Les Amériques* (Librairie Armand Colin, Paris 1964).

Chaunu, Pierre, *Les Philippines et Le Pacifique des Ibériques (XVIᵉ XVIIᵉ, XVIIIᵉ siècles* (S.E.V.P.E.N., Paris 1960).

Ch'en, Jerome and Nicholas Tarling (eds) *Studies in the Social History of China and South-East Asia* (Cambridge University Press, Cambridge 1969).

Cheong, W.E., 'Canton and Manila in the Eighteenth Century', in Jerome Ch'en and Nicholas Tarling (eds) *Studies in the Social History of China and South-East Asia* (Cambridge University Press, Cambridge 1969).

Ch'ien Tuan-sheng, *The Government and Politics of China* (Harvard University Press, Cambridge, Massachusetts 1961).

China, Maritime Customs, *Decennial Reports 1912–1921*, 2 vols (The Statistical Department of the Inspectorate General of Customs Shanghai 1922).

Chrysostom, St John, *Homilies*. In Philip Schaff (ed.) Nicene and Post-Nicene Fathers of the Christian Church, vols. IX-XIV (Eedmans, Grand Rapids, Michigan 1956).

Chu, Samuel C., *Reformer in Modern China, Chang Chien 1853–1926* (Columbia University Press, New York and London 1965).

Chu, Wen-djang, *The Moslem Rebellion in Northwest China 1862–1878* (Mouton, The Hague 1966).

Cicero, *De Re Publica*. (Loeb edition, Heinemann and Harvard 1951).

Cloud of Unknowing, The, Clifton Walters (trans.) (Penguin Books, Harmondsworth, Middlesex 1976).

Coupland, Sir Reginald, *Raffles of Singapore* (Collins, London 1946).

Cox, E.H.M., *Plant-Hunting in China* (Collins, London 1945).

Crow, Carl, *Foreign Devils in the Flowery Kingdom* (Hamish Hamilton, London 1941).

Dagron, Gilbert, *Naissance d'une Capitale, Constantinople et ses Institutions de 330 à 451* (Presses Universitaires de France, Paris 1974).

Dardess, John W., *Conquerors and Confucians, Aspects of Political Change in Late Yüan China* (Columbia University Press, New York and London 1973).

Delumeau, Jean, *Le Catholicisme entre Luther et Voltaire* (P.U.F., Paris 1971).

Demiéville, P., 'Chang Hsüeh-ch'eng and His Historiography', in W.G. Beasley and E.G. Pulleyblank (eds), *Historians of China and Japan* (Oxford University Press, London 1961).

Dermigny, Louis, *La Chine et l'Occident, Le Commerce à Canton au XVIIIᵉ Siècle 1719–1833*, 4 vols. (S.E.V.P.E.N., Paris 1964).

Dunstan, Helen, 'The Late Ming Epidemics: A Preliminary Survey', *Ch'ing-shih Wen-t'i*, vol. III, no. 3 (November 1975) pp. 1–59.

Ebrey, Patrician Buckley, *The Aristocratic Families of Early Imperial China. A Case Study of the Po-ling Ts'ui Family* (Cambridge University Press, Cambridge 1978).

Elvin, Mark, *The Pattern of the Chinese Past* (Eyre Methuen, London 1973).

Encyclopaedia Britannica (London 1957).

Fairbank, John K. (ed.) *The Chinese World Order* (Harvard University Press, Cambridge, Massachusetts 1968).

Fairbank, John King, Katherine Frost Bruner, Elizabeth Macleod Matheson, *The I.G. in Peking, Letters of Robert Hart, Chinese Maritime Customs 1868–1907,*

2 vols. (The Belknap Press of Harvard University Press, Cambridge, Massachusetts 1975).

Fan Yeh, *Hou Han-shu*, vols 5 and 6 (Jen Shou Pen, Erh-shih-liu Shih, Taipei 1971).

Feuerwerker, Albert, 'Industrial Enterprise in Twentieth-Century China: The Chee Hsin Cement Co.', in Albert Feuerwerker, Rhoads Murphey and Mary C. Wright, *Approaches to Modern Chinese History* (University of California Press, Berkeley and Los Angeles 1967) pp. 304–41.

Feuerwerker, Albert, Rhoads Murphey and Mary C. Wright (eds) *Approaches to Modern Chinese History* (University of California Press, Berkeley and Los Angeles 1967).

Finley, M.I., *The Ancient Economy* (Chatto and Windus, London 1973).

Fitzgerald, C.P., *China. A Short Cultural History* (The Cresset Press, London 1954).

Flandrin J.-L., 'L'Attitude à L'Egard du Petit Enfant et Les Conduites Sexuelles dans la Civilisation Occidentale', *Annales de Démographie Historique. Enfant et Société*, (1973) pp. 143–210.

Flandrin, J.L., *Familles: parenté, maison, sexualité dans l'ancienne société* (Hachette, Paris 1976).

Fleming, Peter, *News from Tartary* (Jonathan Cape, London 1936).

Fortune, Robert, *Two Visits to the Tea Countries of China*, 2 vols (John Murray, London 1853).

Frend, W.H.C, *The Rise of the Monophysite Movement* (Cambridge University Press, Cambridge 1972).

Gascon, Richard, *Grand Commerce et Vie urbaine au XVIe siècle, Lyon et ses marchands (environ de 1520–environ de 1580)*, 2 vols (Mouton, Paris, La Haye 1971).

Gaubil, Antoine, *Correspondence de Pékin 1722–1759*, Renée Simon (ed.) (Droz, Geneva 1970).

Gemelli Careri, John Francis, *A Voyage Round the World. A Collection of Voyages and Travels in Six Volumes*, Vol. IV (London 1745).

Gernet, Jacques, *Les Aspects Économique du Bouddhisme dans La Société Chinoise de V^e au Xe siècle*, (École Française D'Extrême-Orient, Saigon 1956).

Gernet, Jacques, *Daily Life in China on the Eve of the Mongol Invasion 1250–1276*, (George Allen and Unwin, London 1962).

Gernet, Jacques, *Le Monde Chinois* (Librairie Armand Colin, Paris 1972).

Giles, H.A., *The Travels of Fa-hsien* (Routledge and Kegan Paul, London 1959).

Gillard, David, *The Struggle for Asia 1828–1914* (Methuen, London 1977).

Goodrich, L. Carrington and Chaoying Fang, *Dictionary of Ming Biography*, 2 vols (Columbia University Press, New York and London 1976).

Goodwin, Godfrey, *A History of Ottoman Architecture* (Thames and Hudson, London 1971).

Graham, A.C., *Two Chinese Philosophers* (Lund Humphries, London 1958).

Guillemain, Bernard, *La Cour Pontificaie d'Avignon 1309–1376* (Editions E. de Baccard, Paris 1966).

Halde, J-B du, *The General History of China*, 4 vols (John Watts, London 1736).

Harris, John, *A Complete Collection of Voyages and Travels* (London 1764).

Hirth, F., and W.W. Rockhill (trans) *Chao Ju-kua, His Work on the Chinese and Arab Trade in the Twelfth and Thirteenth Centuries Entitled 'Chu Fan Chih'* (Imperial Academy of Sciences, St Petersburg 1911).

Ho Ping-ti, 'The Loess and the Origins of Chinese Agriculture', *American Historical Review*, vol. LXXV, no. 1 (October 1969) pp. 1–36.

Ho Ping-ti, 'Lo-yang, AD 495–534 A Study of Physical and Socio-Economic Planning of a Metropolitan Area', *Harvard Journal of Asiatic Studies*, vol. 26 (1966) pp. 52–101.

Ho Ping-ti, *Studies on the Population of China, 1368–1953* (Harvard University Press, Cambridge, Massachusetts 1959).

Hosie, Alexander, *Manchuria, Its People, Resources and Recent History* (Methuen, London 1901).

Hsiao, Ch'i-ch'ing, *The Military Establishment of the Yuan Dynasty* (Council on East Asian Studies, Harvard University, Cambridge, Massachusetts 1978).

Huang, Ray, *Taxation and Government Finance in Sixteenth Century Ming China* (Cambridge University Press, Cambridge 1974).

Hummel, Arthur W. (ed.) *Eminent Chinese of the Ch'ing Period (1644–1922)*, 2 vols. (Government Printing Office, Washington 1943).

Inalcik, Halil, *The Ottoman Empire. The Classic Age 1300–1600* (Weidenfeld and Nicholson, London 1973).

Jankovich, Miklos, *They Rode into Europe* (Harrap, London 1971).

Johnston, David G., *The Medieval Chinese Oligarchy* (Westview Press, Boulder, Colorado 1977).

Jordan, Donald A., *The Northern Expedition, China: National Revolution of 1926–28* (The University Press of Hawaii, Honolulu 1976).

Jung, C.G., *The Practice of Psychotherapy* (Routledge and Kegan Paul, London 1954).

Juvaini, Ata-Malik, *The History of the World-Conqueror*, John Andrew Boyle (trans.) 2 vols (Harvard University Press, Cambridge, Massachusetts 1958).

Kan, Aline, 'The Marriage Institution in Present-Day China', *The China Mainland Review*, vol. 1, no. 3. (December 1965) pp. 1–11.

Kennedy, Paul M., *The Rise and Fall of British Naval Mastery* (Allen Lane, London 1976).

Kent, Raymond K., *Early Kingdoms in Madagascar, 1500–1700* (Holt, Rinehart and Winston, New York 1970).

Kortepeter, C. Max, *Ottoman Imperialism During the Reformation: Europe and the Caucasus* (New York University Press, New York 1972).

Kracke, Jr, E.A., *Civil Service in Early Sung China 960–1067* (Harvard University Press, Cambridge, Massachusetts 1953).

Kurgan-Van Hentenryk, G., *Léopold II et les groupes financiers Belges en Chine. La politique royale et ses prolongements (1895–1914)*, (Académie Royale de Belgique, Brussels 1972).

Lach, Donald F., *Asia in the Making of Europe*, 2 vols (The University of Chicago Press, Chicago and London 1965, 1970).

Lamb, Harold, *Genghis Khan, Emperor of all Men*, (Thornton Butterworth, London 1928).

Lamb, Harold, *Tamerlane, the Earth Shaker* (Thornton Butterworth, London 1929).

Lamotte, Etienne, *Le Traité de la Grande Vertu de Sagesse*, Tome III (Université de Louvain, Institute Orientaliste, Louvain 1970).

Lary, Diana, *Region and Nation, the Kwangsi Clique in Chinese Politics 1925–1937* (Cambridge University Press, Cambridge 1974).

Levi, Peter, *The Light Garden of the Angel King* (Collins, London 1972).

Lewis, C.S., *The Pilgrim's Regress* (Geoffrey Bles, London 1947).

Leys, Simon, *Chinese Shadows* (Penguin Books, Harmondsworth, Middlesex 1978).

Li, Dun J., *The Ageless Chinese. A History* (Scribners, New York 1965).

Libbrecht, Ulrich, *Chinese Mathematics in the Thirteenth Century. The Shu-shu chiu-chang of Ch'in Chiu-shao* (The MIT Press Cambridge, Massachusetts and London 1973).

Liu Mau-tsai, *Kutscha and Seine Beziehungen zu China Vom 2 JH. v. Bis Zum 6 JH. N. CHR* (Otto Harrassowitz, Wiesbaden 1969).

Lo Jung-pang, 'Chinese Shipping and East–West Trade from the Tenth to the Fourteenth Century', in Michel Mollat (ed.) *Sociétés et Compagnies de Commerce en Orient et dans L'Ocean Indien* (Bibliotheque Général de L'École Pratique des Hautes Études, Paris 1970).

Loehr, Max, *Buddhist Thought and Imagery* (Harvard University Press, Cambridge, Massachusetts 1961).

Loehr, Max, 'European Artists at the Chinese Court', in William Watson (ed.) *The Westward Influence of the Chinese Arts* (the University of London Press, London 1972).

Lombard-Salmon, Claudine, *Un Exemple D'Acculturation Chinois: Le Province du Gui Zhou an XVIIIᵉ siècle*, (École Française D'Extrême-Orient, Paris 1972).

Longridge S.S.J.E., W.H. (ed.) *The Spiritual Exercises of Saint Ignatius Loyola* (Mowbray, London 1955).

Macartney, Lord, *An Embassy To China*, J.L. Cranmer-Byng (ed.) (Longman London 1962).

Mancall, Mark, *Russia and China, Their Diplomatic Relations to 1728* (Harvard University Press, Cambridge, Massachusetts 1971).

Marcus, G.J., *A Naval History of England. Vol. I, The Formative Centuries* (Longman, London 1961).

Martini, Martino, 'Description Grographique de L'Empire de la Chine par Le Père Martin Martinius', in Melchisedec Thevenot, *Relations de Divers Voyages Curieux*, Tome second, (Paris 1696).

Maspero, Henri (ed.) *Les Documents Chinois de la Troisième Expedition de Sir Aurel Stein en Asie Centrale* (The Trustees of the British Museum, London 1953).

McCormack, Gavan, *Chang Tso-lin in Northeast China, 1911–1928. China, Japan and the Manchurian Idea* (Dawson, Folkestone 1977).

McCrindle, John Watson, *The Commerce and Navigation of the Erythraean Sea* (Reprint in 1973 of Editions Calcutta and London 1879, 1882).

McCrindle, J.W. (ed.) *The Christian Topography of Cosmas, An Egyptian Monk* (Hakluyt Society, London 1897).

Meilink-Roelofsz, M.A.P., *Asian Trade and European Influence in the Indonesian*

Archipelago between 1500 and about 1630 (Martinus Nijhoff, The Hague 1962).

Memoires Concernant L'Histoire, Les Sciences, Les Arts des Chinois, (Paris 1776).

Metzger, Thomas A., *The Internal Organization of Ch'ing Bureaucracy* (Harvard University Press, Cambridge, Massachusetts 1973).

Migot, Andre, *Tibetan Marches* (Penguin Books, Harmondsworth, Middlesex 1957).

Miller, J. Innes, *The Spice Trade of the Roman Empire 29 BC–AD 641* (Clarendon Press, Oxford 1969).

Mokyr, Joel, *Industrialization in the Low Countries in 1795–1850* (Yale University Press, New Haven and London 1976).

Mollat, Michel (ed.) *Sociétés et Compagnies de Commerce en Orient et dans L'Ocean Indien* (Bibliotheque Général de L'École Pratiques des Hautes Études, Paris 1970).

Morgan, E. Delmar and C.H. Cook (eds.) *Early Voyages and Travels to Russia and Persia* (Hakluyt Societ, London 1886).

Morineau, Michel, 'Quelques remarques sur l'abondance monétaire aux Provinces-Unies', *Annales, Économies, Sociétés, Civilisations*, vol. 29, no. 3 (May–June 1974) pp. 767–76.

Murti, T.R.V., *The Central Philosophy of Buddhism. A Study of the Madhyamika System* (George Allen and Unwin, London 1955).

Naquin, Susan, *Millenarian Rebellion in China, The Eight Trigrams Uprising of 1813* (Yale University Press, New Haven and London 1976).

Needham, Joseph, *Science and Civilisation in China* (Cambridge University Press, Cambridge 1954).

Nef, John U., *War and Human Progress. An Essay on the Rise of Industrial Civilization* (Routledge and Kegan Paul, London 1950).

Nieuhof, Jan, *An Embassy from the East India Company of the United Provinces to the Grand Tartar Cham Emperor of China* (John Ogilby, London 1669).

Nivison, D.S., *The Life and Thought of Chang Hsuch-ch'eng (1738–1801)* (Stanford University Press, Stanford, California 1966).

Obolensky, Dimitri, *The Byzantine Commonwealth* (Weidenfeld and Nicholson, London 1971).

Olschki, L., *Marco Polo's Asia* (University of California Press, Berkeley 1962).

Overmyer, Daniel L., *Folk Buddhist Religion, Dissenting Sects in Late Traditional China* (Harvard University Press, Cambridge. Massachusetts 1976).

Pagel, Walter, *Paracelsus, An Introduction to Philosophical Medicine in the Era of the Renaissance* (S. Karger, Basel and New York 1958).

Pan Ku, *Ch'ien Han-shu*, Vols 3 and 4 (Jen Shou Pen, Erh-shih-liu Shih, Taipei 1971).

Patlagean, Evelyne, *Pauvreté Économique et Pauvreté Social à Byzance 4ᵉ–7ᵉ siècles* (Mouton, Paris, La Haye 1977).

Pepper, Suzanne, *Civil War in China: The Political Struggle 1945–1949* (University of California Press, Berkeley 1978).

Pereira, José, 'Ignazio Arcamone (1615–1682): First Italian Orientalist', *East and West*, New Series, vol. 24 nos. 1–2 (March–June 1974) pp. 153–7.

Pliny the Elder, *Naturalis Historia*, 10 vols (Loeb edition, Heinemann and Harvard 1938–62).

Polo, Marco, *The Travels of Marco Polo* (Penguin Books, Harmondsworth, Middlesex 1958).

Poni, Carlo, 'Archéologie de la Fabrique: la diffusion des Moulins à soie "alla bolognese" dans les Etats vénitiens du XVᵉ au XVIIIᵉ siècles', *Annales, Économies, Sociétés, Civilisations*, vol. 27, no. 6 (November–December 1972) pp. 1475–96.

Popper, Karl, *Unended Quest, An Intellectual Autobiography* (Collins Fontana Books, London 1977).

Propertius, *Elegies* (Loeb edition, Heinemann and Harvard 1962).

Pulleyblank, Edwin G., *The Background of the Rebellion of An Lu-shan* (Oxford University Press, 1955).

Rachelwiltz, I. de, *Papal Envoys to the Great Khans* (Faber and Faber, London 1971).

Ramanan, K. Venkata, *Nagarjuna's Philosophy as Presented in the Maha-Praj-naparamita-Sastra* (Harvard–Yenching Institute, Tuttle, Rutland, Vermont and Tokyo 1966).

Rhodes of Vietnam, *The Travels and Mission of Father Alexander de Rhodes in China and Other Kingdoms of the Orient*, Solange Hertz (trans.) (Newman Press, Westminster, Maryland 1966).

Richthofen, Ferdinand van, *Baron Richthofen's Letters, 1870–1872* (North China Herald Office, Shanghai 1903).

Rozman, Gilbert, *Urban Networks in Ch'ing China and Tokugawa Japan* (Princeton University Press, Princeton, New Jersey 1973).

Saeki, P.T., *The Nestorian Documents and Relics in China* (SPCK, Tokyo 1951).

Schafer, Edward H., *The Golden Peaches of Samarkand* (University of California Press, Berkeley and Los Angeles 1963).

Schram, Stuart, *The Political Thought of Mao Tse-tung* (Praeger, New York 1963).

Schurmann, Herbert Franz, *Economic Structure of the Yüan Dynasty* (Harvard University Press, Cambridge, Massachusetts 1953).

Semedo, F. Alvarez, *The History of that Great and Renowned Monarchy of China* (John Crook, London 1655).

Seneca, *De Beneficiis*, Moral Essays Vol. III (Loeb edition, Heinemann and Harvard 1935).

Shaw, Stanford J., *History of the Ottoman Empire and Modern Turkey. Vol. I, Empire of the Gazis: The Rise and Decline of the Ottoman Empire, 1280–1808* (Cambridge University Press, Cambridge, 1976).

Sinclair, Keith, *A History of New Zealand* (Pelican Books, Harmondsworth, Middlesex 1959).

Snow, Edgar, *The Long Revolution* (Hutchinson, London 1973).

Solzenitsyn, Alexander, *The Gulag Archipelago*, Vol. I, (Collins, London 1976).

Speaight, Robert, *Teilhard de Chardin, A Biography* (Collins, London 1967).

Spence, Johnathan, *The China Helpers. Western Advisers in China 1620–1960*, (The Bodley Head, London 1969).

Spence, Jonnathan D., *Ts'ao Yin and the K'ang-hsi Emperor: Bondservant and Master* (Yale University Press, New Haven and London 1966).

Stein, Sir Aurel, *On Ancient Central-Asian Tracks* (Pantheon, New York 1964).

Stover, Leon F., *The Cultural Ecology of Chinese Civilization* (Mentor, New American Library, New York and Scarborough, Ontario 1974).

Sung Ying-hsing, *T'ien-kung Kai-wu, Chinese Technology in the Seventeenth Century,* E-tu Zen Sun and Shiou-chuan Sun (trans.) (Pennsylvania and London 1966).

Sykes, Sir Percy, *A History of Exploration*, (Routledge and Kegan Paul, London 1950).

Teilhard de Chardin, Pierre, *Man's Place in Nature* (Collins Fontana Books, London 1973).

Teilhard de Chardin, Pierre, *Letters from a Traveller* (Collins Fontana Books, London 1967).

Teilhard de Chardin, Pierre, *The Phenomenon of Man* (Collins Fontana Books, London 1966).

Teilhard de Chardin, Pierre, *The Future of Man* (Collins Fontana Books, London 1970).

Terril, Ross, *800,000,000 The Real China* (Heinemann, London 1972).

Terry, T. Philip, *Terry's Japanese Empire* (Houghton Mifflin, Boston 1914).

Thevenot, Melchisedec, *Relations de Divers Voyages Curieux*, Tome second (Paris 1696).

Thomson, Jr, James C., *While China Faced West. American Reformers in Nationalist China 1928–1937* (Harvard University Press, Cambridge, Massachusetts 1969).

Todd, O.J., *Two Decades in China* (Ch'eng Wen Publishing Company, Taipei 1971).

Trevor-Roper, Hugh, *A Hidden Life. The Enigma of Sir Edmund Backhouse* (Macmillan, London 1976).

Twitchett, D.C., *Financial Administration under the T'ang Dynasty* (Cambridge University Press, Cambridge 1963).

Umnyakov, I., and Y. Aleskerov, *Samarkand. A Guide Book* (Progress Publishers' Moscow 1972).

Veyne, Paul, *Le Pain et Le Cirque. Sociologie Historique d'une Pluralisme Politique* (Editions du Seuil, Paris 1976).

Vishnyakova-Akimova, Vera Vladimirovna, *Two Years in Revolutionary China* (East Asian Research Center, Harvard University, Cambridge, Massachusetts 1971).

Vogel, Ezra F., *Canton under Communism. Programs and Politics in a Provincial Capital, 1949–1968* (Harvard University Press, Cambridge, Massachusetts 1969).

Wallerstein, Immanuel, *The Modern World-System* (Academic Press, New York 1974).

Wang Gungwu, *The Structure of Power in North China During the Five Dynasties* (University of Malaya Press, Kuala Lumpur 1963).

Watson, Burton, *Records of the Grand Historian of China, Translated from the Shih-chi of Ssu-ma Ch'ien*, 2 vols (Columbia University Press, New York and London 1961).

Watson, William (ed.) *The Westward Influence of the Chinese Arts* (The University of London Press, London 1972).

Wells, Calvin, *Bones, Bodies and Disease* (Thames and Hudson, London 1964).

Wheatley, Paul, *The Golden Khersonese* (University of Malaya Press, Kuala Lumpur 1963).

Wheeler, Harold F.B., *The Story of the British Navy* (Harrap, London 1922).

Whiting, Allen S. and Sheng Shih-ts'ai, *Sinkiang: Pawn or Pivot?* (Michigan State University Press, East Lansing, Michigan 1958).

Widmer, Eric, 'Kitai and the Ch'ing Empire in Seventeenth Century Russian Documents on China', *Ch'ing-shih Wen-t'i*, vol. II, no. 4 (November 1970) pp. 21–39.

Widmer, Eric, *The Russian Ecclesiastical Mission in Peking During the Eighteenth Century* (East Asian Research Center, Harvard University, Cambridge, Massachusetts 1976).

Wills, Jr, John E., *Pepper, Guns and Parleys, The Dutch East India Company and China, 1662–1681* (Harvard University Press, Cambridge, Massachusetts 1974).

Wilson, Ernest H., *China, Mother of Gardens* (Arnold Arboretum, Harvard University, Boston 1929).

Wittfogel, Karl A., *Oriental Despotism, A Comparative Study of Total Power* (Yale University Press, New Haven 1957).

Wittfogel, Karl A., and Feng Chia-sheng, *History of Chinese Society: Laio (907–1125)* (American Philosophical Society, Philadelphia 1949).

Worcester, G.R.G., *The Junks and Sampans of the Yangtze* (Naval Institute Press, Annapolis, Maryland 1971).

Worsley, Peter, *Inside China* (Allen Lane, London 1975).

Wright, Arthur F. and Denis Twitchett (eds) *Perspectives on the T'ang* (Yale University Press, New Haven and London 1973).

Wright, Mary Clabaugh, *The Last Stand of Chinese Conservatism. The T'ung-chih Restoration 1862–1874* (Stanford University Press, Stanford, California 1962).

Wu Lien-teh, *Plague Fighter, The Autobiography of a Modern Chinese Physician* (W. Heffer, Cambridge 1959).

Yang Lien-sheng, 'Great Families of Eastern Han', in E-tu zen Sun and John K. Francis (eds.) *Chinese Social History* (American Council of Learned Societies, Washington 1956) pp. 103–34.

Yang Lien-sheng, *Money and Credit in China, A Short History* (Harvard University Press, Cambridge, Massachusetts 1952).

Young, Arthur N., *China's Nation-Building Effort, 1927–1937* (Hoover Institution Press, Stanford University, California 1973).

Young, Arthur N., *China and the Helping Hand 1937–1945* (Harvard University Press, Cambridge Massachusetts 1963).

Young, Ernest P., *The Presidency of Yuan Shih-k'ai, Liberalism and Dictatorship in Early Modern China* (The University of Michigan Press, Ann Arbor 1977).

Yuan T'ung-li, *A Guide to Doctoral Dissertations by Chinese Students in America* (Sino–American Cultural Society, Washington 1963).

Yule, Sir Henry, *Cathay and the Way Thither*, 4 vols (Hakluyt Society, London 1915).

Zahner, R.C., *Zurvan, A. Zoroastrian Dilemma* (Clarendon Press, Oxford 1955).

Zeller, Dom Hubert van, *The Benedictine Idea* (Burns and Oates, London 1959).

Zen Sun, E-tu, and John de Francis (eds) *Chinese Social History* (American Council of Learned Societies, Washington 1956).

Zurcher, E., *The Buddhist Conquest of China* (E.J. Brill, Leiden 1959).

Index

413